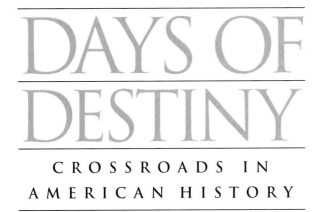

DAYS OF DESTINY

CROSSROADS IN AMERICAN HISTORY

DAYS OF DESTINY

CROSSROADS IN AMERICAN HISTORY

*America's Greatest Historians Examine Thirty-One
Uncelebrated Days That Changed the Course of History*

GENERAL EDITORS

JAMES M. McPHERSON

ALAN BRINKLEY

EDITOR

DAVID RUBEL

AN AGINCOURT PRESS PRODUCTION

THE SOCIETY OF AMERICAN HISTORIANS
To encourage literary distinction in the writing of history and biography

A DK Publishing Book

DK

LONDON, NEW YORK, SYDNEY, DELHI, PARIS,
MUNICH and JOHANNESBURG

Publisher: Sean Moore
Editorial Director: Chuck Wills
Art Directors: Dirk Kaufman, Tina Vaughan
Production Manager: Chris Avgherinos
DTP Designer: Russell Shaw

AN AGINCOURT PRESS PRODUCTION
President: David Rubel

Art Direction and Production: Oxygen Design
Cover and Interior Design: Sherry Williams, Tilman Reitzle

Senior Image Researcher: Julia Rubel
Image Researchers: Martin Baldessari, Deborah Goodsite,
Diane Hamilton, Susan Hormuth, Jennifer Rosen

Copy Editor: Ron Boudreau
Proofreader: Laura Jorstad

For photo credits, see pp. 495–496.
First American edition, 2001

2 4 6 8 10 9 7 5 3 1

Published in the United States by Dorling Kindersley Publishing, Inc.
95 Madison Avenue, New York, New York 10016

© 2001 by Dorling Kindersley Publishing, Inc.

Published in Great Britain by Dorling Kindersley Limited

Color reproduction by Colourscan, Singapore
Printed and bound in the USA by Quebecor World

LIBRARY OF CONGRESS CATALOGING-IN-PUBLICATION DATA

To the best of my ability: the American presidents / James M. McPherson,
editor.—1st American ed.
   p. cm.
Includes index.
ISBN 0-7894-5073-9 (alk. paper)
1. Presidents—United States—History. 2. Presidents—United States—
Biography. 3. United States—Politics and government. I. McPherson,
James M. II. Title.

E176.1 T59 2000
973'.09'9—dc 21

00-021569

CONTENTS

INTRODUCTION

BY JAMES M. McPHERSON
AND ALAN BRINKLEY

ARE THERE PARTICULAR MOMENTS IN HISTORY—"days of destiny," to use the title of this book—on which the future of societies or nations turn? Can the course of history be changed in a moment? These are the questions that have motivated us to invite thirty-one distinguished historians to write the essays that appear in this volume. And as you will see, their answers are highly various.

Through most of the period in which people have been writing history, which is most of the lifespan of human civilization, few would have doubted that an event, or a day, could dramatically transform the world. History was, until relatively recently, perceived as a *story*—a chronicle of great events building, almost inevitably, to some kind of climactic turning point. Examples of such events from American history come easily to mind: the battles of Lexington and Concord in 1775, Abraham Lincoln's election in 1860 and his assassination in 1865, the Japanese attack on Pearl Harbor in 1941, and many others.

This older history mainly examined the public world—political, military, and intellectual events—and the power and authority exercised by elites. It was the story of the extraordinary acts and extraordinary thoughts of exceptional people, and it reflected the prevailing view among scholars and the public alike that there was a profound difference between what was "historic" and what was an insignificant part of the everyday world. Such history, when well presented, easily crossed the boundary between the academy and the popular reader. It had a sharpness of edge and a clarity of purpose, and it rested on the idea of contingency—the belief that individuals make choices among different possible actions and that those choices can have dramatic consequences. Had Jefferson Davis accepted the advice of his secretary of state, Robert Toombs, and refused to fire on

Fort Sumter, the subsequent history of Southern secession might have been different. Had Japanese leaders listened to the warnings of Adm. Yamamoto Isoroku regarding the danger of attacking Pearl Harbor, the course of World War II might have been different.

S UCH EVENT-DRIVEN HISTORY, with its emphasis on choice and contingency, was not without its critics. Beginning early in the twentieth century, Marxist scholars focused on impersonal economic and social forces (industrialization, capitalism, class formation, and class conflict), which they believe determined historical development regardless of the actions of specific individuals. American "progressive" historians such as Frederick Jackson Turner and Charles Beard, writing around the same time, argued that such forces as the availability of free land on the "frontier" and the rise of capitalism had determined the shape of the American past. Nevertheless, the traditional narrative school remained primary until the 1960s, when the writing of history experienced a profound and presumably permanent change.

In that decade, scholars embraced what was, at least at first, known as the new social history. It was not a story-telling but a problem-solving approach to the past. It was not about events but about processes. It drew inspiration from the so-called *Annales* school of French historians (their name derived from an influential scholarly journal in which they published), who argued that history was the story of how deep structures shaped societies over very long periods of time. They proposed a history of the *longue durée* to replace the traditional *histoire événementielle*—the former, a history of gradual, long-term change; the latter, one of "mere events." British labor historians also provided inspiration—most notably E. P. Thompson, whose *The Making of the English Working Class* (1963) prompted a generation of American historians to examine the lives of previously marginalized groups and rescue them, as Thompson had put it, "from the enormous condescension of posterity."

Most of all, perhaps, the new social history was shaped by the social turbulence of the 1960s and the rising demands of previously oppressed groups for dignity and freedom. It should not be surprising, then, that these years also saw the emergence of new areas of scholarship devoted to workers, African Americans, women, Latinos, Native Americans, and other groups whose pasts had never before attracted much notice among historians. The new social history was, as its champions liked to say, a "history from the bottom up," and it brought to the attention of the academy vast new worlds of social experience rooted in the lives of ordinary men and women.

The triumph of the new social history—and of all the related new histories that emerged in its wake—transformed the academic landscape in ways that few historians would today wish to undo. The writing of history became fuller, richer, and far more diverse than it had been, and it reflected more accurately the complexity and variety of the American past. But these benefits came at a cost. The new history, more than the old, broke down into increasingly specialized subfields, each with a relatively limited audience, and its emphasis on structure often robbed it of narrative power and thus of accessibility to nonacademic readers. Lawrence Stone, one of the pioneers of the new social history, eventually began to complain about some of its unintended consequences. As early as 1979, he called for a revival of the "once-despised narrative mode" to enable historians "to make their findings accessible once more to an intelligent but not expert reading public, which is eager to learn." Others during the 1980s, 1990s, and beyond have echoed Stone's plea for a new "narrative synthesis," a format that would incorporate the specialized findings of the new social history and yet leave room for individuals, events, and the sense of drama, irony, suspense, and climax that characterized the historical writing of earlier eras.

THIS BOOK, SPONSORED BY the Society of American Historians, has been edited by two members of its executive board and written by members elected to the society because of their demonstrated capacity to write lucid, significant, and readable history. Each of the essays focuses, at least in part, on a single day in the American past on which a significant event occurred. The authors are scholars with varying interests and sensibilities, and readers will not find here a single, common understanding of history. Yet these essays are premised on the common belief that there is, still, a way for events to inform our understanding of the past; and all of the contributors—many of whom are fully immersed in newer, less narrative forms of history—have accepted the challenge of identifying and describing a "day of destiny" that has had significant consequence, either in causing things to happen or in revealing important historical processes.

Covering a very broad sweep of American history, *Days of Destiny* moves from a June day in 1675, on which Rhode Islanders and Wampanoags parleyed but failed to prevent the devastating clash known as King Philip's War, to another June day in 1973 that saw the beginning of the moral and scientific controversy over biotechnology that is still making headlines thirty years later. In between, it focuses on some of the central themes of American history. Three essays, separated in time by two centuries, examine conflicts between Native Americans and white settlers of European descent, conflicts that shaped much of the American experience. Five essays cluster around the years from 1775 to 1801, during which the nation won its independence and created a new form of government for itself. Five others detail days from the period of the 1830s through the 1860s, during which the United States struggled politically and militarily to resolve disputes over slavery, abolition, emancipation, and Reconstruction. Several essays examine the various ways in which the emergence of modern industrial society created tensions, pressures, and innovation—including controversies over religious beliefs, scientific knowledge, and legal thought. Others look at the growth of the United States as a world power and the emergence of a modern mass culture with first national and then global reach. Overall, the essays in this volume examine the experiences of men and women, of white people and people of color, of the famous and powerful as well as the ordinary. But for all their diversity, these essays also represent the shared conviction of their authors that the past can be made interesting and exciting and can help illuminate the world in which we presently live.

WE HOPE THAT THE STORIES in *Days of Destiny* will suggest to you something of the diversity of historical experience and of the variety of historians' approaches to the past. Most of all, we hope that they will provide you with some of the same stimulation and enjoyment that they have given their writers and editors. This book delivers no final answer to the question of whether there are, indeed, "days of destiny" on which the course of the nation has turned. But it does, we believe, demonstrate the contribution that examining particular events can make to one's understanding of some of the central questions in American history.

★ ★ ★

DAYS OF DESTINY

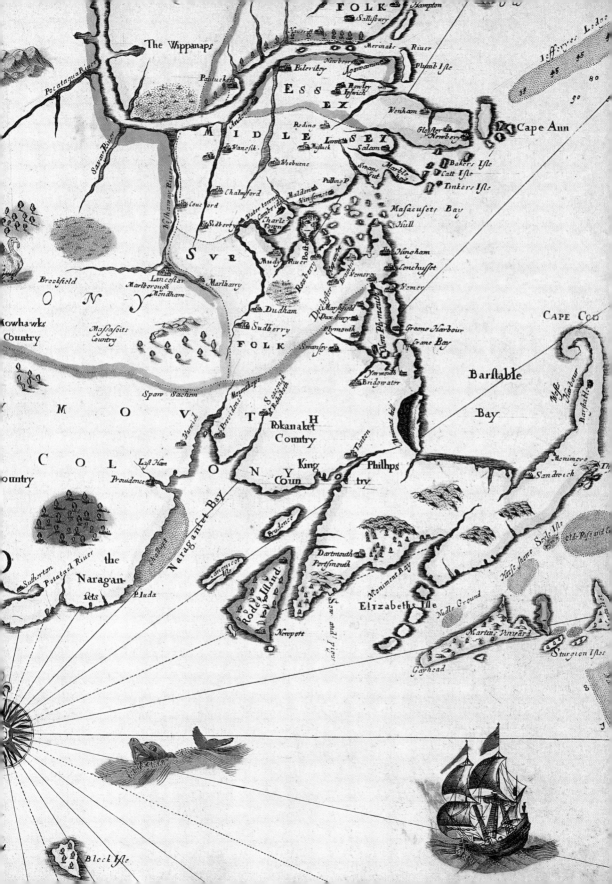

KING PHILIP'S QUARELL

BY JAMES AXTELL

D URING THE EARLY summer of 1675, rumors of war flew through the southern New England colonies like "black birds" (to use the old Indian phrase for bad rumors). The Wampanoag people who lived along Narragansett Bay in the western reaches of the Plymouth Colony were bristling with old and new complaints against their English neighbors and arming themselves. Young warriors were becoming more daring and demonstrative around colonial farms and towns; and the Wampanoag chief, King Philip, let it be known that he was at the end of the short tether on which Plymouth sought to keep him and would break free of it altogether if something weren't done soon.

John Easton—the sixty-year-old deputy governor of Rhode Island, a peace-minded Quaker and Philip's neighbor—was one of the

AT LEFT: *This detail of a 1675 map made by John Seller describes the region northeast of Narragansett Bay as "King Philps Country."*

ABOVE: *The Wampanoags, like their neighbors, used wampum shell beads for currency and ceremonial ornament. This wampum bracelet dates to the time of King Philip and perhaps earlier.*

few Englishmen to take the chief's discontent seriously. Although New Englanders had heard plenty of rumors and rumblings since the end of the Pequot War in 1637, Easton sensed that something was different about the bruits of war in mid-June. "For 40 years time," he noted in the sole account of the meeting, dated February 5, 1676, "reports and jelosys of war had bine [so] veri frequent that we did not think that…war was breking forth." But this time "we had Ca[u]se to think it wold." Especially in Rhode Island, that small maverick colony sandwiched among the more aggressive Puritan strongholds of Connecticut, Plymouth, and Massachusetts, it was apparent that "the English wear afraid and Philop was afraid and both incresed in arems."

So Easton sent a message to Philip inviting him to a preemptive parley, and Philip agreed, meeting a delegation of five Rhode Islanders on June 17 near the ferry opposite Newport. Philip arrived unarmed—dressed most likely in his best buckskin suit, covered with a small fortune in wampum shell beads—but his retinue of forty warriors carried bows and muskets. Through

KING PHILIP

1639? – 1676

Philip (known in his own language as Metacom) was from 1662 the sachem, or chief, of the Wampanoags, an Algonkian-speaking people who occupied parts of present-day Massachusetts and Rhode Island. For forty years, Philip's father, Massasoit, had maintained a stable relationship with the English, but those peaceful relations deteriorated quickly after Massasoit's death. During Philip's fourteen years as the Wampanoag sachem, he was regularly subjected to humiliation by the Plymouth colonists, with whom he remained uncomfortably allied. After his death in battle on August 12, 1676, Philip (shown here in a fanciful nineteenth-century portrait) was beheaded and quartered, and his head was kept on a pole at Plymouth for decades.

interpreters, the parties began a frank, relatively friendly exchange of views. The Rhode Islanders acknowledged that each side blamed the other for the impasse but expressed their desire that "the quarell might rightly be desided in the best way, and not as dogs deside ther quarells." In turn, the Indians "owned that fighting was the worst way" but asked "how right might take plase." When Easton suggested arbitration, the natives objected vehemently, saying that "all English agred against them, and so by arbetration thay had had much rong, mani miles square of land so taken from them," because the English "wold have English Arbetrators." Easton then explained that the arbiters he proposed were Gov. Edmund Andros of New York and any disinterested sachem the Indians chose. This novel suggestion of a bipartisan panel appeared so appealing to the Wampanoags that Easton was certain it would be accepted if officially tendered by the major English disputants.

Thinking they had for the moment spiked the fever of war, the Rhode Island officials prepared to end the meeting without hearing the Indians' indictment of the English, for they "knew what ther Cumplaints wold be." But Philip would not be denied. Perhaps he hoped that by recounting his hardships, he could forestall permanently a war that his tribe, commanding but a few thousand people, was very

The mark of King Philip.

unlikely to win against a united New England population of at least sixty thousand. So Philip proceeded to unfold a long list of grievances, and Easton heard him out, knowing most of them "to be true." It was a unique moment in American history: an Indian chief on the razor edge of war being given a sincere opportunity to explain virtually all the reasons that he and his people had come to such a perilous pass.

BY WAY OF MORAL PREAMBLE, Philip painted a pitiable contrast between the status of the Wampanoags in 1620—when his father, Massasoit, first welcomed the Pilgrims—and his tribe's present circumstances. When the Pilgrims came to the plague-cleared village site of the Patuxets (which they renamed Plymouth), Massasoit "was as a great man and the English as a litell Child." With generosity, the Wampanoag chief "Constraened other indians from ronging the English and gave them Coren and shewed them how to plant and was free [prone] to do them ani good." Perhaps foolishly, in retrospect, he also "let them have a 100 times more land" than the Wampanoags had now. And still, Philip pointed out, land continued to slip from the tribe's hands, through fouler means than fair. The Wampanoags "had bine the first in doing good to the English," he said, "and the English the first in doing rong."

Philip then described a common ploy that he must have experienced himself. Often when an Indian sachem sold land, "the English wold say it was more than [the chief had] agred to" and they would produce a "writing," or English deed, as proof. "Sum of ther kings had dun rong to sell so much," Philip admitted, but this did not excuse English trickery. Some chiefs "being given to drunknes, the English made them drunk and then cheted them in bargens." When this low tactic failed, English settlers often let their livestock persuade the natives to sell out and move. English "Catell and horses" proliferated so much, Philip complained, that even when his people moved thirty miles from "wher English had anithing to do, thay Could not kepe ther Coren from being spoyled, thay never being iused to fence." The Wampanoags naively thought that "when the English [bought] land of them that thay wold have kept ther Catell upone there owne land."

Moreover, when the English sold liquor (illegally) to the Indians, some warriors in their cups and frustration "often did hurt the English Catell"—for which, Philip knew but did not say, they would have to pay a court fine and replace the animals, typically at higher-than-market prices. For all these reasons, the Wampanoags now had "no hopes left to kepe ani land." This was a significant statement on Philip's part because the Rhode Islanders knew how desperate and dangerous those without hope and homesteads could be.

Y ET THE NATIVES' grievances did not end there. Philip also found serious fault with the Rev. John Eliot's "praying Indians" (those gathered in fourteen "praying towns" in Massachusetts) and the administration of English justice throughout New England. On the first count, the Wampanoags, and Philip especially, "had a great fear to have ani of ther indians...Caled or forsed to be Christian indians. Thay saied that such wer in everi thing more mischivous, only disemblers, and then the English made them not subject to ther kings, and by ther lying to rong ther kings." Regarding the second charge, the Wampanoags

The 1621 Peirce Patent (shown here) confirmed the Pilgrims' right to settle and govern Plymouth. It replaced the original Peirce Patent, carried over on the Mayflower, which had assigned to the Pilgrims land in Virginia.

THE NEW ENGLAND COLONIES

The Plymouth Colony was founded in 1620 by a group of separatist English Puritans, the Pilgrims, who had decided that the Church of England was beyond reform. The Crown had given them permission to settle in the New World, but they had sailed off course, landing much farther north than the land they were intended to inhabit. Nine years later, a less radical and better-financed group of Puritans formed the Massachusetts Bay Company, which received a royal charter from Charles I granting it title to most of present-day Massachusetts and New Hampshire. Connecticut and Rhode Island received separate charters from Charles II in the 1660s.

THE WAMPANOAGS

The Wampanoags were what anthropologists call "semi-sedentary"— that is, although they migrated about seasonally, they generally moved from one fixed site to another. Corn was the staple of their diet, supplemented by fish and game. About 1610, their population was estimated at thirteen thousand. Their losses during King Philip's War, though, were so great that after 1676 they ceased to exist as a distinct people.

complained that the prejudice of English judges was severe: Specifically, "if 20 of there [h]onest indians testefied that a Englishman had dun them rong, it was as nothing, [but] if but one of ther worst indians testefied against ani indian or ther king, when it plesed the English that was sufitiant." In short, Easton concluded, "the indians do judg the English partiall against them."

With both of these indictments, Philip reminded Easton of the provocation that had finally pushed the Wampanoags to the brink of war: the execution of three of Philip's leading men by the Plymouth General Court nine days earlier. A jury of twelve Englishmen and six Christian Indians had convicted these men of murdering John Sassamon, a Christian Indian whose battered body had been found in late January underneath the ice of Assawompset Pond near his home at Nemasket (now Middleborough, Massachusetts).

"FOR WE MUST CONSIDER THAT WE SHALL BE AS A CITY UPON A HILL."

—

John Winthrop, sermon aboard the Arbella *as it carried the founders of the Massachusetts Bay Colony to the New World, 1630*

Sassamon, whose neck had been broken, was no ordinary murder victim. After being orphaned in his early teen years by smallpox, he had been raised in Dorchester by adoptive English parents, who schooled him well in the English language and taught him how to read and write. During the Pequot War of 1637, Sassamon served the colonists as a soldier-interpreter, and he won a young Pequot captive for his bride. In 1650, he helped John Eliot establish Natick, the first of the praying towns, working initially as a builder and then as a schoolmaster. In 1653, Eliot, impressed with Sassamon's piety and literacy, sent him to Harvard College for further instruction, and a few years after that, Eliot's now-middle-aged protégé helped prepare a native translation of the Bible that Eliot first published at Cambridge in 1661 on the colony's only presses.

That year, however, both Sassamon's career and Indian-white relations took a turn. Massasoit died, and he was succeeded by his eldest son, Wamsutta (renamed Alexander by the Plymouth authorities). Alexander's allegiances were uncertain, as was his ability to control his warriors. Sassamon became his chief

This speculative woodcut *portrait of Massasoit probably dates from the early nineteenth century.*

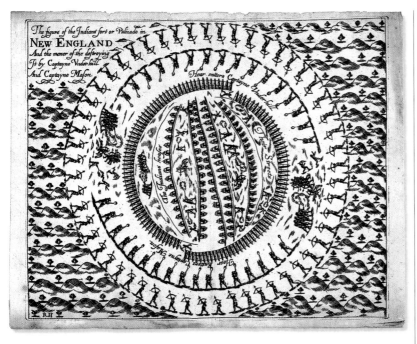

This engraving by John Underhill was published in 1638, the year after the Pequot War that it depicts. The Pequots, who lived at the mouth of the Connecticut River, were the first Indian tribe annihilated by the English. The powerful Pequots and the governments of the Connecticut and Massachusetts Bay Colonies had been competing for control of eastern Long Island's large wampum supply. When war (intentionally provoked by the English) finally broke out, troops from Connecticut surrounded and burned the fortified Indian village shown here, killing several hundred inhabitants.

scribe and interpreter. A year later, shortly after being summoned to Duxbury to appear before the roving Plymouth court, Alexander himself died under mysterious circumstances. Many Indians believed he had been poisoned.

WHEN ALEXANDER'S BROTHER Metacom (Philip) inherited the Wampanoag sachemship, Sassamon stayed on as the king's tongue and even became for a time his "Chief Councellor." Meanwhile, some white colonists became suspicious of Sassamon's change of venue from Natick to Philip's capital at Sowams on the Mount Hope Peninsula. Cotton Mather later reported that Sassamon had "apostatiz[ed] from the profession of Christianity, [and] lived like an heathen in the quality of a Secretary to King Philip." But it's just as likely that Eliot had sent Sassamon to spy on the restless Wampanoags and to urge them to accept the blessings of Christian civility.

As it turned out, Sassamon had little success converting either Philip or his people, and he probably alienated his boss in the attempt. He also angered Philip by putting his translating skills to sometimes questionable use. When Philip asked him—prudently, given the colonial circumstances—for help in drafting a will, Sassamon "made the writing for a gret part of the land to be his but read [the will] as if it had bine as Philop wold." As Easton reported, when this deceit was discovered, Sassamon had to flee the Wampanoag village. He returned to Natick

The seal of the Massachusetts Bay Colony was designed in England and brought over with the first settlers in 1630.

around 1666 and lived there for five or six years before moving to land near Assawompset Pond.

The final bone in Philip's craw was the conviction of his three councilors for Sassamon's murder. The jury's finding was apparently based on the testimony of one of Philip's "worst indians," a would-be Christian named Patuckson, even though this alleged eyewitness had waited three months before coming forward and even then did so, some thought, merely to cancel a debt to one of the accused. At the same time, Philip's loyalists were greatly troubled by the rumor that the three defendants had confessed and then accused Philip of ordering the misdeed; they were justifiably afraid that the English would use the allegation as an excuse to execute Philip and "have his Land." In the days following the June 8 execution, many Rhode Islanders, such as Roger Williams, wished along with John Easton that Plymouth "had left the Indians alone [or] at least not put to death the 3 Indians upon one Indians Testimony, a thing which Philip fears."

This nineteenth-century steel engraving, based on an earlier painting, depicts John Eliot preaching to Indians.

T HE RHODE ISLANDERS were thus not surprised on June 17 when the Indians declined an invitation to lay down their arms. Instead, after Philip had finished his lengthy indictment of English colonial practices, he and the other Wampanoags departed, though "without ani discurtiousnes." The question for the Rhode Islanders now was: What could they do to prevent a terrifying war from erupting in the Plymouth Colony, knowing well that it would probably spread throughout New England? Although Easton understood that the Wampanoags' litany of complaints against their English neighbors was largely justified, he remained surprisingly optimistic—believing that the Indians would accept arbitration and that, to prevent future trouble, the English would grant them "dew propriety" (reserved land), which they could "injoy…without opretion or iusurpation."

On both counts Easton was deluding himself and ignoring the forces that had brought both sides into almost predestinate conflict. Although he had warned the Wampanoags that "the English wear to strong for them," Easton failed to take into account the heavy, hidden costs to the natives of a legacy of perceived injustices, affronts, and threats to their very way of life. Already in 1675 the Wampanoag grievances had historical depth, and with no end in sight, they presaged a long and unhappy future for America's other native peoples.

The most important issue for the Wampanoags was the hemorrhaging of their land. Even the minor colonial poet Benjamin Tompson recognized this, and in 1676 he adopted a native perspective to write a poem blaming both the land-selling chiefs and the land-hungry newcomers:

> They sel our land to english man who teach
> Our nation all so fast to pray and preach:
> Of all our country they enjoy the best,
> And quickly they intend to have the rest.

M UCH OF THE LAND WITHIN PLYMOUTH'S ROYAL GRANT was uninhabitable, as it still is today, and at first the Wampanoags owned the best of the rest. That soon changed, yet not because the colony permitted a lawless land grab. In 1643, the Plymouth General Court prohibited the purchase of native land without its approval and reserved for the tribes certain key sites, such as Mount Hope, whether or not the Indian proprietors of the land wished to sell. A generation later, in 1662, Gov. Thomas Prence agreed with Philip to halt all Indian land sales for seven years. (Prence was largely concerned that land-related complaints would overwhelm the colony's modest legal system.)

John Sassamon!

The sources for the life of John Sassamon, as for much of this story, are few in number and full of holes. We know that Sassamon's parents survived the epidemics that killed so many coastal Indians between 1616 and 1618 and that they chose to live among the English in Dorchester, eventually converting to Christianity during the early 1630s. After they died, Sassamon (probably a young adolescent at the time) was taken in by whites, who taught him how to read and write English. His activities in connection with John Eliot's missionary work made him fairly well known among the English, but no portrait of him exists. All that remains are his name and his mark (shown above).

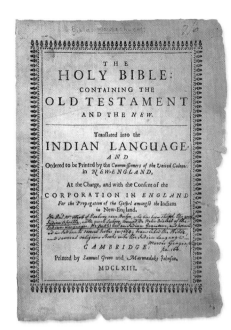

THE
HOLY BIBLE:
CONTAINING THE
OLD TESTAMENT
AND THE *NEW.*

Tranflated into the
INDIAN LANGUAGE
AND
Ordered to be Printed by the *Commiffioners of the United Colonie*
in *NEW-ENGLAND,*

At the Charge, and with the Confent of the
CORPORATION IN *ENGLAND*
For the *Propagation of the Gofpel amongft the Indians*
in New-England.

CAMBRIDGE:
Printed by *Samuel Green* and *Marmaduke Johnfon.*
MDCLXIII.

This is the *English title page from the 1663 edition of John Eliot's Algonkian translation of the Bible. Most of the copies were lost or destroyed during King Philip's War.*

Significantly, it was Philip who broke this moratorium three years later when he sold some land to the town of Rehoboth. Then in 1672, again feeling the need for quick cash, he sold twelve square miles in Taunton for less than a shilling an acre. The price may have smarted, but not as much as the suit for eight hundred pounds—a substantial colonial fortune—that a Rhode Islander laid against him in the Plymouth court after a large land deal initiated in 1661 by his brother Alexander went sour.

Philip also knew firsthand the threat that English livestock posed to native fields, fauna, and purses. Unfenced colonial cows and horses not only trampled and devoured Indian corn but also drove away deer and injured themselves by falling into native deer traps, for which damage the trapper would have to pay dearly. English pigs were only somewhat less objectionable. They too rooted about in native gardens and ruined communal clam beds, but at least when adopted they required little management and served as an easy substitute for deer protein. Indeed, the Indians living in the Plymouth Colony became so adept at hog raising and processing that they began to undercut their English neighbors in the Boston market. Jealous colonists responded by forbidding Indians to mark the ears of their hogs, many of which the English suspected had been stolen by the Indians and passed off as their own. Philip himself received an even sharper slap in 1669, when Portsmouth officials ordered him to remove his herd of pigs from nearby Hog Island, where he and English townsmen had traditionally grazed animals to escape predators. Such treatment must have galled Philip as much as knowing that his native nemeses, the Christian Indians, were being induced to move to praying towns partly by gifts of livestock from English missionaries.

In June 1676, *Edward Rawson, secretary of the Massachusetts Bay Colony, presented engraved brass medals such as this one to the chiefs of loyal tribes fighting alongside the English during King Philip's War.*

ALTHOUGH THE SEPARATIST Pilgrims of Plymouth had never been as keen to proselytize as their neighbors, the Massachusetts Puritans, the Wampanoags from the beginning had been notably resistant to Christianity. In his last negotiation with Plymouth officials, who were seeking to purchase some native land at Swansea, Massasoit had tried to include in the deed a provision requiring the English (as a Puritan minister put it) to abstain from "draw[ing] away any of his People from their old *Pagan* superstitions,

It was money donated by patrons in England that prompted the Rev. John Eliot of Roxbury in 1643 to begin learning the Algonkian tongue. He finished his translation of the New Testament in 1661, printing fifteen hundred copies of it that year. Two years later, when his translation of the Old Testament was finished, he published a thousand copies of the complete Bible text. The opening pages of the Book of Genesis from the 1663 edition are shown here. Eliot claimed that converts could understand his translation, but many others (including some praying Indians) disagreed.

and devilish Idolatry, to the Christian Religion." Neither Massasoit nor, later, his equally adamant sons succeeded in this.

Philip, at least, appreciated the opposition because he had, however briefly, entertained the possibility of conversion himself. In 1664, he had sent to John Eliot for, Eliot noted, "books to learne to read" with John Sassamon "in order to praying unto God." Along with those books, Eliot sent Massachusetts Indian missionaries to persuade the sachem of the benefits of Christianity. As late as June 1674, Philip was known to have slipped into a church service held at the home of the Rev. John Cotton Jr. in Plymouth.

Although Massachusetts Indian commissioner Daniel Gookin lamented that same year Philip's "sensual and carnal lusts," which "hold him fast under Satan's dominions," the sachem's principal objections to praying were less moral than political. According to Eliot's half-historical, half-instructive *Indian Dialogues,* written and published in 1671, the first objection that Philip expressed to the missionaries sent to convert him was that "you praying Indians do reject your sachems, and refuse to pay them tribute…. If I should pray to God, and all my people with me, I must become as a common man among them, and so lose all my power and authority over them." Furthermore, he argued, if all of his people did not join him in converting, "especially such as hate praying to God" would shift their allegiance to other sachems. Thus, "if I be a praying sachem, I shall be a poor and weak one, and easily trod upon by others, who are like to be more potent and numerous."

FURTHER READING

★ James Axtell, *Natives and Newcomers: The Cultural Origins of North America* (2001)

★ Eric B. Schultz and Michael J. Tougias, *King Philip's War: The History and Legacy of America's Forgotten Conflict* (1999)

This buff leather coat belonged to John Leverett, governor of the Massachusetts Bay Colony from 1673 until his death in 1679. It was made from the hide of an ox by an unknown English craftsman. Heavy buff coats such as this were at first worn as additional protection underneath one's armor. When it became apparent, however, that armor offered little protection against bullets, soldiers began using the buff coat as their sole body protection because of the far greater mobility it afforded them.

Philip's concerns were certainly reasonable. Several hundred of his people had already withdrawn from his rule to accept the "yoke of Christ," and in 1670, for the first time, an Indian church within the Plymouth Colony had called a regular minister. This last development did not bode well for Philip's "pagan" empire. In fact, war nearly broke out in the spring of 1671, when Philip stiffly rebuffed the importunities of John Eliot and his Massachusetts Indian missionaries. Equally troubling to Philip were the persistent efforts of the junior John Cotton, who began in 1667 preaching twice a month in various Wampanoag villages. In March 1671, some of Philip's warriors, painted and armed, swaggered through the English town of Swansea, established four years earlier on prime land ceded by the Indians. Swansea was also the English town closest to Philip's own village at Sowams, whose unfenced cornfields made tempting targets for English livestock. Alarmed by the natives' bravado, the Plymouth General Court summoned Philip to Taunton on April 12, 1671, where he was compelled to confess a plot to attack the English, apologize for his "naughty hart," pay a fine, and surrender his English weapons.

As if that were not humiliation enough, five months later Plymouth officials summoned Philip again to answer for having "broken his covenant made with our collonies" by harboring and abetting "divers [foreign] Indians…our professed enimies." Before this second appearance in court, Philip had been persuaded by John Eliot to seek the aid of Massachusetts in arbitrating his grievances against Plymouth, but the effort proved fruitless, much to Eliot's chagrin; only a weak letter was sent to Plymouth's governor reminding him that the colony's relationship with the sachem should be a "naighborly and frindly correspondency." Even this much Governor Prence resented. In the end, after representatives from Massachusetts and Connecticut threw their weight against him, Philip was forced to swear an oath of fidelity to Plymouth and, in order to get his guns back, agree to pay a hefty fine of one hundred pounds and meet an annual quota of five wolves' heads.

Philip managed to pay the fine but only by selling more of his dwindling birthright. "Now," he told Easton four years later at their June 17 parley, the Wampanoags "had not so much land or muny," and they would "as good be kiled as leave all ther liveflyhode."

ONE WEEK AFTER this conference with Easton, some of Philip's warriors attacked Swansea, igniting what descendants of the victors have called King Philip's War. As Easton had foreseen, this conflict between the native and white cohabitants of Plymouth Colony soon engulfed all of southern New England and, a year later, northern New England as well. On one side, the militias of Connecticut, Massachusetts, and Rhode Island joined forces with their Plymouth brethren (and numerous Indian allies) under the royal banner of Charles II, their mutual English king. On the other, the Nipmucks of central Massachusetts, the powerful Narragansetts of western Rhode Island, and tribes of the upper Connecticut River Valley joined the Wampanoags in their quest for short-term revenge and long-term justice.

Relative to the region's population, the war was the costliest in American history. On a proportionate basis, it took more lives and destroyed more property than any other. The English lost more than six hundred fighting men and uncounted civilians; nearly half of their towns

This engraving depicts a battle scene during King Philip's War. Although the colonists' formalized methods of fighting weren't well adapted to the New World, their advantage in firearms was decisive. Seventeenth-century guns weren't particularly accurate, but the noise and smoke that they made unnerved most Indians, even if the bullets didn't kill them.

This war club, made from the ball root of a maple and inlaid with wampum, is believed to have been King Philip's.

In 1710, Mohawk chiefs Ho Nee Yeath (left) and Sa Ga Yeath (right) visited London, where their exotic appearance and manner created a public sensation. On commission from Queen Anne, with whom they had an audience, Dutch artist John Verelst painted the portraits shown here. Paul Revere later borrowed from mezzotints of these paintings to create his own 1772 engraving of King Philip (opposite).

were torched and abandoned; twelve hundred houses and thousands of bushels of grain were burned; eight thousand head of cattle were killed (and, symbolically, often tortured and mutilated to demonstrate the natives' contempt). Even so, the Indians suffered worse: Perhaps nine thousand of Philip's twelve thousand supporters and allies died from wounds, exposure, or starvation; another two thousand fled the region, many to fight another day in another theater; and of the remaining thousand or so, most were captured and sold into foreign or domestic slavery. This conclusive decimation of New England's native population rendered it forever incapable of self-defense and political sovereignty.

FOR ALL HIS COCKEYED OPTIMISM, Easton might possibly have been able to postpone this brutal war, but he could never have prevented it. Not much longer could the Indians have tolerated the "long train of abuses and usurpations" increasingly inflicted upon them by their more numerous, more powerful, and less tolerant English neighbors. (The quotation comes from the Declaration of Independence, written a hundred years later by the descendants of these very New Englanders when *they* could no longer refrain from making their own war of independence.)

Immigrant farmers in search of arable land, along with aggressively Christian refugees seeking to build exclusive "cities upon a hill" (to use John Winthrop's memorable phrase), saw the Indians as impediments to their dreams. So the newcomers framed elaborate rationalizations for dispossessing the natives: They lauded the "providential" epidemics, caused by imported diseases, that regularly reduced native populations and employed every trick in the book, legal or otherwise, to separate the Indians from their land and lifeways.

The English seldom initiated wars to achieve their material and spiritual ends. Instead, they consistently saved moral face by prodding and provoking the natives—who usually knew the odds they faced—into firing the first shot. The English then answered these "attacks" with

Although Paul Revere had no idea what the Wampanoag sachem actually looked like, this 1772 portrait has become the most famous image of Philip.

righteous fury. It was such a successful strategy that, after 1776, the Americans retained it and employed it late into their history. Yet the effectiveness of this manipulation did not blind John Easton, and it should not blind us, to the bald fact that "the English had begun mischif to the indians"—and that the descendants of both, in different coin, have paid the consequences ever since.

★ ★ ★

GEORGE WHITEFIELD.M.A.

Elisha Gallaudet   Sculp. NYork 1774

OCTOBER 23, 1740

WHITEFIELD AWAKENS AMERICA

BY JOHN DEMOS

NATHAN COLE WOULD not forget that morning— not soon, not ever. A full thirty years later, his mind still held all the details of October 23, 1740. He had been up early, as usual, "at work in my field" in the Connecticut farm-village of Kensington, when "on a sudden, about 8 or 9 o'clock, there came a messenger…and [he] said 'Mr. Whitefield had preached at Hartford and Wethersfield yesterday, and is to preach at Middletown this morning.'" Middletown was twelve miles away, and time was short. Cole "dropped my tool that I had in my hand, and run home, and run through my house, and bade my wife get ready quick to go and hear Mr. Whitefield…and run to my pasture for my horse with all my might, fearing I should be too late to

hear him." In another few minutes they were on their way, and "going as fast as I thought the horse could bear."

Periodically, Cole would jump down and run along on foot to give the horse a breather; thus he and his wife "improved every moment to get along, as if we were fleeing for our lives," among a steady stream of friends and neighbors bent on the same objective. "All were in a lather and foam, with sweat and breath rolling out of their nostrils…. [And] every horse seemed to go with all his might to carry his rider to hear the news from Heaven." As thick clouds of dust swirled around them, they crossed a river, with everyone pressing forward pell-mell, and finally reached "the old meetinghouse [where] a great multitude…said to be 3 or 4 thousand people [had] assembled together." There Cole and his wife dismounted, shook off the dust of the road, looked back, "and saw the ferryboats running swift forward and backward, bringing over loads of people…. Men, horses, and boats all seemed to be struggling for life. The land and the banks looked black with people and horses."

AT LEFT: *This engraving of George Whitefield appeared as the frontispiece in a 1774 edition of his memoirs.*

ABOVE: *Whitefield consciously marketed himself, and publications were among his most effective tools. This fourteen-page 1745 pamphlet was written in response to "some passages relating to the Revd. Mr. Whitefield" that had appeared in a recently published book by Boston minister (and Whitefield critic) Charles Chauncy.*

This scene of excitement and tumult, described in the homely yet vivid phrasings of a quite ordinary farmer, was part of an extraordinary religious revival known ever since as the Great Awakening. Its spark, not to say its consuming flame, was indeed the preaching of the Rev. George Whitefield. And Nathan Cole was but one of many to feel its intense heat.

WHITEFIELD HAD BEEN BORN in Gloucester, England, in 1714—the seventh and youngest child of a village innkeeper. His youth was marked by signs of obvious intelligence, strong ambition, and a particular interest in the theater. In due course, he won a place at Oxford as a "servitor" (a category of students from poor families who were obliged to wait on more affluent classmates in exchange for free tuition). There he turned deeply pious, renounced his fascination for the "immoral" world of acting, and decided to become a minister. There, too, he fell under the sway of two fellow students, John and Charles Wesley, leaders of the spiritual movement that would eventuate in the faith (and church) known as Methodism.

After his ordination in June 1736, Whitefield made a further decision, to dedicate himself to the cause of foreign missions. However, while waiting to travel overseas, he began preaching on an occasional basis to various church congregations around London. Almost at once he revealed a prodigious talent. Within a scant few weeks, he was winning admirers and converts by the hundreds—and then by the thousands. In effect, the actor manqué had found a new and far more expansive stage for his powerfully rendered performances.

This rendering *of a mid-seventeenth-century New England farm (albeit one more grand than Nathan Cole might have worked) was engraved in 1761 by James Peake, after a painting by the English landscape artist Paul Sandby.*

Yet even as his fame increased, Whitefield roused the ire of a good many London clergymen whose piety he was not loath to question. As a result, local pulpits were frequently closed to him, and he was obliged to take up a pattern of "field preaching." This was not quite his own invention—others had recently begun experimenting with the same idea—but he developed and perfected it brilliantly. Huge throngs would be gathered in designated outdoor spaces, where Whitefield could preach without official interference.

His London triumphs were but a prelude to what he would soon achieve across the ocean in the British colonies of North America. In the spring of 1738, in the wake of his friends the Wesleys, he sailed for Georgia to found a missionary orphanage; and with this as his base, he began a series of ambitious revival tours. Traveling by whatever means necessary—sometimes by boat, but also by stagecoach and on horseback—he went first to Pennsylvania and New York, then to the Carolinas, and finally to New England. Waves of anticipation preceded him, thanks both to newspaper accounts of his preaching and to a growing network of personal correspondence with and among his followers. (Whitefield himself is said to have written as many as one hundred letters a day to publicize his ongoing endeavors.) The crowds that greeted him at every stop grew correspondingly. As before in London, members of the regular clergy were divided in their response. Some became his eager supporters (and copreachers); some stood aside; some tried strenuously to oppose him.

EVEN BEFORE WHITEFIELD'S ARRIVAL, organized religion in colonial America was in an increasingly fractured state; and his activities (along with the regular clergy's response) exposed the fault lines for all to see. The old Puritan tradition survived in New England, and in some ways it prospered. Yet its leaders bemoaned a "declension" of active piety among the rank and file; many, indeed, spoke darkly of divine wrath and retribution to come. Churchgoing remained very much the norm, but fewer and fewer parishioners approached the sense of inward "grace" that alone was supposed to assure salvation in the afterlife.

THE ORIGINS OF METHODISM

In its beginnings, Methodism expressed a deep protest against the spirit of worldliness and privilege that had come to characterize the established Church of England, especially in university settings. Brothers John Wesley (below) and Charles Wesley (above), along with others in Methodism's founding group, committed themselves to an austere regimen of prayer, pious self-examination, and acts of private charity. Many, like Whitefield himself, kept journals to record their spiritual "exercises" in minute detail. All repudiated the gentlemanly sports and socializing that otherwise typified undergraduate life at Oxford and elsewhere. Their focus was not on fine points of theology and doctrine but rather on the "methods" of religious devotion, hence the name subsequently applied to them.

Other denominations, elsewhere, faced similar problems. In the so-called Middle Colonies of New York, New Jersey, and Pennsylvania, Protestant sects proliferated hugely; Quakers, Presbyterians, Lutherans, Mennonites, Moravians, Dunkers, and a host of other, smaller groups formed a kind of religious crazy-quilt across the landscape. Farther south, Catholics predominated in Maryland, and Anglicans in Virginia and the Carolinas. Among all these groups, secular concerns seemed increasingly to trump spiritual ones. Hardly anyone eschewed religion altogether, but most directed their energies to gaining and keeping a modest level of material comfort (and, in some cases, a good deal more).

With people of every religious persuasion, Whitefield's appeal would prove irresistible and astonishing. And because he cared little for denominational politics, what he offered was open to all. His preaching style was direct, extemporaneous, and blatantly emotional. His words were punctuated with passionate gestures and frequently with tears. He enacted, as well as expounded, his message. His voice was described as being unusually "clear and musical"; it was also powerful enough to be heard across the broad expanse of his "field" meeting sites. His focus was invariably the experience of spiritual conversion and "rebirth"; his approach, then, was intensely personal.

> **"THE GOD THAT HOLDS YOU OVER THE PIT OF HELL, MUCH AS ONE HOLDS A SPIDER, OR SOME LOATHSOME INSECT, OVER THE FIRE, ABHORS YOU, AND IS DREADFULLY PROVOKED."**
>
> —*Jonathan Edwards,* Sinners in the Hands of an Angry God, *1741*—

Moreover, the collective excitement of his audience heightened the effects of his innate charisma. Colonists accustomed to the more restrained ministrations of their traditional leadership were simply—and repeatedly—"overcome." Audience numbers reached perhaps five thousand in Hartford, ten thousand in Philadelphia (among the rest an admiring Benjamin Franklin), and by one estimate over twenty thousand for Whitefield's farewell sermon in Boston. These were extraordinary levels for a small-scale, still premodern society. (For example, the entire

GEORGE WHITEFIELD

1714 – 1770

Among the Americans Whitefield engaged was Benjamin Franklin, whose belief in a vague "deism"—acknowledging God as "prime mover" but not as an active "revealed" presence in human affairs—differed greatly from Whitefield's own intense evangelical piety. Yet over time these two men developed a genuine friendship. Franklin once went to hear Whitefield "resolved he should get nothing from me." But then, "as he proceeded, I began to soften, and concluded to give the coppers [pennies]. Another stroke of his oratory made me ashamed of that, and determined me to give the silver. And he finished so admirably that I emptied my pocket wholly into the collector's dish, gold and all."

population of Boston in 1740 was barely twenty-five thousand.) Even in rural areas, Whitefield's arrival would draw large gatherings of farmers, artisans, and their families, summoned from miles around and often (as Cole's account attests) on very short notice.

HAVING COME TO APPRECIATE his independent status, Whitefield enjoyed the element of sheer movement—here today, somewhere else tomorrow—once describing himself happily as a "Gospel rover." His triumphal 1740 tour of New England included two dozen stops in five colonies, all within the space of just over a month; and his itineraries farther south were no less frenetic. Typically, however, the effects of his visits greatly outlasted his brief personal presence, for there were others eager to forward the cause of awakening. Gilbert Tennent of New Jersey, James Davenport of Long Island, and (most especially) Jonathan Edwards of Northampton, Massachusetts, became powerful itinerants in their own right. Moreover, all across the land, small-town ministers sought to achieve something of the same result at the local level. Occasionally, the banner passed even to unschooled and unordained "exhorters," whose "rantings" and "brayings" would prove a particularly inviting target for opponents of the Great Awakening.

To be sure, none of this commotion was entirely without precedent. As far back as the settlement era (the second quarter of the seventeenth century), revivals of a sort had punctuated religious life in many colonial churches. The very process of migration during the 1630s had lifted the first New England colonists into a high orbit of spiritual excitement; and from time to time in the years that followed, individual ministers had reaped "harvests" of converts within their particular congregations.

The first important glimmerings of a broader revival appeared during the 1720s among the Presbyterian churches of New Jersey and their Dutch Reformed counterparts in Pennsylvania. Then, in 1734, a "glorious work of salvation" began in the Connecticut River Valley. At its source was Jonathan Edwards's Northampton congregation, but other nearby towns were quickly pulled in. Soon thereafter, Edwards published (in both London and Boston) a "faithful narrative" of the valley revivals, which introduced them to a much wider audience.

FURTHER READING

★ Frank Lambert, *Inventing the "Great Awakening"* (1999)

★ Harry S. Stout, *The Divine Dramatist: George Whitefield and the Rise of Modern Evangelicalism* (1991)

This article— taken from an issue of the Boston Gazette *dated September 15–22, 1740—* notes Whitefield's activities that week, culminating with his famous farewell sermon of Sunday, September 21, delivered on Boston Common.

This woodcut portrays Whitefield in 1742 preaching at Moorfields, a park on the edge of London. Whitefield liked Moorfields because crowds gathered there often. It was also a favorite location for shows, many of them indecent.

THESE, CLEARLY, WERE PRECURSORS of the "great alteration" (in Edwards's own phrase) that began with Whitefield's sensational tours. What had heretofore been limited and local was now being described as "general" and "remarkable." Full-fledged spiritual conversions (akin to the modern-day experience of being "born again") were but the most visible sign of a massive, and spreading, public engagement. Regular Sunday services were marked by vivid physical "manifestations" (jerkings, faintings, and other trancelike behaviors, plus recurrent "shriekings and shoutings"). There were also special weekday "lectures," neighborhood prayer meetings, and much ad hoc individual counseling of the "anxious," all serving to stoke the fires still further. Church attendance swelled to levels not seen in generations.

The revivals peaked at different times in different regions: 1740 in New Jersey and Pennsylvania, 1741 in central New England, 1742 a bit farther north, but not until 1745–1746 in the eastern counties of Virginia. In each case, the peak was followed by a sharp drop in intensity and then a long aftermath of reassessment and controversy. Theologians such as Edwards and Charles Chauncy (of Boston) debated the legitimacy of the Great Awakening in a virtual blitz of sermons, learned treatises, and books. Individual churches divided into opposing parties of New Lights and Old Lights—the former enthusiastically supporting the revivals, the latter denouncing their excessive emotionalism and tendency to undermine established authority. Often enough, this led to formal acts of separation, with a single congregation becoming two or three.

Moreover, these disputes helped reshape the contours of prevalent belief. One result was a reinvigoration of traditional predestinarian Calvinism; another was a renewed emphasis on human sinfulness and divine sovereignty. Meanwhile, a new spirit of liberalism also emerged, characterized by a readiness to embrace all believers in a community of shared hope and faith.

THROUGHOUT THE SUCCEEDING CENTURIES, historians, too, have debated the meaning and consequence of the Great Awakening. In some respects it seems a distinctly conservative movement, aimed (as it explicitly was) at reviving an older, more austere, and more demanding form of piety. Yet, taken as a whole, it pointed forward in time: toward the War of Independence, the growth of American nationhood, the establishment of a lasting tradition of evangelical religion, and a host of cultural changes that have increasingly defined our modern society.

It is clear, for example, that the Great Awakening blurred the usual lines of class, age, gender, ethnicity, and race to a degree rarely, if ever, seen before in the colonies. Observers repeatedly commented on the "mixed" character of revival audiences; some, indeed, expressed deep alarm at the apparent threat to traditional hierarchies. At the same time, the Great Awakening gave a strong boost to intercolonial connections. Never before had a single episode been shared so widely—in the North, the South, and in between; in urban centers as well as rural villages; from the maritime-minded coast to the far-off frontier. Subsequent events, such

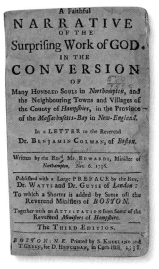

Edwards's Faithful Narrative of the Surprising Work of God in the Conversion of Many Hundred Souls in Northampton *is shown here in its third edition, published in 1738.*

JONATHAN EDWARDS

1703 – 1758

Jonathan Edwards entered Yale before turning thirteen, was graduated first in his class, and then stayed on to study for the ministry. In 1729, he succeeded his grandfather as pastor of the Congregational church in Northampton, Massachusetts, where he struggled for two decades defending Puritan orthodoxy against a rising tide of theological liberalism. In 1737, he published his Faithful Narrative and four years later, Sinners in the Hands of an Angry God, probably the most famous sermon of the Great Awakening. Increasingly, though, his authoritarianism produced unease among the church members, and in 1750 his congregation dismissed him.

Congregationalist minister Charles Chauncy served the First Church of Boston from 1727 until his death in 1787. During that time, he was one of the Great Awakening's leading critics. Chauncy often complained that the revivalists (especially Whitefield) used publicity as a weapon to put antirevivalists on the defensive. "All who did not express a very high Thought of Mr. Whitefield, were lookt upon with an evil Eye," Chauncy wrote at the time of Whitefield's 1740 visit to Boston.

as the French and Indian War and then the Revolution itself, would draw upon (and, in turn, deepen) this nascent sense of common identity. Moreover, the implicitly anti-authoritarian spirit of the revivals—the tendency to question leaders whose spirituality seemed "dead" and the feeling that every individual believer should be guided by his (or her) own inner experience—would help to germinate a growing republican consciousness.

Indeed, the very conduct of the revivals—their strategic and organizational framework—was transforming. In opting to leave the physical confines of long-established churches for fields, public squares, and other outdoor venues, Whitefield took himself and his followers into the dawning world of the market-place. Henceforth, religion would operate more and more as a "product" in direct competition with such secular pursuits as politics, sports, and the theater. From the standpoint of the auditors, Whitefield's sermons were themselves a kind of theater (the first such that many had ever experienced). With the colonies experiencing a kind of early consumer revolution, religious faith became itself another commodity—something to acquire, use, and purvey to others.

WHITEFIELD'S TACTICS in pursuing these goals were no less forward looking. Publicity was, in effect, his watchword from the start. Even as a very young and inexperienced preacher in London, he had sought to use newspapers and other print media to build interest and excitement. Announcements and advertisements of upcoming meetings, reports of his most recent successes, the printing of selections from his personal journal, and the publication of essays of doctrinal "disputation" all figured consistently in his plans. His private diaries show an unbroken attentiveness to matters of public image; time after time, he described in detail the impressions (almost always favorable) he made on others.

Thus did he cultivate a persona to match his broader objectives. And he succeeded in this beyond anyone's wildest expectations (except, possibly, his own). Within a mere half-dozen years, Whitefield had become the first great intercolonial celebrity: a man whose name was known from Maine to Georgia and across the ocean as well. Never before had it even been possible for one individual to acquire fame so broadly and rapidly. But now, as a new age of mass communication began throughout the Western world, it *was* possible—and Whitefield showed the way.

Finally, Whitefield and his fellow preachers of the Great Awakening created a style of religious leadership that has been with us ever since. Before their time, the clergy had been tied to settled churches; afterward, itinerancy was always a possibility—and, for some, an all-consuming vocation. Before, preaching had typically been measured, methodical, formal; afterward, it became increasingly emotional and personalized. Before, the norm was the preacher-scholar; afterward, it was, at least in part, the preacher-performer. Before, the credentials of influential ministers were those of birth, breeding, education, and institutional connection; afterward, they included personal charisma, popularity, and effective public relations. Between Whitefield's time and our own stretches a 250-year tradition of full-bore evangelism, embraced by such figures as Charles Grandison Finney, Dwight L. Moody, Billy Sunday, Oral Roberts, and Billy Graham.

Oral Roberts conducts a tent revival in Virginia in 1954. Since the time of the Great Awakening, the core of revivalism has always been its beliefs in the sinfulness of humankind and the possibility of redemption. The way to avoid eternal damnation, its practitioners have taught, is to surrender to God's will, which usually entails an emotionally wrenching conversion experience. Roberts's pleadings and exhortations often encouraged such experiences.

OPPOSITE:

This 1953 portrait of Billy Graham accompanied the Look article "Barrymore of the Bible" describing the charismatic evangelist as "an uninhibited friend of man who believes in a literal heaven and hell." Once you've heard Graham preach, according to Look, "you cannot doubt his sincerity."

I F WHITEFIELD WAS THE PROTOTYPE for all this (and he has as good a claim as any), then Nathan Cole, rushing across the Connecticut countryside that autumn morning in 1740, was similarly a prototype for the many in our own day who flock to evangelism. To Cole, then, belongs the last word, as—his journey completed, his horse tethered, his clothes dusted off—he turned his face upward in rapt admiration:

> When I saw Mr. Whitefield come upon the scaffold, he looked almost angelical: a young, slim, slender youth, before some thousands of people and with a bold undaunted countenance. And hearing how God was with him everywhere as he came along, it solemnized my mind and put me in trembling fear before he began to preach, for he looked as if he was clothed with authority from the great God. And a sweet solemnity sat upon his brow, and my hearing him preach gave me a heart wound, by God's blessing…. And all the air was love, [and] I saw that everything that was sin fled from the presence of God…. Now I saw with new eyes, all things became new: a new God, new thoughts, and new heart.

★ ★ ★

of expression in my Mo. et al.
and is severe on Dickinson
Mr. Jn.º Rutledge — against any
Concession whatever, that Lord
North has given Us his Ultimatum
with which we cannot agree
treats Dickinsons plan with
the utmost Contempt —
and is so severe that Chase rises
to explain himself —
Col. Lee up again —
Mr. Stone of Maryland — so
disagreeable that one half of the
Congress withdraw —
Mr. Lynch up —
adj.d at Four OClock —
dined with Friend S. Collins, &
supp'd with C. Marshall —

Wednesday: in Congress New York

MAY 24, 1775

SILAS DEANE'S DIARY

BY JACK N. RAKOVE

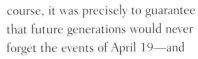

MAY 24 IS NOT, by any account, the most memorable day of 1775. That honor indisputably belongs to April 19, when an anonymous soldier (whether British or American we will never know), standing on Lexington Green, fired the shot heard 'round the world that launched the war for independence. From eastern Massachusetts, express riders immediately carried news of the engagement to neighboring communities in New England and thence to the other colonies. These reports were soon followed by affidavits affirming that the militiamen had acted solely in self-defense when British regulars came tramping through the countryside, searching for the scarce arms and munitions the provisional forces of Massachusetts had been desperately hoarding.

"Hardly a man is now alive," the poet Henry Wadsworth Longfellow later wrote, "Who remembers that famous day and year." But, of

course, it was precisely to guarantee that future generations would never forget the events of April 19—and the preceding evening—that Longfellow wrote his famous 1863 poem "Paul Revere's Ride." Little matter that Revere never did complete his ride, because

> *You know the rest. In the books you have read*
> *How the British Regulars fired and fled,—*
> *How the farmers gave them ball for ball,*
> *From behind each fence and farmyard wall.*

With that first exchange at Lexington, the subsequent clash at Concord, and the long British retreat to Boston, the road to civil war and independence was laid. Events soon tumbled one upon the other in rapid succession: The even deadlier battle of Bunker Hill was fought only two months later on June 17; George Washington took command of the Continental Army on July 3; and on August 23, King George III pronounced the American colonies to be in open rebellion against his and Parliament's rule.

Next to these dramatic developments, the debate that came to a climax on May 24 in

SILAS DEANE

1737 – 1789

*In 1776, while still
a delegate to the
Continental Congress,
Silas Deane was chosen
for a secret mission to
France, becoming the
first U.S. diplomat sent
abroad. Deane's assign-
ment was to solicit
financial and military
aid that would result in
a formal alliance. He
succeeded, signing in
February 1778 a treaty
that he had negotiated
with the help of
Benjamin Franklin
and Arthur Lee. Upon
his return to America,
however, Deane became
the focus of a scandal.
On the basis of insinu-
ations by Lee, he was
accused of having billed
the government for
supplies that France had
presented as gifts. The
accusations ruined his
reputation and caused
him to leave the country.
He spent his remaining
years as an exile, first in
France and then in
England.*

the Continental Congress has been almost completely ignored. One reason is that the best (and virtually only) source for detail on the debate is a rather terse diary kept by Silas Deane of Connecticut. For events of such magnitude as debates in the Continental Congress, one might expect to find extensive records and accounts. Yet, as historians of the period know, members of Congress regularly withheld, even from their most confidential correspondents, news of divisions within their ranks. Delegates often wrote letters describing tensions and disagreements in personal terms, but they were extremely reluctant to reveal anything that might weaken their public show of unanimity.

Diarist Silas Deane was an energetic and quite effective delegate who went on to a more troubled career as a diplomatic commissioner in France. His diary entry for Wednesday, May 24, 1775, begins by noting the election of John Hancock of Massachusetts as acting president of the Second Continental Congress, replacing Peyton Randolph of Virginia. It then describes the renewal of a discussion, begun eight days earlier by John Dickinson of Pennsylvania, relating to "the old affair of the right of regulating Trade"—that is, whether Congress, in the interest of reconciliation, should concede that Parliament could continue to enact navigation laws regulating American commerce. Even though the colonists had already rejected the idea that Parliament had any inherent authority to legislate for

"WHAT A GLORIOUS MORNING FOR AMERICA!"

—

*Samuel Adams, remark (perhaps
apocryphal) upon hearing shots fired
at Lexington, April 19, 1775*

Americans, delegates like Dickinson thought that a voluntary recognition of Parliament's power to regulate imperial trade offered the surest hope for compromise. Trade was the real basis of the British empire, and regulatory powers had to be vested somewhere. Allowing Parliament to enact some navigation laws, if it simultaneously gave up its declared right to legislate for the colonies "in all cases whatsoever," seemed a reasonable price to pay for peace.

Deane's notes reveal little of the substance of this debate—it was, after all, an "old affair," previously agitated—but they do make clear that tensions were approaching the boiling point. The account of the debate ends with this line: "Mr. Stone of Maryland—so disagreeable that one half of the Congress withdraw." Most of the New England delegates, Deane among them, thought concessions pointless and even dangerous.

But Dickinson and other delegates from the Middle Colonies had good reason to be more cautious, for public opinion in their provinces was more divided and less confident of the wisdom of opposing Britain. Until May 24, their suspicion that radicals from New England and Virginia were trying to force events had lurked just beneath the surface; now, according to Deane, it erupted into open condemnation.

Historians have long known that the Second Continental Congress did not find it easy to strike just the right balance between urgent preparation for

The Battle of Lexington, April 19, 1775 *is the first plate in the famous series of Lexington and Concord engravings that Amos Doolittle published in New Haven in December 1775.*

war on the one hand and gestures of accommodation on the other. Some delegates already believed that the prospects for reconciliation were poor; others thought that the colonists could remain unified for war only by keeping the door to peace open as long as possible. Under these circumstances, it was not always possible for delegates to contain their suspicions about one another's motives. In one famous incident later that summer, Dickinson crossed the street rather than greet John Adams, the Massachusetts radical. Dickinson's reaction was caused by the publication in a Loyalist newspaper of an intercepted letter in which Adams mocked him as "a certain great Fortune and piddling Genius" who "has given a silly Cast to our whole Doings" by arguing so strongly for reconciliation.

Yet Deane's spare diary entry offers unique evidence of just how deeply these suspicions were operating in late May as Congress confronted the consequences of the outbreak of war against the greatest military power in the eighteenth-century Atlantic world. That on May 24 tensions ran high enough to cause half the delegates to walk out—apparently the more militant half, because Thomas Stone of Maryland was a moderate—is compelling evidence that Congress was far more divided and uncertain than has often been realized. The delegates were, in fact, at such loggerheads that they could no longer adhere to the decorum expected of speakers and listeners alike. How had Congress, and the colonists more generally, reached this point?

DOOLITTLE'S ENGRAVINGS

A native of Connecticut, Amos Doolittle learned to engrave in metal while serving as an apprentice to a silversmith. When the Revolution broke out, he joined the army, where he met Ralph Earl, an artist with a talent for battle scenes. Using Earl's drawings, Doolittle created a successful series of etchings commemorating the battles of Lexington and Concord. The demand for patriotic prints proved to be so great that Doolittle was soon able to abandon his silver work and support himself with his prints. Although not the first American engraver (as he later claimed), Doolittle was the first in the United States to produce original compositions on a regular basis.

JOHN DICKINSON

1732 – 1808

Before entering public life, John Dickinson (shown here in a 1782 portrait by Charles Willson Peale) studied law in London and practiced it in Philadelphia. He represented Pennsylvania at the 1765 Stamp Act Congress and drafted its declaration of rights and grievances. He also wrote Letters from a Farmer in Pennsylvania *(1768) and the "Declaration…Setting Forth the Causes and Necessity of Their Taking Up Arms" issued by the First Continental Congress. These efforts contributed to his reputation as "the penman of the Revolution." Still hoping for a reconciliation with Britain, though, he voted against the Declaration of Independence.*

M OST MEMBERS OF THE SECOND Continental Congress had also attended the First Congress, convened at Philadelphia in early September 1774. Two great concerns had dominated the political agenda at that time. The more important was the fashioning of a common strategy to persuade Parliament to repeal the Coercive Acts it had imposed on Massachusetts during the spring and summer of 1774. The first of these acts closed the port of Boston to commerce until restitution was made for the tea that local patriots had brewed in the harbor during the famous December 1773 Tea Party. Another, the Massachusetts Government Act, altered the colony's charter in order to strengthen the hand of the Crown—for instance, by limiting town meetings that might otherwise serve as forums for resistance to British policies. The Quartering Act legalized the billeting of troops in civilians' homes, and the last of the Coercive Acts— the Administration of Justice Act, which Americans called the Murdering Act—permitted the royal governor to remand to Britain for trial imperial officials and soldiers charged with capital offenses committed against colonists (rather than allow proceedings against them to continue in Massachusetts courts). The obvious point was to make an example of Massachusetts, a colony that Crown officials had long viewed as a source of irritation—the better to remind the other colonies of the cost of defying imperial policy.

But more than that, the Coercive Acts marked a definitive effort to prove that Parliament was indeed the supreme legislature for the entire British empire and that Americans were obliged to obey its decisions. In effect, the Coercive Acts made good the promise originally contained in the Declaratory Act of 1766. This legislation, which had accompanied the repeal of the Stamp Act, asserted that Parliament had the right to legislate for America "in all cases whatsoever" and pointedly ignored American claims to be bound only by laws enacted by their own assemblies. The sheer scope of the Coercive Acts demonstrated that, insofar as the British government was concerned, there were no limitations on Parliament's authority over the colonies. After May 1774, the phrase "in all cases whatsoever" had to be taken quite literally.

Yet the First Congress did not shrink from the challenge of defying the empire. During two months of debate, it drafted a Declaration of Rights repudiating parliamentary jurisdiction over America. Indeed, the only concession offered by Congress was the acknowledgment that Parliament could continue to regulate imperial trade—and even that sop was justified only on grounds of convenience, not according to right. At the same time, Congress drafted the Association, a plan to suspend the importation and consumption of British goods (and later the exportation of American products to Britain) until the Coercive Acts were repealed and the colonies restored to the political rights they had enjoyed in 1763 at the close of the Seven Years' War.

The second great challenge faced by the First Congress was to stabilize the situation in Massachusetts, lately grown much more volatile.

"THE CAUSE OF LIBERTY IS A CAUSE OF TOO MUCH DIGNITY, TO BE SULLIED BY TURBULENCE AND TUMULT."

—*John Dickinson,* Letters from a Farmer in Pennsylvania, *1768*—

Announcement of the Coercive Acts there had been accompanied by the appointment of a new military governor, Gen. Thomas Gage, whose rule would be enforced by recently dispatched British regulars. The provincial capital of Boston thus became an occupied city—but also something of a besieged one, because Gage did not have enough troops to control all the densely populated and politically mobilized towns surrounding the narrow peninsula on which eighteenth-century Boston sat.

Just as the First Congress convened in early September 1774, word reached Philadelphia of a further ominous development in the Bay Colony. A rumor had spread that Gage would be sending troops into the countryside. In response, militia companies throughout New England were assembling for a retaliatory march on Boston. Massachusetts, the delegates immediately realized, was a tinderbox, a conflagration waiting to happen, and a single spark could doom all prospects for negotiation and reconciliation. The problem was what to do about it. Congress could not afford to

THE OLIVE BRANCH PETITION

In addition to its firm Declaration of Rights, the First Continental Congress also issued one last appeal to the king: the so-called Olive Branch Petition. Drawn up by John Dickinson, it blamed the disorders on the king's ministers and begged George III to prevent Parliament from imposing further tyranny. When the petition reached the king in August 1775, however, he refused to receive it.

In this May 1774 *cartoon, King George's prime minister, Lord North, forces the Coercive Acts (also known as the Intolerable Acts) down the throat of America, which is represented by an Indian whose arms are restrained by other high British officials.*

allow hotheads in Massachusetts to provoke a conflict from which there could be no turning back. Yet how could the delegates ask or expect the people of Massachusetts to turn the other cheek should Gage attempt to rule by force? How could the other colonies deny the legitimacy of Massachusetts acting "on the defensive" in pursuit of its just rights? Finally, a consensus was reached: If force were directed against the residents of Massachusetts, they could, of course, respond in kind.

WHEN THE FIRST CONGRESS adjourned on October 26, 1774, most of its members remained of two minds about the course events might take before the scheduled reassembly of Congress in early May 1775. On the one hand, there was optimism: Although the First Congress had adopted strongly confrontational positions in its Olive Branch Petition to the king and its Declaration of Rights, many delegates hoped that their candor and unanimity would open the eyes of the British government to the depth of American opposition to its policies. To be sure, the ministry of Lord North would have to blink first; but once it did, these colonists believed, a compromise could be worked out. On the other hand, the delegates to the First Congress also understood that events in Massachusetts might spiral out of control, and so long as that colony adhered to a defensive posture—reacting, not provoking—the other colonies were morally and politically obligated to rally to its aid. They hoped that the government "at home" would realize, sooner rather than later, that the better part of valor was discretion—but in no case would they turn back from the militant positions taken at Philadelphia in the fall.

In the meantime, it was essential for American political leaders to preserve the unanimity of the colonies. "The great Point, *at present,* is to keep up the appearance of an unbroken Harmony in public measures, for fear of encouraging Great Britain to Hostilities, which, otherwise, she would avoid," John Dickinson observed in January 1775. "When she has made her Choice, and it proves inimical, I hope every Man of Sense & Virtue in America will draw his Sword." Strong words for an avowed moderate, but they capture the delicate balance in which Americans, for the time being, remained suspended.

Such British signals as reached America during the winter of 1774–1775 were discouraging. Lord North's party had called surprise elections for November 1774 in order to consolidate its control of the House of Commons before the effects of the American boycott could be

*This image of **Frederick North,** second earl of Guilford, accompanied an article published in London's* Town and Country Magazine *in March 1778. The text describes Lord North's career as having shown promise until "a fatal misunderstanding arose between the Mother-Country and the Colonies."*

felt. Meanwhile, the prime minister, his courage screwed up by his king, displayed little interest in reconciliation, as the colony of Massachusetts was declared in a state of rebellion and Parliament passed new laws restraining the commerce of all but four colonies. (Those that were exempted—New York, Delaware, North Carolina, and Georgia—the government mistakenly believed could be detached from the rest.) In Massachusetts, Gage found himself in a precarious position: under instructions from his government to enforce the acts of Parliament and restore order, yet lacking the necessary force to do so in the hostile environment of eastern Massachusetts. Outside occupied Boston, Gage knew, the colonists' provisional forces were gaining strength, and though he doubted these farmers and artisans would be a match for his regulars, he was painfully aware of the limits of his own strength.

On the fateful night of April 18–19, 1775, he sent a strong detachment to the outlying towns of Concord and Lexington, hoping to confiscate American weapons and arrest two key rebel leaders, Samuel Adams and John Hancock. Instead, his troops encountered units of the local militia who, if not yet well trained or disciplined, were brave enough to stand their ground and exchange shots with the British regulars. The war had begun.

With the outbreak of hostilities, reinforcements flocked to join the provisional colonial army in Massachusetts. These new recruits were also poorly trained and poorly armed, but they were enough to persuade Gage that it would be dangerous to send further forays beyond the limits of besieged Boston.

OVERLEAF:

This 1775 map shows the rebel works in and around Boston, as observed by Lieutenant Page of His Majesty's Corps of Engineers. Note the slender nape of Boston Neck, since filled in, which connects the center of town to the mainland. Boston's unusual geography made it an excellent port for oceangoing commerce but also a trap for occupying British forces.

Colonial Mag.

A, N.W. VIEW OF THE STATE HOUSE IN PHILADELPHIA taken 1778

This 1787 line engraving by James Trenchard follows Charles Willson Peale's A N.W. View of the State House in Philadelphia. It was in this building on Chestnut Street, now called Independence Hall, that the Second Continental Congress met. (The First Congress had met in nearby Carpenters' Hall.)

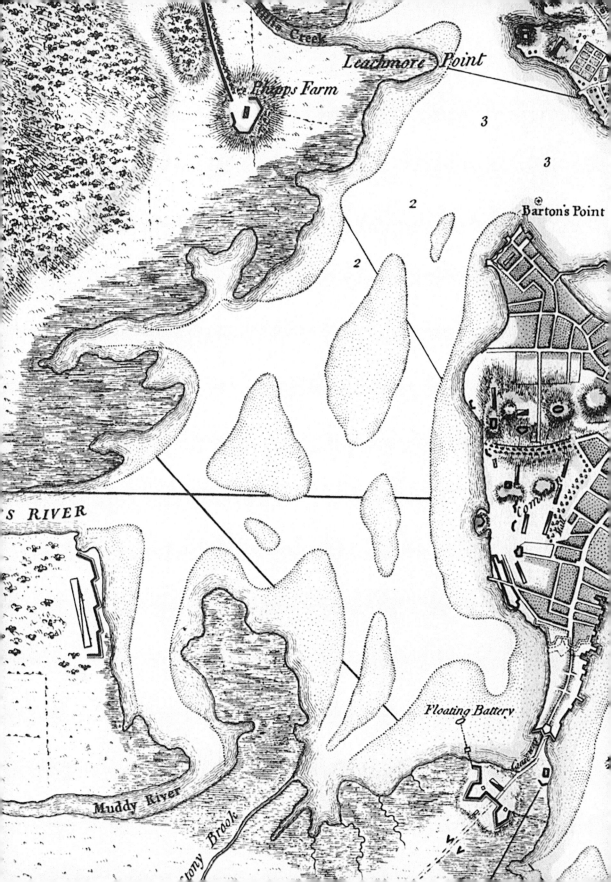

Creek

Leachmore Point

Phipps Farm

3

3

2

Barton's Point

2

S RIVER

Floating Battery

Muddy River

tony Brook

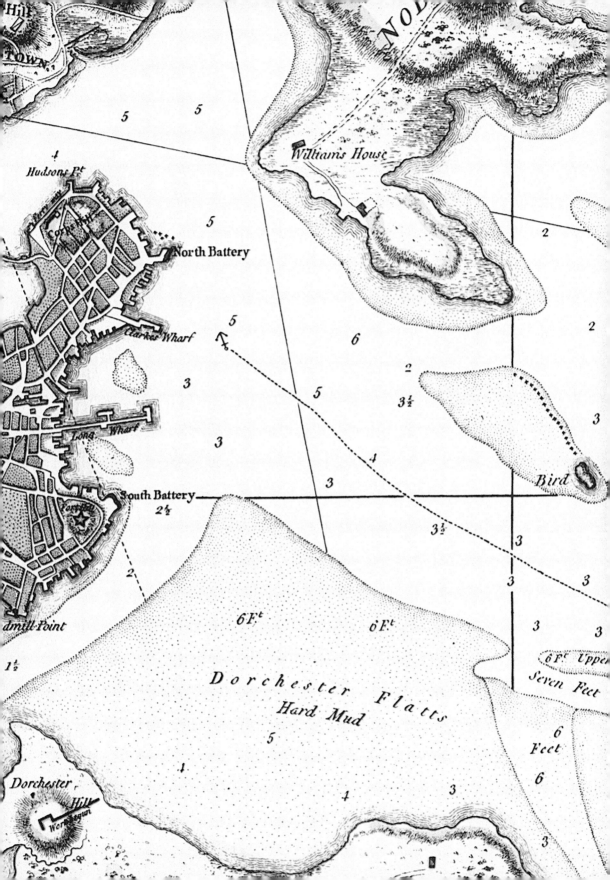

ADAMS AND HANCOCK

The Revolutionary War began with the battles of Lexington and Concord, but Thomas Gage's troops might never have left Boston that night had the general not decided finally to arrest Samuel Adams and John Hancock. Hancock, a merchant, became involved with the Revolution only when the Crown's custom officials began interfering with his thriving shipping business. Adams was more of a genuine radical, exposing British "plots" and writing polemical articles for the Boston newspapers as early as the 1760s.

THIS WAS THE SITUATION as the Continental Congress reconvened in Philadelphia on May 10. The British had *not* blinked; war *had* erupted; and now Congress had to decide not only whether it would adhere to its militant positions but also whether it would mobilize an army in support of Massachusetts. According to our careful diarist, this debate began in earnest on May 16, when Richard Henry Lee of Virginia introduced his "proposals for raising an army." Two delegates from South Carolina, Thomas Lynch and John Rutledge, quickly seconded this motion, with Rutledge seeking to shift the focus by "insist[ing] that previously some other points must be settled, such as do We aim at independancy? or do We only ask for a Restoration of Rights & putting of Us on Our old footing?" Resistance to Parliament had already escalated into an open war against the empire. Now, Rutledge wanted to know, would the colonists' war aims escalate as well?

At this point, John Dickinson intervened. His *Letters from a Farmer in Pennsylvania* had played a critical role in rallying opposition to the Townshend duties of 1767, thus earning him great political credit among the radicals. Yet now he spoke with the voice of moderation, agreeing that Congress should mount "a Vigorous preparation for War" but not at the expense of making every effort to promote reconciliation. In his manner, Deane noted, Dickinson was "very timid" and "is for giving up intirely the Regulating of Trade" (as the First Congress had proposed). He "argues smoothly but sophistically on the Subject," Deane went on, "and gives rather Disgust."

DISGUSTED OR NOT by Dickinson's pleas, the members of Congress put aside these questions, among them the regulation of trade, as they considered for the next week other matters related to defense. Whatever diplomatic strategy Congress ultimately chose, it was evident now that immediate measures were necessary to convert the motley force outside Boston into a true American army. The problems Congress faced included a scarcity of weapons and ammunition, the lack of serious military command experience among the colonists, and the daunting task of protecting an exposed coastline from a British army that could rely on naval transportation to land troops almost anywhere.

However, the basic question raised by Dickinson did not go away: Should Congress relax its 1774 positions in the interest of reconciliation, or should it stand fast in requiring that the first concessions be made by Britain? When Congress finally resumed its discussion of reconciliation on May 23, Dickinson restated his desire that Congress submit new petitions to the Crown and again concede to Parliament the power to regulate trade. This time, though, he added a new wrinkle: Now he wanted Congress to dispatch a diplomatic mission to London, armed with substantive powers to negotiate.

Dickinson's proposal was certainly a bold move, and many delegates worried that it went too far. Skeptics must have wondered whether it was wise to risk so much on such an embassy. For one thing, a mission sent to London would fall under enormous pressure—and be exposed to all sorts of other temptations—to strike a deal, which the American representatives would have to negotiate on their own, unsupervised and unsupported by Congress and the colonial assemblies. Moreover, how could Americans prepare effectively for a war that might still come when they were distracted by the prospect of negotiations abroad? Everyone's natural tendency would be to wait, avoiding prudent military measures in the hope that peace would prevail.

Finally, many delegates felt that they had already made the basic American position more than clear. In its Declaration of Rights, the First Congress had asked that the colonies be restored to the status they enjoyed in 1763, before Parliament and the Crown began imposing the new restrictions—a request that the British government dismissed with contempt. If Congress made further conciliatory gestures now, these could be interpreted as signs of weakness brought on by fear of war. Patrick Henry, already a legendary orator, was sufficiently roused by Dickinson's suggestion that the Americans yield first that he felt impelled to insist that the Declaration of Rights "must never be receded from."

When Congress assembled the next day, the ostensible issue under debate was a motion to permit New York to undertake military preparations for its own defense. Beginning with George Ross of Pennsylvania, some delegates called instead for "a full consideration of the whole Continent." Then Samuel Chase of Maryland interrupted. Here is how Silas Deane recorded the ensuing debate:

This notice, issued two months before Lexington and Concord by the Massachusetts Provincial Congress, requested commanding officers of each regiment of "Minute Men" to "take an exact State of their Numbers and Equipment."

This engraving by Philadelphia printmaker William Russell Birch shows the state of naval engineering during the late eighteenth century as the colonies prepared for war.

THE PATRIOTIC AMERICAN FARMER.

J—N D·K-NS—N, Esq; Barrister at Law.

Who with Attic Eloquence, and Roman Spirit, hath asserted the Liberties of the British Colonies in America.

'Tis nobly done to Stem Taxations Rage,
And raise the Thoughts of a degenerate Age,
For Happiness and Joy, from Freedom spring;
But Life in Bondage is a worthless Thing.

This 1772 woodcut, *entitled* The Patriotic American Farmer, *shows John Dickinson with his elbow resting on the Magna Carta as he holds his own "Farmer's Letters." Dickinson was particularly known for his knowledge of political theory and practical economics.*

Mr. Chase—in his old strain recurs to the old affair of the right of regulating Trade.

Mr. [William] Paca [Md.]—follows him in the same strain.

Mr. [Edmund] Pendleton [Va.]—answers him in particular.

Col. [Benjamin] Harrison [Va.] for letting the Motion [to arm New York] lye, & Consider, at large, in order to end the affair.

Mr. [James] Wilson [Pa.], again for arming New York, speaks earnestly.

Mr. Dickinson in his old Way lengthy, and concludes in his old Way with a Fable.

Mr. [Thomas] Mifflin [Pa.] animadverts with spirit on him and exposes his reasoning &c.

Mr. [Thomas] Johnson [Md.], on a reconciling plan and offers a Motion.

Col. [R. H.] Lee [Va.] for a different mode of expression in the Motion and is severe on Dickinson.

Mr. Jno. Rutledge—against any Concession whatever, that Lord North has given Us his Ultimatum with which We cannot agree—Treats Dickinson's plan with the utmost Contempt— and is so severe that Chase rises to explain himself.

Col. Lee up again.

Mr. [Thomas] Stone of Maryland—so disagreeable that one half of the Congress withdraw.

Mr. Lynch up.

Adj. at Four o'Clock.

EANE'S ENTRY is typically brief, but key phrases do reveal the passion of the debate: Chase and Dickinson going on in their "old strain" and "old Way," to Deane's evident exasperation; Rutledge speaking with "utmost Contempt"; Stone "so disagreeable" as to provoke a walkout. The fact that Dickinson was still "much affected with the loss of his youngest child," as Deane noted elsewhere, apparently did not spare him condemnation.

Deane's provocative entry makes it clear that passions and tensions within the Continental Congress had reached an exceptional depth. In all its history, down to 1789, there is no evidence that emotions in Congress ever again ran quite this high, even at times when delegates were bitterly divided over other issues. Yet Deane does not tell us how the delegates managed to put this moment of turmoil behind them. Whatever conciliatory gestures were made do not appear in the historical record. Perhaps all the delegates needed was a brief cooling off; perhaps a few delegates got together and worked to soothe feelings. What we do know is that when Congress reconvened the next morning, it simply picked up where it had left off. In the days and weeks ahead, it proceeded with the urgent task of military preparation, while continuing to ponder what new appeals might be made to the Crown and Parliament, as well as to public opinion in both Britain and America.

This 1798 stipple engraving, attributed to Edward Savage (after Robert Edge Pine's oil painting), shows the Second Continental Congress voting independence in the Assembly Room of the State House. Although Pine didn't complete his painting until 1785, his rendering—of the setting, at least—is considered highly accurate.

In the last analysis, it was the greater urgency of maintaining a united front that called the delegates back from the brink. In June and July, Congress worked steadily to organize the colonial defenses, hoping that war might be averted yet acting as though it were certain. Meanwhile, the British government showed no sign of shrinking from its original repressive strategy. Lord North still believed that a decisive show of force would persuade the colonists—at least those outside Massachusetts—to back down. Members of Congress had no choice but to respond in kind.

Later that summer, Congress did, in fact, agree to send another Olive Branch Petition to Britain, as Dickinson had wanted. Yet on the critical point of offering new concessions, the Pennsylvania Farmer and his allies lost. Nor would Congress retreat from any of the other key positions it had taken in 1774. The door for accommodation remained open, but a British proposal would have to pass through it first.

Of course, had the British government known of the divisions and tensions besetting the Continental Congress in late May 1775 and had it been a little more flexible, it might well have exploited the political situation to its advantage, deferring or perhaps even avoiding independence. Had the British merely hinted at a willingness to negotiate on favorable terms, for example, Dickinson and many others would surely have jumped at the opportunity. Yet the British were not well informed, and unlike present-day historians, they did not have the benefit of access to Silas Deane's diary. Thus they fumbled in the dark—particularly Lord North, who never developed an artful strategy. Only a handful of British leaders—and none with any power—ever grasped the tantalizing possibility that the Americans might not be as unified as they seemed.

★ ★ ★

FURTHER READING

★ Jerrilyn Greene Marston, *King and Congress: The Transfer of Political Legitimacy, 1774–1776* (1987)

★ Jack N. Rakove, *The Beginnings of National Politics: An Interpretive History of the Continental Congress* (1979)

OCTOBER 19, 1781

THE BATTLE OF YORKTOWN

BY ROBERT MIDDLEKAUFF

AT TWO O'CLOCK IN THE AFTERNOON on October 19, 1781, the army of Gen. Charles Cornwallis marched out of Yorktown, Virginia, to surrender to a combined American and French force under George Washington and Jean de Vimeur, comte de Rochambeau. According to popular tradition, ringing in their ears was "The World Turned Upside Down," a lively tune but now a dirge to the British given the circumstances that framed their astonishing predicament. A verse of "The World Turned Upside Down" captured a part of their mood:

> If buttercups buzzed after the bee,
> If boats were on land, churches on sea,
> If ponies rode men and grass ate the cows,
> And cats should be chased to holes by the mouse,
> If the mamas sold their babies to the gypsies
>   for half a crown,
> If summer were spring and t'other way 'round,
> Then all the world would be upside down.

Not surprisingly, these soldiers, who ordinarily demonstrated discipline and bravery in battle and were accustomed to accepting the surrender of others, did not like their new upside-down situation. An observer, prejudiced to be sure because he was an American, remarked on their "disorderly and unsoldierly conduct—their step was irregular, and their ranks frequently broken" as they made their way to the spot where they were ordered to give up their arms. At this site, their anger became even more obvious as they threw their arms on the pile with violence "as if determined to render them useless." American soldiers soon stopped such behavior, but they did not attempt to restrain a number of British officers who, according to another American observer, "behaved like boys who had been whipped at school. Some bit their lips; some pouted; others cried. Their round, broad-brimmed hats were well-adapted to the occasion, hiding those faces they were ashamed to show." Their commander on the scene was Gen. Charles

AT LEFT: *John Trumbull's* Surrender of Lord Cornwallis at Yorktown *doesn't show the British commander, of course, because Cornwallis wasn't there. In this detail, we see a mounted Gen. Benjamin Lincoln in the foreground, with General Washington behind him and to his left.*

ABOVE: *A contemporary army button.*

O'Hara—standing in for his chief, Earl Cornwallis, who had sent word that he was sick and could not attend. O'Hara observed the usual military proprieties, giving up his sword, which was returned immediately.

Surprise on the British side found no echoes among the Americans, though to be sure they were not practiced in accepting the surrender of their British enemy. After all, Washington's army had never before tasted a triumph so sweet as that at Yorktown; its previous victories were of a lesser order and the most recent more than three years past. Most of Washington's battles, in fact, had ended with his army in dreadful condition, defeated and withdrawing to escape disaster. Yet his army had never surrendered—not at Brooklyn, Kip's Bay, Brandywine, Germantown, or anywhere else. Surviving such defeats was of extraordinary importance, for as long as the army remained in existence, an active force with the willingness and capacity to fight, the Revolution continued. Washington's officers came to express this point with absolute conviction and clarity in the short, stark statement: "The Army is the Revolution."

They had a powerful point, but, of course, the Revolution was much more than the Continental Army, and Washington understood the Revolution better than any of them, perhaps better than anyone in America. As much as he loved his army, he loved more the idea of the

CORNWALLIS

1738 – 1805

Charles Cornwallis was a career soldier who fought well in the Seven Years' War (1756–1763), during which he also succeeded to his father's earldom. He personally opposed the policies that were causing such consternation in the colonies, but that didn't preclude him fighting later to enforce them. He faced George Washington first in New Jersey, pursuing him until the Continentals went into winter quarters in Morristown in January 1777. From 1778, Cornwallis served as second in command in North America to Gen. Henry Clinton. After the war, he drew considerable attention in the British press because of his ongoing debate with Clinton as to which of them should bear the responsibility for the British defeat.

"AN ARDENT DESIRE TO SPARE THE FURTHER EFFUSION OF BLOOD, WILL READILY INCLINE ME TO LISTEN TO… TERMS FOR THE SURRENDER OF YOUR POSTS OF YORK AND GLOUCESTER."

—

George Washington, reply to Lord Cornwallis's request for a cease-fire, October 17, 1781

Revolution as a "glorious cause." He often referred to it using that phrase or as "the common cause" that might bring all Americans together in a grand republican union. Later, in March 1783, when a coup against Congress seemed imminent, Washington seized the opportunity to remind his officers—then encamped with the army at Newburgh, New York—that the purposes of the Revolution were in the province of the civil power, not the military. It was a lesson that he drove home eight months later at Annapolis—where, standing before Congress in a simple ceremony, he resigned his commission. This action demonstrated to all

Washington's conviction that, in a republic, the civil authority is supreme. Lest anyone miss this point, congressional president Thomas Mifflin thanked Washington with these words: "You have conducted the great military contest with wisdom and fortitude invariably regarding the rights of the civil power through all disasters and changes."

Washington had long recognized that the civil power could best protect the great principles proclaimed in the Declaration of Independence. In July 1776, he had ordered the declaration read to his troops as they stood in regimental formation so that they could understand they were fighting for American liberty, which Washington believed would survive only in an American union dedicated to republican ideals. The Declaration of Independence speaks pointedly of governments "deriving their just powers from the consent of the governed," and Washington, throughout his military career, embraced this declaration against arbitrary power. Thus, his victory at Yorktown assured not only the triumph of the army but also the security of the new republic endowed with the consent of the governed.

T HE AMERICAN SOLDIERS WHO SURROUNDED Yorktown in 1781 were not the inexperienced transients who had made up Washington's army in July 1776. To be sure, new men filled the ranks of a number of regiments, but the Continental Army also contained hardened veterans and battle-tested officers. Furthermore, the Americans at Yorktown were not alone. The French army of Rochambeau—recently stationed in Newport, Rhode Island—joined them in a grand combined operation that also included troops under the marquis de Lafayette and the marquis de Saint-Simon. Since April, Lafayette had been leading as many as fifteen hundred American soldiers in Virginia, and in early September Saint-Simon reinforced him with three thousand regulars transported by French admiral François de Grasse from the West Indies.

It was Grasse's sailing to Virginia that led Washington to take his army, then besieging Henry Clinton in New York, to strike Cornwallis, who had recently abandoned the Carolinas (where Clinton had left him in command after the surrender of

The Revolutionary War headdress of a British grenadier.

This broadside, announcing the capture of Cornwallis, was printed in Boston on October 26, 1781, just one week after the British surrender.

COMMUNICATIONS

The preferred methods of communication among military forces in America were packet-boats and dispatch riders. The British used these small ships to send messages up and down the coast, as well as across the Atlantic. Much faster than conventional warships, the packet-boats easily outran the fleets, delivering warnings well in advance of a fleet's arrival. Dispatch riders used fast horses to similar effect. In the southern states, American commanders often chose militiamen as their dispatch riders because, being local, they knew the countryside best.

Perhaps the most significant of *Washington's few previous triumphs were his victories at Trenton in December 1776 and Princeton in early January 1777. In June 1778, he watched as the army of Henry Clinton left the battlefield at Monmouth Court House, but this was more of a British evacuation than an American victory.*

Charleston in May 1780). During the following year, Cornwallis conducted repeated operations against Continental forces, both regular and irregular, yet failed to subdue the countryside or even attract much Loyalist support. Out of touch with Clinton, the commander in chief of the British army in North America, for several months early in 1781, Cornwallis finally emerged from the North Carolina wilderness at Wilmington on April 7. From there, he marched to Virginia, arriving in May 1781. Soon afterward, he settled his exhausted troops in Yorktown, where he took into his command the British troops already in Virginia. His hope, he said, was that Clinton would move southward from New York City to begin combined operations that might end the war.

Washington's decision to attack Cornwallis demonstrated brilliantly his understanding of the importance of sea power, for Grasse commanded twenty-nine ships of the line, a naval force that held the promise of allied mastery of Chesapeake Bay as well as Virginia's offshore waters. Washington had learned of Grasse's sailing from Brest to the West Indies months earlier, in June 1781. He had also been told that Grasse's fleet carried troops and that eventually these ships and soldiers (under Saint-Simon) would be sent to the American mainland. What Washington did not know until mid-August was where Grasse intended to bring his strength to bear. New York was one possibility and Virginia another.

This is the sort of musket that a typical American soldier at Yorktown would have carried.

EIGHTEENTH-CENTURY GENERALS, more than those of later centuries, had to operate in the dark. Washington and his French colleague in Rhode Island, Rochambeau, had grown accustomed to acting without full knowledge of their enemy—and even, sometimes, without full knowledge of each other's activities. At the time word reached Washington on August 14 that Grasse's fleet was on the move from the West Indies to Virginia, he and Rochambeau were engaged in scouting positions from which to launch a joint offensive against New York City. There had been small-scale attacks and minor marches but no success as yet.

The news of Grasse's movement changed everything. Naval superiority in the waters around Virginia offered Washington the means to take charge, perhaps even to trap Cornwallis and regain full control of the South. In Rochambeau, he had an ally who was sympathetic to such ideas. Indeed, Rochambeau was an ideal partner in this venture. He did not know America well, having arrived with his army only the year before, and he spoke no English. Yet he was seven years older than Washington and possessed a distinguished military reputation founded on much European experience. More important, he accepted Washington as his leader. It was the Americans' revolution, he seemed to say, and the French should be subordinate. This disposition spoke well of his judgment as well as of his tact.

Five days after learning of the French movement on the sea, Washington had his Continentals on the move for Virginia. Because he did not want to be intercepted, he hid his intentions from Clinton, which proved easier than might be supposed, though it did require several sorts of disguises. All encouraged Clinton to interpret the Americans' marching as preparation for an attack on New York City, something that had been in the cards for months. To help this assumption seem plausible to Clinton, Washington ordered the repair of roads and bridges in New Jersey, a likely place from which to launch an attack. He also sent some troops toward the city to pose as the vanguard of a large army. Meanwhile, the major elements of Washington's army moved southward, passing through Philadelphia on September 2, followed by the French two days later. When Clinton finally discovered what was afoot, it was too late for him to block the movement, if in fact he felt such a desire.

The march to Head of Elk, Maryland—where ships were collecting to carry the troops, artillery, and supplies to Virginia—depended on the mastery of logistics by Washington and his staff. They proved equal to this assignment, collecting horses, oxen, and wagons to transport both men and equipment. Their routes were carefully chosen, roads and bridges made passable, and magazines with flour, beef, and rum for the army established along the way (in order that the march could remain on a rapid pace).

When the troops reached Chesapeake Bay, the necessary boats and crews were ready to move them. Washington's skill in anticipating such requirements was particularly obvious in his devotion to detail. He gave Gen. Benjamin Lincoln, in charge of the naval transports, sixteen paragraphs of detailed instructions and then added this postscript: "The Tow ropes or Painters [securing lines] of the Boats ought to be strong and of sufficient length otherwise we shall be much plagued with them in the Bay and more than probably lose many of them."

Admiral de Grasse, meanwhile, had landed Saint-Simon and his troops early in September. The British in the West Indies, aware of his intentions, had attempted to warn the fleet at New York, commanded by

ROCHAMBEAU

1725 –1807

Jean de Vimeur, comte de Rochambeau, had a body that was rather stocky, a complexion that was ruddy though not florid, and a manner both direct and friendly. He chose not to exude pride, but he could have, for he was an able soldier. Before coming to America, he had fought in numerous European wars and by 1761 had attained the rank of brigadier general. Rochambeau arrived at Newport, Rhode Island, in July 1780 but had to wait nearly a year for French naval support. Washington found him to be a patient and balanced colleague. After the French Revolution, during which he commanded the Army of the North, Rochambeau was arrested but subsequently spared the guillotine.

This engraving shows Washington conferring with Alexander Hamilton, his onetime secretary and aide-de-camp. After enduring the battle of Long Island and the retreat from New York City, Hamilton joined the general's staff in 1777 and remained with him until February 1781.

This is an example of bar shot. Shipboard artillery fired bar shot not at opposition troops on land but at enemy ships. Its purpose was to snare and rip apart the other ship's sails and rigging.

Adm. Thomas Graves, but Graves failed to catch up with the French until September 5. By this time, though it was not too late for Cornwallis to escape, the net was being drawn more closely around him. As the two navies fought an indecisive battle that day off the Virginia capes, the French admiral Louis Barras, having sailed from Newport, slipped behind the British and landed on the Yorktown peninsula the heavy guns essential to a siege. Graves, who suffered heavy damage inflicted by Grasse, subsequently returned to New York, leaving Cornwallis alone, menaced by French warships in the bay and the advancing troops of Washington and Rochambeau on land.

Aware of his peril, Cornwallis considered fighting his way out and sent patrols up the peninsula to get the lay of the land and to discover the strength of his enemy. The odds were great: Even though Washington and Rochambeau had not yet arrived, the armies of Lafayette and Saint-Simon were not negligible. In addition, the ground did not lend itself to rapid movement, and there were other circumstances to consider: for example, what to do with the Loyalists who had sought his protection and the sick who could not be taken along in a breakout? Or with the small ships and their crews, now sheltered at Yorktown, that would also be left behind? And even if Cornwallis succeeded in breaching the enemy's lines, where could he go? Not north, because Washington's force threatened in that direction; not south to the Carolinas, because he lacked the supplies and provisions to retrace his route to Charleston. Cornwallis also recognized that a breakout battle would yield wounded, making further movement even more troublesome, indeed miserable, and perhaps impossible.

Cornwallis postponed his decision while planning for a move. On September 14, a dispatch from Clinton arrived with a promise of reinforcement by sea. Clinton had written it eight days earlier, before he knew of Graves's rebuff by Grasse's fleet. The dispatch gave Cornwallis hope, and he continued to look toward New York. A few days later, he decided to remain in Yorktown and fight it out until help arrived. But the net closed about him on September 26, when virtually all of Washington's troops arrived at Williamsburg. Two days later, with the French in the lead, the combined army, numbering between seventeen thousand and eighteen thousand soldiers fit for duty, marched to the outskirts of Yorktown and began the siege.

Before Cornwallis occupied Yorktown, which lay on a low bluff above the York River, the village had contained about three thousand people. The York ran deep enough there to allow the passage of large ships, and consequently wharves and warehouses lined the town's waterfront. York-town also boasted several handsome brick houses, a larger number of frame houses, and the usual taverns, public buildings, and church. Artisans, merchants, apprentices, slaves, shopkeepers, and tobacco planters, along with their wives and children, made up the bulk of the population.

Yorktown's defenses were not formidable. Cornwallis had constructed an outer line consisting of a handful of entrenchments about twelve hundred yards from the town. However, there were large gaps in it, and its redoubts were not connected to one another, nor were they initially heavily fortified. With an army of something between nine and ten thousand soldiers, many tired and sick, Cornwallis had not the resources to man extended lines. His abandonment of the outer line two days into the siege spoke to his sense of weakness.

The siege itself followed the classic pattern created by Sébastien Vauban, the illustrious seventeenth-century French military theorist. Vauban's doctrine called for the besiegers to approach their enemy's works by a series of parallel lines. Once the first parallel—that is, a trench with heavily dug-in artillery—was established, the shelling could begin. Once the enemy was softened up, sappers dug zigzag, or approach, trenches, advancing toward the enemy, and then a second, closer parallel, to which the guns were then moved. This process was ordinarily repeated until the besieged surrendered or were overwhelmed by an infantry assault.

The Continental Army, occupying the right side of the semicircle surrounding the town (the French were on the left), dug the first parallel in the early days of October about four thousand feet long and some six hundred yards from the British works. This trench extended from the river on the southeast side of the town to a large ravine. Both French and American troops constructed along it redoubts as well as communication

This plan of the siege of Yorktown was published in Lt. Col. Banastre Tarleton's History of the Campaigns of 1780 and 1781 in the Southern Provinces of North America (1787). *Before the war, according to a contemporary English manuscript, Yorktown was a "delicat village" on a "Sandy Hill." Its houses looked down on a "fine river broader than the Thames." Several of Yorktown's dwellings, made of brick, boasted handsome gardens. Warehouses and wharves crowded its shore.*

OVERLEAF:

This fanciful French etching, published in 1781 not long after the surrender, depicts the small tobacco port of Yorktown as a fortified European city (thereby making its reduction that much more impressive). The engraver apparently fabricated the scene entirely from verbal accounts.

Reddition de l'Armée Angloises Commandeé par Mylord Comte de Cornwallis aux Armees Combineés
et Glocester dans la Virginie. le 19 Octobre 1781. Il s'est trouvés dans ces deux postes 6000 hommes de troupes reç
40 Batimens dont un Vaisseau de 50 Canons qui a eté Brulé 20 Coules Bas: Ce jour a jamais memorables po

A. *Yorck Town*   C. *Armeés Angloise sortant de la place*   E. *Armeé Fr*

mis de l'Amerique et de France aux ordres des Generaux Washington et de Rochambeau a Yorck touvn
ises ou Hessoises et 22 Drapeaux 1500 Matelots 160 Canons de tout Calibre dont 75 de Fonte 8 Mortiers
unis en ce quil assura definitivement leurs independances
Armée naval de France aux Ordres du Comte de Grace   I Riviere d'Yorck.
Baye de Chesapeack

This mechanical drawing of a Vauban-style fortification was created by an unknown artist in 1802.

As a military engineer, Sébastien Le Prestre de Vauban (1633–1707) transformed both the construction of defensive fortifications and their reduction. He was born into the petty nobility but at an early age distinguished himself through his extraordinary talent for siege warfare. He took part in all of France's wars during the reign of Louis XIV, first as a rebel defending towns in the Argonne against government attack, then as a loyalist breaching the rebel defenses.

trenches and depots for stores and ammunition. The last step was to emplace the artillery batteries.

The British recognized what was going on and sought to impede the process with cannonades. By October 9, however, the allied armies had emplaced enough heavy guns to begin replying, and within a few days, as they brought up more and more cannon, superiority was achieved. The French artillery, manned by crews more skilled than the Americans, claimed that they could fire with such accuracy as to put round after round into the British embrasures. The Americans proved remarkably effective as well, and in a few days the British were reduced to returning fire only at night, when it was safe to open the embrasures of their batteries. The bombardment of Yorktown also affected the civilians who had not fled the scene. Many took up residence in hastily built shelters along the river, but they and their houses suffered nonetheless.

WITH FIRE SUPREMACY ASSURED, the allies pushed their trenches forward and on October 11 opened a second parallel about three hundred yards from the British lines. Because of the shrinking distance between the two sides, more of the sappers and supporting infantry lost their lives. Cornwallis had up to this point been frugal in expending his powder and shells. Now he removed those restrictions, and for a few days an unusual amount of American and French blood stained the ground. The allies finally mastered this grievous situation as more and more of their guns moved into the second parallel.

On several occasions, though, the Americans seemed to seek danger and death. As sappers worked and were relieved, there was much movement back and forth in the zigzag trenches and along the parallels as well. Prudence dictated that relief of one work party by another be undertaken as quietly and unobtrusively as possible. Yet warm spirits and the demands of honor evidently disdained this prudence. Alexander

Hamilton, a brave and spirited officer, once marched his troops to a forward trench, where they planted their colors. Hamilton's next order was for them to mount the bank of the trench and go through the manual of arms, ordering and grounding their muskets in full view of the enemy, who had been shooting at them. This spectacle so impressed the British a few hundred yards away that they stopped shooting and no doubt watched in astonishment as these mad Americans performed. Perhaps the British stayed their fire out of admiration for the gallantry on display—certainly Hamilton was a man who valued gallantry and honor—but in this instance, as one of his junior officers observed, he "wantonly exposed the lives of his men."

Indeed there seemed no end of danger and death in these mid-October days. On the night of the fourteenth, the allies carried out simultaneous assaults in darkness on two British redoubts still holding out at the end of the second parallel. The attackers carried unloaded muskets in order to prevent an accidental shot from disclosing their intent. Hamilton led American troops against one of the redoubts; a French officer led French infantry against the other. Both fortifications fell in a few minutes after the attackers forced their way through the abatis surrounding the redoubts.

The next night, the British, who had fought bravely, sortied out and broke into the second parallel. Their raiding party was small, but it managed to spike six guns before retiring. This action, inspired by British pride, was then followed by an escape attempt on the night of October 16. About a thousand men were ferried across the river to Gloucester before a squall made further movement impossible. This small storm didn't last long, but by the time it ended, additional effort was useless. Dawn was near, and in the daylight Washington's big guns would have destroyed troops and boats. Cornwallis had his troops brought back to Yorktown, and he began to reconcile himself to surrender. The allied forces strengthened his resolve by pounding his lines hour after hour.

On October 17, Cornwallis asked for terms. Negotiations consumed most of two days, but on the morning of October 19, agreement was reached. Washington proved to be a generous victor. He allowed British officers to keep their sidearms, and officers and troops were permitted to retain their private effects. To Cornwallis he granted permission to use a sloop to carry

FRONTISPIECE

This etching by John Norman appeared as the frontispiece to a treatise on artillery published in Philadelphia in 1779. It shows a variety of artillery pieces and other ordnance.

This unusual artillery projectile was known as quilted grapeshot. Like all grapeshot, it was an anti-personnel weapon consisting of a cluster of small iron balls.

OPPOSITE:

This print *was the eleventh in a series of small German etchings. Published in 1784 by Daniel Chodowiecki, they show the surrender from a German point of view.*

This flag *belonging to German mercenaries at Yorktown was surrendered along with their arms. It now resides in the West Point Museum.*

FURTHER READING

★ Robert Middlekauff, *The Glorious Cause: The American Revolution, 1763–1789* (1982)

★ Benson Bobrick, *Angel in the Whirlwind: The Triumph of the American Revolution* (1997)

dispatches and some officers and troops to New York. Eighteenth-century convention was to accept the word of captured senior officers that they would not act against their victorious enemy until they had been officially exchanged. Cornwallis gave the usual promise and sailed for New York City in early November.

CLINTON HAD LEARNED of the surrender on October 29. In one of the cruel ironies of the war, he had sailed from New York City with a relief force the same day that Cornwallis's army had marched out of Yorktown to give itself up. To be sure, Clinton had overestimated Cornwallis's ability to hold out and delayed action. Yet he had his own difficulties in New York, and convincing Graves that Grasse, who held Chesapeake Bay with a strong fleet, might be dislodged was only one of them. When Graves finally agreed to the expedition, much time that might have been given to preparations was already lost. The weather refused to cooperate both before and after the fleet sailed, and when it finally arrived off Virginia, Cornwallis's army was in enemy hands. There was nothing to be done except return to New York.

The terrible news carried by a fast packet reached England near the end of the month. When Lord North, the king's first minister, heard of the surrender, he threw up his arms and exclaimed, "Oh God! It is all over." Of course, in a literal sense, the war was not over. The British still had troops in New York, South Carolina, Georgia, Canada, and the West Indies—and in the West Indies and the waters of the Atlantic, the Royal Navy remained a formidable presence.

But despite this military power, Britain no longer possessed the will to carry on the war. It had lasted too long, and the previous summer had brought defeats and discouragement in India and Europe. There was also the matter of the enormous debt incurred since midcentury to pay for North American wars, first against the French and then against the colonists. Taxes were high and seemingly going higher.

Yorktown shook everyone, and Lord North was right: It was too much to go on. The British will to fight had been broken, and though two years would pass before a peace treaty was finally signed, the military phase of the American Revolution in a real sense ended with the surrender of Cornwallis on October 19, 1781. Thus, Washington's victory at Yorktown brought to a triumphal conclusion a war fought to guarantee both American independence and a republican form of government based on "the consent of the governed" from which, according to the Declaration of Independence, all just governmental powers derived.

★ ★ ★

We the People

of the Unite

insure domestic Tranquility, provide for the common defence, promote

and our Posterity, do ordain and establish this Constitution for the Un

Article. I.

Section. 1. All legislative Powers herein granted shall be vested in a

of Representatives.

Section. 2. The House of Representatives shall be composed of Member

in each State shall have the Qualifications requisite for Electors of the most numerous

No Person shall be a Representative who shall not have attained to th

and who shall not, when elected, be an Inhabitant of that State in which he shall

Representatives and direct Taxes shall be apportioned among the several

Numbers, which shall be determined by adding to the whole Number of free Pers

not taxed, three fifths of all other Persons. The actual Enumeration shall be m

and within every subsequent Term of ten Years, in such Manner as they shall

thirty Thousand, but each State shall have at Least one Representative; and

entitled to chuse three, Massachusetts eight, Rhode Island and Providence

eight, Delaware one, Maryland six, Virginia ten, North Carolina five, Sout

When vacancies happen in the Representation from any State, the Ex

The House of Representatives shall chuse their Speaker and other Off

Section. 3. The Senate of the United States shall be composed of two Senator

Senator shall have one Vote.

Immediately after they shall be assembled in Consequence of the first

of the Senators of the first Class shall be vacated at the Expiration of the second

Class at the Expiration of the sixth Year, so that one third may be chosen every se

Recess of the Legislature of any State, the Executive thereof may make temporary a

such Vacancies.

No Person shall be a Senator who shall not have attained to the Age of

not, when elected, be an Inhabitant of that State for which he shall be chosen.

The Vice President of the United States shall be President of the Senate, b

The Senate shall chuse their other Officers, and also a President pro tempo

President of the United States.

The Senate shall have the sole Power to try all Impeachments. When

of the United States, the Chief Justice shall preside: And no Person shall be con

Judgment in Cases of Impeachment shall not extend further than to

July 16, 1787

THE DAY THE CONSTITUTION WAS SAVED

BY GORDON S. WOOD

July 16, 1787, was one of the most decisive days in the history of the United States. On that day, by the slimmest of margins—five states to four, with one state divided—the delegates to the Constitutional Convention in Philadelphia voted to accept equal state representation in the Senate. In other words, every state in the Union, no matter how small or large its population, would be represented by two senators. This decision has made it possible today for Wyoming, with fewer than half a million people, to have the same representation in the Senate as California, with more than thirty million people.

The Great Compromise, as it came to be called, broke a deadlock that had threatened to

destroy the convention. If the compromise had failed, declared many delegates (and many subsequent historians), the Philadelphia Convention would also have failed. And with its failure, the fledging republic of the United States might very well have fallen apart.

The problem was that the Articles of Confederation, adopted by the Continental Congress in November 1777 and ratified in March 1781, had proved inadequate to the task of binding together the thirteen states. In fact, by 1787, the Confederation scarcely existed. Its shortcomings for the most part followed from its severely limited scope and powers. The national government consisted of a single body, the Confederation Congress, in which each state had a single vote. The legislature's mandate (there was no executive or judiciary) dealt principally with foreign affairs (including war and treaty making), domestic matters that crossed state lines (such as fixing standard weights and measures and establishing a post

AT LEFT: *In 1878, British prime minister William Gladstone called the Constitution "the most wonderful work ever struck off at a given time by the brain and purpose of man."*

ABOVE: *The Constitutional Convention was held in the Pennsylvania State House, now known more commonly as Independence Hall.*

More than any other person, James Madison was responsible for the Constitutional Convention that began meeting in Philadelphia at the end of May 1787. His preparation was painstaking: He studied texts that he had on hand and even wrote to Thomas Jefferson (then U.S. minister to France) for more books "that may throw light on the general constitution and droit public of the several confederacies which have existed." Madison's request was answered with more than a hundred additional volumes, which he also studied carefully.

office), and resolving disputes among states. More important, the Congress had no power to raise funds directly and no mechanism to enforce its laws. Even if the Philadelphia Convention had collapsed, it's unlikely that the Confederation could have gathered the states together again. For example, while waiting anxiously for news from Philadelphia, most members of the Confederation Congress stopped attending meetings in New York. The fate of the United States thus rested on what the Constitutional Convention could achieve.

The manner in which the states would be represented in the new national government bedeviled the convention from the start. Indeed, as James Madison recalled, this issue alone threatened the success of the convention more "than all the rest put together." That the role of the states in the new federal government should have been the most serious issue was not surprising. The thirteen states guarded their sovereignty jealously, as demonstrated by the clause in the Articles of Confederation that permitted a single state to veto amendments supported by all the others. And in 1776, the Declaration of Independence had been literally a declaration of the "thirteen united States of America," which claimed that as "Free and Independent *States*, they have full power to levy war, conclude peace, contact alliances, establish commerce, and to do all other acts and things which independent States may of right do."

WHATEVER FEELINGS OF AMERICAN nationalism existed, they paled before people's loyalties to their separate states. Although the United States was new, most of its constituent states had existed as separate colonies for a century or more and had developed symbols and traditions that were emotionally binding. In 1776, when people talked about their "country" or even their "nation," they usually meant Virginia or Massachusetts or Pennsylvania. The development of a national constitution was not a project that attracted the revolutionaries' creative energies, nearly all of which went into their separate state constitutions. Framing governments for individual states, and not for the nation, said Thomas Jefferson in 1776, was "the whole object" of the American Revolution. No one at that time, John Adams recalled, even conceived "of consolidating this vast Continent under one national Government."

The Confederation Congress was certainly not a national government in the usual sense of the term. The Articles of Confederation were

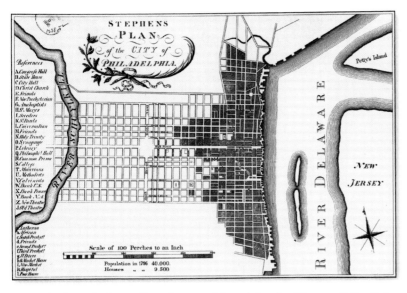

This plan of Philadelphia was printed in 1796, when Philadelphia (with a population of over forty thousand) was still the cultural and commercial center of the United States.

variously described as a "firm league of friendship," a "Treaty of Confederation," and a "council of nations." It was thus a coming together of thirteen sovereign states in an alliance not altogether different from the present-day European Union. Each state annually sent a delegation (called by some states "our embassy") to the Confederation Congress, where it dealt with matters earlier handled by the Crown. The crucial powers of commercial regulation and taxation—indeed, all final lawmaking authority—remained with the states. Some, like Jefferson in 1783, could not even imagine the Confederation remaining permanent; instead, they saw it only as a temporary combination of the states, brought together for the purpose of waging war against the British. With peace, they believed, the Confederation should be allowed to lapse.

By the mid-1780s, however, many other political leaders had concluded that not only was the Confederation too weak to carry out its responsibilities, but also, more alarming, the very state governments in which Americans had placed so many of their hopes had become the principal source of the vices besetting the nation. Since independence, many of the democratically elected state legislatures had passed all sorts of haphazard and unjust laws victimizing the private rights of minorities, especially creditor minorities. Because this legislation was backed by popular majorities in the states, it called into question the fundamental principle of republican government—that majorities should rule—and put the entire revolutionary experiment in doubt.

The Articles of Confederation were engrossed, or written in a large hand, on six parchments sheets that were stitched together and fastened to a wooden roller to form a scroll.

Patrick Henry was a failure as a planter and as a storekeeper before becoming a brilliant success as a revolutionary firebrand. He was less successful in his opposition to the Constitution, which he considered a threat to popular liberties and states' rights.

For many American political leaders, this democratic despotism in the states was the most important source of the crisis of the 1780s that led to the calling of the Philadelphia Convention. Indeed, the abuses of the state legislatures, Madison told his friend Jefferson, "contributed more to that uneasiness which produced the Convention, and prepared the public mind for a general reform, than those which accrued to our national character and interest from the inadequacy of the Confederation."

THE CONVENTION WAS CALLED FOR MAY 14, but spring rains, muddy roads, and other obstacles delayed the start until May 25, when a quorum was finally present. In all, fifty-five delegates representing twelve states attended. Rhode Island, acutely jealous of its local autonomy, wanted nothing to do with efforts to revise the Articles of Confederation and sent no one. Although many of the delegates were young men—their average age was forty-two—most were also experienced, well-educated members of the political elite. Thirty-nine had served in the Continental or the Confederation Congress at one time or another, eight had participated in state constitutional conventions, seven had been governors, thirty-four were lawyers, and one-third were veterans of the Continental Army (that great dissolvent of state loyalties, as George Washington had described it). Although Washington attended the convention and was immediately elected its president, many other Revolutionary War luminaries were absent. Samuel Adams was ill; Thomas Jefferson and John Adams were

This view of Chestnut Street was published as Plate 20 in William Russell Birch's The City of Philadelphia As It Appeared in the Year 1800. *The building on the left, Congress Hall, was the seat of the national legislature while Philadelphia was temporarily the nation's capital.*

abroad serving as U.S. ministers to France and England, respectively; and Richard Henry Lee and Patrick Henry, although chosen as delegates by the Virginia legislature, refused to attend, Henry saying that he "smelt a Rat."

On May 29, the convention finally got down to serious business. Taking the lead, the Virginia delegation presented the first working proposal. Although introduced by Gov. Edmund Randolph, the head of the state delegation, the Virginia Plan was largely the work of thirty-six-year-old James Madison. This short, shy, bookish planter had been contemplating confederations and the problems of American politics for months if not years, and he came to the convention well prepared to initiate a radical reform of the Articles of Confederation.

Certainly the scope of his Virginia Plan was breathtaking. Many Americans expected the convention simply to amend the Articles of Confederation by giving the Congress a few additional powers. Instead, Madison proposed a substantial rearrangement that would allow the new government to exercise direct authority over individual citizens, unmediated by the states. Like most of the states, it would have an executive branch, a bicameral legislature, and an independent judiciary.

The most radical aspect of the Virginia Plan was its disregard for state sovereignty in the makeup of the bicameral legislature. Under the Articles of Confederation, each state had an equal vote in the single-house Congress. Under the Virginia Plan, however, representation in both houses would be proportional—based on population, on contribution of taxes, or on both. The primary difference between the two houses would be that the members of the first house would be chosen by the people of the several states, and these representatives would then choose the members of the second house. Finally, the two houses would jointly select the national executive and the national judiciary. Many of the delegates also presumed that this second house would have sole authority to make treaties and appoint ambassadors. Terms of office were not specified.

In presenting the plan, Randolph argued that, because the vices of the 1780s were mostly due to "the turbulence and follies of democracy," the new federal government had to be protected against not only the pitfalls of the Articles but also those encountered by the individual states. It had to be, according to Randolph, "a strong *consolidated* union, in which the idea of the states should be nearly annihilated." The Articles of Confederation had declared, "Each state retains its sovereignty, freedom and independence, and every Power, Jurisdiction and right, which is not by this confederation expressly delegated to the United States, in

EDMUND RANDOLPH

1753 – 1813

Edmund Randolph studied law with his father, the king's attorney in Virginia, until the Revolution approached. Then he broke with his father, who sailed to England while Edmund cast his lot with the rebels. Randolph served briefly with George Washington before returning to Virginia to help draft the new state constitution. In 1786, he led Virginia's delegation to the Annapolis Convention, called by Virginia and Maryland to discuss commercial matters and attended by five states. It was the report of this convention, urging a more general meeting, that led to the February 1787 resolution of the Confederation Congress authorizing the Constitutional Convention. In the end, though, Randolph was one of three delegates who refused to sign the final document.

Congress assembled." The Virginia Plan, however, granted the new national legislature the authority not only to legislate "in all cases to which the states are incompetent" but also "to negative all laws passed by the several States contravening, in the opinion of the National Legislature, the articles of Union." This authority to veto state legislation was a measure of how disgusted Madison and other convention delegates had become with the foolish and unjust legislation being passed by the states. Madison believed the proposed veto power "absolutely necessary, and…the least possible encroachment on the State jurisdictions."

By a vote of six states to one—with Massachusetts, Pennsylvania, Delaware, Virginia, North Carolina, and South Carolina voting aye, Connecticut voting no, and New York divided—the convention agreed at the outset to make the Virginia Plan the basis for its deliberations. Yet it was not long before the delegates from smaller states—notably New Jersey, lately with a quorum, and Delaware—grasped the plan's nationalist and consolidating implications. Virginia's proposal seemed to swallow the states; it ignored their individual existence and turned them into mere administrative units. Because most of the delegates at Philadelphia were so eager to create a strong central government, they initially ignored these implications of the Virginia Plan. But a number of them soon came to believe that it went too far in eclipsing the states.

THIS ISSUE WAS FORMALLY raised on Saturday, June 9, by William Paterson of New Jersey. A former state attorney general, Paterson was especially bothered by the proposal that seats in both houses of the new legislature be granted according to each state's population or wealth. Proportional representation, Paterson argued, would place majority power in the hands of the most populous states—particularly Virginia, Massachusetts, and Pennsylvania, which as a group contained nearly half the U.S. population. New Jersey, he warned, would never agree to confederate on such terms, to which Pennsylvanian James Wilson retorted hotly that the people of his state would never confederate on a one-state, one-vote basis. "Shall New Jersey have the same right or influence in the councils of the nation as Pennsylvania?" the Scottish-born colleague of Madison exclaimed. "I say no. It is unjust."

Although convention delegates, such as Paterson and Wilson, often understood their conflict as one between small states and large ones, this is somewhat misleading. Madison and Wilson, it's true, were delegates from the large and populous states of Virginia and Pennsylvania, but their opposition to equal representation in the new national legislature was not

JAMES WILSON

1742 – 1798

James Wilson emigrated from Scotland in 1765, at first teaching Greek and rhetoric in Philadelphia and then studying law there under John Dickinson. Wilson was a delegate to the First and Second Continental Congresses and a signer of the Declaration of Independence. As a member of the Confederation Congress, he pressed for an amendment that would allow the Congress to levy a general tax. After the Constitution's ratification, he was named by George Washington one of the first associate justices of the Supreme Court. During the winter of 1796–1797, however, Wilson's finances and health were both ruined as a result of irresponsible land speculation.

based simply on a parochial concern for the interests of their respective commonwealths. Madison and Wilson were more cosmopolitan and far-sighted than that. For them, the real issue was whether any semblance of the old Confederation would foul the new Constitution. As nationalists, they believed that all the ills of the 1780s flowed inevitably from the vicious behavior of the states, and they were worried that equal representation in the new national legislature would effectively perpetuate the state sovereignty that had vitiated the Confederation. They knew that the small states would object, but they believed that these states would eventually have to submit because they couldn't imagine Delaware or New Jersey going it alone in defiance of the other states.

Two days later, on June 11, the convention reaffirmed the principle of proportional representation for both houses. However, the vote regarding the second house, what would become the Senate, was close: six states (Massachusetts, Pennsylvania, Virginia, North Carolina, South Carolina, and Georgia) to five (Connecticut, New York, New Jersey, Delaware, and Maryland). The narrowness of this vote encouraged the small-state caucus. On June 15, Paterson proposed nine resolutions—essentially nine amendments to the Articles of Confederation—that became the New Jersey Plan. Although Paterson's resolutions granted to Congress the powers of taxation and commercial regulation that many had demanded for it, the New Jersey Plan nevertheless continued the basic structure of the old Confederation, with each state equally represented in a single-house legislature. In this proposal, New Jersey was supported by Connecticut, Delaware, and New York. Paterson and his allies were not opposed to a stronger national government; but, as Delaware's John Dickinson warned Madison, they thought the Virginia Plan was "pushing things too far," and the small states would never agree to a complete elimination of state sovereignty.

With two such different proposals before it, the convention had to make a decision. On June 19, it voted for the Virginia Plan against the New Jersey Plan, seven states (Massachusetts, Connecticut, Pennsylvania, Virginia, North Carolina, South Carolina, and Georgia) to three (New York, New

> **"THERE IS PRACTICALLY NOTHING IN THE CONSTITUTION THAT DID NOT ARISE OUT OF THE CORRECTION OF...SPECIFIC DEFECTS OF THE CONFEDERATION."**
>
> —
>
> *Max Farrand,*
> The Framing of the Constitution of the United States, *1913*

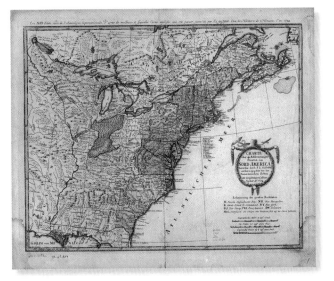

This hand-colored map of the United States, created by F. L. Güssefeld, was published in Nuremberg in 1784.

ROGER SHERMAN

1721 – 1793

Although well known as a conservative, Connecticut superior court judge Roger Sherman was an early advocate of independence from Great Britain. He signed the Declaration of Independence and also helped draft the Articles of Confederation, but his greatest service came at the Constitutional Convention, where he proposed the compromise that kept the convention from disintegrating. Afterward, Sherman served in the House (1789–1791) and the Senate (1791–1793), where he supported Treasury Secretary Alexander Hamilton's program for assumption of the state debt, establishment of a national bank, and enactment of a tariff.

Jersey, and Delaware), with Maryland divided. Although this vote suggested that the new national government would be something other than a league of independent states, the struggle over the precise role of those states in the new framework was far from over. Most of the small-state delegates were good nationalists who did not really want to return to the Confederation; at the same time, they were not willing to have their states' representation in the new government entirely eliminated. Thus, the issue of representation occupied the convention with heated debate over the next month. Throughout that time, as Luther Martin of Maryland later recalled, the delegates "were on the verge of dissolution, scarce held together by the strength of a hair."

AMONG THE DELEGATES MOST STRENUOUSLY advocating proportional representation, in addition to Madison and Wilson, were Alexander Hamilton of New York and Rufus King of Massachusetts (later a senator and presidential candidate from New York). These men claimed that the large states were too divided by manners, religion, and economics to combine against the rights and interests of the small states. Besides, they argued, history had shown that confederations were usually undone by encroachments made by individual parts upon the whole. If the new government were to be strong, the states would have to be kept out of it.

Yet delegates from the small states, especially those from Connecticut, remained committed to equal representation. They countered that the interests of the small states would be overwhelmed by those of their larger neighbors. Indeed, without equal representation in the national government, they warned, states as political entities would eventually disappear, especially given the national government's proposed negative regarding state laws. The small states, Oliver Ellsworth of Connecticut concluded, "would risk every consequence rather than part with so dear a right" as their equal voice in the national legislature. If the small states were willing to break up the convention on this issue, Wilson replied, so be it. Representation on the basis of population, not on "the imaginary beings called *States*," was too equitable and too just to be compromised. "We talk of states, till we forget what they are composed of"—narrow-minded and illiberal politicians.

Several proposals for equal representation were offered and beaten back, but with the small-state delegates refusing to budge and support for proportional representation apparently eroding, more and more delegates began seeking a solution in the suggestion first made by Roger Sherman of Connecticut on June 11—that one house proportionally represent the people and the other equally represent the states. On July 2, when this proposal resulted in a tie vote and a committee was selected to forge a compromise, Madison and Wilson knew their cause was in trouble. If the second house should contain an equal number of members from each state, it would be only a matter of time, they believed, before the states would overawe and dominate the national government.

Gouverneur Morris of Pennsylvania joined Madison and Wilson in vehemently opposing the committee's July 5 proposal that the states should have equal representation in one house of the legislature. These nationalists threatened, they cajoled, and they even predicted ominously that a majority of the American people would refuse to accept such an unjust solution. Sooner or later, they insisted, the small states would have to go along with whatever the majority of Americans wanted. "State attachments and state importance have been the bane of this country," Morris declared. "We cannot annihilate; but we may perhaps take out the teeth of the serpent."

In a last-ditch effort to get the delegates to think about the issue in other than small-state-versus-large-state terms, Madison suggested that the real division in the nation was that between free and slave states. But the more the delegates argued about sectional interests that needed defending, the more sensible the proposal for state equality in the second house seemed. In the end, Madison's arguments notwithstanding, state loyalties and state interests were simply too strong for the proponents of proportional representation to overcome.

This engraving of George Washington addressing the Constitutional Convention was used to illustrate A History of the United States of America, *published in Hartford in 1823.*

FURTHER READING

★ Gordon S. Wood, *The Creation of the American Republic, 1776–1787* (1969)

★ Max Farrand, *The Framing of the Constitution of the United States* (1913)

THE DECISIVE VOTE CAME on July 16, with Connecticut, New Jersey, Delaware, Maryland, and North Carolina in favor of the states' equal representation in the Senate; Pennsylvania, Virginia, South Carolina, and Georgia opposed; Massachusetts divided; and New York not voting because its two Anti-Federalist delegates had gone home and its delegation lacked a quorum. Madison and the other nationalists were dismayed by the vote, seeing equal representation in the second house not as a reasonable compromise but as a momentous defeat. The Virginia delegation immediately asked for an adjournment, and the next morning Madison and his unhappy allies caucused to consider what might be done. Some delegates favored calling a separate convention without the small states present, but most, noted Madison, were reluctantly "inclined to yield," even if their acquiescence resulted in an "imperfect & exceptionable" constitution. Meanwhile, the small-state delegates, having won their point, became more than willing to abandon all other remnants of the old Confederation and consider forming a strong central government. "The whole comes down to this," Charles C. Pinckney of South Carolina had gibed back during a June debate over the New Jersey Plan. "Give N. Jersey an equal vote, and she will dismiss her scruples, and concur in the National system."

Of course, the embodiment of state sovereignty in one house of the legislature did prompt reconsideration of the powers granted that branch of government, and the convention spent a good deal of the next two months adjusting the original Virginia Plan to accommodate these new circumstances. The grant to Congress to legislate "in all cases to which the states are incompetent" was replaced by an enumeration of powers, and much to Madison's chagrin the negative over state laws was replaced by specific prohibitions on state lawmaking. (These became Article I, Section 10, of the final Constitution.)

Other changes also followed from Madison's heightened mistrust of the future Senate. Selection of the executive, for example, was withdrawn from the legislature and vested in an alternative congress, the electoral college, in which each state had the same number of electors as it had representatives and senators combined. Indeed, the reduced confidence that Madison and other nationalists now had in the Senate made them much more willing to enhance the power of the presidency. Because the original proposal to have the Senate by itself make treaties and appoint judges and diplomats now seemed too dangerous, those authorities were transferred to the president, with the Senate retaining only the role of advising and consenting.

Beginning in January 1788, *the* Massachusetts Centinel *printed a small allegorical cartoon to mark each state's ratification of the Constitution. This example—published August 2, 1788—records New York's ratification just one week earlier.*

WHEN THE PHILADELPHIA CONVENTION finally reported the Constitution on September 17, 1787, it was a document very different from the Virginia Plan of May 29. Many delegates, including Madison, were initially unhappy with the result. In fact, in the immediate aftermath of losing the battle over proportional representation, Madison, the so-called Father of the Constitution, judged that the Constitution was destined to fail. Without the power to negative state laws, he complained to Jefferson in September 1787, the new national government "will neither effectually answer its national object nor prevent the local mischiefs which everywhere excite disgusts against the state governments." Even Washington was reported to have said that the Constitution would not last twenty years.

Despite this initial pessimism, Madison soon changed his mind and began working for ratification of the Constitution. With Hamilton and John Jay, he contributed to *The Federalist,* the series of eighty-five essays published in New York in 1787–1788 in defense of the Constitution. He also played key roles in persuading Virginia to ratify the Constitution, adding the Bill of Rights in 1790, and overseeing the final document's implementation as a congressional leader during the 1790s. All these successes were made possible, he later understood, by the compromises contained in the Constitution, the most important of which had taken place on July 16, 1787.

★ ★ ★

Thomas Pritchard Rossiter's The Signing of the Constitution of the United States *(1867) follows in the artistic tradition of John Trumbull's* Declaration of Independence *(1786–1819) and Benjamin West's* The American Commissioners; or, Signing the Treaty of Paris *(1783). Rossiter's work, however, deviates by elevating George Washington above the other delegates and surrounding him with an aura of light.*

JUNE 20, 1790

MR. JEFFERSON'S DINNER PARTY

BY JOSEPH J. ELLIS

IT HAPPENED LATE IN THE AFTERnoon in the private quarters of Secretary of State Thomas Jefferson at 57 Maiden Lane in New York City—the city where the fledgling United States government had gathered during this, its first year of existence. Because June 20, 1790, was a Sunday, government offices were closed, but important political business seldom takes a holiday. This day, Jefferson had proposed hosting a dinner party at which he and two of his colleagues could meet informally to address a pair of nettlesome issues that were currently bedeviling the First Congress: the permanent location of the nation's capital and the fiscal policy of the infant federal government.

"On considering the situation of things," Jefferson later recalled, "I thought the first step towards some conciliation of views would be to bring Mr. Madison and Colo. Hamilton to a friendly discussion of the subject." Perhaps Jefferson thought the genial influences of excellent French wine and gentlemanly conversation would melt away the political differences. In any case, what subsequently transpired, later called the Compromise of 1790, surely places this particular dinner party atop the list of the most meaningful and consequential meals in American history.

Of the two guests, James Madison, at the tender age of thirty-nine, enjoyed a reputation as the most savvy political operator in Congress. He did not look the part. At five feet four inches tall and less than 120 pounds, little Jemmy Madison had the frail and discernibly fragile appearance of a career librarian, forever lingering on the edge of some serious ailment and seemingly overmatched by the demands of ordinary life. He not only looked the epitome of insignificance—diminutive, colorless, sickly—but also was paralyzingly shy, the sort of guest who instinctively searches out the corners of the room.

AT LEFT: The Tontine Coffee House *depicts commercial activity at the corner of Wall and Water Streets in New York City about 1797.*

ABOVE: *This pineapple-patterned pearlware bowl was recovered during archaeological digs at Monticello, Jefferson's home outside Charlottesville, Virginia. It dates from the correct period, but there is no way of knowing whether this particular piece was used to serve Madison and Hamilton.*

In Madison's case, however, appearances were not simply deceptive—they actually supplemented his prowess. Amid the conspicuous orators of Virginia, he was virtually invisible. He seemed to lack a personal agenda because he seemed to lack a personality. Yet the side he championed nearly always won. This was in part because his physical deficiencies drained him of the customary affectations burdening his peers. In contrast, therefore, a Madisonian argument struck powerfully with the force of pure, unencumbered logic. As one English visitor put it: "Never have I seen so much mind in so little matter."

Throughout the spring of 1790, Madison had deployed his logic defensively to block two legislative initiatives in the House. First, he had managed to scuttle plans to locate the nation's capital in Philadelphia or some other site in Pennsylvania; second, he had placed in gridlock the key proposal of Alexander Hamilton's financial plan, the assumption of Revolutionary-era state debt by the federal government.

JAMES MADISON

1751–1836

Among the delegates at the 1787 Constitutional Convention, James Madison was usually the best prepared. His extensive study of past republics and recent stints in the Virginia and Confederation legislatures also made him especially well suited to the work of translating political theory into practice. Shown here in a 1783 portrait by Charles Willson Peale, Madison has since come to be called the Father of the Constitution for the roles he played not only in creating its basic architecture but also in winning its ratification. In general, though, he performed best when operating outside the hurly-burly of public forums. His presidency, for example, which spanned the poorly executed War of 1812, was one of the low points of his long political career.

I F MADISON'S STYLE WAS, in effect, not to have one, then thirty-five-year-old Alexander Hamilton was Madison's complete opposite. At five feet seven inches, he was small like Madison, with a similarly delicate bone structure, but Hamilton's light peaches-and-cream complexion, violet-blue eyes, and auburn hair suggested an animated beam of light compared to Madison's stationary shadow. Whether Hamilton was leading a bayonet charge against the British at Yorktown, collaborating with Madison and John Jay on *The Federalist,* or proposing a visionary fiscal program for the new federal government, he always proceeded boldly, never looked back, and refused to wait for stragglers.

> "A NATIONAL DEBT, IF IT IS NOT EXCESSIVE, WILL BE TO US A NATIONAL BLESSING."
>
> —
>
> *Alexander Hamilton, letter to Robert Morris, 1781*

Hamilton simply took it for granted that the new Constitution had empowered the federal government to manage the nation's economy. As the first treasury secretary, he was determined to unravel the tangled mess of foreign and domestic debt he had inherited and place the government on firm financial footing by restoring public credit. Taking on the debt incurred by the several states during the American Revolution was merely the first prudent step down a road he saw leading to fiscal responsibility and the eventual release of America's latent commercial energies.

H AMILTON AND MADISON'S HOST had nearly ideal credentials to broker a compromise between them. At six feet two-and-a-half inches, Jefferson towered above his guests; and at forty-seven, he was sufficiently their senior to enjoy the sort of respect accorded an elder brother. As a former minister to France and George Washington's current secretary of state, he required no instruction on the international implications of America's fiscal disarray, which made the U.S. government a laughingstock in European capitals and a poor credit risk among international bankers. He recognized that the achievement of Hamilton's fiscal goals was absolutely essential if the new nation were to be taken seriously throughout the world. On the other hand, as a Virginian and Madison's mentor, Jefferson shared his junior colleague's apprehensions regarding the placement of the permanent capital so far from the surveillance of the Old Dominion. He also harbored a Virginia-writ-large view of the American republic as well as a presumption of Virginia's primacy that would be satisfied only if the permanent capital were located somewhere on the Potomac.

Unlike Madison and Hamilton, however, Jefferson had not been involved in the congressional debates on these issues and could therefore claim a measure of detachment. He had spent the spring settling into his new quarters, drafting a report on weights and measures, and recovering from another bout with his periodic migraine headaches. "My duties

This view of New York Harbor and the mouth of the East River (from Long Island) was drawn sometime during the 1770s.

THE JEFFERSON HOUSEHOLD

Jefferson's maître d'hôtel in New York City was a man named Adrien Petit. Jefferson first engaged Petit in Paris and then lured him back to the New World to supervise his household in America. These pages from Jefferson's papers at the Library of Congress record Petit's recipe for coffee and Jefferson's own instructions for making ice cream.

**ALEXANDER
HAMILTON**

1755 – 1804

*In 1789, George
Washington nominated
his former aide-de-camp
to be the nation's first
treasury secretary, a role
that allowed Alexander
Hamilton to pursue both
his nationalist politics
and his passion for
promoting American
capitalist development.
Hamilton left the
cabinet in 1795 but
never Federalist politics.
Even after John Adams
(also a Federalist)
succeeded Washington
in 1797, party members
continued to look to
Hamilton for leadership.
In 1800, when Jefferson
and Aaron Burr tied in
the electoral college,
Hamilton (shown here
in a 1792 portrait by
John Trumbull) used his
influence in the House
to stop Burr. Four years
later, of course, Burr
stopped Hamilton,
killing him in a duel.*

prevent me from mingling in these questions," he observed in a letter to a fellow Virginian just a week before the dinner. "I do not pretend to be very competent to their decision. In general I think it necessary to give as well as take in a government like ours."

THE GIVING AND TAKING ON the permanent location of the capital had been fierce ever since the residency question, as it was called, came before Congress in September 1789. From the start, the likelihood of congressional representatives reaching a consensus on their own was problematic at best because all the regional voting blocs—New England, the Middle Atlantic, and the South—could cite plausible reasons for claiming primacy. By the spring of 1790, no fewer than sixteen sites had been formally proposed, none mustering a majority of both houses. The leading candidates were (in alphabetic order) Annapolis, Baltimore, Carlisle, Frederick, Germantown, New York, Philadelphia, the Potomac, the Susquehanna, and Trenton. Given its geographic centrality, some location in Pennsylvania appeared to have the edge.

"The business of the seat of Government is become a labyrinth," Madison reported to a Virginia assemblyman, "for which the votes printed furnish no clue." What Madison meant was that the congressional record failed to show the extensive political horse trading going on, as different groups of states formed evanescent coalitions to block emerging winners, then realigned to defeat the next comer. Because residency legislation had to pass both houses of Congress, as soon as one option made its way through one house, the other chamber mobilized against it. The *New York Daily Advertiser*, assessing the apparent futility of it all, suggested that Congress surrender the decision to George Washington. While obviously not the republican way, perhaps the only course left was to let the president point to a map and say, "Here."

> "IN ALL LEGISLATIVE ASSEMBLIES THE GREATER THE NUMBER COMPOSING THEM MAY BE, THE FEWER WILL BE THE MEN WHO WILL IN FACT DIRECT THEIR PROCEEDINGS."
>
> —
>
> *Alexander Hamilton,*
> The Federalist, *1788*

The case Madison made for the Potomac was both ingenious and rooted in illusions largely confined to Virginians. On the ingenious side, he argued that Pennsylvania's apparent centrality was a mirage, that the geographic midpoint between northern Maine and southern Georgia was not just the Potomac but Washington's estate at Mount Vernon, a revelation calculated to convey providential overtones.

On the illusory side, Madison shared the Potomac mythology so prevalent among Virginians that this modest river was a gateway to the West. With just a few canal and navigational improvements, Madison argued, a ship could sail via the Potomac all the way from Chesapeake Bay to the Mississippi River and perhaps even to the Pacific Ocean beyond. He quoted from such publications as *Potomac Magazine,* which described the Potomac as the Thames, Seine, and Rhine all rolled into one and its mouth as the world's most perfect commercial harbor, where ten thousand ships the size of Noah's Ark could comfortably dock. After listening to this rhapsodic account, Fisher Ames of Massachusetts spoke for most non-Virginians in Congress when he remarked that Madison had obviously come under some biblical spell and confused the Potomac with "a Euphrates flowing through paradise." Thus, despite Madison's eloquence, by the time of Jefferson's fateful dinner party, the Potomac option had become, as one wag put it, dead in its own water.

COMPARED TO THE POETRY of the Potomac debate, the other intractable argument—whether or not the federal government should assume the states' debt—had a much more prosaic tone. At first blush, it sounded like a wrangle over mere dollars and cents. According to Hamilton's calculations, the total debt of the United States was $77.1 million. About $25 million of this was state debt, largely the legacy of the War for Independence. Hamilton wanted to consolidate this state debt at the national level. Instead of thirteen separate ledgers, there would be just one, allowing the nation's fiscal policy to proceed with much greater coherence.

Madison's chief objection to this apparently sensible plan, emphasized during the House debates, was economic. Most of the southern states, Virginia among them, had already paid off the bulk of their wartime debt. With Hamilton's proposed transfer of payments to the federal level, these states would inevitably lose out when Congress came to levy new taxes to pay off the new federal debt. Madison calculated that Virginia would be charged about $5 million in new taxes after passing

THE FEDERALIST

This volume, published in 1788, collected letters written under the pseudonym "Publius" to encourage ratification of the new Constitution. Of its eighty-five letters, Hamilton wrote about two-thirds, with Madison and John Jay penning the rest. These essays sought to allay widespread fears that the new federal government would tyrannically supersede states' rights and endanger the newly won liberties of individuals. "Publius" responded that a strong federal government was needed to reconcile the conflicting economic and political interests that had undermined the Articles of Confederation. Although not so influential at the time they were written, these letters have since been acclaimed for their expert analysis of the principles upon which the U.S. government was founded.

THE
FEDERALIST,
ON
THE NEW CONSTITUTION,
WRITTEN IN
THE YEAR 1788,
BY
MR. HAMILTON, MR. MADISON, AND MR. JAY:
WITH
AN APPENDIX,
CONTAINING
THE LETTERS OF PACIFICUS AND HELVIDIUS,
ON THE
PROCLAMATION OF NEUTRALITY OF 1793;
ALSO, THE
ORIGINAL ARTICLES OF CONFEDERATION,
AND
THE CONSTITUTION OF THE UNITED STATES,
WITH THE
AMENDMENTS MADE THERETO.

A NEW EDITION.
THE NUMBERS WRITTEN BY MR. MADISON CORRECTED BY HIMSELF.

CITY OF WASHINGTON:
PRINTED AND PUBLISHED BY JACOB GIDEON, JUN.
1818

along only $3 million in debt. He also objected to the reimbursement of pre-1789 government securities at par, another aspect of Hamilton's plan, because it struck him as unjust. The original holders of this government paper, mostly war veterans who had received the notes as pay for their service, had long since sold them to speculators at a fraction of their face value. The men who had shed their blood for independence would therefore gain nothing from redemption at par, while the investment bankers who had preyed on them would turn a tidy profit.

The reference to investment bankers, in particular, suggests a deeper reason for Madison's opposition. In his judgment, under the guise of doing the states a favor, assumption would implicitly grant the federal government sovereignty over the various state economies. As Madison saw it, the issue was less about money than about power, about ultimate political control from afar, and therefore about the true meaning of independence. It seemed eerily similar to the plot hatched not many years earlier by King George III and Parliament to deprive the colonists of their sacred rights and liberties.

The term that for Madison best captured the essence of the conspiracy was *consolidation*. This word referred to the concentration of political and economic power in the central government and ultimately in the hands of those whom Madison derisively called "stockjobbers and moneymen." It evoked the fear, so prevalent during the 1760s and 1770s, that once arbitrary power was acknowledged to reside in distant places, all liberty was lost. At a more primal level, it suggested the unconscious fear of being swallowed up by a larger creature, the terror of being completely consumed, eaten alive.

HAMILTON WAS TONE DEAF to these ideological arguments. While Madison's cast of mind was inherently political, idealizing the dispersal or diffusion of power, Hamilton's frame of reference was doggedly economic. When money was spread out over the populace, Hamilton thought, it was simply money. When concentrated in the hands of investors, however, it was capital. Thus, for Hamilton, consolidation was not a threat but a synergistic fusion of developmental energies. Far from a sinister plot, it was a simply wonderful idea.

As a result, when Madison and Hamilton sat down in Jefferson's rooms to bargain, even Jefferson's finest French wine and most elegant atmospherics were put to a strenuous test. The location of the permanent capital, on the face of it a geographic problem, had become a

Gordian knot that had tightened around powerful sectional interests. Meanwhile, passage of the Assumption Bill, on the face of it an economic issue, had become a clash between agrarian and commercial interests, each fighting for its own vision of America's future and the true meaning of the Revolution. Both sides believed that nothing less than the survival of the infant republic was at stake.

T HE ONLY SURVIVING ACCOUNT of the bargain struck during the early-evening hours of June 20 comes from Jefferson. Written perhaps two years later, by which time Jefferson had concluded that brokering the deal had been the biggest mistake of his political life, the undated memorandum contains some misleading and self-serving features. But since it is the only account we have, the salient passage deserves to be quoted in full:

> *They came. I opened the subject to them, acknowledged that my situation had not permitted me to understand it sufficiently but encouraged them to consider the thing together. They did so. It ended in Mr. Madison's acquiescence in a proposition that the question [i.e., assumption of the state debt] should be again brought before the House by way of amendment from the Senate, that though he would not vote for it, nor entirely withdraw his opposition, yet he would not be strenuous, but leave it to its fatè. It was observed, I forget by which of them, that as the pill would be a bitter one to the Southern states, something should be done to soothe them; that the removal of the seat of government to the Patowmac was a just measure, and would probably be a popular one with them, and would be a proper one to follow the assumption.*

In other words, Madison agreed to permit the core provision of Hamilton's financial program to pass; and in return, Hamilton agreed to use his influence to assure that the permanent site of the national capital would be located on the Potomac.

At least in its outline of events, Jefferson's memorandum accurately described what happened. On July 9, 1790, the House indeed passed the Residence Bill, which approved construction of a

HAMILTON'S REPORT ON THE MINT

About the time that Congress asked Jefferson to prepare a report on weights and measures, it also asked Hamilton for a national coinage plan. The treasury secretary offered his Report on the Mint in 1791, but the U.S. Mint never accumulated enough gold and silver to make coinage feasible on a national scale. Instead, the Bank of the United States, chartered in 1791 at Hamilton's urging, issued banknotes to increase the money supply.

These are *among the various bills and coins that might have lined a gentleman's pockets in 1790.*

*On December 23, 1784,
the Confederation
Congress voted to make
New York City its tenth
meeting place pending
construction of a new
federal capital on the
banks of the Delaware
River near Philadelphia.
Because New York City
had no building suitable
to house the Congress,
a lottery was conducted
to raise funds for the
redesign of the Old City
Hall (later renamed
Federal Hall) at the
corner of Broad and
Wall Streets.*

permanent capital on the Potomac River. (It also provided for a ten-year stay in Philadelphia while the new District of Columbia was being built.) All this was decided by a vote of 32–29. Subsequently, on July 26, the House passed the Assumption Bill by a nearly identical vote of 34–28, Madison voting in the negative but, in keeping with his promise, not opposing the bill's passage in a "strenuous" fashion. Contemporary observers recognized that some sort of secret deal had been struck, even though few knew the specifics of how it had been accomplished or who had been involved. A disgruntled New York City newspaper editor, writing on July 27, was one of those who accurately guessed the essence of the bargain: "The true reason of the removal of Congress from this city will be explained to the people in a few days. To the lasting disgrace of the majority in both houses, it will be seen that the Pennsylvania and Patowmack interests have been purchased with twenty-one and one-half million dollars," which was his figure for the total value of the assumed state debt.

"THE MOBS OF GREAT CITIES ADD JUST SO MUCH TO THE SUPPORT OF PURE GOVERNMENT AS SORES DO TO THE STRENGTH OF THE HUMAN BODY."

—

Thomas Jefferson, Notes on the State of Virginia, *1784*

Yet in two important respects, Jefferson's account of the dinner-table bargain oversimplified the messier reality of the deal. First, an essential piece of business involved recalculating Virginia's assumed debt and its corresponding share of the prospective federal taxes. An act of creative accounting produced numbers that balanced the Virginia debt and taxes at $3.5 million. This rather miraculous coincidence was not a terribly attractive feature of the negotiations, so Jefferson left it out of his account altogether. Second, delegates from Pennsylvania and Virginia had themselves been holding secret meetings for several weeks and had already agreed to a framework for compromise on the residency question. Pennsylvania had agreed to support the

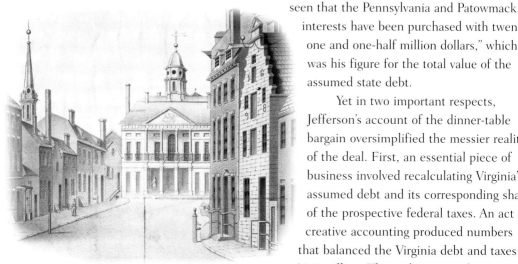

***The work on Federal
Hall,*** *shown here as it
appeared in 1797, was carried
out by Pierre L'Enfant,
the same architect who later
planned the federal capital
on the Potomac.*

Potomac location in return for Philadelphia's designation as an interim site, thinking that once the capital was moved from New York, it would likely never move again. By conveniently ignoring these preliminary negotiations as well, Jefferson was able to give the compromise in his account a romantic gloss, implying that three trusting colleagues had resolved an especially contentious situation by reestablishing the proper atmospherics. In actuality, the Jefferson dinner was but the final act in an ongoing drama that succeeded because its story line had already been developed so well in other secret conversations.

I N THE LONG RUN, OF COURSE, the intricate particularities of the Compromise of 1790 are far less significant than its larger historical consequences. At first, the location of the new capital on the Potomac provided substantial reassurance for the Virginia-writ-large vision of the republic and gave the federal government a decidedly southern accent. For those agrarians like Jefferson who believed cities were sores on the body politic, Washington, D.C., was the perfect capital because— at least in Jefferson's lifetime—it was not really a city at all. For several decades after the government moved there in 1800, it remained a vast and nearly vacant plot of land, so empty that visitors who stopped along the way to ask directions were often astonished to learn they had already arrived and were in fact standing in the capital's very center.

The House of Representatives *met in this chamber in New York City's Federal Hall from the beginning of its first session on March 4, 1789, until August 12, 1790, when it decamped to Philadelphia.*

FURTHER READING

★ Stanley Elkins and Eric McKitrick, *The Age of Federalism: The Early American Republic, 1788–1800* (1993)

★ Joseph J. Ellis, *Founding Brothers: The Revolutionary Generation* (2000)

Jefferson prepared this sketch showing his plan for the new federal city in March 1791. The original District of Columbia land grant comprised a square, ten miles on a side, with property on both sides of the Potomac River. In 1846, however, the federal government returned the land on the western bank to Virginia.

Washington, D.C., embodied the Jeffersonian vision of America in other ways as well. How could one conjure up sinister images of courtiers conspiring in the corridors of power when there were no courts and few corridors and when sessions of Congress were routinely interrupted by the sound of turkey hunters blazing away in the vicinity of Capitol Hill? Nefarious bankers were also nowhere to be found, because the leading banks and investment houses were all located elsewhere, chiefly in New York and Philadelphia. Unlike the leading European capitals—London, Paris, Rome—which gathered together in one metropolis the foremost political, economic, and cultural authorities of each nation, the United States had almost inadvertently decided to segregate these energies. As a result, the residency side of the bargain served for a time as a powerful counterbalance to the urban, commercial, northern-based version of the emerging American nation represented by Hamilton and assumption.

Yet Jefferson realized soon enough, and to his everlasting regret, that the passage of the Assumption Bill had been a truly defining moment in American political history, because it had established the principle of federal sovereignty over the domestic economy. As Jefferson saw it, Hamilton had gotten the better of the deal because his financial program had created what Jefferson called "that Speculating phalanx"—the urban elite of bankers, merchants, and business leaders who became the new commercial aristocracy for an unbridled capitalistic society. Assumption thus proved to be merely the opening wedge for enactment of Hamilton's broad plan to transform America into a modern nation-state whose economic engines were all-powerful—and all located in the North. Once Hamilton's program was institutionalized, Jefferson further realized, it could never be completely dismantled, meaning that the planter aristocracy of the South would be forever placed on the defensive.

This portrait, Thomas Jefferson at the Natural Bridge, *was painted by Caleb Boyle, probably during 1801.*

O N THAT JUNE EVENING, however, Jefferson had no sense of these momentous consequences. Rather, he believed that, like any other effective political compromise, the deal struck by Hamilton and Madison would permit his and Hamilton's competing visions to coexist peacefully, at least for the time being. In fact, the agreement successfully postponed for more than seventy years the fateful conflict, tied to their visions, that eventually erupted in the sectional crisis called the Civil War. By then, of course, through Hamilton's shrewdness, the outcome of that defining moment had already been decided.

★ ★ ★

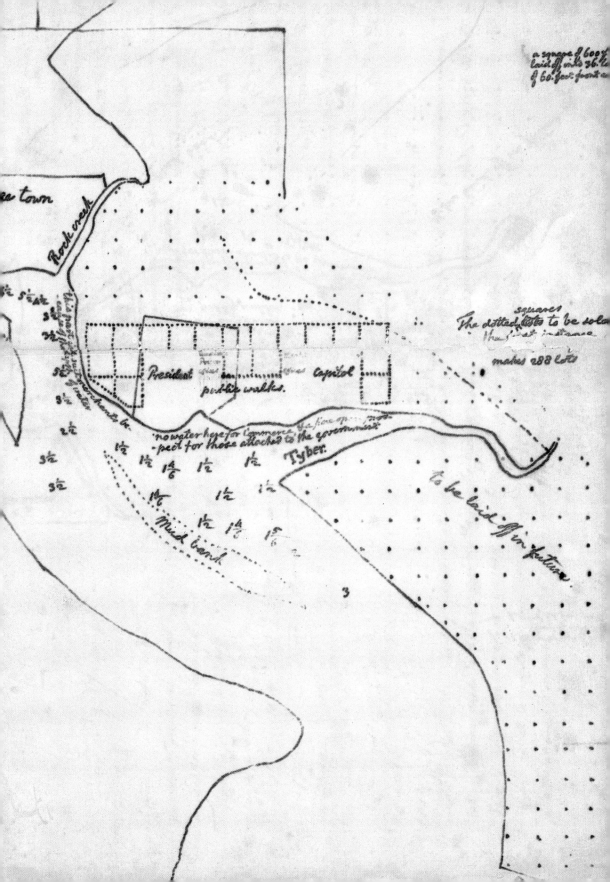

a square of 600 ft
laid off into 36 lots
of 60 feet front a

The dotted lots to be sold
the first instance

squares

makes 288 lots

town

Rock creek

President

public walks.

capitol

no water here for commerce a fine open pros
-pect for those attached to the government

Tyber.

3½ 5½ dk
3½
3½
3½

3½
2½

1½ 1½ 1½ 1½ 1½

3½

3½
3½ 1½ 1½

1½
1½ 1½
1½

Mud bank

to be laid off in future

3

MARCH 4, 1801

THE SECOND AMERICAN REVOLUTION

BY JOYCE APPLEBY

O N MARCH 4, 1801, a tall, narrow-shouldered man in his late fifties emerged from a boardinghouse in the capital city of the United States. He was heading for his inauguration as the country's third president. The nation's second president had decamped earlier that morning in high dudgeon over his defeat, leaving behind only a curt note informing the victor of seven horses and two carriages waiting for him in the White House stables.

Disdaining the company of dignitaries, marching bands, and honor guards, Thomas Jefferson walked with friends and supporters to the Capitol, where Chief Justice John Marshall administered the oath of office. Only a salute from a detachment of the Alexandria militia and the applause of the men and women gathered on the Capitol steps marked the occasion. Pulling some papers from his pocket, Jefferson began to read to

the assembled group of several hundred, delivering his first inaugural address in as inauspicious a manner as he had arrived. Far from finished, the Capitol itself contributed to the day's lack of grandeur— surrounded as it was by scaffolding planks, mud puddles, and hewn stones.

In his inaugural address, Jefferson attempted to transform the vitriol of the recent presidential campaign into proof of the nation's democratic vigor. He downplayed the bitter relations between John Adams's Federalists and his own Democratic-Republican party as mere "animation of discussion," sufficient to worry only "strangers unused to think[ing] freely." Then, acknowledging the depth of the animosity, he asked his fellow citizens to "restore to social intercourse that harmony and affection without which liberty and even life itself are but dreary things." This sentiment found its ultimate voice in Jefferson's famous declaration that day, "We are all Republicans, we are all Federalists." At the completion of his speech, once the crowd had dispersed, the new president returned to his lodgings, where he took a place among his fellow boarders at the noon dinner table.

AT LEFT: *William Russell Birch, the noted Philadelphia printmaker, created this view of the recently completed north (Senate) wing of the Capitol in 1800.*

ABOVE: *Among the many items sold to commemorate Jefferson's 1801 inauguration was this decorative pitcher.*

Joseph Priestley (shown here in a engraving made from a portrait by Gilbert Stuart) is best remembered as one of the discoverers of the element oxygen, which he obtained by heating red mercuric oxide in August 1774.

HISTORIANS AND POLITICAL SCIENTISTS have highlighted the significance of Jefferson's inauguration because it marked the first peaceful transfer of power under the new Constitution, after a hard-fought campaign in which both sides keenly felt the portentousness of the outcome. With coups d'état around the world to remind us of the difficulty of ousting defeated incumbents, such an emphasis is not ill placed, but it hardly does justice to the momentous changes that Jefferson's presidency ushered in.

Writing after his election victory to Joseph Priestley, the famous English scientist then ensconced in rural Pennsylvania, Jefferson had succinctly reprised the differences between his Democratic-Republicans and their Federalist opponents, who looked "backwards, not forwards, for improvement." The Federalists favored education, Jefferson acknowledged, "but it was to be the education of our ancestors," and he noted ruefully that President Adams had actually said that "we were never to expect to go beyond them in real science." Rising to this handsome occasion for expatiating on the subject of the future, Jefferson declared with great gusto: "We can no longer say there is nothing new under the sun. For this whole chapter in the history of man is new. The great extent of our republic is new. Its sparse habitation is new. The mighty wave of public opinion which has rolled over it is new."

"The mighty wave of public opinion" was something of an exaggeration, for Jefferson had won the election with only seventy-three electoral votes to Adams's sixty-five. Still, given the radical platform Jefferson had constructed to run on, we could interpret "mighty" as a reference not to size but to character. Looking back years later, Jefferson

The scientifically inclined Jefferson owned at least two orreries, or operating models of the solar system. He purchased this tabletop model around 1790.

called his election America's second revolution, "as real a revolution in the principles of our government as that of 1776 was in its form." If March 4, 1801, is to earn its place as a day of destiny in American history, then Jefferson's claim must be carefully examined.

THE PRINCIPLES OF government to which Jefferson referred had been clearly spelled out during the two previous presidential campaigns, both of which had pitted Jefferson against Adams, the man who turned out to be the last Federalist president. In 1796 and again in 1800, Jefferson had attacked the Federalists for augmenting federal power and establishing a ruling

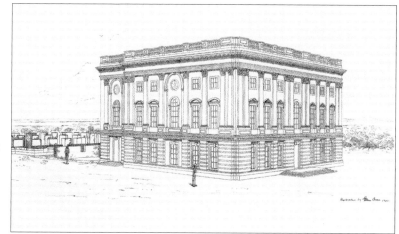

This sketch of the Capitol *under construction first appeared in Glenn Brown's two-volume* History of the United States Capitol *(1900–1903). Brown produced this approximation using numerous primary sources.*

elite at the country's political center. The Federalists wanted to separate from the corruptions of Great Britain, Jefferson pointed out, but not from the example of Britain's hierarchical style of government. Utterly rejecting the Federalists' preferences for an energetic government and a passive electorate, Jefferson championed the new French idea of progress and became an agent of change—profound, transformative change—in the social relations and political style of this country.

When Jefferson called his election "as real a revolution in the principles of our government as that of 1776 was in its form," he also meant to evoke a third revolution: the one that had taken place in France during the 1790s and roiled America's own revolutionary leadership. The 1793 execution of King Louis XVI and subsequent formation of a French republic had enabled Jefferson to reinterpret America's War for Independence as but the first act in an unfolding world revolutionary drama. The Federalists railed against the new French government as the work of dangerous radicals, but Jeffersonians enthusiastically endorsed the Gallic call for "liberty, equality, fraternity." They formed democratic clubs (in imitation of the Jacobins) and began roundly criticizing George Washington's policy of neutrality in the ongoing Anglo-French conflict. Their tumultuous public meetings and dozens of new, partisan newspapers

THE ELECTION OF 1800

Party discipline among Democratic-Republican electors was so strict in 1800 that Jefferson actually tied for first place with his running mate, Aaron Burr. This awkward result tempted some Federalists in the lame-duck Congress (and Burr) to cause mischief. In the end, thirty-five votes were taken in the House before Jefferson was declared president on the thirty-sixth.

THOMAS JEFFERSON

1743 – 1826

For three years, Thomas Jefferson served George Washington as the first secretary of state. Yet Jefferson's constant wrangling with Treasury Secretary Alexander Hamilton, especially over U.S. policy toward Britain and France, steadily soured him on the Federalist administration, from which he resigned in 1793. Jefferson's openness to novelty also put him at odds with the traditional hierarchical views of Washington and John Adams, whom Jefferson opposed for the presidency in 1796 and again in 1800. For Jefferson (shown here in a 1791 portrait by Charles Willson Peale), his battle with the Federalists was a straightforward engagement with darkness in the interests of clarity, a contest between a body of partisans and a party of principled men.

in turn aroused the worst fears of the Federalists, who responded with the repressive Alien and Sedition Acts of 1798.

Thus what began as differences over neutrality turned into a grand debate about free speech and popular political participation. The Federalists maintained that, after voting, citizens should allow their elected officials to govern, while the Jeffersonians articulated a political philosophy that took popular sovereignty literally, insisting on the public's right to engage in vigorous politicking. Such day-to-day involvement challenged venerable notions about how ordinary citizens should behave. Clashes between these opposing groups became even more frequent when Federalists began using the Sedition Act to prosecute the major pro-Jefferson newspapers.

RARELY DO PRESIDENTIAL ELECTIONS produce mandates, and Jefferson's electoral count was far from overwhelming, but the sharpness of the differences between the Democratic-Republicans and the Federalists gave his victory a decisive quality. The two parties had squared off on foreign policy, free speech, the permissible bounds of popular politics, how to interpret the Constitution, whether to limit or energize the federal government, and, most important, whether the future would be markedly different or a replay of the past with different actors. The Jeffersonians said they were fighting to secure the American Revolution. Was America truly the "last, best hope on the world," as the French *philosophe* Anne-Robert Turgot said, or would it slip back into being a pale New World imitation of Great Britain?

With a bold plan for redirecting American political institutions, Jefferson introduced a unique blend of democracy and liberalism in which political participation was extended to the entire white male population but the powers of government were strictly limited. Following this scheme, Jefferson and his successors enlarged the scope of voluntary interactions while limiting what government could do by adopting a strict constructionist view of its powers. American citizens benefited as private persons whose rights were protected, even as the scope of their political power contracted with the diminished scope of government initiatives.

This linen banner *was hand-painted in 1800, most likely for a Jefferson victory celebration.*

This combination of expanding personal rights and shrinking the size of government had not been seen in the world before, though it was implicit in the theoretical writings of Adam Smith and David Hume, which had influenced America's revolutionary leaders. Jefferson devoutly believed in the existence of the natural social harmony that Smith wrote about in *The Wealth of Nations*. Federalists did not share this faith, cleaving to the old wisdom that social order depended upon recognized hierarchies of authority in church and state. Perhaps these deep philosophical differences would have remained buried had events during the 1790s not brought them to the surface of public life.

T HE THOROUGHNESS with which Jefferson exorcised from the government the influence of his opponents still astounds. He removed a whole cohort of young Federalists from civil and military offices; he eliminated domestic taxes; he substantially reduced the national debt; he shrank the size of the bureaucracy despite the nation's growth in population and territory; he hastened the conveyance of land in the public domain to ordinary farmers; and he replaced Federalist formality with a nonchalance in matters of etiquette that gave daily proof that he was a practicing democrat. Not a symbol, a civil servant, or a presidential initiative escaped his consideration as a tool in dismantling the "energetic" and elitist government of his predecessor.

THE INVISIBLE HAND

The "invisible hand" of competition described by Adam Smith in The Wealth of Nations *(1776) exemplified the harmonizing principles that Jefferson saw at work in nature and the world. In Smith's view, a system of perfect economic liberty, operating under the unfettered drives and constraints of marketplace competition, would naturally give rise to an orderly society. Though Smith made this argument on narrow economic grounds, his work was actually broadly philosophical in character.*

This 1825 view *of Jefferson's home, Monticello, shows the west front of the house and its garden.*

Isaac Newton *Francis Bacon* *John Locke*

THE ENLIGHTENMENT

The Enlightenment was a European intellectual movement of the seventeenth and eighteenth centuries that caused revolutionary developments in art, philosophy, science, and politics. Central to Enlightenment thought was the celebration of reason, whose power enabled humans to understand the universe and improve their own condition. Among its principal progenitors were three Englishmen: mathematician Isaac Newton, experimental scientist Francis Bacon, and political philosopher John Locke.

Not content to rely upon government policies alone, Jefferson undertook a radical revision of the etiquette that prevailed at White House dinners. Deriding what he called "the rags of royalty," he made the modesty of person, place, and ceremony displayed on his inaugural day an important feature in his forthcoming administration. He scrapped the traditional protocols for honoring foreign dignitaries and adopted instead measures that embodied republican simplicity and egalitarianism. (For instance, rather than seating guests at state dinners according to rank, as had previously been the practice, he sat them "pele-mele.") By removing the customary props to a structure of ranks and degrees, he weakened the entire edifice of the existing hierarchy. Nor was he reluctant to draw the political implications of his confrontations with the arbiters of polite society. In February 1804, writing anonymously in the *Philadelphia Aurora,* Jefferson announced that since March 4, 1801, there had been no "Court of the United States." He declared, "That day buried levees, birthdays, royal parades, processions with white wands, and the arrogance of precedence in society, by certain self-styled friends of order, but truly styled friends of privileged orders."

> "EVERY MAN'S OWN REASON MUST BE HIS ORACLE."
>
> —
>
> *Thomas Jefferson, letter to Benjamin Rush, March 1813*

The natural social harmony that Jefferson so often rhapsodized about was the one that had dominated the social imagination of English philosophers from the time of Bacon, Newton, and Locke—in Jefferson's estimate, the world's three greatest men. Beneath the myriad of surface variety and detail, these natural philosophers had discovered regularities and uniformities of such lawlike certainty that thinkers began talking about the science of man, a disciplined inquiry that would unlock the social possibilities that centuries of oppression, superstition, and poverty had hidden. This is what made the idea of limited government possible: Human nature had its own organizing principles.

WHERE THE FEDERALISTS looked to the clergy for an articulation of national values, Jefferson extolled natural philosophy and argued that education would promote a new era of political equality. Emphasizing nature's harmonizing principles, best exemplified by the "invisible hand" of the free marketplace that Adam Smith had described, Jefferson looked for ways to cast off the dead hand of the past. Claiming to interpret the laws of nature, he linked the American nation to a grand human destiny, but his association of the rights to life, liberty, and the pursuit of happiness with a uniform human nature boded ill for women, African Americans, and the native tribes whom he believed nature had excluded.

By construing liberty as liberation from historic institutions, Jefferson made America the pilot society for the world. It was not only Americans but all men who sought freedom from past oppression, and this presumed universality of their values gave Americans confidence that retrograde monarchies would in the future turn into republican forms of governance. The assertion that all men are alike in their aspiration to freedom as well as in their capacity to pursue independent lives provided the scientific underpinnings of what became America's national creed. Giving a radical reading to his own Declaration of Independence, Jefferson assumed the presidency in 1801 with a clear sense of what needed to be done to secure the American Revolution from the reactionary program of the Federalists. Hostile to their state building, he looked to the informal interactions of free men to build the country— sharing here Thomas Paine's view, expressed in the opening passage of *Common Sense*, that society "promotes our happiness positively by uniting our affections," while government only restrains "our vices."

THE NATION'S CAPITAL

Jefferson, the first president inaugurated in the District of Columbia, took justifiable pride in the federal city's very existence. Originally, the up-and-coming port of New York City was the nation's capital. But New York, with its polyglot population and tough neighborhoods, frightened Americans, who still lived in an overwhelmingly rural country. Many feared that the piling up of people in large cities would degrade the United States—or, at the very least, sully its politics. Jefferson was among them, and in 1790 he took advantage of a congressional impasse to work out a compromise that moved the capital to a ten-mile-square plot of land on the Potomac, far from dolorous urban influences.

This engraving shows the District of Columbia in 1800 as seen from Capitol Hill looking west down Pennsylvania Avenue.

Jefferson also explicitly detached liberty from its connection to self-denial (a connection made during the Revolution, when self-sacrifice was the watchword) and reattached it to the promise of prosperity. His optimism floated on expectations of material abundance, which he looked for in the expanding frontier of uncultivated land that lay west of the Appalachian Mountains. Too much land, Jefferson believed, fostered the savage condition, but without land, men could not achieve personal autonomy. His draft constitution for Virginia, written in 1776, included a fifty-acre property qualification for voting and simultaneously proposed giving all landless adult white men fifty acres of land. Spurning Thomas Malthus's gloomy predictions about population growth outpacing food supplies, he insisted that, in America, harvests would grow exponentially. The opportunities he saw in the New World enabled him to square the circle of self-interest and community welfare. "So invariably do the laws of nature create our duties and interests," he wrote the French economist J. B. Say, "that when they seem to be at variance, we ought to suspect some fallacy in our reasoning."

English economist and demographer Thomas Malthus was best known for his theory that population growth will always tend to outrun the food supply. In An Essay on the Principle of Population (1798), whose first edition Malthus published anonymously, he argued that population, if uncontrolled, would increase geometrically while food production increased only arithmetically. Therefore, short of stern limits on reproduction, only famine, war, and ill health could be expected to keep the world's population in check.

JEFFERSON HAD THE EXCEPTIONAL good fortune to be followed by two close political allies, James Madison and James Monroe. Both shared his strict constructionist interpretation of the Constitution, his determination to open the world to free trade, and his anti-British foreign policy. After two terms spent dismantling the country's inherited political culture, Jefferson was able to see his own principles worked into the fabric of American national identity over the next quarter century. Recently, historians have focused on Jefferson-the-slaveholder and Jefferson-the-traditional-male in evaluating how revolutionary was his election in 1800. Taking his acceptance of female and African-American disenfranchisement as proof of his lack of reforming zeal, they have used twenty-first-century standards to measure an eighteenth-century man. Race, class, and gender have all gained salience in our time, but it is a grave error of historical judgment to underestimate the difficulty and significance of Jefferson's battle against the prejudices then being directed at ordinary white men. To do so is to misunderstand Jefferson's crusade against the tyrannies of the past and to minimize the conspicuous abuses of a status-conscious society whose elite routinely belittled the self-governing capacity of "the lower orders."

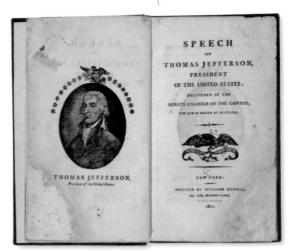

This text of Jefferson's inaugural address was printed by William Durrell of New York City, whose shop at 106 Maiden Lane was just down the street from the house at 57 Maiden Lane that Jefferson occupied while serving as secretary of state.

Beginning in 1813, with each now relieved of his public responsibilities, Jefferson and Adams began to write to each other again. In this famous correspondence, Adams was characteristically crusty, using his words to jab and thrust at the stupidities of the world, while Jefferson calmly steered his own philosophical ship through untroubled waters. Still, he could not resist refighting the election campaign that had resulted in his first inauguration that March day in 1801. He unequivocally characterized their respective parties as "the enemies of reform" and its champions. The two sides, Jefferson continued, split on the question of "the improvability of the human mind, in science, in ethics, in government." "Those who advocated reformation of institutions, pari passu, with the progress of science," he lectured Adams, "maintained that no definite limits could be assigned to that progress." These differences Jefferson summed up in pairs of opposing principles: whether political leaders should be guided by experience or by theory; whether the people should be feared and distrusted or cherished; whether governments should use coercive economic and political force or trust in the people's capacity to act in its own best interest.

One wonders whether Jefferson caught the irony when Adams commented in an August 1816 letter, "Your taste is judicious in liking better the dreams of the Future, than the History of the Past." Their correspondence continued another ten years until death came to both men on July 4, 1826, the fiftieth anniversary of the signing of the Declaration of Independence, which both had helped write. Thinking on his deathbed of his old friend and rival, Adams uttered these last words: "Thomas Jefferson still survives."

FUNERAL THOUGHTS,
EXCITED BY THE DEATH OF
JOHN ADAMS
AND
THOS. JEFFERSON,

Adams died about six o'clock in the evening, not knowing that Jefferson had succumbed in Virginia five hours earlier.

OPPOSITE:

The statue of the third president inside the Jefferson Memorial, Washington, D.C.

I NDEED JEFFERSON DOES. When he stepped before Chief Justice John Marshall that sunny March day in 1801, he was about to make good his claim that the election of 1800 represented a second American revolution. With a clarity of vision, a capacity for leadership, and protégés to follow him, he left us a legacy that still resonates. Where the words *Washingtonian*, *Jacksonian*, and *Wilsonian* direct us to past political regimes, *Jeffersonian* is an adjective still used in contemporary conversation. "Let us return to our Jeffersonian origins," Democratic presidential candidate Gary Hart exhorted a crowd in 1988, while in 1992 an anguished Jerry Brown demanded of his party's convention delegates, "What would Jefferson think?" On the other side of the aisle, Republican pundit John McClaughry asserted in a 1982 *New York Times* op-ed piece that Ronald Reagan was the most Jeffersonian president since Martin Van Buren,

After leaving office in 1801, John Adams gradually restored his relationships with many old friends from the Revolution who had chosen to side with Jefferson in opposing Federalist rule. One such man was Benjamin Rush, who subsequently persuaded Adams and Jefferson to disregard their differences and renew the friendship that they had both previously enjoyed.

a point Reagan himself embellished with his own recommendation that Americans "pluck a flower from Thomas Jefferson's life and wear it in our soul forever." A more recent president, William Jefferson Clinton, recognized his indebtedness to the man whose name he bears by opening his 1992 inaugural festivities at Monticello.

Both critics and champions keep the Jefferson legacy alive. Benignly presiding today in a little Greek temple on the Potomac near the place where in March 1801 he became president, Jefferson's statue profoundly evokes the man and his philosophy and reminds us of the links he forged among American identity and the primacy of natural rights, the politics of limited government, and the belief in a world steadily moving toward liberty and justice for all.

★ ★ ★

MID-FEBRUARY, 1824

THE WAY WEST

BY WILLIAM H. GOETZMANN

I T WAS A SHRIVELING COLD winter in the Rocky Mountains, and the wind blew so hard it was impossible to make a campfire. On the wide floor of the Wind River Valley, the snow accumulated in large drifts, but the conditions didn't faze the Crow Indians or their friends, a small band of fur trappers. Over two days in February 1824, Crow hunters, stripped to the waist and oblivious of the cold, stampeded and killed more than a thousand buffalo. They killed so many, in fact, that the squaws, old men, and children following the hunt couldn't skin and butcher the animals fast enough—so they had to remain with the carcasses all night to keep the wolves from getting at the meat. One of the trappers present, James Clyman, wrote that he saw twenty horseless (and therefore relatively immobile) Indians kill seventy buffalo in a single afternoon.

AT LEFT: *A group of emigrants rests near Colorado Springs. Travelers often took a break from the trail during the middle of the day. The respites were called "nooning."*

ABOVE: *The fashionability of beaver hats among wealthy easterners was one reason that beaver pelts commanded such a high price.*

The Crows must have been delirious with the results of their hunt, but the trappers (or mountain men, as they called themselves) weren't very interested in buffalo. They were determined to find a way across the Rocky Mountains so they could reach the valley of the Green River, the fabled haunt of *their* quarry: the beaver. Clyman's group, led by twenty-four-year-old Jedediah Smith, had left Fort Kiowa on the upper Missouri in September 1823, intending to travel up the Wind River Valley to Union Pass, a route taken by some of John Jacob Astor's fur hunters as early as 1811. However, by the time Smith's men reached that pass in early February 1824, it was choked with snow. Forced to retreat, they moved down the valley and joined the encampment of friendly Crows.

In the aftermath of the grand hunt, once the tribe had settled down, the mountain men asked the Crow hunters whether there was another route across or around the Rockies to reach the Green River (the Seeds-kee-dee in Indian parlance). By his own account, James Clyman spread a tanned buffalo hide across the floor of a warm tepee and made piles of sand to

JEDEDIAH SMITH

1798 – 1831

As a boy, Jedediah Smith worked on a Lake Erie freighter before gradually making his way west. In 1826—soon after he, Bill Sublette, and David Jackson bought out William Ashley's fur-trading company—Smith led a hunting party from the Great Salt Lake across the Mojave Desert to southern California. In the spring of 1827, he returned across the Sierra Nevada, becoming the first white American to enter California from the east and return using an overland route. After the 1827 rendezvous, Smith retraced his route to California, where Mohave Indians killed half of his party. Smith survived, but in May 1831, working the Santa Fe trade, he was killed by Comanches at a water hole near the Cimarron River. This sketch is the only known authenticated portrait of Smith.

represent various mountains. Then, through interpreter Edward Rose, he asked the Crows to show him which way Smith's party might go. The Crows obliged. They indicated a route around the southern end of the Wind River Mountains that would take the trappers to the Sweetwater River. From there, they could follow the Sweetwater southwest to a low pass and thence to the Seeds-kee-dee.

This was a climactic moment in western and Native American history. The Crows had shown Clyman, Smith, and their comrades the location of South Pass, a dip in the Continental Divide that made possible the Oregon Trail, over which roughly three hundred thousand westward-bound emigrants would later travel. For the region's Native American tribes, the revelation of South Pass to these white trappers spelled the beginning of the end of their wild, free way of life. Using the same route, countless settlers, hunters, miners, and missionaries penetrated the West and spread out—building forts and towns, fencing in the range, and displacing the Indians.

ACTUALLY, SMITH'S GROUP WAS NOT the first party of trappers to use South Pass. Robert Stuart's expedition had earned that distinction in October 1812 on its return trip from Astoria, John Jacob Astor's fur-trading outpost at the mouth of the Columbia River. Although Stuart's discovery was announced in all the Missouri newspapers, few early trappers paid much attention to it because the Rockies didn't seem likely beaver country. South Pass itself, a wide saddle of land connecting the Little Sandy River (flowing west) and the Sweetwater (flowing east), was too exposed for beaver. And the newspaper accounts of Stuart's journey revealed little that might help trappers repeat the crossing, because Astor habitually kept his company's maps and other geographical records secret. He viewed them as valuable proprietary information and considered freelance mountain men as much his rivals as the trappers of Britain's two great beaver concerns, the Northwest Company and the Hudson's Bay Company, which hunted down from Canada. Beginning in 1824, for example, the Hudson's Bay Company— led by its governor, George Simpson, and the daring trapper Peter Skene Ogden—attempted to make the country west of the Wasatch Range (in present-day Idaho, Oregon, and Washington) "a fur desert" by trapping out all its beaver.

Following the directions given Clyman by the Crow hunters, Smith and his party reached the Green River on March 20, 1825—a date that Clyman considered significant enough to note specifically in his account. At this point, the trappers split up, with Smith leading seven men farther south along the Green while Clyman and a few others trapped the river's tributaries near South Pass. The Seeds-kee-dee was indeed rich in beaver, and by June 1, the date they had set for a rendezvous on the Sweetwater, the trappers had all enjoyed successful spring hunts. Back on the Sweetwater, Smith found Thomas Fitzpatrick, Alexander Stone, and Solomon Branch but not James Clyman, who was off in a canyon of the Laramie Mountains hiding from hostile Arikaras. (It turned out that the designated rendezvous spot was a famous Indian war ground.)

John James Audubon included this rendering of a beaver in Volume 1 of his Viviparous Quadrupeds of North America (1845).

Smith and most of his men decided to stay in the mountains and continue trapping beaver and exploring, while Fitzpatrick, Stone, and Branch headed back to civilization to sell their furs. To carry their precious cargo down the Sweetwater and North Platte Rivers, the three men quickly fashioned a bullboat from bent saplings and buffalo hides. Before they reached the North Platte, however, the boat capsized, and they ended up caching their furs near Independence Rock, a large granite outcropping on the north bank of the Sweetwater that would later become an important landmark on the Oregon Trail (and a place where hundreds of emigrants carved their names). The rest of the way, they traveled on foot. Meanwhile, Clyman, having survived several Arikara war

William H. Jackson took this photograph of South Pass in 1870. The buildings in the background form South Pass City, a boomtown that sprang up after gold was discovered nearby in 1867.

James Clyman

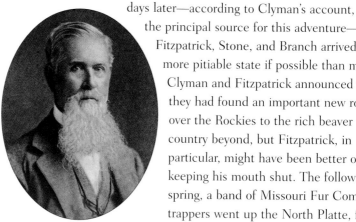

Thomas Fitzpatrick

parties, walked across five hundred miles of prairie to Fort Atkinson, located on the Missouri River at its confluence with the Platte. Ten days later—according to Clyman's account, the principal source for this adventure—Fitzpatrick, Stone, and Branch arrived "in a more pitiable state if possible than myself." Clyman and Fitzpatrick announced that they had found an important new route over the Rockies to the rich beaver country beyond, but Fitzpatrick, in particular, might have been better off keeping his mouth shut. The following spring, a band of Missouri Fur Company trappers went up the North Platte, found Fitzpatrick's cache, and hijacked his furs.

J EDEDIAH SMITH and the others had been sent to the Green River in 1823 by the fur company of Ashley and Henry, founded just one year earlier. Competition among the several fur companies in St. Louis was already fierce, but potential profits were so great that William H. Ashley, the state's first lieutenant governor, and Andrew Henry, a veteran of the upper Missouri River trade, decided to join the sweepstakes anyway. To attract manpower, Ashley had placed a notice in the February 13, 1822, *St. Louis Gazette and Public Advertiser,* asking for "Enterprising Young Men...to ascend the Missouri to its source, there to be employed for one, two, or three years." This call initiated a chain of events that, though at times unfortunate for Ashley, had important positive consequences for the rest of the country.

TO Enterprising Young Men.

THE subscriber wishes to engage ONE HUNDRED MEN, to ascend the river Missouri to its source, there to be employed for one, two or three years.—For particulars, enquire of Major Andrew Henry, near the Lead Mines, in the County of Washington, (who will ascend with, and command the party) or to the subscriber at St. Louis.

Wm. H. Ashley.

February 13 ——98 tf

Historian Don Berry *has called the St. Louis fur traders "a majority of scoundrels."*

That first year, Henry supervised construction of a trading post far up the Missouri at its strategic junction with the Yellowstone. Meanwhile, Ashley launched a keelboat from St. Louis to bring his partner needed supplies and trade goods. Even before Ashley left, though, a cartful of gunpowder, pistols, and rifles exploded, causing some delay. Then the boat had to stop at St. Charles, a short way up the river, to take on a second cartful of munitions, causing further delay. Finally, three hundred miles up the river, one of the boat's masts caught in some trees, causing the ship to flip over on its side and sink with ten thousand dollars' worth of provisions and merchandise aboard—including, of course, the gunpowder, the pistols, and some specially

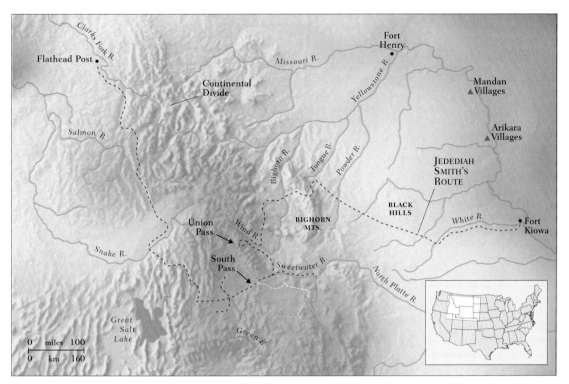

Labels on map: Clarks Fork R., Flathead Post, Continental Divide, Missouri R., Fort Henry, Mandan Villages, Yellowstone R., Salmon R., Arikara Villages, Bighorn R., Tongue R., Powder R., JEDEDIAH SMITH'S ROUTE, BLACK HILLS, White R., Fort Kiowa, Union Pass, Wind R., BIGHORN MTS., South Pass, Sweetwater R., North Platte R., Snake R., Great Salt Lake, Green R.

0 miles 100
0 km 160

Jedediah Smith left Fort Kiowa in September 1823 and arrived at the Flathead Post of the Hudson's Bay Company in November 1824.

made Hawken rifles, the mountain men's favorite weapon. Even worse, the 150 survivors were now stranded hundreds of miles upriver. Within eighteen days, however, the irrepressible Ashley, who was still in St. Louis, had secured another boat to carry them on to the Yellowstone— and, just to be sure that new supplies indeed reached Fort Henry, he himself led an overland party to the Yellowstone. Then, turning around, he floated back down the Missouri in a pirogue to St. Louis, where he immediately began recruiting another band of trappers from the grog shops along the waterfront. Among his chief recruiters that winter were Jed Smith and James Clyman.

In June 1823, having miraculously secured additional credit, Ashley again launched a flotilla of keelboats up the Missouri and again suffered a disaster. About halfway to the Yellowstone, Ashley's convoy stopped to trade for some horses with the Arikaras, also called Rees. After the trade was completed, the Rees attacked Ashley's party—shooting all the horses they had just traded, killing a dozen of the whites, and wounding eleven more. Murderous rifle and arrow fire pinned down many of the whites on a narrow sandbar. Among those trapped were some of Ashley's best men—Smith, Clyman, Edward Rose, Bill Sublette—and they escaped only by giving up their weapons and swimming downstream to the safety of the fast-retreating keelboats. Provoked by the molestation of some Ree

ASHLEY'S MAIN CHANCE

William Ashley was an archetypal Jacksonian capitalist. He was well connected with politicians, other venture capitalists, and a host of newspapermen who followed his every move in the fur business. (Ashley made good copy because disaster seemed to follow him.) After selling his fur business in 1826, he went back to real estate and politics, serving several terms in the U.S. Congress.

The best rifles in early-nineteenth-century America were made by the Hawken brothers of St. Louis.

women by members of a rival fur company, this battle effectively closed the Missouri River above the Arikara village, and a subsequent military campaign in August 1823, led by Col. Henry Leavenworth, failed to reopen it.

Now Ashley, who was a hundred thousand dollars in debt, made a fateful decision. Having had enough of its vagaries, he resolved to abandon the river trade entirely. The other fur companies could have the Missouri and swap goods for furs with the middleman tribes if they wished; *he* was going to deal directly with the mountain men who trapped their own beavers. Moreover, instead of hiring trappers as his employees (as some fur companies had done), Ashley decided to work with them as inde-

The art of Alfred Jacob Miller is one of the few visual records we have of the Rocky Mountain West as it was experienced by the early mountain men. This 1837 work is entitled Trapping Beaver.

pendent contractors, providing them with gunpowder and other supplies in exchange for half their catch. Thus Ashley revolutionized the fur trade in the Central Rockies and began a new phase of capitalism in the West. At the same time, a giant step forward in geographical knowledge also resulted, although much of it was still hearsay and word of mouth.

I N SEPTEMBER 1823, Ashley and Henry sent two parties out from Fort Kiowa on the Missouri River just above its junction with the White. One, led personally by Henry, headed overland to Fort Henry on the Yellowstone River. From there, it moved south to the Powder River country and then on to the Big Horn Mountains, each time without success. Finally, Henry sent John H. Weber south and west over the Big Horn and Owl Creek Ranges into the Wind River basin, there to winter with the same Crows who had earlier sheltered the other Ashley and Henry party, the one led by Jedediah Smith.

When the news of Smith's success, carried by Fitzpatrick and Clyman, finally reached Ashley in St. Louis, the entrepreneur was overjoyed and quickly began outfitting a new expedition to the Seeds-kee-dee, which he led through South Pass. Ashley returned to St. Louis in the fall of 1825 with enough furs to pay off his debts and still have plenty of working capital. He built himself a fine house and took on as his "field partner" Jedediah Smith. (Andrew Henry wanted to leave the business while he still had his scalp.)

Even more important, during his 1824–1825 expedition Ashley had hosted what is generally considered to be the first mountain man "rendezvous," where independent trappers exchanged furs for supplies and other trade goods. The event was so successful that each summer from 1825 until 1841, trappers who had been ranging far and wide all year gathered at a designated place in the heart of the mountains to meet fur company traders with whom they swapped pelts for whiskey, guns, knives, and other products of civilization. Former trappers such as Bill Sublette and Robert Campbell brought wagonloads of these goods out from St. Louis and became rich men. Others made fortunes outfitting the increasing number of wagon trains traveling the Oregon, California, and Santa Fe Trails, and many locals came to believe that the bustling hub city of St. Louis was, as they said, "The Future Great City of the World."

When thirty-two-year-old George Simpson *became governor of the Hudson's Bay Company in 1824, one of the first things that he did was travel to the remote Columbia Department to find out why its balance sheet was so dismal. He decided that the problem was "shameful mismanagement," which he set about correcting with the appointment of Peter Skene Ogden (above) as head of the company's Snake River Expedition. Ogden's efforts were also part of Simpson's larger plan to keep American trappers out of British Oregon by creating a beaver-free buffer zone east and south of the Columbia River and along the Snake River that runs through the Northern Rockies.*

Born in Paris to a prominent French radical, Benjamin Bonneville emigrated to the United States with his family in 1803, when he was seven years old. He attended West Point and was graduated in 1815. In 1821, he was assigned to Fort Smith (in what is now Arkansas), where garrison life bored him. In 1837, Washington Irving published an edited version of Bonneville's western journals that greatly romanticized the captain and his achievements.

OVE FORWARD TO 1831. Using South Pass as their all-important gateway, mountain men had, by the 1830s, searched out every hidden glade and beaver stream in the Central Rockies. But they hadn't yet completed the basic work of western exploration, and there was much about the West that the government didn't know. To learn more, the U.S. Army granted leave in 1831 to Capt. Benjamin Louis Eulalie Bonneville so that he could lead a trapping expedition into the Rockies. Although Bonneville pretended that his goals were purely commercial, his detailed instructions from the War Department made it clear that his pose as a civilian was merely a cover designed to give the U.S. government deniability. From the outset, it was obvious that his mission included learning all he could about the Indians living west of the Rocky Mountains—from the number of warriors in each tribe and the power of their horses to "every information which you may conceive would be useful to the Government." Bonneville was also directed to investigate the natural resources of the country, its climate, and its geography. And there was one more clandestine aspect to his mission, perhaps the most important of all from the government's (and history's) point of view.

Leaving in May 1832 from Fort Osage on the Missouri River (near present-day Kansas City), Bonneville's expedition—outfitted privately, without any government funds—journeyed along the North Platte via the now-familiar route to South Pass and the Green River. Once Bonneville reached the Green, he sent out trapping parties and built a fort on the western bank of the upper Green, about five miles above the mouth of Horse Creek. The mountain men called the fort Bonneville's Folly, because it was so far north as to be nearly useless for trapping beaver during most of the year. What they didn't realize was that Bonneville wasn't in the fur business; he was in the listening post business, and his stout log structure couldn't have been better placed to watch the approaches to South and Union Passes and monitor the activities of the Hudson's Bay Company.

By this time, though, the viability of British operations in the West had been substantially undermined by the arrival of American freelance trappers. The biggest problem for Peter Skene Ogden had become the commercial system under which he and his colleagues labored. The British trappers acted as servants of the Crown and the Hudson's Bay Company, while the Americans were free to speculate in any number of ways as expectant capitalists. The American system made particular sense for independent trappers, whose ranks swelled throughout the 1820s. An important confrontation had taken place in May 1825, when a group of

American free trappers led by Johnson Gardner invaded a Hudson's Bay campsite at Mountain Green, just east of the Great Salt Lake. Although the site was below the Forty-second Parallel (and thus in Mexican territory), Gardner's band raised an American flag and told Ogden that he was trespassing. Gardner also persuaded Ogden's men that, as free trappers, they wouldn't have to share their catch with the Hudson's Bay Company. At this point, Ogden lost control of his Iroquois trappers, and most of them went over to the American side, along with their guns, traps, and furs.

After all, there was more to the exploration of the Rockies than simply adventure. The Americans had to "win the West" as much from the British and the Spanish as they did from the Indians—perhaps even more so—and the outcome of their economic rivalry was crucial in determining the fate of the region.

ONNEVILLE SPENT THE REST of 1832 uneventfully, but the next year he made what would be his most valuable contribution to national expansion: At that summer's rendezvous, he sent a large party led by veteran trapper Joseph Walker southwest to the Great Salt Lake and on to California. Walker's route followed what later became the California Trail. After reaching the Great Salt Lake, he proceeded west and then southwest, following the course of the curving Humboldt River to the marshy "sinks" just east of the Sierra Nevada. Crossing the Sierras via Mono Pass, he and his men became the first whites to view Yosemite. Finally, in late November, they reached Suisun Bay, an inlet of San Francisco Bay, and then the open coast of the Pacific. After spending about a month recuperating in the Mexican provincial capital of Monterey (California still belonged to Mexico in 1833), Walker began the return leg of his journey, this time finding an even better route that arched across the southern end of the Sierras. The low, easy pass he discovered at the end of the San Joaquin Valley, later named Walker Pass, became much used by California immigrants, especially gold seekers in 1849.

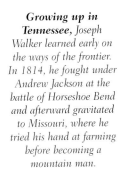

Growing up in Tennessee, Joseph Walker learned early on the ways of the frontier. In 1814, he fought under Andrew Jackson at the battle of Horseshoe Bend and afterward gravitated to Missouri, where he tried his hand at farming before becoming a mountain man.

Meanwhile, in the East, men such as Hall Jackson Kelley were mobilizing public opinion on behalf of westward expansion. In a series of public lectures in Boston, Kelley espoused with great fervor the American settlement of Oregon, which the United States still jointly occupied with

Great Britain. Among Kelley's followers was Nathaniel Wyeth, a Cambridge ice dealer who decided in 1831 that he would go to Oregon himself. With the help of his brother Jacob and his nephew John, Nat Wyeth revived John Jacob Astor's scheme of using ships sent to the Pacific Northwest to control the interior fur trade. Planning to meet his ship, the *Sultana,* at the mouth of the Columbia River, Wyeth and his company set sail from Boston Harbor on March 10, 1832, bound for Baltimore. From there, the party traveled due west over the Allegheny Mountains to the Ohio River and then on to St. Louis. Wyeth knew something of the geography of the West, having studied the map that accompanied the 1814 edition of Nicholas Biddle's *History of the Expedition of Captains Lewis and Clark,* but he was stunned to learn from Bill Sublette in St. Louis how much additional geographical knowledge the mountain men had gathered in recent years.

Joining Sublette's trapping party, Wyeth left Independence, Missouri, on May 3, 1832, reaching that summer's rendezvous at Pierre's Hole (in present-day Idaho) sometime in July. There, Jacob and John Wyeth rebelled against Nat's leadership and turned back. Nat Wyeth, however, continued with the bulk of his men west to the Snake River, whose tributaries they trapped until early fall. Then they headed northwest across the Blue Mountains to Fort Walla Walla on the Columbia River (in present-day Washington). Finally, they floated down

When he died in 1848, *eighty-five-year-old John Jacob Astor was the richest man in America. He made his fortune dominating the North American fur trade and then investing his profits in New York City real estate.*

A wagon train *pulls out of Independence, Missouri, in 1855. Independence was considered the starting point of the Oregon, California, and Santa Fe Trails.*

the Columbia to the British settlement at Fort Vancouver, where they spent the winter of 1832–1833. Nat Wyeth's party thus became the first group to complete the final leg of the Oregon Trail.

THE FOLLOWING SPRING, learning that the *Sultana* had been wrecked at sea, Wyeth made preparations for an overland return to the East. Along the way, near Pierre's Hole, he happened across one of Benjamin Bonneville's lieutenants and on July 2 joined Bonneville's main party. For the next two days, Wyeth and Bonneville made plans for Wyeth to lead a company of Bonneville's men to California. But for some unknown reason, Wyeth changed his mind on July 4 and resumed his journey back to Cambridge. Two weeks later, at the annual summer rendezvous, Bonneville chose Joseph Walker to lead the first important overland train to California, as Wyeth continued east to the Little Big Horn. However, while constructing a bullboat there to carry him to the Missouri, he met and contracted with Milton Sublette, acting on behalf of Thomas Fitzpatrick's Rocky Mountain Fur Company, to haul a load of trade goods to the 1834 rendezvous.

As a commercial venture, the second Wyeth expedition was also a failure. Rival traders under Bill Sublette beat Wyeth to the 1834 rendezvous, and Fitzpatrick, failing to honor his deal, did business with them instead. Yet Wyeth's trip was notable historically because of two missionaries who accompanied him to Oregon. The previous winter, listening to Wyeth recount his experiences in the Pacific Northwest, members of the American Missionary Board had become determined to convert the poor heathen Indians whom Wyeth had encountered. To pursue this work, they recruited Methodist minister Jason Lee, who joined Wyeth's 1834 expedition along with his nephew Daniel. When the Lees reached Oregon, though, they were repulsed by the Flathead Indians, whom they dismissed as "savages," and chose instead to homestead in the Willamette Valley just below Fort Vancouver. The farm and sawmill that they built became the first permanent American settlement in Oregon. So although Wyeth failed in his primary purpose—making money—he did succeed on a much grander scale: completing the Oregon Trail and opening up the Pacific Northwest to the imposing colonizing force of organized Protestant Christianity. By 1836, Pres. Andrew Jackson had become interested enough in Oregon to send a personal representative there to observe conditions with an eye toward strengthening the U.S. claim to the territory. The lengthy period of governmental neglect of the West was coming to an end.

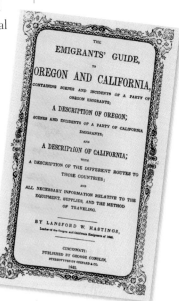

Lawyer Lansford Hastings wrote this 1845 guide to lure emigrants to California, which he hoped to transform from a Mexican province into an independent republic with himself as president. The book touted a new, shorter route over the Rockies of which he had no reliable knowledge.

JOHN C. FRÉMONT

1813 – 1890

The 1842 expedition was not John C. Frémont's first trip beyond the frontier. In 1838, he had assisted the French scientist Jean-Nicolas Nicollet in mapping the upper Mississippi and Missouri Rivers and in 1841 (the year he married Jessie Benton) he explored the Des Moines River for Nicollet, who had instructed Frémont well in astronomy, geology, and topography. Settling in California after the Mexican War, he became a multimillionaire during the gold rush and in 1850 was elected one of the state's first two U.S. senators. This ambrotype was taken by Mathew Brady in 1856, the year that Frémont became the presidential candidate of the new Republican party.

MOVE FORWARD AGAIN TO 1842. That year, Capt. John C. Frémont of the U.S. Army Corps of Topographical Engineers led the first of three mapping expeditions to the West that, along with Lewis and Clark's, remain the outstanding examples in American history of the use of exploration as a diplomatic weapon. In 1842—at the behest of his father-in-law, Missouri senator Thomas Hart Benton—Frémont left St. Louis headed for South Pass, following the South Platte (rather than the usual North Fork route) in order to explore the Front Range of the Rockies. Once across the Continental Divide, Frémont again diverged from the emigrant trail, heading for and climbing what he took to be the highest peak in the Wind River Mountains. It overlooked South Pass and allowed him to map the entire region from its heights. Upon reaching its summit, in a gesture that many took to be the authentic purpose of his mission, Frémont planted in the snow a homemade eagle flag symbolizing American sovereignty over the West.

Benton had wanted Frémont to dramatize the commercial possibilities of the West and spur overland migration, which the senator hoped would provoke his congressional colleagues into action regarding the status of Oregon. Frémont more than complied. With the help of his wife, the former Jessie Benton, whose prose style made the report read like the romance it really was, the captain prepared a document that did more than all the mountain men put together to fire the public's imagination and point the way west. Senator Benton made sure that Frémont's report was widely circulated, and it even became a best-seller. Readers were particularly fascinated by Frémont's unlikely tale (probably invented by Jessie) of a "weary little brown bee," far from its usual haunts, appearing on that Wind River peak just as Frémont planted his flag. In an age of extreme sentimental romanticism, this sort of anecdote had considerable appeal.

The next year, Frémont was determined to accomplish even more. He left St. Louis in the early spring of 1843 with a large contingent that included numerous experienced mountain men (among them Tom Fitzpatrick and Kit Carson), as well as an eccentric German cartographer named Charles Preuss, who hated the outdoors. Frémont had been instructed to conduct a detailed survey of the emigrant trail to South Pass and Oregon beyond. He was supposed to map the route carefully and take notes on the locations of campsites, wood, water, and Indians—but Frémont and his men did much more. After reaching Fort Vancouver and thus completing the assignment, Frémont traveled south up eastern Oregon's Deschutes River and southeast along the Sierras to

the Great Basin, which he was the first to recognize as an enormous depression with no outlet to the sea. When the Pathfinder (as Frémont came to be called) and his men reached the vicinity of Lake Tahoe, they turned west into the Sierras and made a grueling midwinter crossing during which even their local Indian guides began chanting death songs. They finally emerged from the mountains at Johann Sutter's fort on the Sacramento River.

After a stay in California, which Frémont found to be a pastoral paradise, the party set off down the San Joaquin Valley, following the route Joseph Walker had taken a decade earlier, although Frémont crossed the Sierras via Tehachapi Pass (which he mistakenly thought to be Walker Pass). Frémont's men then followed a trail previously taken by Jedediah Smith (during his 1826–1828 circumnavigation of the West) that led them east across the Mojave Desert, where Kit Carson and several others pursued and slew some hostile Indians. At the Las Vegas Meadows, they met Walker, who personally guided them home through the difficult territory of the Southern Rockies.

This is how Johann Sutter's fort on the Sacramento River appeared in 1847. Five years later, Sutter was bankrupt. The gold rush had robbed him of his ranch hands (they had left to become prospectors), most of his livestock had been stolen, and his land was overrun with squatters.

This daguerreotype of Thomas Hart Benton was taken by Mathew Brady sometime during the late 1840s, by which time he had been in the Senate for nearly three decades.

FURTHER READING

★ William H. Goetzmann, *Exploration and Empire: The Explorer and the Scientist in the Winning of the American West* (1966)

★ Robert M. Utley, *A Life Wild and Perilous: Mountain Men and the Paths to the Pacific* (1997)

Upon his return to St. Louis, after completing this incredibly arduous journey, Frémont was immediately confronted with another difficult task: producing not only a report of his travels but also a detailed map that could be used immediately by westbound emigrants. Preuss, of course, handled the bulk of the cartographic chores, creating the first great map of the West, while Jessie Frémont helped her husband craft the accompanying report. This one was even better than the first, becoming a classic of exploration literature and selling fifty thousand copies before the Civil War. Furthermore, Frémont's report made James K. Polk's aggressive trans-Mississippi policy seem even more desirable, and Frémont's opinion of California was equally important.

Because his was one of the first (and certainly one of the most read) books to point out the region's agricultural virtues, it became an important factor in persuading settlers to migrate there. This set the stage for the Bear Flag Revolt of 1846, during which American and some Mexican settlers—aided by Frémont, who happened to be in California at the time—rebelled successfully against Mexican rule. Also influenced by Frémont's work was Brigham Young, who was sufficiently persuaded by the Pathfinder's description of the "bucholic" Salt Lake Valley to lead his Mormon followers there in 1847.

For all the criticism that Frémont has since received from modern historians—for allowing himself, for example, to be called the Pathfinder, even though he was a latecomer to western exploration—the captain did circumnavigate the West and bear its extreme hardships well. He also accelerated the process that culminated in the United States acquiring its

At first, Senator Benton opposed the marriage of his seventeen-year-old daughter to John Frémont. But in the end, he bowed to her adamant will.

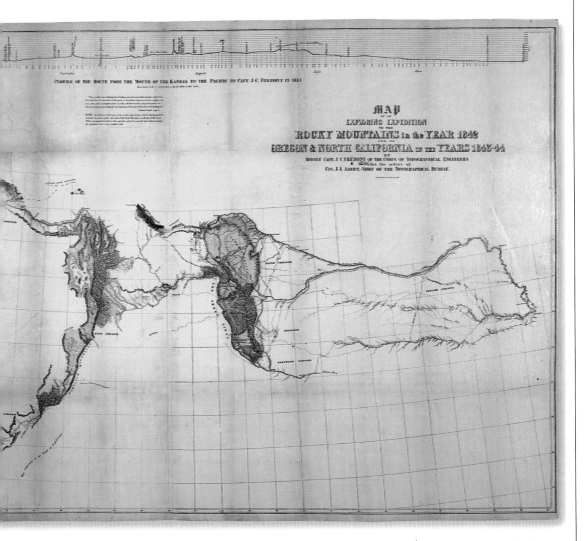

far western territories. By virtue of the 1848 Treaty of Guadalupe Hidalgo, which ended the Mexican War, the United States paid fifteen million dollars (or roughly two hundred million in today's currency) for ceded territory that included, most notably, California. That same year, James Marshall found gold near Sutter's Mill on land along the American River and its tributaries that Frémont himself had crossed just four years earlier. Marshall's discovery started a rush that attracted to California people from all over the world, including Asia and Australia. Thus the West began its cosmopolitan existence. No longer could it be seen as the Crow Indians and mountain men had seen it in 1824—as a vast, empty subcontinent. Henceforth, as historian Jim Holiday has put it, "the world rushed in."

★★★

After finishing the large map that accompanied Frémont's report (above), Charles Preuss used his own and Frémont's field notes to create an emigrant map in seven sections. Preuss's emigrant map was the first accurate chart of its kind, and it guided many novice travelers on their way west.

THE LIBERATOR.

VOL. I.] WILLIAM LLOYD GARRISON AND ISAAC KNAPP, PUBLISHERS. [NO. 1.

BOSTON, MASSACHUSETTS.] OUR COUNTRY IS THE WORLD—OUR COUNTRYMEN ARE MANKIND. [SATURDAY, JANUARY 1, 1831.

THE LIBERATOR
IS PUBLISHED WEEKLY
AT NO. 6, MERCHANTS' HALL.

WM. L. GARRISON, EDITOR.

Stephen Foster, Printer.

TERMS.

☞ Two Dollars per annum, payable in advance.

☞ Agents allowed every sixth copy gratis.

☞ No subscription will be received for a shorter period than six months.

☞ All letters and communications must be POST PAID.

THE LIBERATOR.

THE SALUTATION.

To date my being from the opening year,
I come, a stranger in this busy sphere,
Where some I meet perchance may pause and ask,
What is my name, my purpose, or my task?

My name is 'LIBERATOR'! I propose
To hurl my shafts at freedom's deadliest foes!
My task is hard—for I am charged to save
Man from his brother!—to redeem the slave!

Ye who may hear, and yet condemn my cause,
Say, shall the best of Nature's holy laws
Be trodden down? and shall her open veins
Flow but for cement to her offspring's chains?

Art thou a parent? shall thy children be
Rent from thy breast, like branches from the tree,
And doom'd to servitude, in helplessness,
On other shores, and thou ask no redress?

Thou, in whose bosom glows the sacred flame
Of filial love, say, if the tyrant came,
To force thy parent shrieking from thy sight,
Would thy heart bleed—*because thy face is white?*

Art thou a brother? shall thy sister twine
Her feeble arm in agony on thine,
And thou not lift the heel, nor aim the blow
At him who bears her off to life-long wo?

Art thou a sister? will no desp'rate cry
Awake thy sleeping brother, while thine eye
Beholds the fetters locking on the limb
Stretched out in rest, which hence, must end, for him?

Art thou a lover?---no! naught e'er was found
In lover's breast, save cords of love, that bound
Man to his kind! then, thy professions save!
Forswear affection, or release thy slave!

Thou who art kneeling at thy Maker's shrine,
Ask if Heaven takes such offerings as thine!
If in thy bonds the son of Afric sighs,
Far higher than thy prayer his groan will rise!

God is a God of mercy, and would see
The prison-doors unbarr'd---the bondmen free!
He is a God of truth, with purer eyes
Than to behold the oppressor's sacrifice!

Avarice, thy cry and thine insatiate thirst
Make man consent to see his brother cursed!
Tears, sweat and blood thou drink'st, but in their turn,
They shall cry 'more!' while vengeance bids thee burn.

The Lord hath said it!---who shall him gainsay?
He says, 'the wicked, they shall go away'—
Who are the wicked?——Contradict who can,
They are the oppressors of their fellow man!

Aid me, NEW ENGLAND! 'tis my hope in you
Which gives me strength my purpose to pursue!
Do you not hear your sister States resound
With Afric's cries to have her sons unbound?

* * *

TO THE PUBLIC.

In the month of August, I issued proposals for publishing 'THE LIBERATOR' in Washington city; but the enterprise, though hailed in different sections of the country, was palsied by public indifference. Since that time, the removal of the Genius of Universal Emancipation to the Seat of Government has rendered less imperious the establishment of a similar periodical in that quarter.

During my recent tour for the purpose of exciting the minds of the people by a series of discourses on the subject of slavery, every place that I visited gave fresh evidence of the fact, that a greater revolution in public sentiment was to be effected in the free states—*and particularly in New-England*—than at the south. I found contempt more bitter, opposition more active, detraction more relentless, prejudice more stubborn, and apathy more frozen, than among slave owners themselves. Of course, there were individual exceptions to the contrary. This state of things afflicted, but did not dishearten me. I determined, at every hazard, to lift up the standard of emancipation in the eyes of the nation, *within sight of Bunker Hill and in the birth place of liberty.* That standard is now unfurled; and long may it float, unhurt by the spoliations of time or the missiles of a desperate foe—yea, till every chain be broken, and every bondman set free! Let southern oppressors tremble—let their secret abettors tremble—let their northern apologists tremble—let all the enemies of the persecuted blacks tremble.

I deem the publication of my original Prospectus* unnecessary, as it has obtained a wide circulation. The principles therein inculcated will be steadily pursued in this paper, excepting that I shall not array myself as the political partisan of any man. In defending the great cause of human rights, I wish to derive the assistance of all religions and of all parties.

Assenting to the 'self-evident truth' maintained in the American Declaration of Independence, 'that all men are created equal, and endowed by their Creator with certain inalienable rights—among which are life, liberty and the pursuit of happiness,' I shall strenuously contend for the immediate enfranchisement of our slave population. In Park-street Church, on the Fourth of July, 1829, in an address on slavery, I unreflectingly assented to the popular but pernicious doctrine of *gradual* abolition. I seize this opportunity to make a full and unequivocal recantation, and thus publicly to ask pardon of my God, of my country, and of my brethren the poor slaves, for having uttered a sentiment so full of timidity, injustice and absurdity. A similar recantation, from my pen, was published in the Genius of Universal Emancipation at Baltimore, in September, 1829. My conscience is now satisfied.

I am aware, that many object to the severity of my language; but is there not cause for severity? I *will be* as harsh as truth, and as uncompromising as justice. On this subject, I do not wish to think, or speak, or write, with moderation. No! no! Tell a man whose house is on fire, to give a moderate alarm; tell him to moderately rescue his wife from the hands of the ravisher; tell the mother to gradually extricate her babe from the fire into which it has fallen;—but urge me not to use moderation in a cause like the present. I am in earnest—I will not equivocate—I will not excuse—I will not retreat a single inch—AND I WILL BE HEARD. The apathy of the people is enough to make every statue leap from its pedestal, and to hasten the resurrection of the dead.

It is pretended, that I am retarding the cause of emancipation by the coarseness of my invective, and the precipitancy of my measures. *The charge is not true.* On this question my influence,---humble as it is,---is felt at this moment to a considerable extent, and shall be felt in coming years---not perniciously, but beneficially—not as a curse, but as a blessing; and posterity will bear testimony that I was right. I desire to thank God, that he enables me to disregard 'the fear of man which bringeth a snare,' and to speak his truth in its simplicity and power. And here I close with this fresh dedication:

'Oppression! I have seen thee, face to face,
And met thy cruel eye and cloudy brow;
But thy soul-withering glance I fear not now—
For dread to prouder feelings doth give place
Of deep abhorrence! Scorning the disgrace
Of slavish knees that at thy footstool bow,
I also kneel—but with far other vow
Do hail thee and thy herd of hirelings base:—
I swear, while life-blood warms my throbbing veins,
Still to oppose and thwart, with heart and hand,
Thy brutalising sway—till Afric's chains
Are burst, and Freedom rules the rescued land,—
Trampling Oppression and his iron rod:
Such is the vow I take—SO HELP ME GOD!'

WILLIAM LLOYD GARRISON.

BOSTON, January 1, 1831.

*I would here offer my grateful acknowledgments to those editors who so promptly and generously inserted my Proposals. They must give me an available opportunity to repay their liberality.

DISTRICT OF COLUMBIA.

What do many of the professed enemies of slavery mean, by heaping all their reproaches upon the south, and asserting that the crime of oppression is not national? What power but Congress—and Congress by the authority of the American people—has jurisdiction over the District of Columbia? That District is rotten with the plague, and stinks in the nostrils of the world. Though it is the Seat of our National Government,—open to the daily inspection of foreign ambassadors,—and ostensibly opulent with the congregated wisdom, virtue and intelligence of the land,—yet a fouler spot scarcely exists on earth. In it the worst features of slavery are exhibited; and as a mart for slave traders, it is unequalled. These facts are well known to our two or three hundred representatives, but no remedy is proposed; they are known, if not minutely at least generally, to our whole population,—but who calls for redress?

Hitherto, a few straggling petitions, relative to this subject, have gone into Congress; but they have been too few to denote much public anxiety, or to command a deferential notice. It is certainly time that a vigorous and systematic effort should be made, from one end of the country to the other, to pull down that national monument of oppression which towers up in the District. We do hope that the 'earthquake voice' of the people will this session shake the black fabric to its foundation.

The following petition is now circulating in this city, and has obtained several valuable signatures. A copy may be found at the Bookstore of LINCOLN & EDMANDS, No. 59, Washington-street, for a few days longer, where all the friends of the cause are earnestly invited to go and subscribe.

Petition to Congress for the Abolition of Slavery in the District of Columbia.

To the Honorable Senate and House of Representatives of the United States of America in Congress assembled, the petition of the undersigned citizens of Boston in Massachusetts and its vicinity respectfully represents—

That your petitioners are deeply impressed with the evils arising from the existence of slavery in the District of Columbia. While our Declaration of Independence boldly proclaims as self-evident truths, 'that all men are created equal, that they are endowed by their Creator with certain inalienable rights, that among these are life, liberty, and the pursuit of happiness,'—at the very seat of government human beings are born, almost daily, whom the laws pronounce to be from their birth, not *equal* to other men, and who are, for life, deprived of *liberty* and the free *pursuit of happiness.* The inconsistency of the conduct of our nation with its political creed, has brought down upon it the just and severe reprehension of foreign nations.

In addition to the other evils flowing from slavery, both moral and political, which it is needless to specify, circumstances have rendered this District a common resort for traders in human flesh, who bring into it their captives in chains, and lodge them in places of confinement, previously to their being carried to the markets of the south and west.

From the small number of slaves in the District of Columbia, and the moderate proportion which they bear to the free population there, the difficulties, which in most of the slaveholding states oppose the restoration of this degraded class of men to their natural rights, do not exist.

Your petitioners therefore pray that Congress will, without delay, take such measures for the immediate or gradual abolition of Slavery in the District of Columbia, and for preventing the bringing of slaves into that District for purposes of traffic, in such mode, as may be thought advisable; and that suitable provision be made for the education of all free blacks and colored children in the District, thus to preserve them from continuing, even as free men, an unenlightened and degraded caste.

If any individual should be unmoved, either by the petition or the introductory remarks, the following article will startle his apathy, unless he be morally dead—dead—dead. Read it—read it! The language of the editor is remarkable for its energy, considering the quarter whence it emanates. After all, we are not the only fanatics in the land!

[From the Washington Spectator, of Dec. 4.]

THE SLAVE TRADE IN THE CAPITAL.

'The tender ties of father, husband, friend,
All bonds of nature in that moment end,
And each endures, while yet he draws his breath,
A stroke as fatal as the scythe of death;
They lose in tears, the far receding shore,
But not the thought that they must meet no more!'

It is well, perhaps, the American people should know, that while we reiterate our boasts of liberty in the ears of the nations, and send back across the Atlantic our shouts of joy at the triumph of liberty in France, we ourselves are busily engaged in the work of oppression. Yes, let it be known to the citizens of America, that at the very time when the procession which contained the President of the United States and his Cabinet was marching in triumph to the Capitol, to celebrate the victory of the French people over their oppressors, another kind of procession was marching another way, and that consisted of colored human beings, handcuffed in pairs, and driven along by what had the appearance of a man on a horse! A similar scene was repeated on Saturday last; a *drove* consisting of males and females chained in couples, starting from Roby's tavern on foot, for Alexandria, where, with others, they are to embark on board a slave-ship in waiting to convey them to the South. While we are writing, a colored man enters our room, and begs us to inform him if we can point out any person who will redeem his friend now immured in Alexandria jail, in a state of distress amounting almost to distraction.* He has been a faithful servant of a revolutionary officer who recently died—has been sold at auction—parted from affectionate parents—and from decent and mourning friends. Our own servant, with others, of whom we can speak in commendatory terms, went down to Alexandria to bid him farewell, but they were refused admission to his cell, as was said, 'the sight of his friends made him feel so.' He bears the reputation of a pious man. It is but a few weeks since we saw a ship with her cargo of slaves in the port of Norfolk, Va.; on passing up the river, saw another ship off Alexandria, swarming with the victims of human cupidity. Such are the scenes enacting in the heart of the American nation. Oh patriotism! where is thy indignation? Oh philanthropy! where is thy grief? OH SHAME, WHERE IS THY BLUSH? Well may the generous and noble minded O'Connell say of the American citizen, '*I tell him he is a hypocrite. Look at the stain in your star-spangled standard that was never struck down in battle. I turn from the Declaration of American Independence, and I tell him that he has declared to God and man a lie, and before God and man I arraign him as a hypocrite.*' Yes, thou soul of fire, glorious O'Connell, if thou could but witness the spectacles in Washington that make the genius of liberty droop her head in shame, and weep her tears away in deep silence and undissembled sorrow, you would lift your voice even to tones of thunder, but you would make yourself heard. Where is the O'Connell of this republic that will plead for the EMANCIPATION OF THE DISTRICT OF COLUMBIA? These shocking scenes must cease from amongst us, or we must cease to call ourselves free; ay, and we must cease to expect the mercy of God—we must prepare for the coming judgment of Him who, as our charter acknowledges, made all men '*free and equal!*'

* At the same time this man was sold, another—a husband—was knocked off. The tears and agonies of his wife made such an impression on the mind of a generous spectator that he bought him back.

When a premium of Fifty Dollars is offered for the best theatrical poem, our newspapers advertise the fact with great unanimity. The following is incomparably more important.

PREMIUM.

A Premium of Fifty Dollars, the Donation of a benevolent individual in the State of Maine, and now deposited with the Treasurer of the Pennsylvania Society for promoting the Abolition of Slavery, &c. is offered to the author of the best Treatise on the following subject: 'The Duties of Ministers and Churches of all denominations to avoid the stain of Slavery, and to make the holding of Slaves a barrier to communion and church membership.'

The composition to be directed (post paid) to either of the subscribers—the name of the author in a separate sealed paper, which will be destroyed if his work shall be rejected.

Six months from this date are allowed for the purpose of receiving the Essays.

The publication and circulation of the preferred Tract will be regulated by the Pennsylvania Society above mentioned.

W. RAWLE,
J. PRESTON, } Committee.
THOMAS SHIPLEY,

Philadelphia, Oct. 11.

JANUARY 1, 1831

THE LIBERATOR

BY IRA BERLIN

S AVE FOR THE ANNUAL turning of the calendar, January 1, 1831, seemed little different than any other wintry day in Boston. There seemed nothing remarkable, for instance, about the slight balding young man who walked briskly past the Bunker Hill monument, Faneuil Hall, and other remembrances of America's revolutionary past. Nor did anyone notice that his pace quickened as he turned into Merchants' Hall, or that he mounted the stairs to a nondescript print shop with a mixture of determination and expectation. For more than a week, William Lloyd Garrison—along with his partner, Isaac Knapp, and several of their friends—had been setting type for a new journal that they all hoped would strike a blow at slavery, an evil that degraded millions of Americans and corrupted tens of millions more. For Garrison and his friends, chattel bondage denied the slaves' humanity and contradicted the

AT LEFT: *The first page of the first issue of* The Liberator.

ABOVE: *Shackles of the sort that were used in transporting slaves from Africa.*

principles of the Declaration of Independence as well as the precepts of Jesus Christ. *The Liberator,* they believed, would elevate the slaves and thus restore the nation's highest ideals.

Driven by the belief that all people were created equal and all created in God's image, Garrison worked on through the day, polishing his inaugural editorial. As he put the finishing touches on the first issue of *The Liberator,* Garrison reflected on the enormous task before him. Perhaps to steel himself as well as to assure readers of the depth of his commitment, he concluded the editorial with a ringing affirmation: "I am in earnest—I will not equivocate—I will not excuse—I will not retreat a single inch—AND I *WILL BE* HEARD."

When the issue was at last ready to go to press, Garrison emblazoned the masthead with the words, "OUR COUNTRY IS THE WORLD—OUR COUNTRYMEN MANKIND," capturing the universalism that would characterize his life's work. Now he needed only the cash for paper, ink, and a few other necessary

WILLIAM LLOYD GARRISON

1805 – 1879

Unlike his modest, self-effacing mentor Benjamin Lundy, William Lloyd Garrison wanted to make an issue of himself. "There shall be no neutrals," he once declared; "men shall either like or dislike me." As his biographer Henry Mayer has pointed out, Garrison conceived of himself as a lightning rod that would attract the energy necessary to galvanize his cause. In this regard, he treated his newspaper, The Liberator, as merely an extension of his personality. Garrison's intense, almost manic, prose style gave his editorials the appearance of eruptive spontaneity, yet they were, in fact, quite calculated. It was, according to Mayer, "a deliberate decision, not an irresistible impulse, that led him to write as he did."

supplies. Fortunately, the arrival of an advance payment for some twenty-five subscriptions—courtesy of his friend James Forten, a black Philadelphia sail maker—made it possible for Garrison to proceed.

PUBLICATION OF A RADICAL abolitionist journal was a strange mission for the young man born in December 1805 in the small seaside town of Newburyport, Massachusetts. During the 1780s, through a series of judicial decisions, slavery had been abolished in Massachusetts. So, as a boy, Garrison could have had no direct knowledge of slavery. Nor could he have known many people of African descent, for scarcely a few dozen resided in his hometown. In addition, the tone of the first issue of The Liberator seemed out of character with the twenty-five-year-old who wrote it, for there was nothing in Garrison's physical appearance or demeanor to suggest the steadfast resolve that would lead him to press his beliefs to their logical conclusion.

The tensile strength that Garrison brought to The Liberator had been annealed in most unpromising beginnings. In the early nineteenth century, Adijah and Frances Garrison had migrated to Newburyport from the Maritime Provinces of Canada, seeking economic opportunity and a congenial community for their evangelical beliefs. They found little of the

"THE DANGER OF A CONFLICT BETWEEN THE WHITE AND THE BLACK INHABITANTS PERPETUALLY HAUNTS THE IMAGINATION OF THE AMERICANS LIKE A BAD DREAM."

—*Alexis de Tocqueville,* Democracy in America, *1835—*

former but much of the latter, for Newburyport had been deeply touched by the Great Awakening and its aftermath. Sadly, though, the expansion of Boston had leached the town of its prosperity, making it increasingly difficult for Adijah Garrison to support his growing family. The maritime depression that accompanied the War of 1812 left him unemployed, impoverished, and depressed. He turned to drink and eventually deserted his family, leaving his wife and four young children destitute. Frances Garrison, fortified by her evangelical faith, labored mightily to sustain her children. But, in time, she was forced to place them with kindly neighbors and fellow congregants. Her youngest son, William, was apprenticed to the publisher of the *Newburyport Herald.*

Young William Lloyd Garrison loved the craft of printing as well as the world of words and ideas that sprang from the presses. He read voraciously, which compensated for his lack of formal education, and occasionally tried his hand at poetry and some fiction. But the *Herald* was a Federalist sheet that emphasized politics, and it was from the *Herald* that Garrison took his first political ideas, combining them with an exuberant idealism that had its roots in the radicalism of the American Revolution. (His first public utterance—delivered on July 4, 1824, at a meeting of the local debating society—celebrated the global expansion of American revolutionary principles as "freedom's awakening triumphant call.") Garrison's views were also shaped by his mother's evangelical moralism and his own stiff-necked sense of rectitude. Principle, not expedience, would be his guide, and the identification and eradication of sin his quest.

Garrison was born in a house on School Street in Newburyport. His next-door neighbor was Newburyport's Presbyterian church. This photograph shows the house as it appeared during the 1890s.

This heady mixture manifested itself when, upon completing his apprenticeship in 1825, the nineteen-year-old Garrison took up the editorship of his own newspaper in Newburyport. Before long, he was denouncing Thomas Jefferson as "the great Lama of Infidelity" (for Jefferson's flirtation with deism) and proclaiming his own continuing attachment to the Federalist party, even though it had lost its electoral franchise nearly a decade earlier. In championing the candidacies of the few remaining Federalists, Garrison demonstrated his resolute commitment to loyalty no matter the cost, but as his candidates failed, so did his editorship. In 1828, with the collapse of his journalistic career in Newburyport, Garrison left for new opportunities in Boston.

WHILE GARRISON'S unfashionable attachment to Federalism won him few new friends, his moralism gained him entry into Boston's expanding universe of benevolent reform. On the rise in Boston were Christian missionaries, temperance advocates, pacifists, vegetarians, and proponents of all manner of human betterment from feminism to socialism. As yet another foot soldier in the evangelical war against sin, Garrison quickly secured the editorship of a temperance journal and, when that publication also failed, attached

This is what a print shop in Massachusetts would have looked like during the 1820s.

himself to a kindly Quaker named Benjamin Lundy, the peripatetic publisher of an irregular antislavery sheet grandly entitled *The Genius of Universal Emancipation.*

For years, Lundy had traveled the slave states making the case for abolition. Carrying (almost literally) his press on his back, he lived from hand to mouth as he published his journal. For the most part, he labored in near-total anonymity, unnoticed except by like-minded members of the Society of Friends and appreciative people of color. Accepting Garrison as a junior partner marked a sharp break for Lundy, who was very much a loner. In fact, the association did not last long, but it was fateful, because in Lundy's cause Garrison found his life's work and in Lundy's methods he found his own metier. Garrison's egalitarianism and moralism gained a new, clearer direction as he came to appreciate through Lundy the evil that was chattel bondage.

There is a small controversy about Garrison's birth date. Like many nineteenth-century Americans, he didn't know the exact day, or even year, of his birth. Eventually, he came to accept December 12, 1805. This engraving shows him in 1825, when he would have been about twenty years old.

O PPOSITION TO SLAVERY WAS itself relatively new in the United States, as it was everywhere in the world. Until the end of the eighteenth century, slavery had few principled enemies. From antiquity onward, nearly every society practiced slavery, and every authority—religious and secular—sanctioned it, often with elaborate codes affirming the legitimacy of the slave master's rule. In a world where hierarchy was ubiquitous and inequality the norm, slavery had long been considered at one with God and nature, and few voices were raised against slave ownership.

The American and French revolutions changed that. The doctrine that "all men are created equal," asserted first in the American Declaration of Independence and then reiterated in the French Declaration of the Rights of Man, initiated a transformation of slavery from a universally accepted convention for extracting labor and assuring obedience into a hideous relic of the past. Henceforth, it was not equality that would be the anomaly but slavery. In the new United States, leading revolutionaries—Jefferson, Washington, and Franklin, to name just the most prominent—condemned slavery. Some, like Jefferson, bemoaned it while continuing to exercise the practice; others, like Washington, freed their slaves; still others, like Franklin, formed manumission societies and urged slavery's total liquidation.

Yet slavery survived and flourished, even as its legitimacy was called into question. At the end of the Revolution, it could still be found

This ad offering cash for slaves was posted in Charleston, South Carolina, in May 1835.

in every part of the new United States, deeply rooted at the base of the American economy and tightly woven into the fabric of society. Even in the northern states, opposition to slavery remained a novelty, and abolitionists moved with caution. Although slavery fell quickly in northern New England, where slaves were numerically few and their labor economically marginal, emancipation proved more difficult in southern New England and the middle-Atlantic states. The 1780 Pennsylvania Emancipation Act freed not a single slave on emancipation day—March 1 of that year—and proposed to eliminate slavery only by freeing the children of slaves born thereafter once they reached the age of twenty-eight. Moreover, at the time of the enactment of the Pennsylvania statute, the legal liquidation of slavery had not yet begun at all in Connecticut, Rhode Island, New Jersey, or the largest northern slave state, New York.

This issue of Lundy's journal was published in July 1830.

As in Pennsylvania, emancipationists in these states dared not challenge slavery directly; instead, they settled for the gradual, piecemeal emancipation of slaves, while assuring grumbling slaveholders of fair compensation for their lost property. Gradualism therefore guaranteed that the death of slavery in the North would take not years, or even decades, but generations to accomplish. More important, it signaled the impossibility of abolition in the South, where slaves were more numerous and believed to be an essential element of the plantation economy. Indeed, even as the work of abolition commenced, the number of slaves in the United States grew, increasing from about half a million at the beginning of the American Revolution to well over one million by 1810.

T HE FEEBLE NATURE of the assault on slavery had much to do with the fact that slavery had become identified with people of African descent. Whatever white Americans thought of slavery in principle, they had no desire to live with black people who were free. As many white Americans explained it, circumstance—the very experience of enslavement—had degraded black people, making them unfit for full participation in the new republic. And some whites simply believed that black people ranked below them on the scale of civilization.

BENJAMIN LUNDY

1789 – 1839

Benjamin Lundy was by trade a saddler. He lived in Ohio, but his business dealings regularly took him across the Ohio River to Wheeling, Virginia, where he became familiar with the institution of slavery and the conduct of slave trading. In 1815, he organized the Union Human Society, one of the first groups to discuss openly possible ways to end the practice of slavery. In January 1821, he began publishing The Genius of Universal Emancipation. *Much of his time thereafter was spent traveling around in search of suitable places for freed slaves to settle— including Canada, Mexico, and Haiti.*

This woodcut *of a supplicating male slave was created in 1837 to illustrate John Greenleaf Whittier's antislavery poem "Our Countrymen in Chains."*

White slaveholders, who had a deep material interest in chattel bondage, made much of this perceived inferiority of black people as well as the feared destabilizing effects of emancipation. They promoted the ideas that free blacks would not work, that they would demand political rights and seize power, and that they would intermarry with whites and destroy white posterity. Perhaps even more telling is that many of the white opponents of slavery shared these sentiments. The very laws that liberated northern slaves often carried with them proscriptions regarding the liberty of former slaves, denying them the rights to vote, to sit on a jury, to testify in court, to carry a gun, and to travel freely. And where legislative enactments dared not tread, informal practice (newly established, but anointed with the force of custom) served the same function. By general consensus, white employers barred free blacks from trades they once practiced openly as slaves, and white citizens denied them entry into public places, excluding them from churches, schools, and militia musters. Some communities "warned out" free people of color, and when they would not leave voluntarily, they were often ridiculed and assaulted, physically as well as verbally. The desire to rid the nation of black people—particularly free blacks—spurred a movement to deport or "colonize" them, with Africa being the logical destination.

The obstacles faced by free blacks in the young republic led some opponents of slavery, styling themselves realists, to conclude that abolition was possible only upon removal—or, in their words, "pending repatriation." The realists denied any racial animus toward people of African descent. Indeed, they maintained that once repatriated, black people could enjoy without prejudice the rights promised by the Declaration of Independence. African Americans transported to Africa would not only regain their birthright, it was believed; they would also become agents of the expansion of American republicanism, Christianity, and commercial capitalism. With the founding of the American Colonization Society in 1817 and the establishment of the colony of Liberia soon thereafter, "Negro removal" became the central feature of American antislavery activity.

Yet colonization had other faces. Some advocates simply wanted to rid the United States of all its black people. Many of these were white supremacists who despised people of color. Other colonizationists were slaveholders who wanted to deport free blacks and thereby strengthen the institution of slavery. These people believed that eliminating free blacks would allow slaves to be content with their lot, making them better workers and more obedient servants. By depriving slaves of a model of black freedom, the threat of servile insurrection would also likely wither—assuring white slaveholders of economic prosperity, political stability, and an undiluted posterity.

For their part, black people had no doubt about the meaning of colonization. To them, colonization was little more than a plot to perpetuate chattel bondage and bolster white supremacy. Asserting their claims to American nationality, many denounced the logic of repatriation. "This is our home, and this is our country," proclaimed a coalition of black Philadelphians led by James Forten and Bishop Richard Allen of the African Methodist Episcopal Church. "Beneath its sod lie the bones of our fathers; for it some of them fought, bled, and died. Here we were born, and here we will die."

L IKE MANY OTHER OPPONENTS of slavery, Benjamin Lundy was wedded to the colonizationist cause as the only practical means of securing the slaves' freedom. But Garrison had no such attachment, and as he accompanied Lundy around the nation, the pair of them proselytizing against slavery, Garrison discovered that the alleged beneficiaries of colonization wanted nothing to do with the scheme. He listened ever more attentively as men like Forten and Allen denounced colonization as a slaveholders' trick, and he found himself swept up by the power of their logic: If black people could be free and equal in Africa, why not in America? In this way, the African-American critique of colonization (and black people's demand for equality) became central to Garrison's understanding of slavery and race. He carried these ideas with him when he returned to Boston and made them his own. Thereafter, black people became his strongest supporters and most loyal allies.

The inaugural issue of *The Liberator* borrowed much from the protests of black leaders. Apologizing for his previous support of the

RICHARD ALLEN

1760 – 1831

Richard Allen was born into slavery in Philadelphia. Soon after his birth, though, his family was sold to a farmer in Delaware, where he spent his youth and served as a wagon driver in the American Revolution. When he was seventeen, Allen became a Methodist convert. When he was twenty-six, he bought his freedom and returned to Philadelphia, where he preached occasionally at St. George's Methodist Episcopal Church. He also held prayer meetings at St. George's attended by African-Americans. When white church officials placed restrictions on these meetings, a dissatisfied Allen decided to organize his own Methodist church. In 1787, he turned an old blacksmith shop into the first church for blacks in the United States.

"pernicious doctrine of *gradual* abolition"—a belief he now admitted to be "full of timidity, injustice, and absurdity"—Garrison demanded an immediate end to slavery and the resurrection of the principles asserted in the Declaration of Independence. In condemning slavery as a sin, he unsheathed the weapons that would become the signatures of his egalitarian campaign. There would be no groveling for political favor, with the implicit willingness to compromise—for the immoral nature of slavery would not allow for compromise. There would be no call for slaves to rise up and throw off their chains, with the explicit threat of bloodshed—for violence would beget only more violence. Instead, there would be relentless reassertion of the principle of human equality and persistent denunciation of the evil of slaveholding. White and black could not be distinguished in the eyes of God; therefore, they should not be distinguished in the eyes of the law. Is it possible that "all men are born equal, and entitled to equal protection, excepting those whose skins are black and hair wooly?" *The Liberator* editorialized. Garrison then concluded his opening editorial with this stern warning:

> *I will be as harsh as truth, and as uncompromising as justice.
> On this subject, I do not wish to think, or speak, or write,
> with moderation. No! No! Tell a man whose house is on fire to
> give a moderate alarm; tell him to moderately rescue his wife
> from the hands of the ravisher; tell the mother to gradually
> extricate her babe from the fire into which it has fallen;—but
> urge me not to use moderation in a cause like the present.*

The first issue of *The Liberator* sparked a small fire that grew, as more issues were published, into a blaze extinguished only by civil war. In the process, Garrison forced a nation to confront, for the first time, its most pressing moral dilemma—race—and inspired a tradition of social commitment and moral agitation that became a model for others from Frederick Douglass to Martin Luther King Jr. He also personified the difference between conventional partisan politics (which seeks, through the process of compromise, to identify a mutually acceptable middle ground) and movement politics (which stakes out a principled position on the periphery and then attempts to draw conventional politicians to its cause). Lastly, Garrison elevated the work of social reform into a profession, which men and women from Susan B. Anthony to Ralph Nader would find worthy as an occupation. On that New Year's Day in 1831, though, Garrison's work was just beginning.

*This subscription
notice appeared
on the back of an
1831 pamphlet
containing one of
Garrison's antislavery
stump speeches.*

WHEN COMPARED TO the stirring editorial, the rest of *The Liberator's* first issue seems relatively tame. There were poems, short stories, meditations, and pleas for subscribers. Garrison published the text of a petition against slavery in the nation's capital, then being circulated in Boston, and urged readers to sign it. He also reprinted an article on the District of Columbia slave trade (taken from a Washington newspaper) that, like the petition, emphasized how slavery in the seat of their national government made hypocrites of all Americans. "That District," Garrison sneered, "is rotten with the plague, and stinks in the nostrils of the world." Elsewhere, he announced a fifty-dollar prize for the best essay on "The Duties of Ministers and Churches of all denominations to avoid the stain of Slavery." Garrison informed his readers of the arrival in North Carolina of *Appeal to the Colored Citizens of the World,* a pamphlet written by black revolutionary David Walker urging black people to rise up against slavery and racial subordination, and he took note of several other matters of local and national import. But the miscellany that filled the back pages of *The Liberator* hardly disguised its single-minded preoccupation.

The appearance of The Liberator challenged not only the institution of slavery in the South but also the antislavery movement in the North and the structure of racial inequality upon which both rested. In doing so, it naturally aroused opposition of the sort one might expect from such a

THE FINANCING OF *THE LIBERATOR*

Although subscription revenues underwrote some of the costs of publication, The Liberator *was largely dependent upon the largess of sympathetic donors. In 1839, William Lloyd Garrison formalized the arrangement, establishing a committee, made up of staunch but reputable abolitionists, to manage and improve the paper's finances. A "very much relieved" Garrison was thereafter able to concentrate solely on his editorial duties.*

This scene, *painted in 1852, shows a typical slave market of the time. Congress had acted in 1807 to ban the importation of slaves (beginning January 1, 1808), but it left alone the domestic slave trade, which flourished.*

In July 1835, a mob in Charleston, South Carolina, raided the post office there. Mail sacks were taken out through a forced window and torn open in the street. The crowd burned all the abolitionist mail it found, including copies of The Liberator.

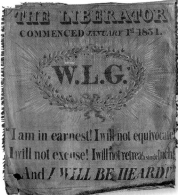

Banners such as this one often decorated the walls at antislavery meetings.

radical assault on the foundations of American society and the conventions of master over slave, white over black. The same year that The Liberator appeared, the District of Columbia tried to prevent its circulation by prohibiting free blacks from removing copies from the post office. Meanwhile in Raleigh, North Carolina, a grand jury indicted Garrison for distributing incendiary literature, and the Georgia legislature offered a five-thousand-dollar bounty for anyone arresting Garrison and bringing him to the state to face charges of libel. Other threats emerged closer to home as Garrison was pelted with eggs and epithets; condemned as a fanatic, lunatic, and worse; and, according to one account, targeted for assassination. In October 1835, an antiabolitionist mob shouting "Hang him on the Commons" nearly lynched Garrison on the streets of Boston.

But Garrison did not frighten easily. Unmoved by the torrent of abuse, he gathered around him a small group of disciples attracted by the depth of his egalitarian commitment and his unshakable willingness to defend his principles against all comers. For the most part, his followers were young men and women—among them Lydia Marie Child, Abbey Kelly, Samuel May, and Henry C. Wright—who took seriously the promise of the American republic. Like Garrison, they were appalled by the nation's failure to practice the ideals it celebrated and by the rank injustice they believed was rooted in a government whose founding charter delayed the close of the slave trade for two decades, required the return of fugitive slaves, and assigned slaves the status of only three-fifths of a man. Using The Liberator as their platform, they denounced the republic, its founders, and its icons. Declaring the Constitution "a covenant with death and agreement with hell," they publicly burned copies to demonstrate their contempt for the government that most Americans believed represented the apotheosis of liberty.

BEYOND THIS SMALL COTERIE, at least at first, the Garrisonian assault on slavery won few converts. But the issuance of *The Liberator* broke the silence on slavery—for if Lundy's opposition to chattel bondage was barely audible, Garrison's broadcasts could not be escaped. *The Liberator* also removed colonization as a legitimate avenue of antislavery activity, eventually replacing it with the principle of immediate emancipation. Already by 1833, when the Garrisonians established the American Anti-Slavery Society, their leader had become the central figure in the war against chattel bondage and *The Liberator* the unparalleled voice of the antislavery movement.

This *mezzotint* *by John Sartain, taken from a portrait by Manessah C. Torrey, shows Garrison at thirty, four years after the founding of* The Liberator.

I N THE YEARS THAT FOLLOWED, Garrison's influence extended beyond the radicals he had initially attracted into the moderate reform community at large. These newcomers to the antislavery cause included many who did not share Garrison's animosity toward both the American republic and conventional political partisanship. Rather than repudiate the Constitution, they embraced it and worked within its system to build political parties that might overturn slavery through electoral means. Noting that the Constitution never actually used the word *slave,* they aimed to restore what they claimed to be the Founding Fathers' antislavery intent. By 1840, political abolitionists such as Joshua Giddings of Ohio and William Slade of Vermont had used antislavery platforms to secure seats in Congress, and that same year James G. Birney ran for president as the candidate of the Liberty party, the first political party dedicated to the eradication of slavery.

Although Garrison distanced himself from politicians who wanted to ride the antislavery issue to power and blistered political abolitionists for their willingness to dance with the devil, he did nothing to discourage their assault on slavery. On occasion, he even raised a glass of ice water to toast their successes, making it clear for whom he would have voted (if he had considered it ethical to vote under the present system, which he did not). Likewise, antislavery politicians tended to keep their distance from Garrison and his followers; yet none would deny the strength they all drew from the assault on slavery he had unleashed on January 1, 1831. In late 1864, soon after his reelection, Abraham Lincoln invited Garrison to the White House. Later, the president was heard to remark that he considered himself "only an instrument" in the struggle for emancipation, adding, "The logic and moral power of Garrison and the antislavery people of the country and the army, have done it all." The Liberator had been heard.

★ ★ ★

FURTHER READING:

★ Ira Berlin, *Many Thousands Gone: The First Two Centuries of Slavery in North America* (1998)

★ Henry Mayer, *All on Fire: William Lloyd Garrison and the Abolition of Slavery* (1998)

Elizabeth Cady Stanton and her daughter, Harriot. from a daguerreotype 1856

JUNE 20, 1848

THE SENECA FALLS CONVENTION

BY CHRISTINE STANSELL

O N July 20, 1848, in the little country town of Seneca Falls in upstate New York, a convention of several hundred excited women and a few score men issued, among other demands for women's rights, a call for votes for women. This inspired proposal, although made by a modest gathering in a small provincial town, ultimately had momentous consequences. Daring, even outrageous at the time, the call for suffrage came to galvanize women's politics in the United States; and during the next fifty years, the fight for woman suffrage would become the center-piece of a popular, powerful, and innovative movement. This long effort, set off by the deliberations at Seneca Falls, would eventually undo, from top to bottom, deeply established ideas about the relevance of sexual distinction the business of governing the country.

AT LEFT: *Seneca Falls resident Elizabeth Cady Stanton was one of the principal organizers of the 1848 women's rights convention.*

ABOVE: *Stanton's comrade, Lucretia Mott of Philadelphia, used this design (adapteded from the popular abolitionist* Am I Not a Man and a Brother? *motif) on her stationery.*

The Seneca Falls declaration had been long in the making. It emerged from a fitfully articulated history of women's grievances stretching back at least as far as 1792, when the bold British writer Mary Wollstonecraft, inspired in part by Parisian women's activism during the French Revolution, published *A Vindication of the Rights of Women,* a remarkable indictment of women's low social position. Closer to home, the gathering was motivated by years of controversy within the trans-Atlantic abolitionist community over the proper role of women in its agitation against slavery, the great issue of the day. Many northern women were already active, passionately so, in the fight against slavery, and conflict over whether or not their activities should be limited—should respectable women be permitted to speak in public before audiences that included both sexes?—split the movement in the late 1830s. The nub of the issue was whether a woman had the right to follow the dictates of her own conscience into the theater of public protest—a radical, even transgressive act in an age that viewed a woman's "exposing" herself to public scrutiny as tantamount to prostitution.

RADICALS WITHIN THE ANTISLAVERY ranks, led by William Lloyd Garrison, backed the many women who demanded a greater role for themselves. At the same time, "gradualists," prominently represented by New York City merchant Lewis Tappan, lined up with the clergy to send the women back home to perform the gentler work (so lauded by American culture) of turning family members and neighbors against slavery through prayer, persuasion, and sweet female influence. A ruckus between these two factions broke out in London at the 1840 meeting of the World Anti-Slavery Convention. There the moderates carried the day after a bitter floor fight. The women members of the American delegation were barred from participating in the proceedings and allowed only to observe the convention from behind a curtain in the meeting hall's balcony.

In 1830, *Lucretia Mott counseled a young William Lloyd Garrison, "If thou expects to set forth thy cause by word of mouth, thou must learn to lay aside thy papers and speak from the heart."*

Two of the women present were Lucretia Mott, a distinguished middle-aged Quaker preacher, and Elizabeth Cady Stanton, a young newlywed who had traveled to the London meeting on her honeymoon. The pair had already taken to each other on the voyage over, during which Henry Stanton, already showing signs of a cold and critical nature, reproached his bride for her gaiety in company, her boldness in mixing with the renowned delegate aboard (among them Liberty party presidential candidate James G. Birney), and her fearlessness in professing her views before people who knew much more than she did. But Lucretia Mott found the younger woman's exuberance captivating—the expression of an "open generous confiding spirit,"

Lewis Tappan
was among those who believed that women should not be allowed to participate openly in the deliberations of the antislavery movement.

as she wrote soon afterward in a letter to Mrs. Stanton. Stanton herself was enchanted. Mott seemed to be, as Stanton would later describe her, a creature emancipated from any fear of scorn or denunciation, who entirely trusted her own opinions: "It seemed to me like meeting a being from some larger planet, to find a woman who dared to question the opinion of Popes, Kings, Synods, Parliaments, with the same freedom that she would criticize an editorial in the *London Times.*"

Temperamentally drawn to each other, the two also struck up what would prove to be a significant political alliance. Witnessing the acrimony in London, they became even more vigorous in the conviction, born of years of experience in antislavery work, that grievous wrongs, if perpetrated against women, would be excused by even the most high minded of people. Years later, Stanton recalled that on the evening after the floor fight, she and Mott walked arm in arm back to their hotel, rehearsing the events of the day and determined, once they returned to the States, to hold a meeting devoted solely to the question of women's rights.

T HEIR PLAN LAY FALLOW for eight years. Philadelphia, where James and Lucretia Mott lived, was a long way from upstate New York, where the Stantons settled, and both women were busy with antislavery work. Mott was also occupied with her preaching, and Stanton soon had to cope with the cares of motherhood and the burden of managing a large household with few servants. Adding to Stanton's difficulties was the frequent absence of her husband, Henry, who often traveled on antislavery business. Not until 1848 did Lucretia Mott and Elizabeth Stanton have the opportunity to renew their ambitions. That

In 1840, Lucretia Mott was one of seven American delegates to the World Anti-Slavery Convention whose credentials were rejected because they were women. Elizabeth Cady Stanton, though not a delegate herself, had traveled to London on her honeymoon because her new husband, Henry, was one. In Benjamin R. Haydon's rendering of the convention, Henry Stanton can be seen in the first row, seated second from the right.

Although generally overshadowed by her famous, more serious sister, Martha Wright provided a touch of lightness often lacking in her colleagues. Susan B. Anthony once described Wright as "clearsighted, true and steadfast almost beyond all other women."

summer, while visiting her sister Martha Wright in Auburn, New York, Mott became caught up in a local Quaker schism, supporting a rebellious group of Friends who broke away from a local meeting hostile to abolitionism. A few weeks later, on July 13, she got together with Stanton at the home of some like-minded Friends in Waterloo, not far from Seneca Falls.

Stanton and Mott's interest in sponsoring a women's rights gathering was promptly rekindled; and with Martha Wright and two other Quaker women (Jane Hunt and Mary Ann McClintock), they set to work around a tea table organizing a meeting. They had calls placed the next day in several local newspapers and the abolitionist *North Star*, published by Frederick Douglass in nearby Rochester, announcing a two-day convention to be held the following week in Seneca Falls, beginning on Wednesday, July 19. From the outset, these five women aimed for something grand and momentous. Stanton proclaimed the event "the first women's rights convention that has ever assembled," and although she knew little of the history of women's rights—no one really did—she happened to be right.

In her later account of the preparations, Stanton emphasized how politically naive and innocent the women were: "Having no experience in the *modus operandi* of getting up conventions, they felt as helpless and hopeless as if they had been suddenly asked to construct a steam engine," Stanton related in her *History of Woman Suffrage* (1881–1886), the official account she compiled with Susan B. Anthony and Matilda Gage. Stanton's characterization, though, was something of an overstatement. In truth, the

This announcement appeared on page two of the North Star's *July 14, 1848, issue. The newspaper's lead article described a festival recently held in Rochester to celebrate the end of slavery in the French West Indies.*

Woman's Rights Convention.

A Convention to discuss the Social, Civil and Religious Condition and Rights of Woman, will be held in the Wesleyan Chapel at Seneca Falls, New York, on Wednesday and Thursday, the 19th and 20th of July instant.

During the first day, the meetings will be exclusively for women, which all are earnestly invited to attend. The public generally are invited to be present on the second day, when Lucretia Mott, of Philadelphia, and others, both ladies and gentlemen, will address the Convention.

tea-table group included women whose organizing skills had been honed by years of abolitionist and church activity and whose fortitude in the face of disapproval had just been tested in the recent Friends schism. Certainly, these women showed no timidity in throwing together a meeting in just six days' time. They rented the Wesleyan Methodist Chapel for the gathering—Wesleyan Methodists, who were explicitly antislavery, tended to be more supportive of women's rights— and printed up flyers. Using the Declaration of Independence as a model, they also drew up a Declaration of Sentiments and several resolutions to be debated at the meeting. "When, in the course of human events, it becomes necessary for one portion of the family of *man* to assume among the people of the earth a position different from that which they have hitherto occupied," the declaration began, "...a decent respect to the opinions of mankind requires that they should declare the causes that impel them to such a course."

It was at the house of Jane Hunt (above) *in Waterloo that Stanton and Mott renewed their friendship.*

Stanton, Mott, and the others worried that attendance would be low. It was high summer: a busy time on the farms, hot and slow in town. Yet on July 19, a substantial crowd converged on the chapel, some arriving in genteel carriages, humbler travelers in farm wagons, and locals on foot. "At first we travelled quite alone," a sewingwoman who came with some friends recalled, "but before we had gone many miles we came on other waggon-loads of women, bound in the same direction. As we reached different cross-roads we saw waggons coming from every part of the county, and long before we reached Seneca Falls we were a procession." Men came, too. The plan had been to exclude them from the first day of the event, but when even the intrepid Elizabeth Stanton quailed at the prospect of presiding over the unorthodox gathering, a quick caucus decided to admit the men and turn the podium over to James Mott. Some three hundred people packed into the chapel for two days of speeches, declamations, and deliberations.

On July 14, the five ladies met again, this time at the home of Mary Ann McClintock (above), to set the agenda for the convention.

THERE WAS A CONVICTION in the hall that history was in the making. The spring of 1848 had already seen revolutions in Europe, and the crowd's awareness of these must surely have contributed to the participants' sense that they were kicking off the traces of illegitimate government and could "do and dare anything," as Stanton put it. Two months earlier in New York City, Mott had given a speech extolling the revolutions—which, she knew, included women bent on raising the question of rights for their sex. "The spirit of freedom is

Throughout 1848, U.S. *newspapers kept readers informed of events across the ocean, which made American reformers hopeful that all forms of entrenched privilege might soon be overthrown. This wood-cut from a March 1848 issue of the* Illustrated London News *shown women on the streets of in Paris selling the feminist daily newspaper* Voix des Femmes.

arousing the world; and the press universal will echo the glad sound," Mott had exulted. At the Seneca Falls convention as well, one can detect in the language of tyranny, usurpation, and entrenched despotism a faint echo of the defiant clarion calls that were then being issued from the barricades in Paris and Prague. "The history of mankind is a history of repeated injuries and usurpations on the part of man toward woman, having in direct object the establishment of an absolute tyranny over her," the Declaration of Sentiments asserted.

The deliberations at Seneca Falls ranged far beyond previous articulations of the injustices being perpetrated against women—including those of Mary Wollstonecraft. The structure of the law, a subject never addressed by Wollstonecraft, was a particular target at Seneca Falls: The common law of coverture, adopted virtually wholesale from British practice by the new United States, followed the premise that a woman was legally "covered" by her husband or father, meaning that women were the subjects of men and not persons in their own right, as least as far as the legal system was concerned. Married women, for

"THIS IS THE AGE OF REVOLUTIONS.... BY THE INTELLIGENCE, HOWEVER, WHICH WE HAVE LATELY RECEIVED, THE WORK OF REVOLUTION IS NO LONGER CONFINED TO THE OLD WORLD, NOR TO THE MASCULINE GENDER."

—New York Herald, *reporting the Seneca Falls convention, July 1848*—

instance, could not hold property in their own names, nor could they retain their own earnings. Divorce was similarly an economic and social disaster for women, denying them not only whatever money they might have contributed to the marriage but also custody of their children. The obvious analogy, that married women were to their husbands what slaves were to their masters, applied even to successful relationships.

All marriages, according to the Declaration of Sentiments, were founded on a profound corruption of liberty: that a woman was legally compelled "to promise obedience to her husband, he becoming, to all intents and purposes, her master—the law giving him power to deprive her of her liberty, and to administer chastisement."

The political grievances that took form at Seneca Falls had long simmered in Stanton's mind and, more generally, in the minds of many enlightened middle-class women. Although many of those attending the convention would have been respectable married ladies, insulated from the worst depredations of worthless husbands and unsympathetic courts, the urgent need to change the law of coverture would have been on all their minds because of the well-publicized debates that had recently accompanied passage by the New York state legislature of the Married Women's Property Act. This law, enacted in April 1848, was the first in the country to guarantee a married woman's right to own property apart from her husband. Stanton, the daughter of a judge, knew many of the legal reformers who had pushed for the law in Albany, and several later attended the convention in Seneca Falls. Stanton had closely followed their work, and she went on to make the abolition of coverture a pillar of her feminist thinking.

OTHER CONVENTION GRIEVANCES were more diffuse. The participants were careful not to denounce expressly the widespread cultural belief in a "woman's sphere," that supposedly hallowed world of home and family where female power and influence were dominant. Yet the convention did repudiate some of that tradition's central tenets. It protested the fact that women were barred from colleges and universities, although in this the Declaration of Sentiments was not altogether accurate: Mount Holyoke, while still a seminary, did offer advanced course work, and Oberlin had begun admitting women in 1837, although not to higher degree programs. Because professional schools were also closed to them in 1848, women could not become theologians, ministers, physicians, or lawyers. Furthermore, in the few fields that did employ women, such as school teaching, the pay was scanty. With few exceptions, women could not even participate in church governance—a particular irritant because church congregations were heavily female.

This portrait appeared as the frontispiece to Henry Stanton's 1885 memoirs Random Recollections.

ELIZABETH CADY STANTON

1815 – 1902

Born to a judge in Johnstown, New York, Elizabeth Cady received the finest education available to a young woman in the early 1830s, attending Emma Willard's Academy in Troy. Still, she always regretted being denied a full college education. Although her father opposed her engagement to Henry Stanton, ten years her senior, the couple was married in 1840. Upon their return from London, the Stantons lived in Boston until 1847, when they moved to Seneca Falls. It was particularly after this move that, deprived of the intellectual and social life she had enjoyed in Boston, Mrs. Stanton (shown here in 1848) began to resent her domestic confinement.

The culprit in all these abuses was man, the despot. The framers of the Declaration of Sentiments, emboldened by years of listening to passionate antislavery rhetoric, described the fundamental tyranny of man's treatment of woman in severe language: "He has usurped the prerogative of Jehovah himself, claiming it as his right to assign for her a sphere of action, when that belongs to her conscience and to her God." The meaning of man in this passage was intended to be generic and abstract, so that the precise identity of the male perpetrators remained vague. The absence of more concrete charges perhaps allowed the men in attendance to sign on to the Declaration of Sentiments, apparently wholeheartedly.

How might they have felt, listening for two days to these denunciations? A bit discomfited, perhaps, but, it seems, not riled. One must remember, of course, that these men were abolitionists, Quakers, and reformers—veterans of life in a region that had been "burned over" by evangelical revivals. They were attuned to what they saw as a spiritual rebirth, which had done much to inspire glowing hopes that America might indeed become a true republic, where all manmade fetters on human dignity would be sundered. The extension of this sentiment from slaves to women must have seemed to the men in the audience, at least during those two days, an unfolding of America's promise rather than a personal challenge.

The text of the Declaration of Sentiments did signal, however, a striking and powerful departure from customary reform ideas. The pattern of the declaration's specific grievances was, unquestionably, designed to hold actual male people responsible for women's oppression. A half century before, Mary Wollstonecraft had been too steeped in the misogynist thinking of her era to approach an analysis so sympathetic to women. Although a feminist, Wollstonecraft didn't like other women much, and she tended to blame them (their thwarted characters, their bad educations) for the handicaps they faced. In her *Vindication*, there was even the hint, the implicit suggestion, that the male character, at its most reasonable and virtuous, was the model toward which women should strive. In contrast, the Declaration of Sentiments

> "THERE EXISTS, IN THE WORLD OF MEN, A TONE OF FEELING TOWARDS WOMEN AS TOWARDS SLAVES."
>
> —*Margaret Fuller,* The Dial, *July 1843*—

LUCRETIA MOTT

1793 – 1880

Born into the family of a Nantucket sea captain, Lucretia Coffin became interested in women's rights while teaching at a Quaker boarding school in Poughkeepsie, New York, where she was paid only half of what the male teachers earned simply because of her sex. When her family moved to Philadelphia, she moved with them and was followed there by another teacher at the Quaker school, James Mott, whom she married in 1811 (and with whom she is pictured above). Together, the Motts became active in the antislavery movement. They boycotted all goods produced by slave labor and often used their Philadelphia home to hide runaway slaves.

offered a firm defense of women as they were, poised to exercise their God-given capacities were it not for the fact that men held them down.

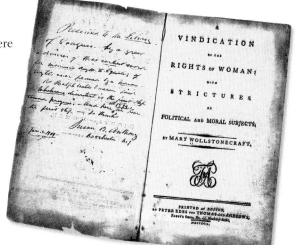

BEYOND THE CALL FOR THE ABOLITION of coverture, though, the remedies proposed in the Declaration of Sentiments were nearly all vague. The resolutions appended to the declaration were mostly variations on the preamble's call for the moral enlightenment of both sexes (especially men). There was one resolution, however, that was precise and political: the demand for votes for women, Elizabeth Cady Stanton's special contribution. The idea was startling. Decades earlier, female activists had briefly raised the notion of suffrage during the French Revolution, but they were crushed. In the early weeks of 1848, a small group of militant Parisian women had protested their exclusion from the universal suffrage declared by the provisional government, but they were jailed for their efforts. In the United States, virtually no one had even broached the subject, although a handful of women in New York had indirectly touched upon it when they complained, in petitions to the state legislature advocating the Married Women's Property Act, that they suffered taxation without representation. In general, however, female disenfranchisement seemed so natural and normal, and women seemed to fall so entirely outside the boundaries of the political community, that no one even thought to comment on it.

Today, the wholesale disenfranchisement of half the population of a nation founded on republican principles seems wildly illogical. Yet the classical republican ideas that fired the revolutionaries of 1776—and remained embedded in the political culture of the United States—were predicated on the idea that independent men of virtue and reason would represent the political interests of their households within the national polity. The household members for whom each of these men spoke and voted were considered to include adult women as well as children, slaves, and apprentices. So, although universal white manhood suffrage was achieved by 1848, the prospect of women voting challenged deeply ingrained notions of proper government. Even Stanton's fellow organizers balked that last day at introducing the suffrage resolution, concerned that it would make them seem ridiculous, even among such right-thinking

Susan B. Anthony
presented this first edition of Wollstonecraft's Vindication *to the Library of Congress in 1904.*

MARY WOLLSTONECRAFT

Born in 1759, Mary Wollstonecraft grew up in a family ruled by an abusive father who made her acutely aware of the degradations suffered by women because of their dependent position in society. Because her father was also a wastrel, she worked from an early age to support herself and her siblings. Arriving in London in 1788 determined to be a writer, she fell in with a group of radicals that included Tom Paine and the artist William Blake. Taking to heart their faith in the rights of man, she reapplied their doctrines in her 1792 work "vindicating" the rights of woman. The prevailing social system, according to Wollstonecraft, produced coquettish women trained to flatter and tyrannical men raised to accept slavish submission.

OPPOSITE:

This photograph of Lucretia Mott was taken sometime during the early 1850s, when her fame was near its height.

Even Mott's silk needle-craft workbag bore an antislavery motif.

people as the convention participants. When the resolution came to the floor, it was argued hotly before it came to a vote. The great antislavery orator Frederick Douglass, however, threw his considerable moral weight behind Mrs. Stanton's proposal, and it passed by a small majority. It was the only resolution not to be unanimously approved.

Had Stanton not presented this resolution, the sentiments of Seneca Falls would most likely have melted into what had been, up to that point in the Atlantic world, a halting, episodic tradition of women's protest. It may be easy today to see votes for women as an automatic outgrowth of modern democracy, but during the second half of the nineteenth century, woman suffrage proved to be an enormously contentious issue. Vociferous suffrage movements—all of them indebted to the unorthodox proposition enunciated at Seneca Falls—were launched across the globe but stymied repeatedly, in most cases until after the First World War; indeed, women in France were not enfranchised until after the Second World War. In the United States, ratification of the Nineteenth Amendment was blocked until 1920, and even then suffrage did not immediately force the deep changes regarding a women's place in the polity that the Seneca Falls advocates had envisioned.

FOR ONE THING, until the civil rights movement brought about the end of African-American disenfranchisement, huge numbers of women still could not vote. In addition, both white and black women long remained "covered" in ways that the Seneca Falls participants would have deplored. Because of the lingering legal premise that women needed to be protected from the burdens of public duties, they were excused from jury service, for example, in many states up through the 1960s. Nonetheless, it was the protest ventured on July 20 by those sitting in the pews of the Wesleyan Methodist Chapel that opened up the space for questioning, with critical detachment and even scorn, conventional ideas about the fitness of women for citizenship—ideas once so imbued with the patina of common sense and tradition that they seemed to smack of the authority of Nature itself.

★ ★ ★

FURTHER READING

★ Bonnie S. Anderson, *Joyous Greetings: The First International Women's Movement, 1830–1860* (2000)

★ Ellen Carol DuBois, *Feminism and Suffrage: The Emergence of an Independent Women's Movement in America, 1848–1869* (1978)

MARCH 6, 1857

THE DAY OF DRED SCOTT

BY SEAN WILENTZ

THE GLOOMY GROUND-FLOOR Supreme Court chamber, deep inside the U.S. Capitol, was, for once, packed with spectators and newspaper reporters. Congress had adjourned three days earlier, so the Senate rooms just above the courtroom were silent. At eleven o'clock in the morning, as scheduled, the nine black-robed justices filed in, led by the crevice-faced Chief Justice Roger B. Taney, two weeks short of his eightieth birthday. Expectant mutterings from the onlookers died down as Taney, his voice low and tremulous with age but fixed in its purpose, began reading the Court's designated opinion in the fractious and portentous case of one Dred Scott, a slave.

Scott, the plaintiff, was hundreds of miles away, living in St. Louis—still in bondage more than a decade after he had begun legal efforts to secure his freedom. The defendant, John F. A. Sanford, a hitherto obscure St. Louis and Manhattan merchant, had years earlier taken up the matter on behalf of his sister, Scott's formal owner, Irene Emerson. Sanford (whose name was misspelled on the case docket as "Sandford") was also absent from the courtroom: He was languishing in a New York insane asylum, where he would die two years later.

In the principals' stead stood their attorneys, each of whom was a consummate political insider. Sanford was represented by the proslavery U.S. senator from Missouri, Henry S. Geyer, along with the even more imposing Reverdy Johnson, a Maryland politician and renowned constitutional lawyer who was also a good friend of Chief Justice Taney. On Scott's behalf (working pro bono) stood Montgomery Blair, a prominent Washington lawyer with strong connections to Missouri, and another imposing constitutional expert, George Curtis of Massachusetts. Geyer and Johnson commanded the sympathies of the Court's prosouthern

AT LEFT: *G. P. A. Healy painted this official portrait of Chief Justice Roger B. Taney in 1858.*

ABOVE: *This Supreme Court desk was most likely used at the time of the* Dred Scott *case in the chambers of Justice John A. Campbell, but tradition also associates it with Chief Justice Roger B. Taney.*

conservative majority, but their adversaries also had influence, particularly with Associate Justice Benjamin R. Curtis, George Curtis's brother. In addition, neither Blair nor George Curtis was an antislavery radical—Blair was a moderate Free Soil Democrat, Curtis an old-school Whig—which many observers thought worked to Scott's advantage. The odds against the slave winning his freedom were enormous, but the exact outcome of the trial was uncertain.

Scott's shallow hopes evaporated as Taney, speaking for two hours in barely audible tones, delivered an opinion that was as furious in its implications as it was flat in its rhetoric. Not only had the Court majority decided against Scott, denying him his freedom; it had also found that Negroes, free or slave, were not and had never been citizens of the United States and that they possessed "no rights which the white man was bound to respect," including the right to bring suit in a federal court. Furthermore, Taney declared, consideration of Scott's case made it clear that Congress was powerless to prohibit slavery in the federal territories—meaning that the fragile Missouri Compromise of 1819–1821, abrogated in 1854 by the Kansas-Nebraska Act, had been unconstitutional all along.

This ruling, from which two justices (John McLean of Ohio and Benjamin Curtis) dissented, promulgated as a matter of federal law the most extreme proslavery position in a sectional debate that had already reached a fever pitch. In his barely contained anger—the anger of a southern gentleman aggrieved at Yankee interference—Taney supposed that, with a single emphatic stroke, he and his colleagues could suppress the slavery question once and for all. Instead, he rendered a decision so one-sided that it was denounced the

Reverdy Johnson was elected to the U.S. Senate from Maryland in 1845. He resigned four years later (the same year this engraving was published) to become Zachary Taylor's attorney general. Although a staunch advocate of states' rights, Johnson was nevertheless instrumental in preventing Maryland's secession in 1860–1861.

CENTER:

From 1810 until 1860, the justices heard oral arguments in the Old Supreme Court Chamber, located in the Capitol beneath the Senate. The room has recently been restored to its appearance at the time of the Dred Scott *decision.*

next day by the *New York Tribune* (admittedly a Republican antislavery newspaper) as "entitled to just so much moral weight as would be the judgment of a majority of those congregated in any Washington bar-room." Later reaction to the decision, both pro and con, was even more passionate, and it soon became clear that the deceptively dry drama of March 6, 1857, had brought the nation one large step closer to bloody civil war.

D RED SCOTT COULD HARDLY HAVE imagined that his suit would become so important or that he would become so famous. Probably born in Virginia at the dawn of the nineteenth century, Scott had been the property of one Peter Blow, a planter who moved in 1830 from Alabama to St. Louis, where he started an unsuccessful hotel venture and died two years later. At some point, either just before or just after Blow's demise, Scott was sold to Dr. John Emerson, who in late 1833 was appointed an assistant surgeon in the U.S. Army.

Over the next ten years, acting as Emerson's personal servant, Dred Scott bounced from one army post to another, starting out at Fort Armstrong in Illinois, then moving with Emerson to the Iowa Territory, the Wisconsin Territory, Louisiana, and finally in 1840 back to St. Louis, where he stayed with Emerson's wife, Irene, while the doctor took up his latest military assignment in Florida. After quitting the army, Emerson rejoined his wife and slaves and moved them up the Mississippi River in 1843 to Davenport, Iowa. He died shortly thereafter (purportedly of consumption, but quite possibly of syphilis). Scott—who had

A moderate, Montgomery Blair served as Abraham Lincoln's first postmaster general. He began free city mail delivery before being forced from the cabinet by the Radical Republicans.

"SLAVERY IS FOUNDED IN THE SELFISHNESS OF MAN'S NATURE— OPPOSITION TO IT IN HIS LOVE OF JUSTICE."

—

Abraham Lincoln, speech, October 1854

ROGER B. TANEY

1777 – 1864

As a young Federalist lawyer, Roger B. Taney defended the landed gentry from whence he sprang, having been born into a family of wealthy Maryland slaveholders. During the 1820s, though, he threw his support behind Andrew Jackson, becoming Jackson's attorney general in 1831. Two years later, when Secretary of the Treasury William Duane refused to carry out the president's order to re-move all federal deposits from the Second Bank of the United States, Jackson replaced Duane with Taney, who ordered the removal. Although the Senate later refused to confirm Taney as treasury secretary, Jackson rewarded his loyalty in 1835, when he nominated Taney to succeed the late John Marshall as chief justice of the Supreme Court.

meanwhile taken a wife, Harriet, back in Wisconsin—was turned over on loan to Irene Emerson's brother-in-law, Capt. Henry Bainbridge, who appears to have taken Dred and Harriet Scott with him to Texas.

By the time the Mexican War broke out in May 1846, though, the Scotts were back in St. Louis, now hired out to one Samuel Russell. We know this because on April 6, 1846, after trying unsuccessfully to purchase their freedom (with funds from an unknown source), Dred and Harriet Scott filed petitions in county court demanding their freedom.

How Dred Scott, an illiterate slave, came to launch his suit remains a mystery, although recent research suggests that Harriet Scott's friends in a local black church may have made the couple aware of the possibility of legal action. Indeed, after their sojourns in a free state and in territories where slavery had been banned, the Scotts were in a remarkably strong legal position to claim freedom for themselves and for their young daughter, Eliza. Repeatedly, Missouri courts had ruled that any slave taken by his or her master into a free state or territory was automatically free. By long-settled precedent, all that Scott's lawyers had to show was that he had been taken to live on free soil and that he was still being claimed as a slave by his master (or, in this case, his mistress). The case should have been open and shut—or would have been, had bad luck and politics not intervened.

In June 1847, Scott lost his initial trial on the technical grounds that his lawyers failed to produce a witness who could testify that Irene Emerson still claimed ownership of Scott. The Missouri Supreme Court ordered a retrial, but two continuances (one caused by a major fire, the other by a cholera epidemic) delayed the new proceeding until January 1850. At that time, a St. Louis County Court jury, upholding Missouri legal precedent, found for the Scotts. But Mrs. Emerson was loath to lose her slaves, so her brother John Sanford filed an appeal with the state supreme court.

MEANWHILE, IN THE WAKE of the Mexican War, controversies over slavery had begun to traumatize American politics. The Wilmot Proviso, introduced by northern congressmen in August 1846, had sought to ban the extension of slavery into territories acquired from Mexico as a result of the war. It had divided Congress sharply along sectional lines (and was eventually blocked by the southern-dominated Senate). The creation of the Free Soil party two years later deepened the divisions, not only in Washington but also around the country. Southern proslavery spokesmen, led by the venerable John C.

Calhoun, began demanding positive protections for slavery in all the federal territories; less radical southerners (along with their northern friends) advocated letting residents of the territories decide the matter for themselves.

In 1850, Henry Clay and other congressional moderates brokered a compromise with costs and benefits for all concerned. The price that the North had to pay for the admission of California as a free state (and other southern concessions) was the Fugitive Slave Law. This law compelled northern officials to aid in the capture and return of runaway slaves; it also enraged antislavery northerners, who deeply resented the presence of slave catchers in their cities, hunting down blacks who weren't always runaway slaves. Amid this mounting turmoil, in 1852, the case of *Scott v. Emerson,* which had begun so quietly in 1846 and seemed so cut and dried, came before the Missouri Supreme Court. There, legal precedent flew out the window, and brazen political arguments held sway.

The high court quickly reversed the county court's decision and declared on March 22, 1852, that Scott was indeed still a slave. "Times are not now what they were when the former decisions on this subject were made," Chief Justice William Scott declared, adding that in recent

This 1855 engraving depicts Henry Clay introducing the resolutions that became the Compromise of 1850. The speech Clay delivered on January 29, 1850, was the last of significance in his long legislative career, which began with his election to the Senate in 1806.

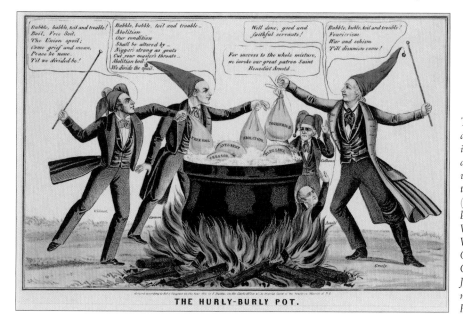

THE HURLY-BURLY POT.

This 1850 cartoon attacks the sectional interests then disrupting national unity. It singles out those represented (from left to right) by Free Soiler David Wilmot, abolitionist William Lloyd Garrison, South Carolina senator John Calhoun, and newspaperman Horace Greeley.

Justice John McLean

Justice Robert C. Grier

years antislavery opinion had reached the point at which it threatened "the overthrow and destruction of our Government." Unwilling "to show the least countenance to any measure which might gratify this spirit," he concluded, the Court had no choice but to find in favor of the plaintiff, Mrs. Emerson.

ESPITE THIS DISAPPOINTMENT, Dred Scott and his lawyers would not be deterred. On November 2, 1853, with aid from the family of Peter Blow (Scott's former owner), the slave brought a new suit in federal court, charging John Sanford with wrongful imprisonment in the hope of winning his freedom under federal law. After months of legal skirmishing, Scott's case finally went to trial in May 1854. At the end of the trial, in his charge to the jury, the presiding judge, Robert W. Wells, instructed the jury members that, because the Missouri Supreme Court had already ruled Scott a slave, they had no alternative but to uphold the state's judgment. This the jury swiftly did, paving the way for Scott's appeal to the U.S. Supreme Court. His argument was that Judge Wells had erred in his interpretation of the law.

The Court heard oral arguments in February 1856 and sat through another round in December before arriving at its final decision in March.

This image was taken from an 1857 daguerreotype of Dred Scott.

The delays were suspicious: At first, some justices had simply wanted to postpone the matter until the bitter 1856 presidential election was over, but others outside the Court (especially Republicans such as former Illinois congressman Abraham Lincoln) believed that Taney and his allies were engaged in a massive conspiracy to elect conservative Democrat James Buchanan and force slavery into the territories. Like many conspiracy theories, theirs may have been a little far-fetched—one of the dissenting justices, John McLean, had been among those voting for the initial delay—but the possibility of a conspiracy appeared much more plausible when on March 4, 1857—Buchanan's inauguration day—the president-elect, elegantly dressed and all smiles, halted atop the dais on which he would be sworn in to engage in a whispered conversation with Chief Justice Taney. Minutes later, Buchanan delivered an inaugural address that bid the country to heed the Court's upcoming decision.

We will never know what Taney said to Buchanan, but historians have discovered that Buchanan already knew how the Court was going to rule. Departing drastically from the unwritten rules that separate the three federal branches, Buchanan's fellow Pennsylvanian, Justice Robert C. Grier, had informed the incoming president fully about how the case was proceeding behind the justices' closed doors. When Buchanan in his inaugural address urged public support for the decision—whatever that decision might be—he knew very well it would uphold the southern position on slavery. Call it conspiracy or mere collusion, but Buchanan and Taney and the rest of the Court majority were certainly working closely together to achieve the outcome they desired.

Justice Samuel Nelson

IT WOULD HAVE BEEN EASY for the Court to have followed a different course, one that kept Scott in bondage without further inflaming sectional passions over slavery. On the eve of the decision, one of the justices, Samuel Nelson of New York, drafted an opinion that would have avoided controversy by simply declaring that the federal bench had no business interfering with Missouri slave law and that because the Missouri court had already ruled Scott a slave, he would remain one. But Taney, pushed by his fiercely proslavery colleagues Peter V. Daniel of Virginia and John A. Campbell of Georgia, was determined to force a confrontation—and, with his ruling, he did.

The majority decision unequivocally promoted sectional politics at the expense of supposedly nonpartisan judicial decision making. Yet the overtly political purpose of Taney's ruling made it vulnerable on both legal and historical grounds. Because his judgments relating to the Missouri Compromise went well beyond the legal issues in *Scott v. Sandford* (and well beyond the historical facts as well), critics immediately dismissed these passages as obiter dicta—that is, extraneous commentary without any binding legal force. Furthermore, Taney's arguments about black noncitizenship in

Justice Benjamin R. Curtis

early America were demonstrably false. "At the time of the ratification of the Articles of Confederation," Justice Curtis wrote in his uncompromising dissent,

all free native-born inhabitants of the States of New Hampshire, Massachusetts, New York, New Jersey, and North Carolina, though descended from African slaves, were not only citizens of those States, but such of them as had the other necessary qualifications possessed the franchise of electors, on equal terms with other citizens.

Over the ensuing decades, to be sure, blacks, North and South, had seen a steady erosion of their civil and electoral rights. Nevertheless, Curtis argued, blacks were constituent members of the nation and could not now be blithely declared noncitizens with no rights whatsoever.

Proslavery southerners could not have cared less about these historical details. "A prize, for which the athletes of the nation have often wrestled in the halls of Congress, has been awarded at last, by the proper umpire, to those who have justly won it," the *Richmond Enquirer* exulted. "The nation has achieved a triumph, sectionalism has been rebuked, and abolitionism has been staggered and stunned." Other proslavery newspapers, such as the *Charleston Mercury,* expressed their delight at the decision but tempered their words with a prescient sense of dread and caution. "The Abolitionists are not at all abashed or dismayed," the *Mercury* wrote; "on the contrary, they accept this repulse as another blow in the work of imparting compactness and strength to their organization, and, from the fire that consumes *Dred Scott,* they appear to anticipate a conflagration which will again set the popular sentiment of the North in a blaze of indignation."

In fact, many nonradical northerners welcomed the *Dred Scott* decision almost as much as southerners did. To conservative Democrats, Taney's ruling was a political gift—which, by ending the agitation over slavery, might heal their splintered party. To those northern whites (probably a majority) who believed that blacks, if undeserving of slavery, were inferior creatures, Taney's remarks about black noncitizenship sounded eminently correct. And to many northern businessmen,

TOP: *This cover sheet— prepared on March 6, 1857— summarizes the disposition of the* Dred Scott *case as "dismissed for want of jurisdiction."*

BOTTOM: *The Supreme Court's judgment in* Dred Scott v. Sandford, *signed by Taney on March 6.*

especially those with ties to the South, the *Dred Scott* decision augured a much-desired restoration of calm to the nation's markets. "The people, who reverence the Constitution and the laws, and who only need to be shown the truth to adopt and obey it, will hail the decision with satisfaction and will regard [it]...as almost the greatest political boon which has been vouchsafed to us since the foundation of the Republic," New York City's *Journal of Commerce* declared.

Although a longtime opponent of slavery, Abraham Lincoln said little in public about the issue before 1854.

OF COURSE, TO THE GROWING northern antislavery movement, centered now in the infant Republican party, Taney's majority opinion was a deliberate falsification of the Constitution and of history—less an opinion, the *New York Independent* bellowed, than "a horrible hand-book of tyranny." But at least one prominent abolitionist, the former slave Frederick Douglass, agreed with the *Charleston Mercury* that the "devilish decision" and its immediate aftermath had actually strengthened the movement for slavery's overthrow. "I have no fear," Douglass told the assembled members of the American Anti-Slavery Society in May 1857, "that the National Conscience will be put to sleep by such an open, glaring, and scandalous tissue of lies as that decision is, and has been, over and over, shown to be."

Other Republican orators and candidates also seized on the decision to press their antislavery appeal, none more eloquently than Abraham Lincoln. In 1858, Lincoln opened his bid for the U.S. Senate with an address that would in time become famous as the "House Divided" speech. According to Lincoln, should the Democrats remain in power, slavery would be nationalized—and he offered Taney's decision as proof positive. "We shall lie down pleasantly," Lincoln intoned, "dreaming that the people of Missouri are on the verge of

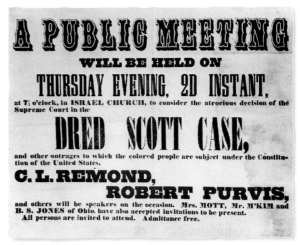

Lucretia Mott was among those scheduled to speak at the public meeting "to consider the atrocious decision of the Supreme Court" announced by this poster.

making their state free; and we shall awake to the reality, instead, that the Supreme Court has made Illinois a slave state." The logical deduction from *Dred Scott,* Lincoln pointed out, was that "what Dred Scott's master might lawfully do with Dred Scott, in the free state of Illinois, every other master may lawfully do with any other one, or one thousand slaves, in Illinois, or in any other free state." From there, it was but a short step to a second *Dred Scott* decision legalizing slavery in every state.

FURTHER READING

★ Don E. Fehrenbacher, *The Dred Scott Case: Its Significance in American Law and Politics* (1978)

★ Eric Foner, *Free Soil, Free Labor, Free Men: The Ideology of the Republican Party Before the Civil War* (1970)

NEVERTHELESS, BY THE TIME LINCOLN made these remarks, proslavery southerners and their northern sympathizers had lost their euphoria over *Dred Scott v. Sandford.* Taney's decision could not, they realized, enforce itself. Masters could bring slaves legally into all U.S. territories, but without a formal legalization of slavery, how could those masters' rights be protected? Northern Democrats—most notably Lincoln's 1858 opponent, Sen. Stephen A. Douglas—grasped at the argument that, if the people of a territory did not want to institute slavery, they could simply fail to give it protective legislation. Southerners, however, were not easily placated. Proslavery men grew increasingly angry at many northern Democrats (including Douglas) for their opposition to the admission of Kansas in 1858 under a disputed proslavery constitution. In the light of the Kansas struggle, northern conservative assurances regarding *Dred Scott,* about local protections and popular sovereignty, sounded to southerners at best unreliable and at worst evasive. Led by Sen. Jefferson Davis of Mississippi, southern Democrats began attacking Douglas and his allies as heretics and demanded nothing less than a federal slave code for all

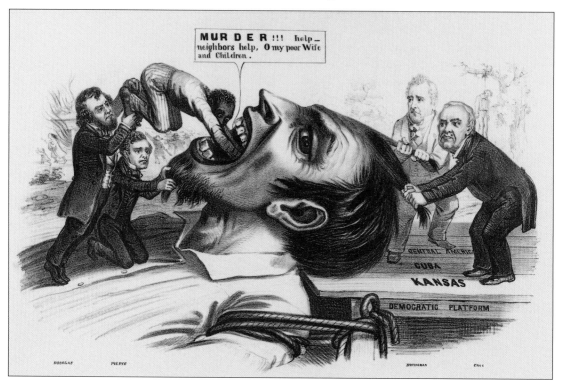

This 1856 cartoon blames the Democrats for the violence overspreading Bloody Kansas. Here, presidential nominee James Buchanan and Sen. Lewis Cass restrain a Free Soiler (bound to the "Democratic Platform"), while Sen. Stephen A. Douglas and Pres. Franklin Pierce force a slave down his throat.

the territories, to be enforced by federal officials. In 1860, Abraham Lincoln (whom Douglas had defeated in 1858) ran for president as a Republican. He proclaimed that the slave code demand confirmed the aim of the slaveholders to be the eventual nationalization of their odious peculiar institution. Lincoln's candidacy galvanized northern antislavery opinion and shocked proslavery southerners to the point where, upon Lincoln's election, they severed the Union. Thereafter, following a civil war of unanticipated duration and ferocity, capped by Lincoln's martyrdom, passage of the Thirteenth and Fourteenth Amendments rendered *Dred Scott v. Sandford* null and void.

D RED SCOTT DID NOT LIVE to see the denouement of the drama in which he played so central a part, but he did finally experience freedom. Shortly after March 6, 1857, the sons of Peter Blow purchased the Scotts from Mrs. Emerson and set them free. For nine months, Dred Scott enjoyed a certain celebrity in antislavery circles, until he died of consumption in St. Louis on February 17, 1858.

Roger Taney, though, did live long enough to see his decision backfire, placing in motion forces that would settle the slavery question exactly as he had hoped it would not be settled. If Scott lived to enjoy a touch of renown, Taney lived to endure vilification. And even after the ancient chief justice died in 1864, Sen. Charles Sumner of Massachusetts and his fellow Radical Republicans continued the personal attacks, declaring that Taney had "degraded the judiciary of the country, and degraded the age." Sumner had no doubt but that "the name of Taney is to be hooted down the page[s] of history."

Actually, Taney's fate has not been quite so risible. Legal scholars have found much to praise in his long career on the bench, not least his decisions on economic matters. But in the end, his name is inextricable from *Dred Scott* and the shame of March 6. Even conservative jurists and scholars have come to regard *Dred Scott* as the Court's most regrettable decision of the nineteenth century, if not of all time. Subsequent history will no doubt provide future scholars with similar examples of politics overcoming jurisprudence, and other names will be, like Taney's, hooted down through history. But none is likely to surpass Taney's in ignominy. He will be forever stained by the ruling that one current Supreme Court justice—interestingly enough, Antonin Scalia—has ridiculed as the paragon of judicial error, an aggressive decision that left the Court "covered with dishonor and deprived of legitimacy."

★ ★ ★

After Taney's death, northern congressmen arose en masse to oppose a pro forma appropriation of funds for the completion of the chief justice's official bust. Nevertheless, the marble bust (shown here) was eventually completed by sculptor Horace Stone.

Lewisville take possession of London
Hights if Practicable by Friday Mornin
Keeps from on his left and the road
between the Eva of mountain and the
Potomac on his right. He will as far
as practicable Cooperate with Gen McLaw
& Genl Jackson in intercepting the retreat
of the Enemy.

VII Gen D. H. Hill's division will form
the rear guard of the army pursuing
the road taken by the main body of the
Army. The reserve artillery Ordnance
and supply trains will precede Gen
Hill

VIII Gen Stuart will detach a squad
of Cavalry to accompany the Commands of Gen
Longstreet Jackson and McLaws and with the main body of the
Cavalry will cover the route of the army & bring up all stragglers
that may have been left behind.

IX The commands of Gen Jackson McLaws & Walker after accom
plishing the objects for which they have been detached will join the
main body of the army at Boonsboro or Hagerstown

X Each Regiment on the march will habitually carry its
axes in the Regimental ordnance waggons for use
of the men at their encampments to procure wood

By Command of Gen R. E. Lee

R. H. Chilton
A. A. General

for Gen D. H. Hill
Maj Gen D. H. Hill
Comdg division

SEPTEMBER 13, 1862

THE LOST ORDERS

BY JAMES McPHERSON

Saturday, September 13, 1862, was far from an ordinary late-summer day for Cpl. Barton W. Mitchell of the Twenty-seventh Indiana Volunteer Infantry. Early that morning, his regiment had been ordered to stack arms and take a break in a meadow just east of Frederick, Maryland. The Twenty-seventh was part of the XII Corps of the Army of the Potomac. Its soldiers had experienced hard fighting and marching that summer, though they had not been present two weeks earlier at the second battle of Bull Run (or Manassas, as the Confederates called it). The Army of the Potomac under Maj. Gen. George B. McClellan was now probing toward the South Mountain gaps in western Maryland, looking for Gen. Robert E. Lee's Army of Northern Virginia. Lee had invaded Maryland a week earlier in a climactic effort to conquer a peace, and part of his army had camped four days earlier in the very field where Corporal

Mitchell and his buddy, Sgt. John M. Bloss, flopped down in the welcome shade of trees along a fence line. September 13 was a sultry day, and the two tired soldiers hoped to catch forty winks before their regiment resumed its march. As he turned over, however, Mitchell noticed a bulky envelope lying in some tall grass nearby. Curious, he picked it up and discovered inside a sheet of paper wrapped around three cigars. As Bloss went off to hunt for a match, Mitchell noticed that the paper contained writing under the heading "Headquarters, Army of Northern Virginia, Special Orders, No. 191" and was dated September 9. This caught his surprised attention, and his eyes grew wider as he read through the orders studded with names that Northern soldiers knew all too well—Jackson, Longstreet, Stuart—and signed "R. H. Chilton, Assist. Adj.-Gen. By command of Gen. R. E. Lee."

"As I read, each line became more interesting," Mitchell said later. "I forgot those cigars." Bloss and Mitchell took the document to their captain, who excitedly passed it on to his regimental commander, who took it to Col. Samuel E. Pittman, division headquarters

AT LEFT: *This is the sheet of paper that Corporal Mitchell found wrapped around three cigars in a meadow near Frederick, Maryland.*

ABOVE: *A forage cap of the sort worn by Union troops at Antietam.*

Robert Hall Chilton
was graduated forty-eighth in the fifty-member West Point Class of 1837. During the Mexican War, his career received an important boost at Buena Vista, where he valiantly carried to safety the wounded Jefferson Davis, then a colonel of Mississippi volunteers. Following Fort Sumter, Chilton resigned his commission and joined the Confederate army with the rank of lieutenant colonel. As Lee's adjutant, he would have had duties similar to those carried out by a CEO's assistant in today's corporate business world.

adjutant. By an extraordinary coincidence, Pittman had known R. H. Chilton in the prewar U.S. Army and recognized his handwriting. The orders *were* genuine. Pittman rushed to McClellan's headquarters and showed him the paper. According to one report, the Union commander exclaimed after reading Lee's orders, "Now I know what to do!" In a telegram to Pres. Abraham Lincoln dated noon on September 13, McClellan reported, "I think Lee has made a gross mistake, and that he will be severely punished for it…. I have all the plans of the rebels, and will catch them in their own trap."

McClellan's elation proved to be overly optimistic, in part because his own movements in response to this remarkable windfall were characteristically slow and cautious. Nevertheless, Maj. Walter J. Taylor of Lee's staff referred after the war to the significance of these lost orders: "The God of battles alone knows what would have occurred but for the singular accident mentioned; it is useless to speculate on this point, but certainly the loss of this battle-order constitutes one of the pivots on which turned the event of the war."

By "the event of the war," Taylor meant the battle of Antietam (called Sharpsburg by the South), which occurred four days later. The loss and finding and verification of Lee's orders certainly was a "singular accident"; the odds against such a chain of coincidences occurring must have been a million to one. Yet it did occur, and this sequence of events became, according to Taylor, "one of the pivots" on which both the battle and the war turned. What *were* these orders? How were they lost? Why were they so important?

T O ANSWER THESE QUESTIONS, we must turn back the clock several months. During the first half of 1862, Union arms had won a string of victories along the Atlantic and Gulf Coasts as well as in the river systems of Tennessee, Mississippi, and Louisiana. In addition, the North had consolidated its control of Maryland, Kentucky, Missouri, and western Virginia (soon to become the new state of West Virginia). In eastern Virginia, the Army of the Potomac had advanced up the peninsula between the York and James Rivers to within six miles of Richmond. By June 1862, the days of the Confederacy seemed numbered.

But that month, Robert E. Lee assumed command of the Army of Northern Virginia and Braxton Bragg took over the Army of Tennessee. Both men immediately launched counteroffensives that, within three months, took their armies from imminent defeat to imminent success, with Bragg invading Kentucky and Lee crossing the Potomac into

Maryland after winning major victories in the Seven Days' Campaign (June 25–July 1) and at Second Manassas (August 29–30). This startling reversal of momentum caused Northern morale to plummet. "The feeling of despondency is very great," one friend of McClellan wrote after the Seven Days' battles. Reacting to this decline in spirits, Lincoln lamented, "It seems unreasonable that a series of successes, extending through half a year, and clearing more than a hundred thousand square miles of country, should help us so little, while a single half-defeat [the Seven Days' Campaign] should hurt us so much."

Unreasonable or not, it was a fact. The peace wing of the Democratic party stepped up its attacks on Lincoln's policy of trying to restore the Union by war. Branded disloyal Copperheads by Republicans, these Peace Democrats had long insisted that Northern armies could never conquer the South and that the government should seek an armistice and peace negotiations. Confederate military success during the summer of 1862 boosted the credibility of these arguments.

Rather than give up and negotiate a peace, however, Lincoln and the Republican Congress acted to intensify the war dramatically. In July, the president called for three hundred thousand more three-year volunteers; meanwhile, Congress passed a militia act that required the states to provide specified numbers of nine-month militia and imposed

This Federal artillery battery was photographed in June 1862 at Fair Oaks, Virginia, during the failed Peninsular Campaign.

Confederate troops march through Frederick, Maryland, on September 12, 1862. This rare image of enemy troops in Union territory was taken by a local merchant and amateur photographer named Rosenstock, a portion of whose sign can be seen at the bottom of the image.

GEORGE B. McCLELLAN

1826 – 1885

On July 27, 1861, a week after the Union army's failure at First Bull Run, Lincoln decided to remove Maj. Gen. Irvin McDowell as commander of the Division of the Potomac. The man he chose to replace McDowell was George B. McClellan, an 1846 graduate of West Point and a major general for all of two months. In a letter to his wife written the same day, McClellan displayed characteristic vanity: "I find myself in a strange & new position here—Presdt, Cabinet, Genl Scott & all deferring to me—by some strange operation of magic I seem to have become the power of the land. I almost think that were I to win some small success now I could become Dictator."

a draft to make up any deficiencies in the quotas. The same day (July 17) that Lincoln signed this militia bill, he also signed a confiscation act punishing treasonous Confederates by seizing their property, including their slaves.

Slaves constituted the principal labor force in the Southern economy. Thousands built fortifications, hauled supplies, and performed fatigue labor for Confederate armies. From the onset of the war, Radical Republicans who understood this had urged a policy of emancipation. Such a blow, they believed, would strike at the heart of the rebellion and convert the slaves' labor from a Confederate to a Union asset.

By the summer of 1862, Lincoln had come to agree with them. But he doubted the constitutionality and effectiveness of congressional confiscation, a cumbersome process that would have required proof in court that a given slaveholder had engaged in "rebellion." At the same time, he believed that, as commander in chief, he had the power during time of war to seize enemy property being used to perpetuate hostilities against the United States. Slaves were such property. Therefore, on July 22, Lincoln told his cabinet that he intended to issue an emancipation proclamation as a "military necessity, absolutely essential to the preservation of the Union. We must free the slaves or be ourselves subdued…. Decisive and extensive measures must be adopted…. The slaves [are] undoubtedly an element of strength to those who [have] their service, and we must decide whether that element should be with us or

A pair of Union field binoculars.

against us." Most of the cabinet agreed, but Secretary of State William H. Seward advised postponement of the edict "until you can give it to the country supported by military success." Otherwise, Seward argued, the world might view the president's proclamation "as the last measure of an exhausted government, a cry for help…our last *shriek* on the retreat."

This advice persuaded Lincoln to await a more propitious moment, but when that moment might come was anyone's guess. With the Confederate invasions of Maryland and Kentucky that fall, Northern morale fell even lower. "The nation is rapidly sinking just now," New York lawyer George Templeton Strong wrote in early September. "Stonewall Jackson (our national bugaboo) about to invade Maryland, 40,000 strong. General advance of the rebel line threatening our hold on Missouri and

Kentucky…. Disgust with our present government is certainly universal."

Democrats hoped to capitalize on this disgust in the November congressional elections, and Republicans feared the prospect. "After a year and a half of trial," wrote one, "and a pouring out of blood and treasure, and the maiming and death of thousands, we have made no sensible progress in putting down the rebellion…and the people are desirous of some change." The Republican majority in the House was vulnerable. Although there were 105 Republicans to just 43 Democrats, 30 other seats belonged to border-state Unionists who sometimes voted with the Democrats. Thus, even the normal loss of seats in an off-year election might endanger the Republican majority—and 1862 was scarcely a normal year. With Confederate invaders in two border states ripe for the plucking and Lee threatening Pennsylvania, Democrats seemed likely to gain control of the House with their platform of an armistice and peace negotiations. Such an outcome, Lincoln knew, would cripple the Northern war effort.

Black refugees in Virginia ford the Rappahannock River during the summer of 1862. Once the Union began conducting military operations in the South, it became commonplace for runaway slaves to attach themselves to Union forces moving through a region.

R OBERT E. LEE WAS ALSO WELL AWARE of the Northern political situation. It was one of the factors that had prompted his decision to go ahead with the invasion of Maryland despite the poor physical condition of his army after ten weeks of constant marching and fighting that had produced thirty-five thousand Confederate casualties and thousands more stragglers. "The present posture of affairs," Lee wrote Confederate president Jefferson Davis on September 8 from his headquarters near Frederick, "places it in [our] power…to propose [to the U.S. government] the recognition of our independence." Such a "proposal of peace," Lee declared, "would enable the people of the United States to determine at their coming elections whether they will support those who favor a prolongation of the war, or those who wish to bring it to a termination."

Henry John Temple, the third viscount Palmerston, became Britain's prime minister in 1855. This etching (left) was created from the last photograph ever taken of him. The photograph of Foreign Secretary John Russell (right) was taken sometime between Palmerston's death in 1865 and Russell's own in 1878.

Lee didn't mention the foreign policy implications of his invasion, though these were considerable as well. Newspapers in the North and South, as well as in Britain, were full of rumors and reports of imminent British and French intervention to end the American war. At the very least, it was believed, these two nations would soon be granting diplomatic recognition to the Confederacy. The Union naval blockade of the Confederate coastline had interrupted cotton exports to Europe, shutting down textile factories and throwing thousands out of work in Britain and France. An end to the fighting would reopen foreign trade and bring a renewed flow of cotton from the South. Beyond these commercial reasons, powerful leaders and portions of the public in both countries sympathized with the South. When news of the Seven Days' battles reached Paris, for example, Emperor Napoleon III instructed his foreign minister, *"Demandez au gouvernement anglais s'il ne croit pas le moment venu de reconnaître le Sud."*

B RITISH SENTIMENT ALSO SEEMED to be moving in this direction. The U.S. consul in Liverpool reported that "we are in more danger of intervention than we have been at any previous period…. They are all against us and would rejoice at our downfall." The Confederate envoy in London, James Mason, anticipated "intervention speedily in some form." News of Second Manassas and the invasions of Maryland and Kentucky strengthened the Confederate cause abroad. Early that fall at Newcastle, Britain's chancellor of the exchequer gave a speech in which he declared that "Jefferson Davis and other leaders have made an army; they are making, it appears, a navy; and they have made what is more than either; they have made a nation."

More cautiously, the British prime minister, Viscount Palmerston, and his foreign secretary, John Russell, discussed a plan under which

THE COPPERHEADS

Why the Peace Democrats who opposed Lincoln's war policy were called Copperheads is a matter of some speculation. It may have been because they wore in their lapels Indian heads cut from copper pennies. It may also have been because some Peace Democrats in the Midwest wore the pennies around their necks to show their preference for hard money. In either case, Republicans certainly considered them venomous and disposed to strike without warning.

Britain and France would offer mediation to end the war on the basis of Confederate independence—if Lee's invasion of Maryland brought another Confederate victory. Union forces "got a complete smashing" at Second Bull Run, wrote Palmerston to Russell on September 14, "and it seems not altogether unlikely that still greater disasters await them, and that even Washington or Baltimore may fall into the hands of the Confederates. If this should happen, would it not be time for us to consider whether in such a state of things England and France might not address the contending parties and recommend an arrangement on the basis of separation?" Russell concurred and added that if the North refused the offer of mediation, "we ought ourselves to recognize the Southern States as an independent State."

U.S. minister to Great Britain Charles Frances Adams realized that he couldn't stop the construction of Confederate ships by British shipyards, but he did quietly gather evidence for a future tribunal. One piece was this photograph of the steamship Old Dominion *being refitted as a blockade-runner.*

Northern leaders were certainly alarmed by the political and diplomatic dangers provoked by Lee's invasion, but even more pressing was the military crisis. The Union force that had lost Second Bull Run was an ill-matched amalgam of troops from Maj. Gen. John Pope's Army of Virginia, Maj. Gen. Ambrose Burnside's IX Corps (transferred from North Carolina), and parts of McClellan's Army of the Potomac (transferred from the failed Peninsular Campaign). McClellan disliked Pope and was sulking because he had been forced to withdraw from the peninsula. This caused him to drag his feet when ordered to send troops to Pope's aid and also influenced the conduct of his subordinates. Two of his strongest corps, for example, although within hearing of the guns along Bull Run, never made it to the battlefield.

This photograph, taken shortly after the battle, shows the principal street in the crossroads hamlet of Sharpsburg, Maryland.

ROBERT E. LEE

1807 – 1870

Virginian Robert E. Lee was an exemplary product of the Southern aristocracy's proud military tradition. In 1829, he was graduated from West Point second in his class (as McClellan would be in 1846), and he served with distinction in the Mexican War, entering Mexico City with Winfield Scott in 1847. During the secession crisis, he declined an offer from Scott, then the army's general in chief, to become the Union's chief field commander. Instead, he resigned his commission and joined the Confederacy.

Lincoln considered McClellan's behavior "unpardonable," and a majority of the cabinet wanted him to cashier the general. But Lincoln also recognized McClellan's organizational skills and the remarkable hold he had on the affections of the army, which had been demoralized by its recent defeats. The president therefore gave McClellan command of all Union troops in the theater with instructions to meld them into the Army of the Potomac and move out to fight the invaders. To those cabinet members who protested, Lincoln conceded that McClellan had "acted badly in this matter," but "he has the Army with him…. We must use what tools we have. There is no man in the Army who can lick these troops of ours into shape half as well as he."

E VENTS CONFIRMED LINCOLN'S JUDGMENT. A junior officer wrote that when the soldiers learned of McClellan's appointment to command the combined forces in and around Washington, "from extreme sadness we passed in a twinkling to a delirium of delight…. Men threw their caps in the air, and danced and frolicked like schoolboys…. The effect of this man's presence upon the Army of the Potomac…was electrical." McClellan indeed reorganized the army and licked it into shape in a strikingly short time. But then he reverted to his wonted caution and tendency to overestimate the strength of his enemy. He clamored for reinforcements, particularly the twelve thousand troops garrisoned at Harpers Ferry, but General in Chief Henry W. Halleck refused to release these men.

Halleck's refusal created a risky opening for Lee. The Harpers Ferry garrison threatened his line of supply through the Shenandoah Valley, but it was not nearly strong enough to withstand the focused might of his Army of Northern Virginia. So on September 9, Lee dictated those fateful Special Orders No. 191, which sent nearly two-thirds of his army to Harpers Ferry in three widely separated columns under the overall command of Stonewall Jackson. The

opportunity: a large supply of artillery, rifles, ammunition, provisions, shoes, and clothing for his ragged, shoeless, hungry troops. The problem: During the three to five days it would take to complete the operation, McClellan might get between his columns and destroy them in detail.

Yet two of Lee's hallmarks as a commander were his ability to judge an opponent's qualities and his willingness to take risks. He had twice before divided his army in the face of the enemy and twice had gotten away with it. Lee estimated McClellan to be "an able general but a very cautious one. His army is in a very demoralized and chaotic condition and will not be prepared for offensive operations—or he will not think it so—for three or four weeks. Before that time I hope to be on the Susquehanna."

Yet, as fortune would have it, on September 13 Corporal Mitchell's sharp eyes changed everything. We will never know how the orders, one of eight copies sent to various division commanders, were lost. They probably fell out of the pocket of a careless staff officer in Maj. Gen. Daniel Harvey Hill's division. In any case, these orders gave McClellan a good idea of the location of the scattered enemy units. Although he advanced with caution, the Union commander moved much faster than Lee had expected.

AT LEFT: *By 1887 when this Kurz & Allison chromolithograph was published, the fighting at Burnside Bridge had become in the popular imagination a glorious event.*

This map shows the disposition of the Union and Confederate forces around Sharpsburg on September 17, the day that they fought the battle of Antietam.

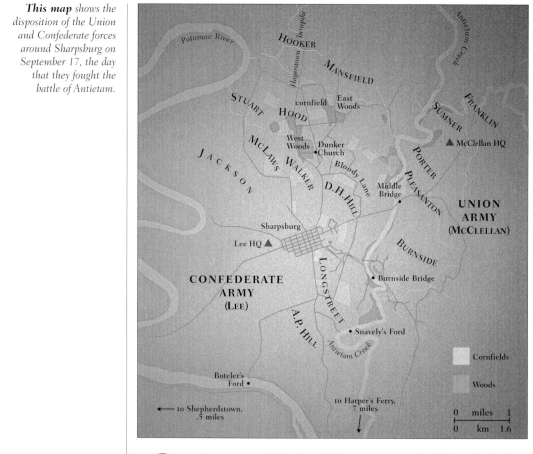

These are the sort of small-arms projectiles that would have been used by the armies at Antietam.

O N SEPTEMBER 14, three Union corps smashed through thinly defended gaps in the South Mountain range west of Frederick, endangering the rear of one of the Confederate divisions besieging Harpers Ferry. Lee prepared new orders for a retreat to Virginia but changed his mind when a dispatch came from Jackson stating that he would capture Harpers Ferry the next day. Jackson proved to be as good as his word, and after reducing the Northern garrison he marched to rejoin Lee and reunite the Army of Northern Virginia. Meanwhile, Lee, who had come north for a showdown battle, decided to stay and fight McClellan, even though his forty thousand men were outnumbered by seventy-five thousand Union troops. (For his part, McClellan continued to believe that *he* was the one outnumbered.) With the return of Jackson's detachment, Lee deployed his Army of Northern Virginia along a series of ridges east of the village of Sharpsburg, Maryland, with its left flank on the Potomac and its right on Antietam Creek.

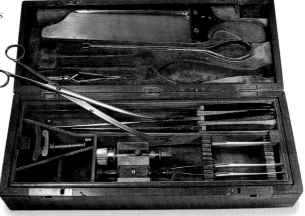

After taking the time to deploy his own troops and artillery deliberately (and thus giving Lee the time to consolidate most of his forces), McClellan attacked at dawn on September 17. His plan called for a one-two punch against the Confederate left and right, followed by an advance of reserves through whatever holes were created in the Southern lines. The Union attacks were poorly coordinated, however, enabling Lee to shift troops as needed from quiet sectors to threatened points. During the early-morning hours, assaults by six Union divisions against portions of six Confederate divisions under Jackson's command were contained on the Confederate left by vicious fighting in locales that became forever famous: the Cornfield, the West Woods, Dunkard Church. Meanwhile, on the Confederate right, Burnside tried to force his corps across a bridge over the Antietam rather than simply ford that shallow stream. In the center at midday, two Union divisions broke through Confederate defenses along a sunken farm road known thereafter as Bloody Lane, but McClellan failed to exploit this success because he feared Lee's

This instrument case was carried by a Union army surgeon in the Civil War. Soft lead .58-caliber bullets generally made rather large holes and, more often than not, shattered bones. With antiseptic surgery still years away, the amputation of limbs was usually the only way to save an injured man's life. Saws were used to create a clean cut that could be sealed quickly and relatively cleanly. An experienced surgeon, called on to perform hundreds of amputations in a day, could relieve a soldier of a limb in as little as two minutes.

"THERE IS NOT A BARN, OR FARMHOUSE, OR STORE, OR CHURCH, OR SCHOOLHOUSE, BETWEEN... SHARPSBURG AND SMOKETOWN THAT IS NOT GORGED WITH WOUNDED—REBEL AND UNION."

—*U.S. Sanitary Commission report, September 1862*—

nonexistent reserves. Burnside finally forced his way across the bridge in the early afternoon and advanced toward Sharpsburg, threatening Lee's rear and his retreat route across the Potomac. But about 4 P.M., Maj. Gen. A. P. Hill's division, which had remained at Harpers Ferry to mop up after the surrender, arrived after a forced march and hit Burnside's flank, halting the Union advance.

The sun then set on the deadliest single day of the Civil War—indeed, in all American history. Some six thousand men lay dead or dying, and another sixteen thousand were wounded. The next day, despite

OVERLEAF:

On October 2, 1862, *Lincoln traveled to the headquarters of the Army of the Potomac to confer with McClellan. This photograph was taken on the second day of the conference. McClellan is the officer facing the president.*

FURTHER READING

★ James M. McPherson, *Battle Cry of Freedom: The Civil War Era* (1988)

★ Stephen W. Sears, *Landscape Turned Red: The Battle of Antietam* (1983)

receiving his sought-after reinforcements, McClellan chose not to renew the attack, and that night Lee retreated to Virginia. Although McClellan failed to follow up, he nevertheless claimed a victory.

And indeed the battle of Antietam was a victory, strategically if not tactically, as President Lincoln confirmed on September 22, when he called a special meeting of his cabinet to announce that "the time has come" to issue a preliminary Emancipation Proclamation. "The action of the army against the rebels has not been quite what I should have best liked." Nevertheless, he said, Antietam was the victory he had been waiting for. On the following day, his proclamation was published throughout the North, and it has since echoed down the ages. It declared that in all states still in rebellion on January 1, 1863, the slaves in those states "shall be then, thenceforward, and forever free."

Meanwhile, news of Antietam traveled by ship across the Atlantic (there was no functioning undersea cable yet). "These last battles in Maryland have rather set the North up again," Prime Minister Palmerston wrote to Foreign Secretary Russell in early October. "The whole matter is full of difficulty, and can only be cleared up by some more decided events between the contending armies…. I am very much come back to our original view that we must continue to be lookers-on till the war shall have taken a more decided turn."

A month after this correspondence between Palmerston and Russell, congressional elections were held across the North. Antietam had drawn much of the sting from the antiwar Democrats, and although their party did make some gains, Republicans retained control of the House by a comfortable margin. Even so, a shift of an average of 1 percent of the vote in sixteen districts in nine states would have given the Democrats a 91–86 edge in the next House (with nine border-state Unionists filling out its ranks). A Confederate success at Antietam would surely have produced that margin and more.

No one can say what might have happened had Corporal Mitchell not noticed that envelope lying in the grass on September 13. Lee would probably have been granted more time and opportunity to achieve the goals of his invasion. Britain and France might have recognized the Confederacy, Democrats might have won control of the House, and Lincoln might have kept the Emancipation Proclamation in his drawer—all with incalculable consequences. Yet Mitchell did find the orders, and though he and Bloss were both wounded at Antietam, they survived to witness Union victory in a war whose outcome may have hinged, as Lee's adjutant believed, on the "pivot" of their discovery.

★ ★ ★

Columbia, on Monday the fourth day of December, one thousand eight hundred and sixty-five.

Joint Resolution proposing an amendment to the Constitution of the United States.

Be it resolved by the Senate and House of Representatives of the United States of America in Congress assembled, (two-thirds of both Houses concurring,) That the following article be proposed to the legislatures of the several States as an amendment to the Constitution of the United States, which, when ratified by three-fourths of said legislatures, shall be valid as part of the Constitution, namely:

Article XIV.

Section 1. All persons born or naturalized in the United States, and subject to the jurisdiction thereof, are citizens of the United States and of the State wherein they reside. No State shall make or enforce any law which shall abridge the privileges or immunities of citizens of the United States; nor shall any State deprive any person of life, liberty, or property, without due process of law; nor deny to any person within its jurisdiction the equal protection of the laws.

Section 2. Representatives shall be apportioned among the several States according to their respective numbers, counting the whole number of persons in each State, excluding Indians not taxed. But when the right to vote at any election for the choice of electors for President and Vice President of the United States, Representatives in Congress, the Executive and Judicial officers of a State, or the members of the Legislature thereof, is denied to any of the male inhabitants of such State, being twenty-one years of age, and citizens of the United States, or in any way abridged, except for participation in rebellion, or other crime, the basis of representation therein shall be reduced in the proportion which

JUNE 13, 1866

EQUALITY BEFORE THE LAW

BY ERIC FONER

O N JUNE 13, 1866, Thaddeus Stevens, the majority floor leader in the House of Representatives and the nation's most prominent Radical Republican, rose to address his congressional colleagues. His subject was the Fourteenth Amendment to the Constitution— which, after months of deliberation and innumerable drafts and redrafts, was about to receive final approval by Congress. Its purpose was to secure the fruits of Union victory in the Civil War by guaranteeing equal civil rights for the freed slaves and loyal governments in the South.

Born during George Washington's administration, Stevens had enjoyed a public career that embodied, as much as anyone's, the struggle against the "Slave Power" and for equal rights for black Americans. In 1837, as a delegate to Pennsylvania's constitutional convention, he had refused to sign the state's new frame of government because it abrogated the right

of African Americans to vote. As a member of Congress during the 1850s, he had fought against the expansion of slavery and, during the secession crisis, opposed compromise with the South. Once the Civil War began, he was among the first to advocate the emancipation of slaves and the enrollment of black soldiers.

During the era of Reconstruction that followed the war, Stevens insisted that the South was a "conquered province," which Congress could govern as it saw fit. He was the most prominent advocate, for example, of distributing land to former slaves so that they might have an economic foundation for their freedom. Like other Radicals, he believed that Reconstruction was a golden opportunity to purge the nation of the legacy of slavery and create a society whose citizens enjoyed equal civil and political rights, secured by a powerful and beneficent national government. "The whole fabric of southern society must be changed," he declared, "and never can it be done, if this opportunity be lost." Stevens's speech on June 13 was an eloquent statement of this political creed:

AT LEFT: *The text of the Fourteenth Amendment approved by the House of Representatives on June 13, 1866.*

ABOVE: *This 1868 Harper's Weekly cartoon poked fun at the president's intransigence with regard to Reconstruction.*

THADDEUS STEVENS

1792 – 1868

For generations, Thaddeus Stevens was vilified as the evil genius who had wrecked Andrew Johnson's benevolent plans for Reconstruction and turned the South over to the ravages of "black rule." More recent scholarship, though, has treated him more kindly. Born with a clubfoot (then considered a mark of evil), Stevens (shown here in a photograph taken by Mathew Brady around 1858) felt at home among dissenters and outsiders of many sorts, including the Amish who populated the area of Pennsylvania in which he lived. He never married but lived for years with a black housekeeper, choosing neither to confirm nor deny long-standing rumors about their relationship. A master of parliamentary tactics, he was respected in the House for his honesty and his imperviousness to criticism and flattery.

In my youth, in my manhood, in my old age, I had fondly dreamed that when any fortunate chance should have broken up for awhile the foundation of our institutions, and released us from obligations the most tyrannical that ever man imposed in the name of freedom, that the intelligent, pure and just men of this Republic…would have so remodeled all our institutions as to have freed them from every vestige of human oppression, of inequality of rights, of the recognized degradation of the poor, and the superior caste of the rich…. This bright dream has vanished [quoting Shakespeare's The Tempest] "like the baseless fabric of a dream." I find that we shall be obliged to be content with patching up the worst portions of the ancient edifice, and leaving it, in many of its parts, to be swept through by the…storms of despotism. Do you inquire why, holding these views and possessing some will of my own, I accept so imperfect a proposition? I answer, because I live among men and not among angels.

A few moments later, the Fourteenth Amendment was approved by the House. The result was never in doubt because, with the southern states still unrepresented, the Republican party commanded an overwhelming majority. The final vote was 120–32, well above the required two-thirds majority. Three days later, having been approved by the Senate shortly before the House vote, the amendment was sent to the states for ratification. It became part of the Constitution on July 28, 1868.

THE FOURTEENTH AMENDMENT prohibited the states from abridging the equality before the law of American citizens, provided for a reduction in representation in Congress should any state deprive male citizens of the right to vote, excluded Confederates who had previously taken a constitutional oath from holding state or federal office, and prohibited payment of the Confederate debt. It was one of the most important lasting consequences of the immense changes produced by the Civil War and the subsequent political crisis of Reconstruction, especially the struggle between the president and Congress over control of Reconstruction policy.

In late May 1865, six weeks after he succeeded the martyred Abraham Lincoln, Pres. Andrew Johnson announced his plan for reuniting the nation, launching the era of presidential Reconstruction. Although a staunch Unionist from Tennessee, Johnson was an inveterate racist and a firm defender of states' rights. The essentials of his Reconstruction plan allowed white southerners to establish new state governments—which were required by Johnson to abolish slavery, repudiate secession, and abrogate the Confederate debt but otherwise accorded a free hand in controlling local affairs. When these new governments quickly enacted the repressive Black Codes, most northern Republicans turned against the president. As one observer put it, the Black Codes seemed designed to "restore all of slavery but its name." Meanwhile, the election of "rebels" to leading offices in the South and reports of violence directed against both freed people and northern visitors reinforced the conviction that Johnson's plan played into the hands of the southern Democrats.

When the Thirty-ninth Congress (elected in November 1864) finally assembled in December 1865, Radical Republicans, led by Stevens, called for abrogation of the Johnson-authorized state governments and the establishment of new ones based on equality before the law and universal manhood suffrage. The Radicals, however, didn't control the Republican party. Occupying the political middle ground was the moderate Republican majority, led in Congress by Sen. Lyman Trumbull of Illinois and Sen. John Sherman of Ohio. Unenthusiastic about black suffrage—which they viewed as a political liability in the North and an experiment whose outcome couldn't be predicted in the South—Trumbull, Sherman, and their allies were nonetheless fully committed to ensuring "loyal" governments in the former states of the Confederacy and protecting the elementary rights of freed slaves in a society organized on the basis of free labor rather than slavery. Eventually, however, Johnson's policies, and the actions of the state governments created under his supervision, drove them into the Radicals' arms, uniting the entire Republican party against the president.

Much of the ensuing debate over Reconstruction revolved around the problem, as Trumbull put it, of defining "what slavery is and what liberty is." The Civil War had greatly enhanced the power of the national state. Especially because of the service of two hundred thousand black men in the Union army and navy, the war had also put the question of black citizenship on the national agenda. By early 1866, moderates had concluded that equality before the law—enforced, if necessary, by national authority—had become an inevitable consequence of emancipation and a condition for restoring the South to full participation in the Union. These principles

This December 9, 1865, Harper's Weekly *cartoon illustrates the refusal of the clerk of the House (at Thaddeus Stevens's request) to seat new members sent by the former states of the Confederacy.*

Alexander Stephens *of Georgia, once the Confederate vice president, was among those former rebels sent to Congress in 1865 by reactionary southern legislatures authorized under President Johnson's original Reconstruction plan.*

were embodied in the Civil Rights Act of 1866, a precursor to the Fourteenth Amendment that outlined the rights all Americans were to enjoy regardless of race. These included the rights to make contracts, bring lawsuits, and enjoy equal protection of the security of person and property. Johnson's veto of this measure and its repassage by Congress in April 1866 marked the final breach between the president and the Republican party. It was the first time in American history that a significant piece of legislation became law over a president's veto.

BEYOND IMPELLING congressional Republicans to devise their own Reconstruction plan, Johnson's intransigence persuaded them to write their understanding of the consequences of the Civil War into the Constitution, there to be secure from shifting electoral majorities. The result was the Fourteenth Amendment, adopted by Congress after months of committee deliberations and a series of alterations on the House and Senate floors. Some Republicans wished to disqualify leading Confederates from voting; others wanted to include both "universal amnesty" for "rebels" and "universal suffrage" for black men. But these proposals failed to win the support of most Republicans. In its final form, the amendment was a compromise on which all Republicans could unite.

This process of compromise, however, as Stevens's June 13 speech suggests, resulted in a text that didn't fully satisfy the Radicals. The Fourteenth Amendment, as enacted, didn't abolish existing state governments in the South, nor did it guarantee blacks the right to vote; indeed, in one section, it offered each southern state, once readmitted to the Union, the alternative of allowing black men to vote and retaining the state's full representation in Congress or continuing to disenfranchise blacks and suffering a loss of representation proportionate to the black percentage of the state population. (No penalty applied, however, when women were denied the right to vote, an omission that led many advocates of women's rights to oppose ratification of the amendment.)

The Fourteenth Amendment had five sections in all, three of which have little importance today—those barring Confederates from office, dealing with the Confederate debt, and reducing a state's representation in Congress if men are denied the right to vote. (This last provision was never enforced, even during the decades when southern states disenfranchised most black voters.) Nonetheless, the Fourteenth Amendment has since become, after the Bill of Rights, the most important constitutional change in the nation's history. Its heart was

ANDREW JOHNSON

1808 – 1875

During the secession crisis, Andrew Johnson of Tennessee was the only senator from a seceding state who remained loyal to the Union—but that was not for lack of love of the South. He simply loved the Constitution (and hated the southern planter aristocracy) more. President Lincoln rewarded his loyalty in March 1862 when he appointed Johnson military governor of Tennessee and again in 1864 when he made Johnson, a Democrat, his running mate on a unity presidential ticket. By that time, Johnson had begun to champion emancipation as a necessary war measure, but he never relinquished his extremely racist views and, as president, showed little concern for the fate of the freed people.

Section 1, which declared that all persons born or naturalized in the United States were both national and state citizens. Section 1 also prohibited states from abridging the "privileges and immunities of citizens"; depriving them "of life, liberty, or property without due process of law"; and denying them "equal protection of the laws." It thus established, as Thaddeus Stevens told the House, the principle that state laws "shall operate equally upon all." Later he added, "I can hardly believe that any person can be found who will not admit that...[it] is just."

In clothing with constitutional authority the principle that equality before the law, regardless of race, could and should be enforced by the national government, the Fourteenth

Amendment permanently transformed the definition of American citizenship and refashioned relations between the federal government and the states as well as those between individual Americans and the nation. We live today in a legal and constitutional system shaped profoundly by the Fourteenth Amendment.

D URING THE 1866 CONGRESSIONAL ELECTIONS, ratification of the Fourteenth Amendment became the central issue of the campaign. That fall, the president embarked on an unprecedented speaking trip across the North, known as the "swing around the circle." Its primary purpose was to drum up support for candidates associated with Johnson's National Union party—mostly northern Democrats who supported the president's Reconstruction policies. Yet Johnson also took the opportunity to rally whatever opposition to ratification he could. Again and again, he called for reconciliation between North and South, insisting that suffrage requirements and citizens' rights should be left to the states. Johnson also engaged in impromptu debates with hecklers, intimating that Stevens and the other Radicals were traitors. For their part, Republicans defended the amendment as necessary to secure the emancipation of the slaves and prevent Confederates from controlling the South.

The focus of the 1866 midterm campaign was the widening breach between the president and Congress. During his "swing around the circle," Johnson delivered a series of ill-considered speeches in which he blamed the Radicals for recent racial violence in the South. The speeches made him look foolish and contributed to the defeat of congressional candidates who supported his Reconstruction plan.

This March 1868 woodcut shows the House of Representatives in session.

The outcome of the midterm elections was continued Republican dominance in Congress and a clear mandate for Stevens and the Radicals. Johnson, however, continued his intransigent opposition to the amendment, urging southern legislatures to refuse to ratify it. And during the winter of 1866–1867, every southern state, except Tennessee, indeed rejected the amendment. With southern state governments thus having thoroughly discredited themselves in the eyes of nearly all Republicans, moderate and radical alike, party leaders concluded that only by establishing entirely new governments in the South could Reconstruction be accomplished. In March 1867, on the penultimate day of its postelection session, the Thirty-ninth Congress passed, over Johnson's veto, the Reconstruction Act of 1867. This gave the right to vote to black men in the South and launched the short-lived period of Radical Reconstruction during which, for the first time in American history, a genuine interracial democracy flourished. In March 1870, the Fifteenth Amendment, prohibiting any state from depriving citizens of the right to vote because of race, became part of the Constitution. What Republican leader Carl Schurz called "the great Constitutional revolution" of Reconstruction was complete. "Nothing in all history," exulted abolitionist William Lloyd Garrison, equaled "this wonderful…transformation of four million human beings from…the auction-block to the ballot-box."

I N GENERAL, THE ACTS AND AMENDMENTS of Reconstruction reflected the intersection of two products of the Civil War era: the newly empowered national state and the idea of a national citizenry enjoying equality before the law. In fact, rather than embodying a threat to liberty (as Jefferson had perceived it), the federal government had now become "the custodian of freedom," declared Charles Sumner, the abolitionist senator from Massachusetts. The rewriting of the Constitution during Reconstruction promoted a sense of the document's malleability and further suggested that the rights of individual citizens

CONGRESSIONAL RECONSTRUCTION

Northern voters' overwhelming repudiation of Johnson's policies in the 1866 congressional elections inaugurated the era of congressional Reconstruction. With all the seceding states (except Tennessee) having rejected the Fourteenth Amendment, Congress decided to begin Reconstruction anew, dividing the South into five military districts and setting new, more stringent requirements for states to meet before being restored to representation in Congress.

were intimately connected to federal power. This was a substantial departure from the pre–Civil War period, when disenfranchised groups were far more likely to draw inspiration from the Declaration of Independence than from the Constitution. (After all, the only mention of equality in the original Constitution came in the clause granting each state an equal number of senators.)

For example, the Bill of Rights, ratified in 1791, defined civil liberties in terms of state autonomy. Its language—"Congress shall pass no law…"—reflected the Jeffersonian belief that concentrated power was a threat to freedom. The Reconstruction amendments, however, which included the Thirteenth Amendment abolishing slavery, assumed that rights required political power to enforce them. These amendments, therefore, not only authorized the federal government to override state actions that deprived citizens of equality but also concluded with sections empowering Congress to "enforce" the amendments with "appropriate legislation." The Reconstruction amendments, especially the Fourteenth, transformed the Constitution from a document primarily concerned with federal-state relations and the rights of property into a vehicle through which members of vulnerable minorities could stake a claim to substantive freedom and seek protection against misconduct by all levels of government.

Limiting the privileges of citizenship to white men had long been intrinsic to the practice of American democracy. In 1857, in deciding *Dred Scott v. Sandford*, the Supreme Court had declared that no black person could be a citizen of the United States. Racism, federalism, a belief in limited government and local autonomy—Reconstruction challenged all these principles of nineteenth-century political culture. So deeply rooted were they, in fact, that only during an unparalleled crisis could they have been superseded, even temporarily, by the vision of an egalitarian republic embracing black Americans as well as white under the protection of the federal government. Indeed, it was precisely for this reason that the era's laws and constitutional amendments aroused such bitter opposition. The underlying principles—that the federal government possessed the power to define and protect citizens' rights, and that blacks were equal members of the body politic—were striking departures in

MENDING THE FAMILY KETTLE.

This cartoon from Frank Leslie's Illustrated Newspaper *was published on June 16, 1866, three days after the House vote on the Fourteenth Amendment. The woman holding the child is Columbia, the cartoonist's personification of the nation. "Now, Andy," she is saying, "I wish you and your boys would hurry up that job, because I want to use that kettle right away. You are all talking too much about it."*

American law. It isn't difficult to understand why President Johnson, in one of his veto messages, claimed that federal protection of African-American civil rights, together with the broad conception of national power that lay behind it, violated "all our experience as a people."

RECONSTRUCTION PROVED FRAGILE and short lived. Its end is usually dated at 1877, when federal troops were withdrawn from the South (as a consequence of the contested 1876 presidential election) and white-supremacist Democrats regained control of southern state governments. But retreat from the idea of equality was already underway prior to 1877, as traditional ideas of racism and localism reasserted themselves during the early 1870s and violence disrupted the southern Republican party. This transition accelerated after 1877, when Supreme Court interpretation of the Fourteenth Amendment increasingly eviscerated its promise of equal citizenship. Deciding the 1873 Slaughterhouse Cases, for example, the Court severely restricted the rights protected under the amendment, ruling that these comprised only those rights that owed their existence to the federal government—such as traveling on navigable waterways, running for federal office, and being protected on the high seas. Clearly, *these* rights were of limited concern to most former slaves. All other rights, the Court ruled, were derived from state, not national, authority, and with these the amendment had "nothing to do."

Next came the 1883 Civil Rights Cases, which invalidated a federal law prohibiting unequal treatment of blacks in public accommodations on the grounds that the Fourteenth Amendment barred only *legal* discrimination, not the actions of private individuals. Finally, the Court's famous 1896 decision in *Plessy v. Ferguson* decreed that state-mandated racial segregation didn't violate the Fourteenth Amendment's equal protection clause because "separate" could be equal. By the turn of the twentieth century, therefore, the states had been given carte blanche to nullify the Reconstruction amendments and civil rights laws. A new system of racial subordination was put in place in the South, centered on the elimination of black voting, racial segregation, and the severe restriction of blacks' economic opportunities. And these blatant violations of the Fourteenth and Fifteenth Amendments occurred with the acquiescence of the North, as reflected in the Supreme Court rulings.

Although Frederick Douglass had promoted suffrage for women as early as the 1848 Seneca Falls convention, his efforts during Reconstruction to secure the voting rights of freedmen caused some woman suffragists to conclude that he was colluding in their own disenfranchisement, winning the vote for black men at a cost of the vote for all women.

Meanwhile, the Court made use of the Fourteenth Amendment in a manner that Thaddeus Stevens could never have imagined—as a barrier against governmental regulation of corporate behavior. In 1886, in *Santa Clara County v. Southern Pacific Railroad*, the Court declared that a corporation was a "person" under the law and thus couldn't be deprived of the "privileges and immunities" specified in the amendment's first section. This principle underpinned a long legal era during which the Court held that "liberty of contract"—the right of corporations to operate without state interference such as regulation of working conditions, limitation of working hours, and so on—was the real intention of the Fourteenth Amendment. Not until the late 1930s did the Court abandon this liberty-of-contract jurisprudence.

This November 1866 woodcut illustrated the impasse in the nation;s capital. The Johnson caricature (left) says, "Look here! One of us has got to back." The Stevens figure responds, "Well, it ain't me that's going to do it—you bet!"

The Fourteenth Amendment's checkered history, however, is also the history of evolving American ideas about civil rights and civil liberties. During the first half of the twentieth century, the Court slowly took up the work of applying Fourteenth Amendment protections to the citizens' rights enumerated in the Bill of Rights. That is, the Court began to rule that states must respect the same civil liberties that the first ten amendments to the Constitution protect against federal intrusion. This process, called "incorporation" by legal historians, began shortly after World War I, when the Court responded to extensive censorship by wartime authorities with an opinion that obligated states under the Fourteenth Amendment to refrain from unreasonable restrictions on the freedoms of speech and of the press. Soon afterward, it invalidated state laws that required all students to attend public schools and prohibited teachers from instructing in languages other than English (measures directed against schools established by churches and immigrant groups). The amendment's guarantee of equal liberty, it declared, included the right to bring up children and practice religion free from governmental interference.

During the 1950s and 1960s, led by Chief Justice Earl Warren, the Court again turned to the Fourteenth Amendment as a source not only for the racial justice envisioned by its framers but also for a vast expansion of civil liberties for all Americans. In 1954, in the *Brown v. Board of Education* decision that overturned *Plessy*, the Warren Court ruled that state-sanctioned racial segregation violated the Fourteenth Amendment's equal protection clause because separation was inherently unequal. In subsequent decisions, it struck down state laws that sought to destroy civil rights organizations by requiring them to disclose lists of

FURTHER READING

★ Eric Foner,
The Story of American Freedom (1998)

★ Howard N. Meyer,
The Amendment That Refused to Die: The History of the Fourteenth Amendment (2000)

OPPOSITE:

OPPOSITE:

*"**Now, Andy,** take it right down," advises the bartender offering Johnson "Extract Const. Amend." in this October 27, 1866, Harper's Weekly cartoon. "More you look at it, worse you'll like it."*

their members; and in *New York Times v. Sullivan* (1964), it greatly expanded the legal protections given newspapers and other media by requiring that plaintiffs in libel suits prove that the defamatory remarks in question were made out of either malice or a "reckless disregard" for the truth. Reversing its long history of compliance with racial injustice, the Supreme Court had become by the end of the 1960s the Congress's leading ally in the struggle for racial justice.

The Warren Court continued the process of incorporation until the states were required to abide by virtually every clause in the Bill of Rights—from such literal guarantees as protection against unreasonable searches and seizures and the right to a speedy trial to inferred rights, including the right of indigent defendants to publicly appointed legal counsel. During this period, the Court struck down numerous state and local measures, including some mandating prayer in public schools, that violated the First Amendment's ban on government support for religion.

Meanwhile, generating even greater controversy, it discovered under the aegis of the Fourteenth Amendment some entirely new rights that the states couldn't abridge. Most dramatic of these was the right to "privacy," embodied in the 1965 *Griswold* decision overturning a Connecticut law that prohibited the use of contraceptive devices and in *Roe v. Wade* (1973), which created the constitutional right to terminate a pregnancy. This "rights revolution" undertaken by the Warren Court elevated the status of the Fourteenth Amendment until it became the major constitutional provision to which aggrieved groups of all sorts—blacks, women, gays, welfare recipients, the elderly, the disabled—appealed in seeking to expand their legal rights and social status.

*In this **May 1954** wire-service photograph, taken on the steps of the Supreme Court, Mrs. Nettie Hunt explains to her three-year-old daughter the significance of the Brown ruling.*

Today, amid the continuing controversies over abortion rights, affirmative action, the rights of homosexuals, and many other issues, the Court's interpretation of the Fourteenth Amendment remains a focus of judicial as well as political debate. An imperfect compromise when added to the Constitution during Reconstruction, the amendment has since become the most powerful bulwark of the rights of American citizens. We haven't yet created the "bright dream" of which Thaddeus Stevens spoke in his June 1866 speech, but thanks to the reinvigoration of the Fourteenth Amendment by the twentieth-century Supreme Court, more Americans enjoy more rights and more freedoms today than ever before in our history.

★ ★ ★

Extract Const. Amend.

OCTOBER 5, 1877

"I WILL FIGHT NO MORE FOREVER"

BY ELLIOTT WEST

ABOUT FOUR IN THE AFTERNOON on October 5, 1877, a man on horseback rode slowly from behind some dirt entrenchments and approached a knot of army officers waiting on a nearby low ridge. The place was northern Montana, about forty miles from the Canadian border. The man was one of the Nee-me-poo, the Real People, called the Nez Perces by whites. He wore a gray blanket over one shoulder and carried a rifle across his saddle pommel. Beside him walked a few other men, their hands resting lightly on the horse as they spoke lowly, urgently.

The ground that these men crossed, slushy from recent snowfalls, was also torn and blood soaked from fighting six days earlier, when several hundred of the soldiers had stormed the surprised Nez Perce camp. An army surgeon had heard that day "the bullets hum all the notes of

AT LEFT: *Chiefs Yellow Wolf and Peopeo Tholekt pose for amateur historian Lucullus V. McWhorter as they would have appeared stripped for battle three decades earlier during the 1877 Nez Perce War. Yellow Wolf holds the club and rifle he used at that time.*

ABOVE: *A drinking horn that accompanied the Nez Perces on their flight to Canada.*

the gamut, fit music for the dance of death," while a Nez Perce warrior recalled his people being cut down as though "hail [were] leveling the grass." The Real People had rallied and driven their attackers back, producing a standoff, but now—with his people hungry, their options gone, and more soldiers arriving—the horseman was prepared to end it. He was Heinmot Tooyalakekt (Thunder Rising to Loftier Mountain Heights), though the army officers knew him as Joseph. Dismounting, he offered his rifle to a one-armed bearded man, but that officer gestured toward another soldier, younger and mustachioed, who accepted the weapon.

Chief Joseph's surrender thus ended what was arguably the most remarkable of all the Indian wars of the late nineteenth century. Even Gen. William Tecumseh Sherman, then the nation's highest-ranking military officer, marveled at the Nez Perces' bravery and "almost scientific skill" at warfare. During their extraordinary trek in search of freedom, the Nez Perces had led army pursuers across more than fifteen hundred miles of the West's most difficult terrain. In each encounter—except, of course, the last—they had

CHIEF JOSEPH

1840 – 1904

Joseph would always say that when he surren- dered, he was promised repatriation to Idaho. Instead, the Nez Perces were sent to the Indian Territory (now Okla- homa), where the stench of betrayal hung over them. In 1885, those who agreed to accept Christianity were permitted to return to Lapwai, while Thunder Rising and others who refused conversion were sent to northeastern Washington. Although he petitioned several times, Joseph (shown here in November 1877) was never allowed to go home. He traveled east a few times, staying at the Astor Hotel and attend- ing the opening of Grant's Tomb. On his last trip in 1903, while eating buffalo steaks with Nelson Miles and Theodore Roosevelt, he asked the president to protect the Nez Perces from miners flocking to a new gold discovery.

outmaneuvered and outfought the larger, better-equipped forces sent against them. Even more incredible, they had done all this while moving and protecting hundreds of noncombatants and all of their belongings. An equivalent feat during the recently completed Civil War would have been for the men of a small Virginia village to have retreated with their women, children, elderly, and farm stock all the way from Richmond to Denver while being chased by Union troops.

That cold October afternoon was also an ending for the Indian peoples generally. By the time of Thunder Rising's surrender, the forces set loose by an intruding white culture had cut away the last supports of Native American independence. The country crossed by the Real People in their run for freedom, like all North America, had provided the stuff of life to native peoples for millennia. Now, however, this land had been placed irrevocably under the control of others.

The Nez Perces' long march was merely the final dramatic act in a centuries- old struggle in which the lives of Indians and whites had become inextricably interwoven. In the years following that cold October afternoon, as victor and vanquished alike

This shirt *belonged to Chief Joseph.*

lived out the implications of their mutually tangled histories, some Indian peoples would still reach toward independence. But they would be forced to do so by means other than warfare, because that battle was over.

THE 1877 FLIGHT OF THE Real People began in their homeland of eastern Oregon and western Idaho—where they had lived, according to tradition, since Coyote slew a great monster and cut out its heart, scattering the butchered pieces across the West. Wherever some part of the monster had landed, a different people had sprung up— the Flatheads, Pend Oreilles, Crows, Cayuses, Blackfeet, and others. Then Coyote rinsed his hands, and where he sprinkled the bloody wash- water, there the Nee-me-poo appeared. According to the tribe's oral tradition, Coyote assured them that, although never numerous, they would be "very, very manly."

For centuries, the Real People lived in small autonomous bands along the Clearwater, Grande Ronde, lower Salmon, and middle Snake Rivers. Their territory included rugged lava canyons, sweeping plateaus, and magnificent meadows where the men hunted and the women dug camas root, a staple of the regional diet. To the west rose the Wallowa Mountains and to the east the Bitterroot Range of the Rockies. Within this rather isolated country, the ways of the Nee-me-poo varied little until the early eighteenth century, when the tribe first acquired horses. Soon the Real People ranked among the West's most accomplished breeders, trading their mounts with other tribes and making regular forays across the Rocky Mountains to hunt bison on the Great Plains.

Relations between the Nee-me-poo and white Americans were friendly from first contact. This took place in September 1805, when a band of starving whites was welcomed into a Nee-me-poo camp with bison meat, salmon, and general hospitality. One member of that expedition—led, of course, by Meriwether Lewis and William Clark—was sufficiently moved to call the Real People "the most friendly, honest and ingenious" tribe of all he had met. Clark himself had praise for the Real People, whom he called (in his corrupted French) the Nez Perces, or Pierced Noses, confusing the Nee-me-poo with another tribe whose members wore shell ornaments in their nostrils.

The Nez Perces took this friendship with whites as a binding pledge of mutual support and protection, observing it for the next three-quarters of a century. Yet they might not have been quite so loyal had they lived in a territory less isolated from the juggernaut of white westward expansion, which gained momentum during the 1840s and brought calamitous

This buckskin jacket *was worn by a U.S. Army officer during the period of the Indian wars. Its appearance, so unlike that of an officer's standard uniform jacket, demonstrates the degree to which the cultures of the two groups, soldiers and Indians, had merged.*

"IF YOU TIE A HORSE TO A STAKE, DO YOU EXPECT HE WILL GROW FAT? IF YOU PEN AN INDIAN UP ON A SMALL SPOT OF EARTH… HE WILL NOT BE CONTENTED."

—*Chief Joseph, quoted in* The North American Review, *April 1879*—

changes to more exposed Indian peoples. In the wake of the 1849 gold rush, for example, California's native population rapidly collapsed. Many bands were hunted down and killed; others saw their lands taken, their economies destroyed, and their children stolen and sold into de facto slavery. Similarly, the white settlers who flooded into Oregon during the 1840s and 1850s brought with them epidemics that devastated the local

In this photograph
*of the Nez Perces
who negotiated the
controversial treaty of
1863, Hallalhotsoot
can be seen seated in
the center, holding
a cane. Among the
whites, Hallalhotsoot
was known, revealingly,
as Lawyer.*

tribes, who were also being pushed steadily off the best land. On the
Great Plains as well as in the Great Basin, a massive overland migration
of some three hundred thousand people between 1841 and 1865 chewed
up substantial habitats along the Platte, Arkansas, Humboldt, and other
rivers that had been essential to the livelihoods of the Sioux, Cheyennes,
Arapahoes, Kiowas, Comanches, Shoshones, and other seminomadic
hunting-and-gathering peoples. After 1859, gold and silver strikes in
Colorado, Arizona, and New Mexico brought in so many miners, farmers,
and stock raisers that the intricate economies of native groups were disrupted all the way from Nebraska to the Mexican border. In each case,
the horrific stresses and abuses initiated by invading whites eventually
triggered violent indigenous reactions, from nasty
skirmishes and raids to full-blown wars.

Yet it was not until 1860 that the
Real People finally began to feel the
force of these changes. Gold strikes
that year in Idaho drew the usual rush
of prospectors (as well as farmers and
stockmen hoping to mine the miners),
and with these newcomers came the
usual demands that nearby Indian lands
be opened to white settlement. Five
years earlier, the Nez Perces had agreed
to a treaty that included the sale of some
of their land to the whites, but that same

C ENTER:

***The Old Spalding
Mission** stood originally
on a bank of Lapwai
Creek. It was later
moved and turned
into a museum.*

treaty had also guaranteed them a large portion of their traditional homeland. In 1863, however, a new treaty was signed that conveyed to the whites nine-tenths of the guaranteed territory (in exchange for annual payments and promises of economic development). As with many such treaties, however, what seemed a clear agreement on its face concealed a much muddier situation.

Henry Harmon Spalding was once described by a fellow missionary as "a sincere, though not always humble Christian."

THE NEZ PERCES WERE BY THIS TIME divided along lines increasingly familiar to other western tribes. Since the arrival of Henry Harmon Spalding in 1836, Christian missionaries had been working among the tribes of present-day Idaho, insisting not only on their conversion but also that they adopt European-American modes of living (most notably the practice of agriculture). Some Nez Perce bands simply kept their distance and continued hunting and horse raising as they had in the past; others, however, accepted the new faith, took up farming, and clustered near to the Christian missions on the Clearwater River. It was these mission Nez Perces who signed the 1863 treaty, and it was their land that the new treaty protected. All other Nez Perce bands would have to move to the new Lapwai reservation and live there on the same terms as their converted tribesmen.

Taking advantage of this sort of schism was nothing new for the U.S. government. Since colonial times, whites had negotiated with native factions inclined toward accommodation, then claimed that the resulting treaties applied to disinclined factions as well. The consequences of such a policy were predictably tragic, and over time the feeling of powerlessness it generated in many native peoples led them to seek hope and consolation with powerful new apocalyptic religious movements. These movements typically fused traditional native beliefs with Christian millennial notions, especially the prediction of an imminent judgment day, to produce a gospel of native pride and cultural renewal that absolutely rejected white culture and religion.

THE DREAMERS

Brig. Gen. Oliver O. Howard once described the Dreamer prophet Smoholla as "a large-headed, hump-shouldered, odd little wizard of an Indian." Smoholla knew well, though, the effects of white immigration. All his children and grandchildren had died from disease, and his people, the Wallulas, had shrunk in number from two thousand to fewer than three hundred. Smoholla's new teaching promised an imminent rising of all Indian dead accompanied by an instant vanishing of all whites.

A group of Nez Perce Dreamers poses where they lived prior to the 1877 war. Apocalyptic religions such as the Dreamer faith had sprung up before among Indians facing white encroachment—most famously in 1809–1810, when the Shawnee prophet Tenskwatawa (Tecumseh's brother) promised the banishment of whites if his teachings were followed. And in 1890, the Ghost Dance religion, inspired by the Paiute shaman Wovoka, spread from the Great Basin to tribes as far away as Texas and the Dakotas.

As tensions rose and tribal divisions deepened, many Indians of the Pacific Northwest, including some of the Nez Perces, turned to the Dreamer religion. Most prominent of the Dreamer converts was Tu-ke-kas, known to whites as Old Joseph. Tu-ke-kas had been one of the first Nez Perces to accept Spalding's call to Christ, but when the treaty of 1863 surrendered his band's homeland at the base of the Wallowa Mountains, he had furiously renounced his conversion and adopted the Dreamer faith. Joining him were his sons Ollokot and Thunder Rising. It was the latter, Young Joseph, who assumed leadership of the band upon his father's death in 1871.

Along with several other bands of Nez Perces, Young Joseph's group denied that the 1863 treaty applied to them and refused to leave their beloved Wallowa country, even as swelling numbers of white settlers brought a sharp competition for resources, occasions of mutual misunderstanding, and violent incidents born of simple meanness. This situation simmered for fourteen years. In the meantime, as was typically the case, assaults, killings, and rapes by whites went virtually unpunished.

B Y THIS TIME, MOST NATIVE PEOPLES in the United States had been either maneuvered or forcibly corralled into confinement. Between the 1830s and the 1860s, more than forty tribes from the East, the Great Plains, and the Southwest were removed to the confines of the Indian Territory. During the late 1860s, the Southern Cheyennes and Arapahoes were defeated and sent there as well, joined in 1875 by the Kiowas and the Comanches. Although the Northern Cheyennes and western Sioux mangled George A. Custer's command at the battle of the Little Big Horn in June 1876, these tribes, too, had by the following spring either surrendered or fled to Canada.

These Sioux arrows were collected by the cavalry troops who came upon the remains of Custer's command two days after the battle of the Little Big Horn.

At this point, in the immediate wake of its successful suppression of the Sioux, the government insisted that all nontreaty Nez Perces give up their homelands and move to the Lapwai reservation for good. The officer the army placed in charge of pressing this demand was Brig. Gen. Oliver Otis Howard, a Civil War veteran who had lost his right arm at Fair Oaks during the Peninsular Campaign. A devout Christian, Howard was appalled by the Dreamer religion and thus doubly determined to compel the Nez Perces to move, literally, closer to Christ.

At a council held in mid-May 1877, Young Joseph, recognized by his people as a skillful diplomat, tried to work out a compromise with Howard, but the parley ended when another chief, Toohoolhoolzote, spoke scornfully of whites as men who "measure the earth, and then divide it" and swore that he would never leave the land that "is part of my body." Howard had Toohoolhoolzote arrested, and although he later honored the request of the other chiefs that Toohoolhoolzote be released, he also gave them this ultimatum: Report to the reservation within thirty days or face the consequences.

During the next month, the various nontreaty bands reluctantly prepared to comply. As the deadline neared, however, the accumulated stress—from the soured friendship, the abuses and land grabs and violations of trust, the intertribal resentments, and the clash of spiritual visions—flashed into violence. At first, a few young warriors settled a grudge by killing four white settlers. Then many more Nez Perces rampaged for two days through the valley of the Salmon River, killing thirteen more whites, raping two women, and burning several houses. Stunned, Joseph and several other older leaders gathered their people together and sought refuge at the village of White Bird, a prominent headman. They hoped to secure a truce. Instead, early on June 17, a hastily assembled collection of more than a hundred troopers and civilian volunteers attacked the sleeping camp. As they would many times during the months ahead, the Nez Perces outmatched their opponents.

This pictograph of the Little Big Horn fight was drawn on muslin by White Bird in 1894–1895.

With one rapid counterburst, about sixty-five warriors, many of them badly hung over from stolen whiskey, turned the attackers' flank, and within an hour the white command was routed. Thirty-four whites died, while the Nez Perces suffered only one man wounded.

The fight at White Bird Canyon, and especially the army's humiliation, ended any serious chance of reconciliation. Howard soon arrived with more troops and caught up with the bands along the Clearwater River, where he attacked with another superior force. This time, with shrewd maneuvers and astonishing marksmanship, the Nez Perces kept the whites pinned down for two days while they considered their options. The choices they faced were the same ones confronting all western tribes in conflict with the whites: The nontreaty bands could continue to struggle against what was, ultimately, immeasurably greater power, or they could surrender and face retribution, confinement to the reservation, and the loss of their cultural autonomy. Instead, they chose a remarkable third option: They ran for it.

The Nez Perces struck out eastward over the Rockies via Lolo Pass. It was the same route Lewis and Clark had taken seventy-two years earlier when, bellies empty and hands out, they had come down to the Nee-me-poo camp and been given food and hospitality. Now the Real People used this pass to leave the place where they had sprung up as sprinkled blood from the Heart of the Monster. They numbered more than 500 women, children, and elderly, but never more than 150 fighting men. They brought with them two thousand horses and the basic provisions for a new life.

A cartridge belt of the sort worn by cavalry officers during the Nez Perce War.

THUS BEGAN THE NEZ PERCES' extraordinary odyssey. Their plan was to follow the tribe's old hunting route to the northern Great Plains, where they hoped to find refuge among their allies, the Crows. Because Joseph had long played a highly visible role as a negotiator—and because, at the end of the war, he was one of the few surviving leaders—some historians have portrayed Heinmot Tooyalakekt as the dominant figure in this entire drama. He wasn't. Always the Nez Perces operated as autonomous bands, and once the fighting began, the tribe's diffuse leadership shifted toward those known for their strategic and military skills: Looking Glass, White Bird, Lean Elk, Toohoolhoolzote, Yellow Bull, Joseph's brother Ollokot, and others.

OLIVER O. HOWARD

1830 – 1909

At the start of the Civil War, West Point graduate Oliver Otis Howard resigned his regular army commission so that he could lead a volunteer regiment from his home state of Maine. After Antietam, he was promoted to the brevet rank of major general and in July 1864 given command of the Army of Tennessee. He took part in Sherman's March to the Sea and also in the Carolina Campaign of early 1865. After the war, Pres. Andrew Johnson appointed Howard, who was genuinely interested in the welfare of the freed slaves, to run the new Freedmen's Bureau. Howard (shown here in 1886) also helped found Howard University, which bears his name in recognition of his service to African Americans.

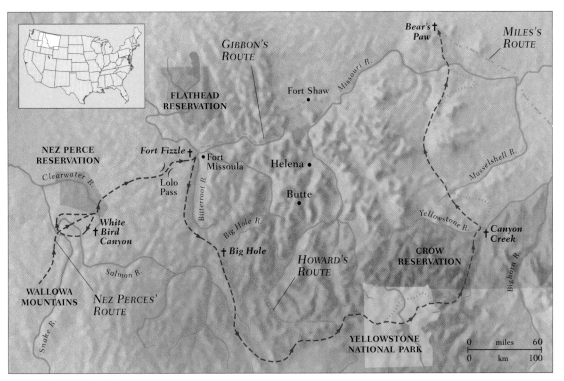

In late July, as the bands descended Lolo Pass toward Montana's Bitterroot Valley, they found soldiers and volunteers waiting for them in a makeshift fort at the narrow neck of a canyon through which the Lolo trail passed. Using a hunting trail apparently unknown to the whites, the Nez Perces simply bypassed what locals soon were derisively calling Fort Fizzle. Settlers in the valley below panicked, but under firm admonitions from their leaders, the Nez Perces did no damage, kept mostly to themselves, bought some supplies in a nearby town, and moved peacefully southward along the Bitterroot River.

With the army apparently lagging far behind, the Real People—who took to calling Howard "General Day After Tomorrow"—were lulled into a disastrous illusion of safety. On August 7, they stopped to rest in the lush valley of the Big Hole River—not knowing that Col. John Gibbon's command had been ordered out of Fort Shaw, Montana, to join the chase and was now closing in on them. At dawn on August 9, Gibbon attacked with a combined force of nearly two hundred troopers and Montana volunteers. Bellowing and cheering, they fired volley after volley into the Nez Perce lodges and clubbed and shot warriors as they stumbled toward their weapons. Soon rifle flashes lit up teepees from within as soldiers fired at their occupants. The air became thick with smoke and bloodmist. Some

This map shows the Nez Perces' route from White Bird Canyon to the Bear's Paw.

Like his brother, Ollokot adopted the Dreamers' distinctive hairstyle, suggestive of a flame or perhaps a lofting prayer.

women hid children under bison robes and grabbed knives to join the fight; others ran for the river, where a few were spared and the rest shot as they tried to hide among the reeds. After twenty hellish minutes, the soldiers had driven most of the men to the northern edge of the camp.

Here Looking Glass and White Bird rallied the warriors. One recalled an enraged White Bird shouting, "Are we going to run to the mountains and let the whites kill our women and children before our eyes?" The counterattack came as the soldiers, thinking the fight was over, were just beginning to torch the Nez Perce lodges. The warriors' furious assault forced Gibbon to pull his men back onto a sparsely wooded rise, where for more than thirty-six hours Nez Perce riflemen peppered them with a relentless fire. In the meantime, the rest of the tribe built travois for the wounded and hurried once more along the trail. Gibbon would later call the battle of the Big Hole a victory—in fact, he even wrote an epic poem to commemorate it—but thirty of his men died and another forty were wounded, many severely. The Nez Perce also took heavy losses, of course—including two of their finest warriors, Rainbow and Five Wounds. Yet they got away clean—that is, without pursuit—and managed to seize more than two thousand rounds of army ammunition in the process.

THE BANDS CONTINUED THEIR FLIGHT in an understandably soured mood, moving south and east through the high desert of far eastern Idaho. Howard drew close once but fell behind again when his mules were stolen. Finally, in late August, the Nez Perces climbed into some of the most remarkable terrain in all of North America—the geyser basins, deep canyons, bubbling mudpots, and thick forests of the newly created Yellowstone National Park. There, in a surreal encounter between the old and new Americas, they killed one tourist, seized several others, and came within a hair of giving this remarkable story a truly bizarre twist when they nearly crossed paths with a vacationing William T. Sherman. They remained in Yellowstone for more than two weeks—lost, some would say, but more likely considering their options and refreshing their horses on the lush late-summer grasses. Meanwhile, the army stepped up its effort to intercept the bands. Col. Samuel D. Sturgis was dispatched to the eastern edge of the park, where he waited with six companies of the refurbished Seventh Cavalry for the Nez Perces to emerge. With Howard behind and Sturgis ahead, the army didn't see how the Nez Perces could escape.

A bayonet trowel recovered at the Big Hole battlefield. Gibbon's troops used these to dig in following the Nez Perce counterattack, and the colonel later credited the trowels with saving their lives.

It was John Gibbon's command, ordered to rendezvous with Custer's Seventh Cavalry, that discovered the carnage of the Last Stand.

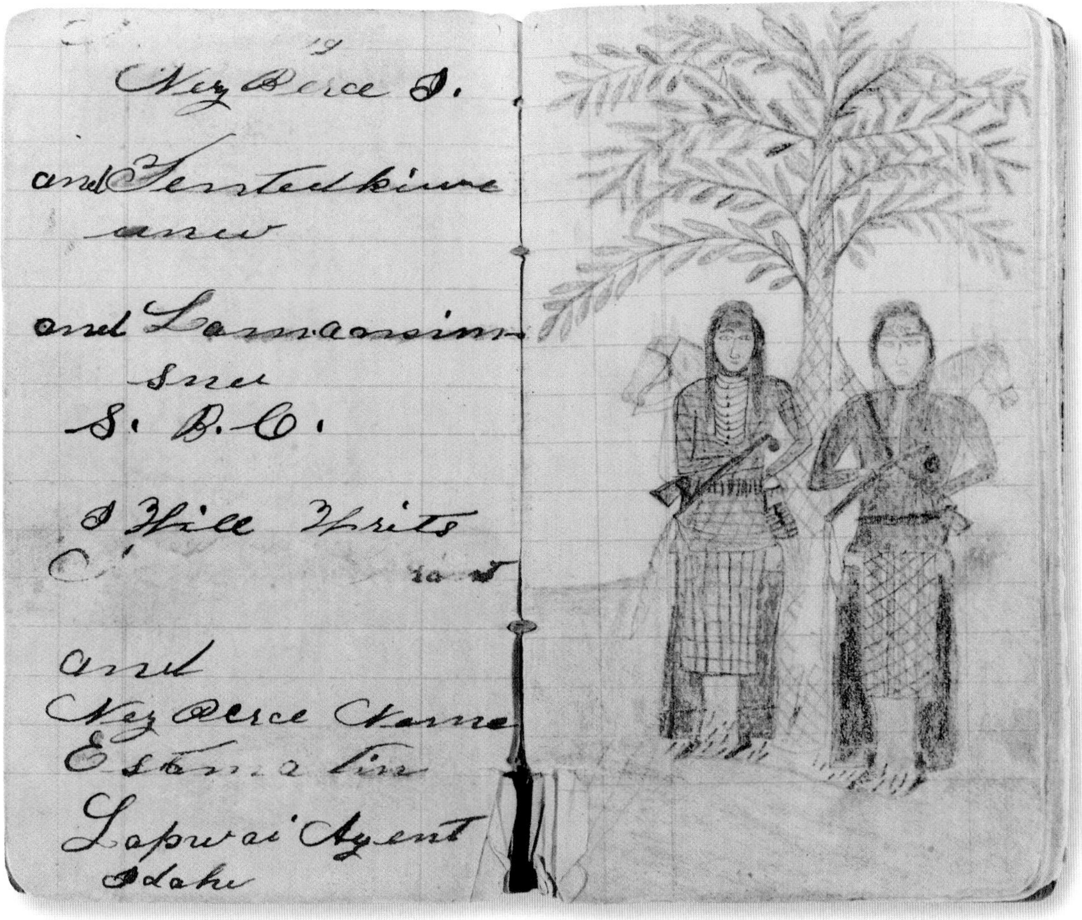

Nez Perce I.

and Tenteedkive anew

and Lamaonsinn snee

S. B. C.

I Will Write

ic vt

and Nez Perce Channe Estimatin Lapwai Agent Idahe

An anonymous Nez Perce created a pictorial record of the war in a leather-bound journal called the Cash Book. This portrait of two Nez Perce warriors matches, in quality of composition, the best pictographic work of its time. Both men are holding war clubs with stone heads sewn into rawhide pouches (the momentum of the loose heads made their blows more powerful).

Then, stunningly, they did. With a brilliant feint, the Nez Perces pulled Sturgis out of position and, by a route still debated, rode out of the mountains along the Clarks Fork River, a principal tributary of the Yellowstone. Here they traveled from one fantasy of the West (the land of unspoiled natural beauty) into another (the land of progress and savagery redeemed). In the great valleys where Nez Perce hunters had chased bison for generations, they now found towns, ranches, and other boasts of civilization.

About this time, in early September, they also learned that their old allies, the Crows, would not be helping them. In fact, some Crows were already serving as scouts for the army units marching against them. The disappointment brought on by such news must have been crushing for the Nez Perces, who had traveled a thousand miles from the Wallowa Mountains only to find that no refuge awaited them. Weary from three months on the move, burdened by their wounded, chased by enemies, and abandoned by friends, what could they do now? Their answer was

After the Civil War, as the nation raced toward its urban industrial future, a nervous public began experiencing a profound romantic urge to preserve virgin spaces from the touch of modern life. These places were typically found in the West, where most easterners believed the land was full of natural beauty and untroubled by human complication. In response, the federal government created Yellowstone, the first national park, in 1872. Yellowstone included hunting grounds of the Bannocks and Crows, but all Indian peoples were banned from the park so that the illusion of a "natural" state might be maintained. This photograph from the 1870s shows tourists enjoying Heart Lake.

as audacious as their original decision to leave Idaho. They would head for the one place where the U.S. Army couldn't follow them: Canada. Four months earlier, in May 1877, Sitting Bull's followers had found refuge there, and now the Real People would join them. They chose a direct route north across the Montana plains.

First, however, they had to leave the valley of the Yellowstone, and that meant ascending the steep bluffs along its northern side. The only practical way of doing this was to follow a trail that ran along Canyon Creek up to a narrow defile. On September 13, the Nez Perces were ascending this trail when Sturgis and his men arrived on the scene. After their earlier embarrassment, they were hungry for a fight. Once again, however, the Nez Perces showed that they possessed the cooler nerve. As hundreds of women and children hurried up the canyon, marksmen well placed among the rocks kept the greener, more anxious soldiers pinned down and off balance. For hours, these warriors held the army at bay, allowing their families the critical time they needed to climb above the rimrock and begin the race northward.

Over the next two weeks, the army groped for its quarry, as if feeling for a clever cat in a darkened room. The Nez Perces were by this time desperately short of food, but they knew that a sustained hunt was impossible. They had to keep moving. On the Missouri River, they came across some soldiers guarding a large freight shipment. Twice they offered to buy food and twice were refused. Finally, they attacked and took some of what they wanted. Now the Canadian border was just eighty crow-flying miles away.

ONCE AGAIN, THOUGH, the Nez Perces allowed an apparent calm to lull them into a false sense of security. General Day After Tomorrow was indeed far behind them, but not so Col. Nelson A. Miles, who joined the chase on September 18, when he left the Tongue River Cantonment with nearly four hundred men marching rapidly northwest. On September 29, the Nez Perces stopped to rest on Snake Creek, just east of some isolated laval mountains called the Bear's Paw and less than forty miles south of the Canadian border. The nights this far north were already quite cold, and the Nez Perces were just beginning to stir on the morning of September 30 when scouts rushed frantically into the camp, shouting that soldiers were close behind.

It was not long after dawn that Miles's Cheyenne and Crow scouts had found the Nez Perce trail, and two miles from Snake Creek the colonel had ordered a charge. Although nearly as unprepared as they had been at the Big Hole, more than a hundred Nez Perces managed to reach their horses and flee northward while warriors directed a withering defensive fire against the three cavalry companies leading the raid. More than half of these soldiers were either killed or wounded—including all the first sergeants and all but one of the officers. Yet the Nez Perce losses were heavy as well: twenty-two killed, among them Ollokot and Toohoolhoolzote, and Looking Glass died from a sniper's bullet the next day. Almost as disastrous, virtually all the horses were either stampeded or captured.

The confrontation settled into a grueling standoff. The Nez Perces threw up protective embankments, digging rifle pits for the men and caves for the women and children. The troopers set up their own marksmen and lobbed occasional artillery shells into the Indian camp, to little effect. Meanwhile, under the cover of darkness, some of the besieged slipped away—including, at the end, White Bird. In all, more than two hundred Nez Perces joined Sitting Bull in Canada.

Among those who remained, Joseph once again came to the fore. At first, he attempted to negotiate a way out for his people. But when a cold front brought a bitter north wind and snow, the suffering of the Nez Perces deepened considerably. On October 4, the last handfuls of dried bison meat were given to the children, and that night Howard finally arrived. He had brought with him as herders two

A hunter stands atop a mountain of slaughtered bison. After 1870, when it was discovered that bison leather made excellent factory gaskets, professional hunters began killing the beasts by the hundreds of thousands. They started on the southern Plains and moved steadily northward. By 1884, even Montana's herds had been reduced to nearly nothing.

OVERLEAF:

Lucullus V. McWhorter's fascination with the Nez Perce War began shortly after he moved his family from Ohio to Washington's Yakima River Valley in 1903. Over the next four decades, he worked diligently, collecting both primary sources and artifacts. He interviewed surviving participants and photographed important people and locations. This is one of eight views he took of the Bear's Paw in 1932.

This photograph of Looking Glass, the only one that has survived, was taken in 1871.

A page from the November 17, 1877, Harper's Weekly.

CHIEF JOSEPH'S SPEECH (AS RECORDED BY C. E. S. WOOD)

"Tell General Howard I know his heart. What he told me before I have in my heart. I am tired of fighting. Our chiefs are killed. Looking Glass is dead. Toohoolhoolzote is dead. The old men are all dead. It is the young men who say yes or no. He who led on the young men is dead. It is cold and we have no blankets. The little children are freezing to death. My people, some of them, have run away to the hills, and have no blankets, no food; no one knows where they are—perhaps freezing to death. I want to have time to look for my children and see how many of them I can find. Maybe I shall find them among the dead. Hear me, my chiefs. I am tired; my heart is sick and sad. From where the sun now stands I will fight no more forever."

of the Christianized Nez Perces, and on October 5, Captain John and Old George began acting as intermediaries. After shuttling back and forth between the camps for four hours, Captain John finally returned with Chief Joseph's answer, which Captain John communicated to the army officers through an interpreter. The words attributed to Thunder Rising are among the most famous in American history. Joseph spoke of his people's long ordeal, of their dead, and of the hungry survivors shivering beside the Bear's Paw. He said he was tired and heartsick and wanted most to search for his missing children, to "see how many of them I can find." Then he ended his message with a resonant pledge of peace: "From where the sun now stands I will fight no more forever." Shortly after this answer was delivered, Joseph himself rode out of the Nez Perce camp and handed his rifle to Miles.

TODAY, THUNDER RISING IS BEST REMEMBERED for this poignant surrender speech and its brief, eloquent farewell to a cherished way of life. But as is so often the case with such mythic moments, a closer look reveals a number of subtler, broader meanings. As it turns out, Joseph's exact words are difficult to authenticate. For one thing, because Joseph spoke no English, whatever he said had to pass first through Captain John and then through the army interpreter. And there is no evidence that the words uttered by this interpreter were actually written down before Howard's official report was drafted a few days later. And the man who drafted this report was no ordinary scribe.

Lt. Charles Erskine Scott Wood, Howard's aide-de-camp, entered the 1877 Nez Perce campaign with a sympathy for the Indians and a romantic sensibility to match. He was also something of a poet with a flair for words, hence his work drafting Howard's reports. So whose words have come down to us from that snowy day on Snake Creek? The gist of the speech and its spirit are probably Joseph's, and perhaps each of his phrases was translated and recorded faithfully. Or perhaps Wood polished the interpreter's account of Joseph's words, smoothing here and rearranging there. Or perhaps the lieutenant edited more extensively for the Victorian ear. Or maybe he made the whole thing up.

Or we can look at this puzzle another way: Perhaps in the chance encounter between these two men, Chief Joseph and Lieutenant Wood, something was passed and something set in motion. Joseph, through Wood, was able to communicate to white Americans, in a language they could understand, the Real People's dignified acceptance of this most bitter turn in their lives. And Wood, through Joseph and the ordeal of his people, could express his own ambivalence and that of other Victorian Americans toward the meaning of this day.

Seen this way, October 5, 1877, was a pivot in relations between native and white Americans and their mutual perceptions of each other. It was not a turning point in a story that might have taken another course. Had the Nez Perces made it to Canada, they likely would have been forced back across the border and onto a reservation just as Sitting Bull and his band were in 1881. Their run for freedom certainly changed nothing in the balance of power between whites and Indians.

NELSON A. MILES

1839 – 1925

Nelson Miles was a clerk in a Massachusetts crockery store when the Civil War broke out. Joining a regiment of volunteers, he fought at Fredericksburg and at Chancellorsville, where his bravery earned him the Congressional Medal of Honor. By 1865, wounded four times, he had become a hero and risen to the rank of major general. After the war, the ferociously ambitious Miles remained determined to engage an enemy (he wrote to his wife that he had "Indians on the brain"). In 1874–1875, he commanded the troops that pacified the Kiowas, Comanches, and Southern Cheyennes along the Red River, and in 1876–1877, he led the winter campaign that pummeled the Sioux after Custer's defeat.

Joseph's surrender was, however, both an end and a beginning. For three centuries, starting with the first bloody clashes in New Mexico and Virginia, Native Americans had pushed back against white intruders. Now that fight was finished. Except for intermittent resistance from Apaches in the far Southwest, Indian peoples in the United States would never again go to war against the federal government. The white invaders had given the Indians three choices: adopt our ways, submit to the reservation system, or be destroyed. By October 5, 1877, all the choices had been made, and the master strategy seemed accomplished.

However, as usual, history and human nature proved much messier than planned. The conquering whites and those they vanquished found themselves increasingly snarled together. Indians had borrowed from their opponents—notably the horse Joseph rode and the firearm he handed to Miles—to create magnificent cultures of free-roaming resistance to whites. Similarly, they had declared spiritual independence through religions, like the Dreamer faith, that appropriated traditions from the very missionaries they defied.

So on that day beside Snake Creek, even as the military phase of the Indian struggle ended, a new stage of resistance began. Indian peoples henceforth applied their adaptive energies to preserving their cultural integrity and religious rights—not by arms, but through political and legal processes. Appealing to principles claimed in common with white authorities, many have since reached toward economic independence through enterprises that draw on established Indian traditions, from ranching to cooperative manufacturing to running casinos.

White Americans, meanwhile, have come to identify with the same lands, animals, and peoples they once sought to conquer. They have created islands of the wild, starting with Yellowstone, and promised themselves that these enclaves will be forever free of the same civilization they previously struggled to carry westward. They have also come to identify with the Indians themselves—who, once defeated, were transformed into symbols of a wild nobility said to be at the heart of the national character.

C. E. S. Wood

1852 – 1944

Charles Erskine Scott Wood's romanticism and sympathy for the Nez Perces only deepened after he left the army in 1884. He moved out to Oregon and, having collected both a Ph.D. and a law degree during his final years in the army, he set up a law practice in Portland, where he became a vocal social critic (but not one so strict that it interfered with his financial success). He kept in touch with Joseph and sent his son to spend several summers with the exiled chief in Nespelem, Washington. He also wrote prolifically—essays, stories, and scores of poems that often celebrated Indians as everything the confining, dollar-chasing new America was not.

This rifle belonged to Geronimo. His Chiricahua Apaches held out the longest before submitting to the whites in 1886.

Howard and Joseph met for the last time in 1904, when this photograph was taken.

N OW IN FILM, SONG, ART, advertising, and countless other expressions of the popular culture, white America confronts the muddy ambiguities of its final victory. Arguments over sports mascots and other public images remind us how we once exploited that which we have since come to admire. As in all the Indian wars, the pursuit of the Nez Perces was a campaign to confine an independent people and suppress their religion undertaken by a nation ostensibly dedicated to liberty and justice. In the many decades since 1877, our nation has continued to wrestle with this central glaring contradiction in the story that ended at Snake Creek.

Thunder Rising's words still needle us with disquieting questions regarding the sincerity of American values. And the entanglement of Joseph's words with those of the white man who conveyed them reminds us of the entwined destinies of all who fought beside the Bear's Paw—and all of us ever since.

★ ★ ★

FURTHER READING

★ Bruce Hampton, *Children of Grace: The Nez Perce War of 1877* (1994)

★ Alvin M. Josephy, *The Nez Perce Indians and the Opening of the Northwest* (1965)

AFFIRMING THE SEXUAL DIVISION OF LABOR

BY ALICE KESSLER-HARRIS

WHEN IT CAME DOWN ON February 24, 1908, the U.S. Supreme Court decision in *Muller v. Oregon* produced a burst of approbation. Headlines trumpeted the unique position in which the Court had placed women: "Supreme Court Holds Woman Above Man in Law," the *Washington Post* declared. Influential liberal magazines such as *The Outlook* described the decision as "A Victory for Posterity." The leading women's groups celebrated—particularly the National Consumers' League, which had helped prepare the decisive brief in the case. Its members were ecstatic because the Court's ruling had explicitly affirmed what everyone knew to be common sense: Gender distinctions justified treating women differently before the law.

The *Muller* case was a simple one, involving an Oregon statute that limited the number of hours women (but not men) could work operating certain types of mechanical equipment. In its ruling, the Court sustained the law, thereby affirming the constitutionality of legislation that placed women in a separate legal category—or class—from men. The *Muller* decision proved to be so important that the precedent it set prevailed for more than half a century. During that time, the legislative agenda *Muller* fostered shaped the daily lives of men, women, and children throughout the country.

EXCESSIVE AND DEBILITATING work, of course, was not an issue that threatened women alone. Around 1900, ten- and twelve-hour workdays—and sixty- or even seventy-hour workweeks—were not uncommon for both men and women; and because the pace of industrialization had accelerated during the late nineteenth century, working conditions everywhere had become nearly intolerable. Most unskilled laborers found themselves confined to unsanitary and often dangerous workplaces, while even skilled working men gradually lost

AT LEFT: By 1900, nearly six million women earned their livings in factories, retail stores, and other people's households (as domestic workers). This 1908 photograph shows the interior of a factory employing women to make shoes.

ABOVE: The NWTUL, founded in 1903, was one of the principal groups through which women worked for reform.

control over the process of production and the pace of their work. Women, disproportionately unskilled, were especially vulnerable. Because single women were thought to be only temporary members of the labor force and married women merely secondary wage earners, women were generally denied the job training that prepared men for good jobs. Most apprenticeships, for example, were closed to females, and employers tended to hire them to fill only the lowest-paid and most exploitative jobs.

The results were everywhere evident. Department store saleswomen stood on their feet for long hours; female garment and textile workers were crowded into unventilated, lint-infused workplaces where they contracted tuberculosis and spread smallpox at alarming rates; female factory workers were forced to operate unguarded machinery that endangered their weary fingers and sometimes, if they weren't careful, pulled them in by their long hair. The below-subsistence wages they were paid produced visible malnutrition and, according to some social critics, drove more than a few women into prostitution.

Many early American manufacturers, especially in New England, relied on young unmarried women for their labor pool. Farmers' daughters, in particular, were actively recruited to work the twelve-hour days. This early-nineteenth-century woodcut shows a young woman working as a pin maker.

During the years just prior to the *Muller* decision, the particular vulnerability of women workers forced its way into public consciousness. By this time, young women had already been part of the industrial labor force for several generations, having worked in the earliest U.S. textile and paper mills as well as at shoe binding and in the garment industry. However, when nineteenth-century industrialization moved jobs such as washing laundry out of the home and into small factories, women of all ages supplied the labor. By 1900, women made up a noticeable 20 percent of the nation's industrial workforce, and most young women now spent several years in the labor force before marrying and having children.

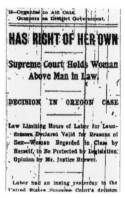

The **Washington Post** *printed this front-page story on February 25, 1908. The article ran below the masthead but above the fold.*

Although the employment of young women wasn't considered too disturbing, the plight of married women and the mothers of young children was. By the turn of the twentieth century, it had become clear that, increasingly, married women and young mothers had no economic choice but to work outside the home, often under arduous conditions. (African-American women had long worked at difficult jobs outside the home in great numbers, but white social activists and their friends in organized labor didn't take much notice until large numbers of white married women began to join them.) In 1900, 6 percent of white married women in the United States earned wages outside the home; a decade later, that figure had nearly doubled. The surge was obvious to everyone and produced a great deal of anxiety that women would become overworked and too sickly to sustain a normal family life. Women's wage work thus seemed a threat not only to their own health but also to that of society.

MANY SKILLED LABORERS RESPONDED to deteriorating conditions at work by organizing unions. They wanted to ameliorate the most dangerous working conditions, reduce the number of working hours, and earn enough pay to support their families— but few men and even fewer women obtained these benefits. Although most states permitted the organization of trade unions, no worker had the guaranteed right to join one, and employers were free to fire any worker who did. State laws also severely restricted the kinds of activities in which organized workers could engage. Strikes, for example, were not legal if they deprived employers of property (which was their point); with the implicit support of courts and state governments, most employers routinely hired thugs to brutalize any workers who dared to strike. Twice during the 1890s, organized workers suffered spectacular and well-publicized defeats—in 1892, when Andrew Carnegie used eight thousand state militia to break up a strike at his Homestead, Pennsylvania, steel mills; and in 1894, when Pres. Grover Cleveland used federal troops to end the Pullman strike, which had shut down rail traffic into and out of Chicago. These incidents reminded everyone, especially workers, of the power that employers had to resist collective action.

In the case of the Pullman strike, most of the violence was precipitated by a federal court injunction requiring the strikers to return to work, and this was often so: Court injunctions typically gave employers the legal cover they needed to use violence to break a strike. Nearly all of these injunctions relied on the prevailing interpretation of the Fourteenth Amendment's due process clause— which had become, in the hands of the late-nineteenth-century Supreme Court, an effective weapon that employers could use to prevent unions from obstructing their businesses. Another legal principle cherished by late-nineteenth-century employers was the "freedom of contract" doctrine that had been found in the Fourteenth Amendment's

OVERLEAF:

Lewis W. Hine *took this photograph,* Little Spinner Girl in Globe Cotton Mill, Atlanta, Georgia, *in early January 1909. At the time, Hine was working as an investigator for the National Child Labor Committee, an advocacy group funded by Progressives. Now and then resorting to subterfuge to gain access to the worst sweatshops, Hine produced a collection of photographs that educated the public of his generation and now constitute a remarkable visual record of the working class at the turn of the twentieth century.*

State militiamen *enter Homestead, Pennsylvania, after the governor's declaration of martial law.*

This 1908 cartoon *shows Labor shackled by the chain of "Bryanism," which AFL president Samuel Gompers has tied to it. Though known for keeping the AFL neutral, Gompers chose to support Democratic nominee William Jennings Bryan in 1908 because federal courts had begun issuing injunctions against strikes and boycotts, the chief weapons of voluntarism, and the Democrats had adopted an anti-injunction platform plank.*

privileges and immunities clause—which, according to a number of court decisions, guaranteed "the fundamental right of the citizen to control his or her own time and faculties." Prior to *Muller,* state and federal courts ruled consistently that states could not regulate work hours or working conditions because doing so would infringe on the individual's constitutional right to negotiate his or her own contract free from government interference.

To escape such damaging court rulings, the American Federation of Labor, then the largest and most respected U.S. trade union coalition, adopted a new strategy that it called voluntarism. The idea was to control wages and employment conditions through the economic leverage of organized working people. Instead of asking for legislative or judicial relief, labor emphasized such new and old tactics as union labels, boycotts of unfair employers, and strikes.

Whatever its merits for men, voluntarism made female industrial workers decidedly unattractive candidates for organization because they had so little economic power. Unskilled or at best semiskilled, they were easily replaced and thus in a poor position to negotiate. When they had no choice but to accept low pay and acquiesce to employers' demands for extra work, male coworkers accused women of dragging down all wages. In addition, male trade unionists believed like everyone else that most women were just passing through the workforce. If men helped women to organize at all, they did so reluctantly.

ALTHOUGH MOST TRADE UNIONS continued to discount legislative solutions during the early years of the twentieth century, independent advocates agitating on behalf of the working poor did pursue legal remedies, especially for women and children. They specifically hoped to extend to other states advances already made in Massachusetts, where an 1874 law limiting the number of hours women and children could work had successfully withstood state supreme court review. This had encouraged a dozen other states to look for loopholes in the freedom-of-contract doctrine and pass laws regulating working hours and conditions for both men and women. The results of these efforts, though, were mixed: The laws were generally weak, and although some were upheld, many were struck down by state courts, which held them to be violations of workers' and employers' freedom of contract. In 1893, when Illinois tried to establish an eight-hour workday for women, the state's high court rejected the effort decisively. Still, many ambiguities concerning the application of freedom-of-contract law remained until 1898, when the U.S. Supreme Court entered the fray.

That year, in its landmark *Holden v. Hardy* decision, the Court upheld a Utah law limiting the workday of miners on the grounds that their health was at stake. Thereafter, some states began seeking health-related rationales to justify laws protecting workers whose overtired or diseased bodies could put their own or the public's health and safety at risk. The states of Nebraska, Pennsylvania, and Washington specifically applied the Court's new interpretation to women, passing regulations that limited the number of hours women could work on the grounds that the government had a legitimate interest in protecting women's more fragile health because of their singular ability to reproduce. Each of these laws was later upheld in state supreme court.

Meanwhile, the U.S. Supreme Court set another important precedent regarding freedom of contract in 1905, when it decisively limited the use of the health rationale for men. In *Lochner v. New York,* the Court overturned a New York State law limiting the number of hours bakers (who were predominantly men) could work. By a seven-to-two majority, the Court declared the New York law unconstitutional because it interfered with the rights of bakery owner Joseph Lochner and his employees to contract freely *without serving any larger public purpose.* The deciding factor, the Court said, was that the law protected "neither the safety, [nor] the morals, nor the welfare of the public."

This freedom-of-contract roadblock affirmed the labor movement's decision not to pursue legislative action, at least where working men were

Miners *were the focus of much important labor activity at the turn of the twentieth century. Four years after* Holden v. Hardy, *150,000 anthracite coal miners in Pennsylvania went on strike for higher pay, shorter hours, and recognition of their union. The often violent protest continued from May until December, when winter cold, dwindling coal supplies, and pressure from Pres. Theodore Roosevelt forced mine management to accept a settlement largely favoring labor.*

> "THIS IS AN ERA OF OR-GANIZATION. CAPITAL ORGANIZES, AND THEREFORE LABOR MUST ORGANIZE."
>
> —
>
> *Theodore Roosevelt, speech, October 14, 1912*

concerned. But other reform-minded men and women increasingly pursued the legal logic of sex differentiation, arguing (as had Nebraska, Pennsylvania, and Washington) that exceptions to freedom-of-contract law should be made for women because wage work threatened their health; the health of future generations; and the safety, morality, and welfare of the American family. Demanding even more laws to protect women from the most difficult working conditions, these activists organized themselves first locally and then nationally through such groups as the General Federation of Women's Clubs; the National Women's Trade Union League; and, most powerfully, the National Consumers' League.

I N FEBRUARY 1903, THE OREGON LEGISLATURE passed one such law prohibiting employers from hiring women to work more than ten hours a day operating mechanical equipment in certain commercial businesses (including steam laundries). A year and a half later, Curt Muller, the prosperous owner of a small chain of Portland laundries, told Emma Gotcher that she could not leave before meeting her quota for the day. Faced with the choice of working overtime or possibly losing her job, Gotcher finished her work and then complained to the office of the Oregon labor commissioner. Two weeks later, the county court cited Muller for criminal misconduct.

Instead of paying the fine and letting the case drop, Muller decided to fight the judgment. He didn't like any law that hampered

In September 1909, the National Women's Trade Union League held its second convention in Chicago. That winter, the NWTUL also played an important role in the New York City shirtwaist strike that built up the garment workers' unions.

his flexibility as an employer, and a consortium of laundry owners who felt the same way was willing to fund and otherwise back his appeal. To handle the litigation, Muller retained distinguished Portland lawyer and former Southern Pacific Railroad counsel William D. Fenton, who opposed the judgment on constitutional grounds. He argued, not surprisingly, that Oregon's 1903 law improperly interfered with his client's right to contract freely with his employees. That Gotcher was a woman, Fenton insisted in his brief, made no difference because women were "entitled to the same rights, under the Constitution, to make contracts with reference to [their] labor as are secured thereby to men." The general right of any person "to pursue any lawful calling" was not one that could be abridged by the state. Yet, Fenton continued, this was precisely what Oregon had done in the name of protecting women's health, thereby sacrificing a woman's right to her own labor "in an attempt to conserve the public health and welfare."

The county trial judge had sympathized with Muller—but because Muller had, after all, admitted to violating the law, the judge had found him guilty. Fenton's appeal to the Oregon Supreme Court failed to overturn that judgment, but it did clarify the issues involved. Rooting its June 1906 decision in *Holden v. Hardy,* the state supreme court reasoned that because the health of the workers was at stake, the regulation of women's hours was legal. Once again Muller appealed, this time to the U.S. Supreme Court.

S EEING A TEST CASE IN THE MAKING, the Oregon Consumers' League contacted its parent organization, the National Consumers' League—whose executive secretary, Florence Kelley, was an early and eager advocate of protective labor legislation. Kelley had been an architect of Illinois's unsuccessful 1893 eight-hour law, and now she saw the opportunity to establish a beneficial precedent, settling the issue once and for all.

By the time Kelley got involved, Fenton had already submitted to the Supreme Court a detailed brief, based on precedent, defending his client's freedom to contract. Oregon's attorney general knew he needed help, so he encouraged Kelley to approach Joseph Choate, a distinguished lawyer friend of his. Rebuffed, Kelley immediately turned to the lawyer she most trusted—someone who could argue persuasively that the public interest in preserving women's health overrode whatever private rights inhered in freedom of contract. That person was Louis Brandeis, brother-in-law of Josephine Goldmark, director of legislation and law for the National Consumers' League.

FLORENCE KELLEY

1859 – 1932

After her graduation from Cornell in 1882, Florence Kelley continued studying social problems at the University of Zürich, where she became a socialist and translated into English Friedrich Engels's 1887 study The Condition of the Working Class in England in 1844. *Returning to America, she began working in 1891 at Chicago's Hull House settlement, where she later met William English Walling. In 1899, Kelley became secretary of the National Consumers' League and moved to New York City, where she took up residence at Lillian Wald's Henry Street Settlement. In 1909, she joined the biracial civil rights group, led initially by Walling, that founded the NAACP.*

In 1907, Brandeis was a distinguished professor of law at Harvard with a reputation for defending progressive legislation, particularly laws that regulated transportation monopolies and insurance companies. When Kelley and Goldmark came to call, he quickly agreed to participate in the case on two conditions: He wanted Oregon's attorney general to remain the attorney of record, and he insisted on having the facts necessary to make the argument that long hours threatened women's health. The thesis that Kelley, Goldmark, and Brandeis subsequently developed asserted that the maternal destiny and physical constitution of women—along with their greater vulnerability to fatigue as a result of their dual roles as paid and unpaid workers—gave the state reasonable cause to limit their liberties and deprive them of due process. Goldmark and a team of ten young social scientists conducted research that produced hundreds of pages of supporting material. Using this data, Goldmark and Brandeis wrote the 113-page argument that has since come down to us as the Brandeis Brief.

Drawing on the Court's *Lochner* rationale, the Brandeis Brief acknowledged that, for the Oregon law to be constitutional, the state had to demonstrate the existence of a public interest substantial enough to override the parties' freedom of contract. The brief then laid out an authoritative basis for arguing that such an interest did exist where women workers were concerned. To prove the special dangers that long hours of work posed to women (because of their physical constitutions and the negative impact of overwork on childbirth), Goldmark and Brandeis cited dozens of medical authorities and social science experts from the United States and abroad. The Supreme Court was impressed. Unanimously, it upheld the Oregon law.

UNEXPECTEDLY, THE MAJORITY decision was written by Associate Justice David J. Brewer, one of the Court's more conservative members. Previously, Brewer had voted often to uphold the rights of employers and corporations, so many expected him to embrace Fenton's freedom-of-contract appeal. But Brewer also believed strongly in a woman's special place, and liberty, he acknowledged, especially in the case of women, wasn't absolute. Therefore, citing the painstakingly assembled data in the Brandeis Brief, he concurred that a "woman's physical structure and the performance of maternal functions place her at a disadvantage in the struggle for subsistence," adding that "as healthy mothers are essential to vigorous offspring, the physical well-being of woman becomes an object of public interest and care in order to preserve the strength and vigor of the race." Noting as well the family's need for

LOUIS BRANDEIS

1856 – 1941

Louis Brandeis was the son of Bohemian Jews, who had emigrated from Prague in 1849 and settled in Kentucky. He was educated in the Louisville public schools and at Harvard Law, where in 1877 he was graduated first in his class. Practicing in Boston, he became known as "the people's attorney" because he often defended the interests of working people for no pay. Nominated to the Supreme Court by Woodrow Wilson in January 1916, he was opposed by the business lobby and anti-Semites but eventually confirmed in June. Even after his appointment, however, Brandeis remained secretly active in social causes, funding them quietly through his friend Felix Frankfurter.

the services of women, Brewer sharply distinguished *Muller* from other cases that involved legislation protecting men. "The two sexes differ in structure of body, in the functions to be performed by each, in the amount of physical strength, in the capacity for long-continued labor," he wrote. Finally, he insisted that woman—who "has always been dependent on man"—"is properly placed in a class by herself, and legislation designed for her protection may be sustained, even when like legislation is not necessary for men and could not be sustained."

With the Court's decision, advocates of protective labor legislation for women won a great victory, but it came at some cost. Carefully refusing to sustain laws ameliorating the conditions faced by all workers, the Court invoked the police power of the state only to protect a traditional view of women and family life. In so doing, it transformed women into wards of the state—who, like children, had a special need for protection because of their weakness. As the *New York Herald* reported on February 25, 1908, the day after the decision came down, "legally she is in a class by herself." The tone of such coverage made it clear that much of the public found the outcome not only appropriate but also desirable. A leading reform magazine greeted the decision with a declaration that although the Court had nominally addressed "a constitutional question, it is really a vast social question that the Court has answered."

The labor movement joined in the general expression of satisfaction, but its leaders had more pressing concerns. Just three weeks earlier, the Supreme Court had resolved the famous Danbury Hatters' Case (formally *Loewe v. Lawlor*) by declaring that unions, already barred from organizing boycotts against the clients of their employers, could be assessed triple damages for such actions, as could the individual union members who participated in them. Unions responded to this decision, which threatened their very existence, by organizing public protest meetings designed to renew the commitment to voluntarism. American Federation of Labor leaders were busy with this work on February 24, the day that the *Muller* decision came down. The AFL leadership, therefore, embraced the *Muller* judgment because it was consistent with their views of women and of family life and because it finally resolved the troublesome issue of women workers. The women reformers who had backed the *Muller* case generally mistrusted male trade unionists, but even they welcomed the AFL's tacit support for new labor legislation regulating the working hours of women.

The group of nine justices *that decided* Muller v. Oregon *was known as the Fuller Court after Chief Justice Melville Fuller.*

David J. Brewer, *appointed to the Court by Pres. Benjamin Harrison in 1889, generally joined conservative justices in resisting the trend toward greater power and responsibility for the federal government. Yet, writing the majority opinion for* In Re Debs *(1895), he upheld the constitutionality of federal court injunctions then being used against labor strikes.*

During the early 1910s, both the number of strikes and the number of women joining unions increased dramatically. An important catalyst was the strike staged by shirtwaist workers in New York City beginning in November 1909. (These pickets were photographed early in 1910.) Similar strikes followed in Philadelphia and Chicago, promoting union membership, and by 1920, nearly one-half of the women in the clothing trades were organized. Through these unions, the Amalgamated Clothing Workers of America and the International Ladies' Garment Workers Union, women finally entered the mainstream of the American labor movement.

THE MAJORITY OF WOMEN ACTIVISTS cheered *Muller* because, at the turn of the twentieth century, they shared the common assumption that men should be the primary breadwinners in the family; and, like male unionists, they applauded the decision's acknowledgment of women's maternal roles. Women activists also accepted the Court's rationale that women had weaker constitutions; less physical strength; and bodies that were more susceptible to fatigue, toxins, and muscular damage. The few men and women who were worried by the Court's vision of women as dependent and sickly remained in the shadows, along with those who feared that the decision would further diminish the labor movement by dividing it along gender lines.

Some of these fears were calmed by the suggestion that labor legislation for women might serve as an "entering wedge" for protective legislation benefiting all workers, but the sexually divisive rationale behind *Muller* prevented that from happening. Between 1908 and 1917, nineteen states and the District of Columbia passed laws limiting the number of hours women could work and otherwise restricting their labor. Much of this new legislation was justified on the basis of *Muller,* and the court cases that sustained these new laws all turned on versions of the Brandeis Brief (which the National Consumers' League had assiduously circulated). But where Brandeis and Goldmark had attempted to persuade the Court that social science data could allow it to become more generally involved in resolving social issues, their successors narrowed the focus of the litigation, emphasizing (and sometimes exaggerating) the role of sex differences in order to ensure success. Even Brandeis and Goldmark focused their approach. After *Muller,* Goldmark expanded her research into the effects of fatigue on women; and in 1909, she and Brandeis used this new data to persuade the Illinois Supreme Court (in the case of *Ritchie and Company v. Wayman*) to sustain a tenhour law for women. As the Supreme Court had in *Muller,* the Illinois court cited sex distinctions as the grounds for its decision, with Judge John Hand declaring that "women's physical structure and the performance of maternal functions place her at a great disadvantage in the battle of life." Other decisions followed, all of which relied heavily on the construction of women as a separate class before the law.

Of course, this rationale did little to protect men in the workplace. In 1916, Oregon passed a law requiring employers to pay overtime to any man or woman working in excess of ten hours a day. (The law effectively applied only to men, because women were already forbidden to work such long hours.) Defending the law before the Court, Harvard law professor Felix Frankfurter tried to apply the principles contained in the Brandeis Brief to men, but he was not persuasive. In its 1917 *Bunting v. Oregon* decision, the Court ignored the law's implicit regulation of men's hours and permitted the overtime pay on other grounds.

FURTHER READING

★ Sara M. Evans,
Born for Liberty: A History of Women in America (1989)

★ Alice Kessler-Harris,
Out to Work: A History of Wage-Earning Women in the United States (1982)

WHATEVER ITS GOOD INTENTIONS (we can certainly give credit for those) and whatever immediate benefits women workers received (reduced hours and safer workplaces were two), the strategy of isolating women as a legal class soon began to impact them well beyond the workplace and in ways that were not always positive. In 1915, for example, a New York court (in the case of *People v. Schweinler*) sustained a law that prohibited women from working at night—much to the dissatisfaction of women printers, who protested that the law threatened their livelihoods and deprived them of the extra wages they could earn at night.

Emboldened by the new case law, other state legislatures began denying women the opportunity to hold jobs that might expose them to close and possibly salacious contact with men. These were often jobs that required contact with strangers, such as delivering telegrams, operating elevators, and collecting tickets on streetcars. Encouraged by unions, some state lawmakers even enacted seemingly arbitrary restrictions on women's

work around machinery or with heavy objects, thereby excluding women from wide ranges of industrial work. As these legal restrictions replaced weaker customary restraints on women, the sexual division of labor affirmed by *Muller* was exacerbated, and growing numbers of women were crowded into a restricted universe of permissible jobs.

Nor did the courts see fit to compensate women for limiting their workplace choices—for instance, by offering them wage protection. In 1916, the Supreme Court—unpersuaded by Felix Frankfurter's argument that women's health could not be sustained without adequate income—barely upheld in *Stettler v. O'Hara* Oregon's meager attempt to provide women with a minimum wage. And six years later, the Court turned back

Lewis W. Hine took this photograph of a girl working in a Tampa, Florida, box factory on January 28, 1909. In his notes, he recorded, "I saw 10 small boys and girls working. Has a bad reputation for employment of youngsters, but work is slack now."

> **"IF WE WOULD GUIDE BY THE LIGHT OF REASON, WE MUST LET OUR MINDS BE BOLD."**
>
> —
>
> *Louis Brandeis,*
> New York State Ice Co.
> v. Liebmann, *1932*

the District of Columbia's effort to set a minimum wage for women. In *Adkins v. Children's Hospital,* the majority conceded the need to protect women's physical well-being but saw no reason to intervene in the wage bargain. "The physical differences must be recognized in appropriate cases, and legislation fixing hours or conditions of work may properly be taken into account," Associate Justice George Sutherland wrote for the majority. But if women were to be guaranteed a minimum wage for their labor, that would restrict the liberty of an employer to pay as much or as little as he wished. His freedom of contract would thus be violated.

AS THE YEARS PASSED, even as the Supreme Court slowly backed away from freedom-of-contract law, the principle that women constituted a special legal class endured. When a Massachusetts court affirmed the exclusion of women from juries in 1931, it drew on Brewer's argument in *Muller.* There was no difference, the Massachusetts court held, between denying women the right to make certain kinds of labor contracts and denying them the right to serve on juries. Such a law "violates no rights or privileges secured to women by the Fourteenth Amendment," Associate Justice John M. Harlan asserted with regard to a similar case, *Hoyt v. Florida,* reviewed by the Supreme Court in 1961.

In 1948, acting in *Goesaert v. Cleary,* the Court sustained Michigan's ban on women working as bartenders. Writing for the majority, Felix Frankfurter (whom Franklin Roosevelt had appointed to the Court in 1939) invoked the argument his mentor Louis Brandeis had made that it was proper for women to be treated as a separate class. Acknowledging that major changes had taken place in women's lives during the forty years since *Muller*—but forgetting the degree to which Brandeis himself had relied on the Court's perception of the social good—Frankfurter insisted that "the Constitution does not require legislatures to reflect sociological insight, or shifting social standards, any more than it requires them to keep abreast of the latest scientific standards." When in 1956 Oregon denied women the right to wrestle publicly (and thus professionally), the Supreme Court upheld the law on the same grounds, taking "judicial notice of the physical differences between men and women" (just as Brandeis had requested) and asserting that "there should be at least one island on the sea of life reserved for man and that would be impregnable to the assault of woman." The state of Texas came to the same conclusion when in 1960 it decided to exclude women from an all-male university. Sex was a reasonable basis for classification, the courts agreed, in part because it had already been applied so widely in cases beyond employment and labor law.

The caption *to this July 1955 wire-service photo of women wrestling professionally in Chicago was headlined "Strictly Legal," but that wouldn't be the case for long.*

For nearly sixty years—until Title VII of the Civil Rights Act of 1964 initiated a reconsideration of women's legal status—court decisions affirmed and legitimized the popular wisdom of 1908. They altered the relationship of working women to the state and in doing so renegotiated the terms of their citizenship. These rulings also played a decisive role in perpetuating and reinforcing the sexual division of labor, contributing to the wage gap between men and women and significantly enhancing gender divisions within the family. Arguably, too, they affirmed male prejudices against working women and changed the course of the labor movement by providing male leaders with a basis for excluding female workers. By offering a persuasive rationale for excluding women from the Fourteenth Amendment's equal protection clause, the *Muller v. Oregon* decision canonized the belief, prevalent in 1908, that women and men could reasonably be treated differently before the law.

A ND YET WE CAN DRAW more benign conclusions as well. For instance, the *Muller* decision empowered a generation of women to organize on behalf of progressive labor legislation. Groups such the National Consumers' League recruited and trained women in every state and many local communities—women such as NCL lobbyist Frances Perkins, who went on to play central roles in shaping and enacting the revolutionary welfare legislation of the 1930s. And even as *Muller*'s negative impact became more obvious, it fueled organizational engagement among women who recognized and opposed the decision's stigmatization of women as weak. This struggle to discard the burdensome legacy of *Muller* informed the women's liberation movement of the 1960s, many of whose leaders saw that achieving sex equality demanded first and foremost the reversal of the sex-difference jurisprudence that still limited a woman's ability to work at the occupation of her choice.

By 1971, the *Muller* decision had run its course. That year in *Phillips v. Martin Marietta*, the Supreme Court—taking into account dramatic changes in women's workforce participation, their demands for equality before the law, and changes in family structure and responsibility—grudgingly agreed that gender probably no longer constituted an appropriate legal classification. The burden of *Muller v. Oregon* was finally lifted.

★ ★ ★

This African-American woman was photographed at work in a laundry in 1909 or soon thereafter. While the rhetoric of sisterhood was an important part of the early-twentieth-century women's movement, the well-educated and often well-to-do white women who led the movement for protective laws rarely reached out to understand and accommodate the needs of people of color.

Tree where negro was
Lynced.

AUGUST 14, 1908

THE END OF ACCOMODATION

BY DAVID LEVERING LEWIS

ON THE NIGHT OF August 14, 1908, a race riot convulsed Springfield, Illinois. In the town where Abraham Lincoln, the Great Emancipator, lay peacefully entombed, a white mob of thousands swept through black neighborhoods like a plague of locusts, howling, "Lincoln freed you, we'll show you where you belong!" The alleged rape of a white woman by a well-spoken young black man was the immediate cause of the riot, but its tremendous explosive power was fueled more by economic and demographic circumstances. Springfield's population in 1908 was only 10 percent African American, but the black community was growing rapidly, and working-class blacks were competing actively with whites for both jobs and living space. Boardinghouse keeper Kate Howard's bawling charge to the mob—"What the hell are

W.E.B. Du Bois
29
Black Heritage USA

you fellas afraid of?…Women want protection!"—led to more than eighty injuries, six fatal shootings, two lynchings, and the flight of some two thousand African Americans. Finally the National Guard restored order, but after the conflagration in Springfield, Illinoisans and other northerners could no longer claim that the race problem was an unfortunate feature of life exclusive to the former Confederacy. The problem of race was now a fully American dilemma.

There was shock outside the South and much smug comment within it. In Illinois, excuses were made: "It was not the fact of the whites' hatred toward the negroes," the *Illinois State Journal* suggested, "but of the negroes' own misconduct, general inferiority or unfitness for free institutions that were at fault." Even the governor of the state was heard to wonder whether an elderly black businessman had not invited his own lynching by resisting the white rioters. Invidious rationalizations such as these held fearful significance for the nation, said peripatetic millionaire socialist William English Walling, who raced to the city with his Russian

AT LEFT: *During the August 14, 1908, race riot in Springfield, an African American was lynched on this street corner.*

ABOVE: *The Springfield riot set in motion events that resulted two years later in the founding of the NAACP by, among others, W. E. B. Du Bois. The U.S. Postal Service released this stamp honoring Du Bois in January 1992.*

WILLIAM ENGLISH WALLING

1877 – 1936

As a young man, William English Walling was captivated by the idea of ridding American society of its disparities of wealth and power. While studying at the University of Chicago in the mid-1890s, he became a socialist, and during the Russian revolution of 1905, he fell in love with Anna Strunsky, a Russian Jewish immigrant whose revolutionary politics had made her unwelcome in her homeland. Their romance caught the fancy of American society pages, but like the socialist movement itself, the marriage foundered on the shoals of World War I. Walling's support for U.S. intervention alienated his wife, and after the war, he drifted increasingly rightward.

wife, Anna Strunsky, just as the violence was subsiding. Two years earlier, the handsome twenty-nine-year-old Walling had dashed off to St. Petersburg after news of Bloody Sunday, the massacre of peasants and workers before the Winter Palace, reached him in Paris. His mother's people had been Kentucky slaveholders, but the aristocratic Walling was a passionate reformer, a disciple of the magnetic social activist Robert Hunter, and a member of the American Socialist party.

"Race War in the North"—Walling's article in the September 3, 1908, edition of *The Independent*—threw down the gauntlet to those who cared about civil liberties and fair treatment. If the Springfield riot had occurred thirty years earlier, the North would have been outraged, Walling wrote. Instead, "mitigating circumstances" were offered up everywhere, and although the real cause of the riot was obviously "race hatred," Walling asserted, "we at once discovered that Springfield had no shame." But then neither did the nation. According to Walling, the issue was clear, the moment historic: "Either the spirit of the abolitionists, of Lincoln and of [Elijah P.] Lovejoy, must be revived and we must come to treat the negro on a plane of absolute political and social equality, or [southern politicians James K.] Vardaman and [Benjamin] Tillman will soon have transferred the race war to the North." The article's final words about the widening persecution of African Americans took the form of an anguished question: "Yet who realizes the seriousness of the situation, and what large and powerful body of citizens is ready to come to their aid?"

A T THE TIME WALLING made this appeal, the current ground rules for race relations in America were those written by Booker T. Washington in collaboration with the leaders of the white South and powerful industrial and philanthropic elements in the North and East. Washington, the founder of Tuskegee Institute, and his Tuskegee Machine represented the belief among civil rights advocates that black people should consent to social and political subordination until economic self-improvement enabled them to lay claim to the citizenship rights possessed by whites. Opposition to Washington's doctrine of accommodationism was growing, however, and the Springfield riot persuaded many more blacks, as well as whites, that the cause of African-American equality demanded a more activist approach than Washington and his allies were willing to take. Indeed, the Springfield race riot set in motion a chain of events that led, within two epic years, to the founding of the National Association for the Advancement of Colored People (NAACP), the first activist civil rights organization.

In the meantime, Walling counted on his close friend in the Liberal Club—socialist scribe, investigative journalist, and muckraker novelist Charles Edward Russell—to help him put together an organization populated by "fair-minded whites and intelligent blacks." As it happened, Russell had already met a man who far exceeded Walling's requirement for an "intelligent" African-American collaborator. At New York City's Republican Club, Russell had listened to a judge, a minister, and a public official discourse on the race problem. Then William Edward Burghardt Du Bois spoke and "eclipsed the rest." The author of *The Souls of Black Folk* would become the star of Walling's interracial coalition, bringing into the organization the small but highly influential body of men active in Du Bois's militant Niagara Movement.

Before Du Bois's advent, however, it was settlement house pioneer Mary White Ovington, another socialist, who supplied the initial organizational spark. Several weeks after reading Walling's article in *The Independent*, Ovington took in a lecture given by Walling at Cooper Union. There she heard him declare in the course of his talk on Russian politics that the race situation in America was worse, in some respects, than anything in tsarist Russia. Afterward, she pressed him to stage a meeting, which he finally called for the first week of January 1909. Although Russell was detained elsewhere, Ovington attended, along with social worker Dr. Henry Moskowitz.

At this first informal meeting, held in Walling's apartment on West Thirty-ninth Street, Walling, Ovington, and Moskowitz made two decisions: They chose Lincoln's Birthday as the day on which they would launch a public campaign to mobilize biracial support for African-American rights, and they agreed to invite Oswald Garrison Villard to become the group's fifth member. Recalling that event thirty years later, Villard wrote, "No greater compliment has ever been paid to me."

A manifesto, or "call," was soon prepared, with Walling writing the initial text and Villard serving as the ideal final draftsman in light of his greater social distinction and ownership of the *New York Evening Post* and *The Nation*. Villard was an egocentric man of limited personal warmth, but he tended to express himself in writing with passion and generosity. Reeling off the mounting outrages against the race of Africans in America, in the North as well as the South, he infused "The Call" with righteous wrath:

If Mr. Lincoln could revisit this country he would be disheartened by the nation's failure [to assure each citizen equality of opportunity].... In many States Lincoln would find justice enforced, if at all, by judges elected by one element in a community to pass upon the liberties and lives of another. He would see the black men and women, for whose freedom a hundred thousand of soldiers gave their lives, set apart in trains, in which they pay first-class fares for third-class service, in railway stations and in places of entertainment, while State after State declines to do its elementary duty in preparing the negro through education for the best exercise of citizenship.

Silence in the face of such outrages, Villard went on, meant tacit approval. "This government cannot exist half slave and half free any better today than it could in 1861," he warned, and in conclusion he summoned "all the believers in democracy to join in a national conference for the discussion of present evils, the voicing of protests, and the renewal of the struggle for civil and political safety."

As "The Call" circulated, Walling, once he got going, became a powerhouse, bringing into the small group the cream of white progressive reform. He also backed enthusiastically Ovington's recommendation that their Committee on the Status of the Negro include two prominent African-American clergymen of her acquaintance, and by March 1909 the group had swelled to fifteen members, three of whom were black. Having thus grown too large to fit comfortably into Walling's apartment, the committee shifted its proceedings to the more spacious home of the Liberal Club on East Nineteenth Street, where it held its first formal meeting sometime in the middle of March. According to the minutes of

A native of New York City, *Mary White Ovington became active in the campaign for African-American civil rights in 1890, after hearing Frederick Douglass deliver a speech as a Brooklyn church. She held various positions with the NAACP until 1947, when she retired as a board member, ending nearly four decades of service.*

Booker T. Washington *believed that African Americans should abstain from politics until they had accumulated enough wealth through patient, humble industry to ensure the success of their demands for equal treatment.*

that meeting (the first for which any formal minutes exist), plans were already underway for the public conference described in "The Call." The first National Negro Conference would be held on May 31 and June 1 at the Charity Organization Society hall in Lower Manhattan, not far from Astor Place. Significantly, Booker Washington's name was not among those listed as sponsors of the event.

O N THE DESIGNATED MONDAY morning of May 31, 1909, the high-ceilinged auditorium of the Charity Organization hall was filled to capacity with a distinguished audience keenly aware of the history about to be made. Here, for the first time since the great abolitionist meetings of the 1850s and the suffrage conclaves held in the aftermath of the Civil War, had come together white and black people, men and women, in united purpose to resurrect the interrupted advance of civil rights. William Hayes Ward, the editor of *The Independent*, gave a ringing keynote address. His newspaper, along with Villard's, had been among the rare white clarions of racial fair play. Now, he told the capacity audience, it was imperative to draw battle lines; it was time to proclaim to the nation the "absolute divergence of view between the ruling majority in the South…and ourselves."

The three hundred or so men and women in the hall included experienced social uplifters, affluent dabblers in reform, descendants of abolitionists, public-minded academics, and suffragists—with women comprising nearly one-third of those in attendance. (Their perfumes and lotions, some noted, combined memorably with the acrid body odors released as the warm day advanced.) The presence of Fanny Garrison Villard (Oswald's mother) and other women associated with the female suffrage campaign was an encouraging augury because, although overt discord between white women and black men had greatly abated since the bitter days immediately after the Civil War (when Frederick Douglass had colluded in sacrificing female suffrage for the half loaf of ballots for black men), some tension still existed below the surface. However, as Du Bois himself observed later, "The curiosity of the spectators was toward the darker and less known portion of the audience."

The conference opened with a morning of speeches enunciating its principal theme: the basic humanity of black people, especially as it related to their mental and biological parity with whites. One after another, four learned white academics stepped to the podium: Columbia anthropologist Livingston Farrand; Cornell neurologist Burt G. Wilder; Columbia political economist Edwin Seligman; and, closing the charged morning session, Columbia philosopher John Dewey, whose instrument-

OSWALD GARRISON VILLARD

1872 – 1949

Oswald Garrison Villard's father, Henry Villard, emigrated to the United States from Germany in 1853 and worked as a journalist in New York City before making his fortune as a railroad executive. Oswald's mother, Fanny Garrison Villard, was the daughter of antislavery activist William Lloyd Garrison and herself a social reformer of note. It was Henry who, in 1881, bought the New York Evening Post, *which Oswald inherited on his father's death in 1900. In keeping with his pacifist views, Oswald opposed American intervention in World War I. His position, however, generated such enmity among the* Post *readership that he was forced to sell the newspaper in 1918.*

W. E. B. Du Bois

1868 – 1963

William Edward Burghardt Du Bois, educated at Fisk University between 1885 and 1888, became in 1896 the first African American to receive a doctorate from Harvard. From 1897 until 1910 (when he became editor of The Crisis*), Du Bois taught economics and history at Atlanta University, where he developed his concept of the Talented Tenth. Du Bois believed in leadership from the top, provided by college-educated men and women of color located largely in the urban North and committed to full and immediate equality for blacks. He wrote most famously of this class in his seminal essay "Of Mr. Booker T. Washington and Others," published in* The Souls of Black Folk *(1903).*

alist verdict on racism was that it deprived society of "social capital." Professor Wilder meanwhile presented an array of charts, photographs, and measurements rebutting the "alleged prefrontal deficiency in the Negro brain" and thought it reassuring to tell the audience that indeed "many white brains have lateral or ventral depression of the prefrontal lobe." The turn of the twentieth century was an era in which many educated whites still believed that black people had been created separately and that Darwinian evolution had passed them by. The science of the day had only just begun to adduce evidence that the biological and mental variations within races were as great as those among them. Wilder's remarks were therefore relatively enlightened, and for this reason Du Bois chose to abide by the etiquette of black gratitude for white solicitousness. Writing animatedly in the June issue of *The Survey,* a liberal opinion magazine in the mold of *The Nation,* he declared that the two-day conclave had found the Negro to be fully human and the opposing argument to be "utterly without scientific basis."

With this heartening evidence of biological and mental equivalency in the air, both races took lunch together at the nearby Union Square Hotel so as to get to know one another. Even in large northern cities, though, interracial meals were rare and never risk free. The previous year, the progressive Cosmopolitan Club had sponsored a well-attended biracial dinner at Peck's Restaurant on Brooklyn's Fulton Street only to have it compromised the next morning by salacious accounts in the New York press, the *New York Times* included. To Ovington's immense relief, lunch at the Union Square Hotel went smoothly.

> "THE PROBLEM OF THE TWENTIETH CENTURY IS THE PROBLEM OF THE COLOR LINE."
>
> —W. E. B. Du Bois, speech, 1900—

THE NATIONAL NEGRO CONFERENCE reassembled that afternoon at Cooper Union, where Du Bois took a turn at the podium. His text was entitled "Politics and Industry." He didn't say so directly, but the unmistakable impression he gave was that he believed the matter of proving Negro intellectual parity to be of secondary importance. What did matter was the habit of white progressives—in their well-intentioned zeal to improve the housing, employment, health, and morals of black people—to mistake effects for causes. Du Bois argued specifically that black people had lost their self-respect and become almost a different species in the eyes of many whites, not because they were forced to live in squalid conditions but because they were no longer citizens—civil persons—in the South and elsewhere. They had thus been degraded by a new slavery that could never be abolished until African Americans had the ballot. In Du Bois's view, economic power would come once political power had been regained and not the reverse, as Booker Washington maintained.

Encouraged by the fiery Du Bois, the black men and women who had bantered and deferred so nicely over lunch on Monday seemed to the whites by Tuesday to have abandoned their desire for consensus. Du Bois caught this altered mood in his account for *The Survey*: "The black mass moved forward and stretched out their hands to take charge. It was their problem. They must name the condition." How could there be such a thing as "too much racial agitation?" demanded Boston newspaper publisher William Monroe Trotter and antilynching crusader Ida B. Wells-Barnett after a white participant seemed to say as much. And Trotter didn't stop there: Regarding the subject of Pres. William Howard Taft's announced intention to appoint to his new administration only those African Americans regarded as trustworthy by the South, Trotter demanded that Taft be censured; he was later joined by J. Milton Waldron, founder of the National Negro American Political League of the District of Columbia, in doggedly raising objection after objection and proposing amendment after amendment, which combined with other wrangling over semantics and points of order to carry the final session of the conference well into the evening.

Before the proceedings were gaveled to a close near midnight, however, the conference did vote into being the National Committee for the Advancement of the Negro (NCAN), precursor of the NAACP. Earlier that evening, Walling, acting as chairperson, had fumbled badly, but Villard had stepped into the leadership breach and pounded out the final resolutions that were approved by the full conference. Wells-Barnett, a firebrand feminist from Chicago, spoke with special passion for those who favored the boldest declaration without any hint of diplomacy. She must have been the woman Du Bois later described as leaping to her feet when someone proposed inviting Booker Washington to serve on a prospective committee, crying "in passionate, almost tearful earnestness—an earnestness born of bitter experience—'They are betraying us again—these white friends of ours.'" Afterward, in a philosophical mood, Villard concluded that "these poor people who have been tricked so often by white men" ought not to be

OVERLEAF:

A sizable crowd watches the 1893 lynching of a black man accused of murdering a three-year-old white girl. Although most lynchings were carried out by small groups with little visibility, some (such as this one) were remarkably well publicized, often attracting large audiences.

Among the women attending the 1909 National Negro Conference was Inez Milholland, who is pictured here four years later in Washington, D.C., leading the March 1913 woman suffrage parade.

SCIENTIFIC PHILANTHROPY

In 1889, Scottish-born industrialist Andrew Carnegie, who rose from poverty to become the nation's greatest steel baron, wrote "Wealth," an essay in which he argued that well-to-do citizens had a moral obligation to return some of their wealth to the community. Chief among the "scientific" principles he established was: Help those willing to help themselves. He listed these seven fields of philanthropy as the "wisest": universities, free libraries, hospitals, parks, convert halls, swimming baths, and church buildings.

The London journal Punch *published this cartoon in May 1901, soon after Carnegie gave one million pounds to support free education.*

blamed for being so fractious, yet the experience had been "none the less trying." It was the unflappable Russell who "saved us from being blown up," Ovington wrote later.

Although Du Bois privately knew better and admitted that much work remained, writing in *The Survey* for public consumption and the benefit of institutional solidarity, he sounded positively euphoric:

> *So the conference adjourned. Its net result was the vision of future cooperation, not simply as in the past, between giver and beggar—the older ideal of charity—but a new alliance between experienced social workers and reformers in touch on the one hand with scientific philanthropy [as espoused by Andrew Carnegie] and on the other with the great struggling mass of laborers of all kinds, whose condition and needs know no color line.*

THE THOUSAND OR SO men and women who streamed out of the Cooper Union mass meeting that night had voted to reprimand the president of the United States, demand strict enforcement of civil rights under the Fourteenth and Fifteenth Amendments, appeal for African-American access to the ballot on the same terms as other citizens (though female suffrage was not addressed), and call for equal educational opportunities for all Americans in all the states.

Yet it was the resolution establishing a Committee of Forty on Permanent Organization that set off the most fireworks, even though Villard had drafted the resolution with particular care. The chief problem was that, when Du Bois read the list of committee members in the closing minutes of the conference, the names of Ida Wells-Barnett, Monroe Trotter, and Milton Waldron were noticeably missing. All three were stunned and angry, but none more so than Wells-Barnett, who had been told earlier that her name headed the list. In a later autobiographical account, she vividly described her experience standing with Du Bois in the near-empty hall, surrounded by a knot of dismayed whites, as the race radical, confirmed feminist, and sole African-American member of the nominating committee apologized to her for agreeing that her views be represented by one of the white notables from Chicago's Hull House settlement. Supposedly, Du Bois and several others then pleaded with her to accept reinstatement, but she refused and departed, eyes glistening. "Of course, I did a foolish thing," she recalled regretfully. "My anger at having been treated in such a fashion outweighed my judgment."

Villard thus succeeded in populating the Committee of Forty according to his own purposeful design. Because the Forty would determine the ideological mold of the new organization, choosing its board of directors and hiring its staff, the New York publisher knew that he would have to control its members if he were to consolidate his position as the group's ringmaster. Furthermore, as a practical matter, he was certain that no civil rights organization would be credible if led by radicals and that an alliance with Booker Washington, thus far left out of the proceedings, was necessary. In an attempt to repair relations with the Tuskegee principal, Villard promised him, "It is not to be a Washington movement, or a Du Bois movement," and Villard further accommodated the Great Accommodator by continuing to exclude from NCAN leadership positions such crusading African Americans (and bitter Washington critics) as Trotter, Waldron, and Wells-Barnett. (For similar reasons, Villard also tried to minimize the role of Du Bois, with much less success.) Little wonder that Wells-Barnett declared later that Washington had seemed to sit among them during the Cooper Union proceedings.

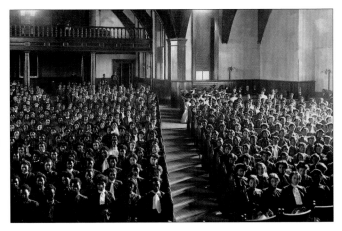

Students fill a lecture hall at Tuskegee Institute shortly after the turn of the twentieth century.

For Du Bois, however, the two-day conference marked the beginning of the end of the Era of Accommodation and the twilight, he believed, of the Tuskegee Machine and its influential white patrons. "The answer long forced on the American world has been: Let them alone; do not agitate; do not let loose dangerous forces and passions," he thundered in *The Survey*. But now the passions were finally loosed, and the great problem of the twentieth century—the problem of the color line, in Du Bois's memorable phrase—was about to be attacked, vigorously and collectively.

Following the adjournment of the National Negro Conference, Du Bois understood that he was expected by many, if not Villard, to play a major role in marshaling the new civil rights coalition. On his shoulders, he believed—and on those of the so-called Talented Tenth minority, which he had nurtured—would rest their race's destiny. It was, Du Bois wrote long afterward, "the opportunity to enter the lists in a desperate fight aimed straight at the real difficulty: the question as to how far educated Negro opinion in the United States was going to have the right and opportunity to guide the Negro group."

THE TUSKEGEE MACHINE

Booker T. Washington founded Tuskegee Institute in 1881 to provide industrial education for blacks and train black teachers. The racial philosophy he developed there, supported by philanthropic whites in the North, dominated the cause of civil rights until the advent of Du Bois's Niagara Movement. The Tuskegee Machine's defining moment came in 1895, when Washington delivered his Atlanta Compromise speech favoring racial accommodation at the Cotton States Expo. "In all things that are purely social," he told his white audience, "we can be as separate as the fingers, yet one as the hand in all things essential to mutual progress."

**IDA B.
WELLS-BARNETT**

1862 – 1931

*In 1887, while teaching
school near Memphis, Ida
B. Wells bought a railroad
ticket and sat in a section
reserved for whites. When
she refused to move, she
was literally thrown off the
train. (She subsequently
sued the railroad for
damages, winning at first
but then losing on
appeal.) Four years later,
she helped found the
militant newspaper* Free
Speech, *in which she
wrote scorching editorials
denouncing whites for
lynching black men in the
name of preserving white
chastity (but for the actual
purpose of eliminating
economic competition).
After a mob burned her
office and threatened to
kill her, Wells took her
crusade overseas, touring
England in 1894. The
next year, she married
lawyer Ferdinand Lee
Barnett, with whom she
had four children while
continuing her social
protest work.*

Although Washington said little in public about the work of the fledgling National Committee for the Advancement of the Negro, his numerous surrogates cajoled, intimidated, and seduced well-placed men and women of color who might have otherwise displayed interest in or support for the new civil rights organization. Among whites, the work of the Forty was similarly undermined by conflicting interests and clashing egos. John Milholland's Constitution League, for example, forerunner of the American Civil Liberties Union, pursued competing claims on white liberal resources. And within the National Committee itself, Villard had come to dislike Walling and was positively contemptuous of Du Bois.

Yet because Villard prided himself on never failing in a cause to which he had publicly committed himself and because Du Bois believed that the fate of his people hung in the balance, these two imperious men exerted themselves through editorials, public addresses, and personal suasion to solidify their respective bases in the weeks leading up to the second meeting of the organization in May 1910. And indeed their efforts were desperately needed: During the past twelve months, the political status of African Americans, already slipping during the final years of Theodore Roosevelt's tenure, had become even more grim under Taft, who had virtually ceased appointing African Americans to federal jobs. Meanwhile, throughout the South, Jim Crow practices were being set in legislative concrete, and in the country at large, ninety-two black men and several black women would be lynched by year's end.

The NAACP's monthly journal of opinion, The Crisis, *created by Du Bois, debuted in November 1910.*

WHILE THE 1909 CONFERENCE had focused on black people's humanity, the National Committee's 1910 gathering—held May 12–14, again in the Charity Organization hall—emphasized the effects of racial disenfranchisement. The broad sense of urgency Du Bois and Villard had successfully conveyed was reflected in a growing cast of celebrity boosters—including philanthropist Susan P. Wharton, lawyer Clarence Darrow, and anthropologist Franz Boas. Money also began to arrive, some of it even coming from past supporters of Booker Washington, as indicated by the donation Henry Street Settlement founder Lillian Wald secured from investment banker Jacob Schiff.

After shaking hands publicly on opening day, Villard and Du Bois collaborated masterfully in managing three days of highly pressured sessions, and on May 14 in the great hall of the Charity Organization Society, they celebrated together their greatest achievement: the formal creation of the nation's oldest extant civil rights organization, the National Association for the Advancement of Colored People. (*Colored* was chosen for the association's name, rather than *Afro-American* or *Negro*, because of the group's intention to promote the interests of dark-skinned people everywhere.) Exactly twenty-one months had passed since the August 1908 Springfield riot, and in that time white and black progressives had come a long way. Now they launched together an organization whose creation marked the beginning of the end of the formal acceptance of second-class citizenship by the black leadership class in America. And henceforth, it was now clear, race relations would be seen as a major issue confronting all Americans and not merely those in the unreconstructed South.

★ ★ ★

FURTHER READING

★ W. E. B. Du Bois,
*The Autobiography of
W. E. B. Du Bois:
A Soliloquy on Viewing
My Life from the Last
Decade of Its First
Century* (1968)

★ David Levering Lewis,
*W. E. B. Du Bois:
Biography of a Race,
1868–1919* (1993)

This photograph of Du Bois *was taken sometime around, or just before, the National Committee's 1910 conference.
Although the organization was altered somewhat when its constitution was approved in 1911, the basic shape of the
National Association for the Advancement of Colored People emerged at this time.*

JANUARY 1, 1913

THE ROUTINE ARREST THAT LAUNCHED A REVOLUTION

BY GEOFFREY C. WARD

HISTORIANS OF THE ARTS in America remember the winter of 1913 mostly for the February 17 opening of the Armory Show, an exhibition of some thirteen hundred artworks held at the Sixty-ninth Regiment Armory on Manhattan's Upper East Side. The event was meant both to showcase the canvases of the native Ashcan school and to introduce the American public to European modernists, but the homegrown art on display was quickly eclipsed by the more adventurous work of such overseas painters as Marcel Duchamp, Wassily Kandinsky, Fernand Léger, Henri Matisse, and Pablo Picasso. Most critics, and a good many of the ninety thousand curiosity seekers who passed through the show's eighteen crowded galleries, came away scornful of what one writer called this

"alien disgorging of a curdled imagination." But American art would never be the same, as painters and sculptors found themselves struggling to come to terms with the developments abroad.

Still, a strong case can be made that the event of 1913 that had the most impact on the development of a genuinely *American* art form had already occurred, a little more than six weeks earlier, in the wide-open Storyville district of New Orleans. Shortly after midnight on January 1, 1913, as church bells rang in the new year, cheerful revelers stumbled in and out of the tonks and whorehouses that lined the muddy streets, singing, dancing, embracing, shooting off fireworks. Two plainclothes detectives stood quietly in the shadows at the corner of Rampart and Perdido to see that things didn't get too far out of hand. Somewhere in the crowd were four small boys, members of a ragged street quartet who had been singing and dancing for tips until the midnight celebration drowned them out.

As the policemen watched, one of the boys broke away from the rest, pulled a big .38

AT LEFT: *At the time this publicity still was taken in 1931, Armstrong had risen from the streets of New Orleans to become the most influential musician in jazz.*

ABOVE: *This Hot Five rendition of "West End Blues"— recorded on June 28, 1928—is considered by many jazz critics the peak of Armstrong's art.*

revolver from beneath his shirt, and gleefully emptied its chambers into the air. The crowd scattered at the echoing sound of the gunfire, and before the laughing boy could reload, one of the detectives grabbed him. "Oh Mister, let me alone," the boy begged, "just take the pistol." Instead, the policeman marched his weeping eleven-year-old captive to the New Orleans Juvenile Court, where he was locked into an empty cell until he could appear before a judge the following morning. The dark cell terrified him; he was "sick and disheartened," he remembered. "What were they going to do to me?" The next morning, he found himself anxiously peering out through the barred window of a jolting horse-drawn Black Maria, on his way to the Colored Waif's Home, a grim institution for New Orleans delinquents on the outskirts of town, to which he had been committed for an indefinite term.

KING OLIVER

1885 – 1938

In his youth, Joseph "King" Oliver worked as a servant for white families in New Orleans while developing a cornet style that held sway until the arrival of Louis Armstrong. In 1910, after performing with various early jazz bands, Oliver (shown here in a photograph taken about 1905) joined one of the city's leading groups, fronted by trombonist Kid Ory. (When Oliver left for Chicago in 1919, Armstrong took his place in Ory's band.) The high point of Oliver's career came in 1923, when he cut forty remarkable sides with Armstrong in Chicago. According to Armstrong, "No trumpet player ever had the fire that Oliver had. Man, he really could punch a number."

NO PLAQUE MARKS THE SPOT where that arrest was made, but the frightened boy was Louis Armstrong, and had he not been locked up that night, the whole course of American music might have been very different. Jazz—that quintessentially American amalgam of blues and black religious music, ragtime and military marches, Italian opera and minstrel tunes and countless other elements absorbed by black and Creole musicians in New Orleans and then compacted into something altogether new—was already flourishing in the city of its birth at the time of Armstrong's arrest, and it would soon begin its steady spread across the country. Yet no one can say how the music might have developed if the man who created what jazz historian Dan Morgenstern has called its "mature working language" had been denied his chance to play it.

This 1910 photograph *shows Johnny Fischer's Marching Band playing on North Rampart Street in New Orleans. It was by following such street parades that Armstrong became familiar with the music of King Oliver.*

Those who recall Armstrong only as the genial entertainer who was a fixture on television variety shows during the 1950s and 1960s may find it hard to see him as the genuine revolutionary he once was. But American music without Louis Armstrong would have been like American literature without Mark Twain, cubism without Picasso, movies without Sergei Eisenstein or D. W. Griffith. His innovations became the common musical coin of the Western world, and they're still heard every day in the hardest rock and the softest elevator music; in the scores for Broadway musicals and Hollywood films and in the sound of symphonic brass players; in television themes and country-and-western tunes and in the playing of every jazz musician who picks up a horn—whether or not he or she knows enough to acknowledge the debt. There is still truth in what Miles Davis said some fifty years after Armstrong first ventured into a recording studio: "You can't play anything on a horn that Louis hasn't played—I mean even modern."

Located at the corner of Basin and Iberville, Anderson's was the most lavish club in Storyville and one of the few in the district large enough to showcase a full-size dance band. Its bar, half a city block long, was manned by a dozen bartenders. Every other building on the block was a brothel.

ARMSTRONG WAS "brought up around music," he remembered, and showed an early interest in joining in. At seven, he blew a long tin horn to announce the progress through the streets of a junk wagon belonging to his first employer. At ten, he struggled to teach himself to play a battered cornet bought from a pawn shop with his employer's help. Meanwhile, he adopted cornetist Joe "King" Oliver as his hero, following street parades for miles in the hope that Oliver would allow him to carry his gleaming horn for a block or two. At eleven,

The Colored Waif's Home Brass Band, photographed in 1913. Louis Armstrong, then twelve years old, sits just behind band manager Peter Davis.

Armstrong began singing tenor in a boy's quartet, and he was performing with this group on the night that he got into trouble. But he was still a wild fatherless boy from a still wilder neighborhood—known as the Battlefield because of the mayhem that routinely took place on its streets—and he was already considered by the courts an "old offender," because he had been picked up several times for minor transgressions. "You had to fight and do a lot of ungodly things," Armstrong once explained when asked about his youthful misbehavior, "to keep from being trampled on." Most of the heroes in his neighborhood were pimps and gamblers, and Armstrong had even thought vaguely of someday becoming a cardsharp himself—one who "didn't steal too much," he said.

"I do believe that my whole success goes back to that time [I was arrested]," he once wrote. "Because then I *had* to quit running around and begin to learn something." Life at the Colored Waif's Home changed everything for him, taught him discipline, and offered him a way up and out of the turbulent world into which he'd been born (and from which there might otherwise have been no escape). "Me and music got married in the Home," he said.

The Colored Waif's Home to which Armstrong was sent was the creation of Capt. Joseph Jones, a black cavalry veteran who had set out single-handedly to provide delinquent black boys with an alternative to jail. "In those days," Captain Jones recalled many years later, "there were a great many youngsters in the city who were supposed to be 'bad,' but it seemed to me they were just kids who never had a chance." Nonetheless, the home was a threadbare place, run along strict military lines. The boys were made to drill with wooden rifles several times a week; meals often consisted of nothing more than bread and molasses; and those who tried to run away could expect to be flogged.

Joseph Jones bought this cornet in a pawnshop and loaned it to Armstrong so that he could continue to play after leaving the Waif's Home. Jones told his former charge to bring the horn back once he'd earned enough money to afford one of his own, and Armstrong did. The cornet now resides in the Louisiana State Museum.

But the home also had a marching band led by an able educator named Peter Davis, one of that legion of unsung African-American teachers for whom segregation was simply a spur to greater effort. A strict disciplinarian, Davis allowed only the most reliable inmates to play in his brightly uniformed outfit. (Because the funds the band raised performing in parades and at picnics and garden parties helped keep the institution running, Davis couldn't risk too many poor performances.)

On one of his return visits to New Orleans, the now-famous Armstrong, joined by his current backing group, sat in with his old, renamed outfit: the Municipal Boys Home Band. The hatless man standing on the right is Peter Davis.

From the moment Armstrong arrived, he wanted to be in that band, but Davis wouldn't hear of it. "Mr. Davis thought that since I had been raised in such bad company," Armstrong explained, "I must also be worthless." The boy enrolled in singing classes, where his teachers took note of his extraordinary gift for harmony, while day after day he sat wistfully watching the band rehearse. After a six-month probationary period, Davis finally relented and allowed Armstrong to join the group. He started the boy off playing the lowly tambourine, then the snare drum, then the alto horn and bugle, and finally the cornet—on which Armstrong quickly developed what one old-timer recalled as "a good solid tone," remarkable in one so young. "Pretty soon I was the leader of the band," Armstrong remembered, "twenty kids, and we played pretty good.... We'd hire out to those big social clubs—the Tammany Social Club, the Broadway Swells, the Moneywasters.... We used to play in that hot sun and...parade for miles and miles and we'd be so tired, and our little lips were sore for a week. But we was glad just to be out in the streets around people."

Nineteen-year-old
Louis Armstrong poses
with his mother,
Mayann, and his sister
Beatrice in 1920.
Armstrong's father,
Willie, had abandoned
the family around the
time of Louis's birth
(and perhaps even before
that). Armstrong
remained close to his
mother until her death
in 1927. He once said
that the only time in his
life that he wept was
when her coffin
was closed.

Much later, Armstrong would give a great deal of credit to Peter Davis for starting him on his way: "He was one of the finest persons I have met in my life," Armstrong wrote. "Even when he would get angry with you, there would be a little something that would make you feel you would definitely do the right thing next time without him saying another word to you." But no teacher, however skilled or inspiring, could have done more than nurture Armstrong's genius, what he modestly called his "gift." For all his genuine deference toward men such as Peter Davis and Joe Oliver who helped him over the years, it seems clear, almost from the moment of his release from the Waif's Home in the spring of 1914, that his destiny was musical revolution.

NEW ORLEANS BRASS BAND MUSIC was a collective art. The cornetist played the lead, but he was only the first among equals, stating the theme around which the clarinetist was expected to weave obbligato embellishments while the drummer kept time and the trombone player offered countermelodies from below. Yet first among equals seems never to have been enough for Louis Armstrong. At fourteen, while working a series of menial day jobs to feed and house his mother and sister, he also began a sweaty late-night apprenticeship in music, playing the blues for whores and their customers in Storyville tonks. It took him only a few months to prove himself more inventive than a good many older musicians: "It never did strike my mind," a cornetist who heard him then recalled, "that the blues could be interpreted in so many different ways." He spent the next three summers playing for dancers—and honing his skill at reading music—aboard steamboats that plied the Mississippi River. Along the way, he developed both the huge warm tone that would make his playing instantly recognizable and a fondness for playing what he called "figurations"—ornate, crowd-pleasing, clarinetlike improvisations that were the envy of his baffled contemporaries. "I didn't never understand Louis Armstrong," recalled one trombonist who tried to play with him in street parades during those years, "because that son-of-a-gun he…wouldn't never once play straight with you. But everything he put in there, by Ned, it worked." Armstrong also listened to recordings of other kinds of music, including operatic arias by Enrico Caruso—all of which turned up in his playing over the years.

By the summer of 1922, when Joe Oliver asked the twenty-one-year-old Armstrong to leave New Orleans and join him at the Lincoln Gardens on Chicago's South Side, jazz had already been a national craze for nearly five years. It had been introduced on records in 1917 by five white men from New Orleans who called themselves the Original Dixieland Jazz Band and whose version of it was raucous, often frenetic, and still closely related to ragtime and the vaudeville stage. Its message, one early practitioner recalled, was, "Let's all get loaded and see how nutty we can sound."

In 1919, Armstrong played with Fate Marable's band aboard the SS Sydney. He's seated fourth from the left, next to Marable at the piano.

The music that Oliver and Armstrong played was different. They also wanted their audiences to have a good time: Oliver was a master at producing vocal imitations with a profusion of mutes, while Armstrong sang and danced and clowned on the bandstand. (He could never quite understand why critics in later years urged him to perform with more "dignity," because for him art and entertainment would always be inextricably linked, equal parts of what he sometimes called his "hustle.") But their music was far more relaxed and flowing than that of the ODJB and its legion of imitators, and it was built around thrilling duet breaks—brief solos played while the band unexpectedly fell silent—during which Armstrong seemed always able to predict just what his boss was about to play and then provide the perfect complement to it. No one seemed to know for sure how they managed this feat, but news of it brought musicians flocking to the club—including so many

Both Armstrong and Bix Beiderbecke played at one time on this Mississippi steamboat, the SS Capitol.

JASS

The indigenous music of turn-of-the-twentieth-century New Orleans was originally called jass *(and even sometimes* jasz) *before the term* jazz *became standardized. Leading the shift was the Original Dixieland Jass Band, which hurriedly changed its name in January 1917 after hearing that small boys were scratching the J's off its posters.*

young white ones that a special weekly Midnight Ramble show was scheduled to accommodate them. Among those who crowded in during the summer of 1923 were pianist and future songwriter Hoagy Carmichael and cornetist Bix Beiderbecke: "We took two quarts of bathtub gin and a package of muggles [marijuana cigarettes]," Carmichael remembered, "[Armstrong] slashed into Bugle Call Rag. I dropped my cigarette and gulped my drink. Bix was on his feet, his eyes popping.… 'Why,' I moaned, 'why isn't everybody in the world here to hear that?' I meant it. Something as unutterably stirring as that deserved to be heard by the world."

IT SOON WOULD BE, because a few weeks earlier Armstrong and Oliver had recorded for the first time. (The younger man's power was already so great that the engineer insisted he stand well back from the recording horn, lest his sound overwhelm that of his mentor.) Within a year, bandleader Fletcher Henderson lured Armstrong to New York to join his dance orchestra at the Roseland Ballroom. Henderson gave Armstrong very little room to show what he could do, rarely more than sixteen bars, but—to quote Dan Morgenstern again—those brief appearances stand out on the band's recordings "like poetry in a sea of doggerel." Before Armstrong's arrival, trumpet player Max Kaminsky recalled, most New York City bands, including Henderson's, were still playing "oompah and ricky-tick, breaking up the rhythm into choppy syncopation." By the sheer inventiveness of his playing, however, and his

This ad appeared in the Chicago Defender *in June 1922, just as Oliver was preparing to send for Louis Armstrong.*

willingness to turn virtually any kind of tune (even a polka) into raw material for jazz, Armstrong changed all that, moving the music away from the old two-beat feel toward a flowing, evenly distributed 4/4 that would eventually become the pulsing heart of big band swing—which one writer later called simply "orchestrated Armstrong." "No one [in New York] knew what swing was till Louis came along," Kaminsky wrote. "It's more than just the beat, it's conceiving the phrases in the very feeling of the beat, molding and building them so that they're an integral, indivisible part of the tempo. Others had the idea of it, but Louis could do it; he was the heir of all that had gone before and the father of all that was to come."

And this new rhythm was only the first of his revolutionary contributions to American music. The infectious jazz that had come boiling up out of New Orleans was still a collectively improvised *ensemble* form. Next, by the sheer power of his musical imagination, Armstrong turned it into a soloist's art. In a series of some sixty-five recordings made between 1925 and 1928 with pickup bands he called his Hot Five and Hot Seven, Louis Armstrong established, once and for all, his supremacy as the most important solo instrumentalist in the history of the music. Although these recordings are mostly rooted in the polyphonic tradition of New Orleans, it's perfectly clear from the opening chorus of the very first side that Armstrong himself is always firmly in charge. By the time he completed this series—as the wife of his friend and drummer Zutty Singleton recalled—his role had expanded until the rest of the musicians were reduced to something like a choir, present mostly to comment on his eloquent preaching.

There were purely technical reasons for Armstrong's supremacy. He could play faster than any other jazz trumpeter of his generation, and he had phenomenal endurance, once hitting 280 high C's in a row as a delirious audience counted cadence with him. He also possessed astonishing power in the highest register. In an era when brass players rarely ascended above high C, Armstrong routinely ended performances with a full-bodied—and prolonged—high F.

Armstrong (standing) with Oliver in Chicago in 1922. Two years later, Armstrong left King Oliver's Creole Jazz Band, and in 1927 Oliver suffered again when he gave up a booking at New York City's Cotton Club. Duke Ellington took the gig instead, and it proved to be the turning point of Ellington's career.

A publicity photograph of Louis Armstrong's Hot Five from 1925. To the right of Armstrong are Johnny St. Cyr and Johnny Dodds, who played with Armstrong in Fate Marable's steamboat band; Kid Ory; and Lil Hardin, who had become Armstrong's second wife in February 1924.

B UT NONE OF THAT would have made him the most important figure in jazz history had he not been a supreme musical logician as well. It was he, more than anyone else, who showed his fellow musicians how to move beyond abbreviated breaks to construct full-length solos. Bix Beiderbecke and fellow cornetist Esten Spurrier hailed Armstrong as the father of what they called the "correlated chorus," and Spurrier later did his best to explain what he and Beiderbecke had meant: "Play two measures, then two related, making four measures, on which you played another four measures related to the first four, and so on ad infinitum to the end of the chorus. So the secret was simple— a series of related phrases." Of course, the secret was anything but simple. Armstrong's genius, wrote the late jazz critic Martin Williams, was that he could "take any piece, add a note here, leave out a note there, condense or displace this melodic phrase a bit, rush this cadence, delay that one, alter another slightly and transform it into sublime melody, into pure gold."

By 1928, when Armstrong recorded his masterpiece "West End Blues," he was regularly demonstrating, in the words of composer and conductor Gunther Schuller, that jazz "had the potential to compete with the highest order of previously known expression." Musicians now very nearly worshiped him—Duke Ellington once lamented that he couldn't have Louis Armstrong play for him on *every* instrument—and when the Melrose Bros. Music Company published *Louis Armstrong's 50 Hot Choruses for Cornet* and *Louis Armstrong's 125 Jazz Breaks for Cornet* with introductions claiming that "hundreds of jazz cornetists…have adopted the Armstrong style of playing," they were actually understating their case: Musicians of all kinds, and in much larger numbers, were busily adopting the Armstrong style.

Having taught the music world how to swing, having brought the jazz soloist front and center and expanded the range and emotional power of his horn, Armstrong now went on to work his magic on American popular singing as well. His voice—a fairly smooth tenor in his youth, sandpaper and gravel in his middle and late years—was unmistakable. And what he did with it was unprecedented: He brought the old New Orleans practice of scatting, or singing nonsense syllables to improvised melodies, into the musical mainstream; he infused the most inane lyrics with honest, blues-inflected feeling; and he brought to singing the same freedom that had already transformed the way instrumentalists played.

Armstrong created the material for this book by playing all of the breaks into a Dictaphone. These recordings were carefully transcribed by the publisher, then subsequently lost.

"LOUIS? HE'S THE CAUSE OF THE TRUMPET IN JAZZ."

—*Dizzy Gillespie,* Down Beat, *July 9, 1970*—

No singer was more grateful for this liberation than his friend Bing Crosby, who once called Louis Armstrong "the beginning and the end of music in America." Without Armstrong, it's fair to say, there would have been no Billie Holiday, no Ella Fitzgerald, and no Sarah Vaughan; no Frank Sinatra, no Nat Cole, no Ray Charles, no Tony Bennett.

AND OVER MORE THAN HALF A CENTURY on the road, against odds that would have crushed a less resilient man, Armstrong helped foster still another revolution, this time contributing immeasurably to the welfare of his country and not merely to the enrichment of its music. He had been born black and poor in an America whose white majority considered black people less than human and their music less than art. Yet through the inventiveness of his playing, the majesty of his sound, and the

FURTHER READING

★ Louis Armstrong, *Satchmo: My Life in New Orleans* (1954)

★ Gary Giddens, *Satchmo: The Genius of Louis Armstrong* (1988)

radiance of his personality—he liked to say that he had enlisted himself in the "cause of happiness"—Armstrong forced thousands of white Americans to reassess their most basic prejudices. "Louis opened my eyes wide and put to me a choice," remembered one white southerner who had heard Armstrong play a 1931 college dance in Austin, Texas, and was stunned to find himself for the first time in the presence of someone who was at once African American and undeniably a genius. "Blacks, the saying went, were 'all right in their place.' But what was the 'place' of such a man, or the people from whom he sprung?"

One afternoon in 1928, Armstrong was strolling through his South Side Chicago neighborhood with an ardent young admirer, tenor saxophonist Bud Freeman, when they stopped to listen to some street musicians play "Struttin' with Some Barbecue," a tune Armstrong had recently recorded with his Hot Five. The trumpet player was laboring his way through Armstrong's solo, note for note. When the man finished, Armstrong applauded politely, then stepped closer and murmured, "Man, you're playing that too *slow*."

"How would *you* know?" asked the trumpet player, indignant.

"I'm Louis Armstrong. That's my chorus you're playing."

When he passed by the next day, the musicians had put out a hand-lettered sign next to their tin cup: PUPILS OF LOUIS ARMSTRONG.

So are we all.

★ ★ ★

JUNE 20, 1917

THE GREAT DEMAND

BY NANCY F. COTT

EMISSARIES FROM the new-born Russian constitutional government, which had just overthrown Tsar Nicholas II, arrived in Washington, D.C., in late June 1917 to confer with Pres. Woodrow Wilson. The United States stood on a war footing. Half a million army recruits were being readied for the French front, and enthusiasm for joining the Great War against Germany ran high (although some dissenters spoke up as the country teemed with preparedness). On June 20, crowds along Pennsylvania Avenue welcomed the Russian envoys as heroes. President Wilson intended to use all his powers of persuasion to keep the Russian republic in the war—allied with the United States, Britain, and France against the German empire.

At the gates of the White House, though, a greeting unintended by Wilson met the visitors:

AT LEFT: The National Woman's Party pickets first appeared outside the White House on January 10, 1917. This photograph was taken on January 23.

ABOVE: This 1917 "jailed for freedom" pin was one of ninety-seven presented by the National Woman's Party to demonstrators who had been sent to jail.

a line of women holding purple, white, and gold flags that rippled slightly in the warm summer breeze. As the Russian delegation neared, the women hoisted a ten-foot-long banner inscribed, "To the Russian envoys: …We the women of America tell you that America is not a democracy. Twenty million American women are denied the right to vote. President Wilson is the chief opponent to their national enfranchisement. Help us make this nation really free. Tell our government that it must liberate its people before it can claim free Russia as an ally."

The presence of the women pickets outside the president's mansion was not new. These "silent sentinels," as they saw themselves, had been there every day since January 10, the lettering on their banners calling democracy's bluff at the very seat of the national government. "We demand an amendment to the Constitution of the United States enfranchising women," their central banner read. "Mr. President, how long must women wait for liberty?" asked another. Through winter and spring, they had walked the same path as curious onlookers alternately cheered and jeered them.

Official Program
WOMAN SUFFRAGE
Procession

Washington
D.C.
March 3, 1913

O F ALL THE STARTLING INNOVATIONS that opened the twentieth century—from airplane flight, to the theory of relativity, to modernism in art—none was as socially significant as this: women's assertion of themselves in public. The spirited pickets at the White House included artists, reformers, political radicals, college graduates, wage earners, and professionals, as well as housewives and matrons. They came not from the huge federation of woman suffrage advocates known as the National American Woman Suffrage Association (NAWSA), which counted two million members, but from the National Woman's Party (NWP), a group of perhaps one hundred thousand, proud to be called "militant." Young or old, rich or just getting by, these women resisted conventional expectations. Many identified with contemporary movements to overturn accustomed forms in politics, education, art, styles of living, occupational choices, and relations between the sexes. They wanted liberty in their choice of political representation as in other areas of their lives, and that meant they wanted the vote.

These militant women introduced a new spirit into the suffrage movement. They had burst onto the nation's capital in March 1913 on the day before Wilson's first inauguration with a suffrage parade of such unprecedented scale and pageantry that when Wilson arrived at Union Station, there were no crowds to greet him. He'd been upstaged by eight thousand white-robed women marching in formation down Pennsylvania

THE 1913 MARCH

As the leaders of NAWSA's Congressional Committee in 1912, Alice Paul and Lucy Burns wanted to call attention to the dormant federal suffrage amendment, faithfully introduced at the start of each congressional session but not debated in either house since 1887. They began their campaign by staging an immense parade in the capital (right) on March 3, 1913, the day before Woodrow Wilson's first inauguration. Paul, Burns, and their colleagues wanted to show the president-elect that women expected to win the vote during his administration.

WE DEMAND
AMENDMENT T
CONSTITUTION O
UNITED STA
EN FRANCHISIN
WOMEN OF THIS

Avenue with flags and banners flying, led by lawyer Inez Milholland riding a white horse. Their daring caused many in the crowd (and around the country) to reconsider the long-simmering cause of voting rights for women. But these restless "New Women" of the period also aroused antagonism as they sought political freedoms equivalent to those enjoyed by men. Male hecklers, shoving and throwing stones, turned the 1913 parade into a near-riot, which the many police on hand did little to quell. Secretary of War Henry L. Stimson eventually had to call out cavalry troops from nearby Fort Myers to clear the line of the parade.

Besides defying public propriety, the National Woman's Party insisted on an amendment to the U.S. Constitution as the means to achieve the vote for women. When it was founded in 1913 by Alice Paul and Lucy Burns (under the original name of the Congressional Union), the group left behind the state-by-state campaigning pursued by NAWSA. Its methods also distinguished this more militant band from the large mainstream of suffragists. Paul, who became the mastermind behind the group's new strategies, believed that a constitutional amendment could be enacted quickly if the Democratic party, then in control of both houses of Congress and the presidency, would favor the issue. When the Democrats failed to respond actively, Paul decided to punish the party, and her organization worked to defeat Democratic congressional candidates in 1914 and again in 1916. When 1917 opened with the Democrats still in power and Wilson beginning a second term in the White House, the National Woman's Party determined upon its dramatic White House vigil.

Congress's declaration of war in April 1917 raised the stakes for any White House protest. Despite the war emergency, Paul's determined group remained outside the president's mansion. The National Woman's Party refused to take a stand on the war, emphasizing that it existed only to gain the vote for women. This neutrality kept in its ranks those suffragists who opposed U.S. entry into the war, but it also made the

CONGRESSIONAL UNION FOR WOMAN SUFFRAGE

Mass Meeting

BELASCO THEATRE
Sunday, December 12
3:30 P. M.

SPEAKERS

Mrs. Sara Bard Field, Oregon ⎱ ENVOYS OF WOMEN
Miss Frances Jolliffe, California ⎰ VOTERS

Senator George Sutherland, Utah
Representative Frank W. Mondel, Wyoming
Miss Maud Younger, California
Mrs. O. H. P. Belmont, New York
Chairman, Mrs. Margaret Zane Cherdron, Utah

TICKETS 25c, 50c, 75c, $1, $1.25, $1.50
1420 F Street N. W.

The Congressional Union,
formed originally as a NAWSA
auxiliary, broke ties with the larger
group in 1914.

ALICE PAUL

1885 – 1977

Born into a prominent Quaker family, Alice Paul studied at Swarthmore College and the New York School of Philanthropy before traveling to England in 1907. During the next three years, while serving as a caseworker for a London settlement house, she became active in the militant suffrage movement being led by Emmeline and Christobel Pankhurst. Paul (shown here in 1917) learned during that time how to generate publicity and then take advantage of it. When she launched her own full-time suffrage career in 1912, she gathered about her many young women who had also worked with the Pankhursts in England and were eager to move beyond NAWSA's conservative tactics.

TO THE RUSSIAN ENVOYS
President Wilson and Envoy Root are deceiving Russia.
They say We are a democracy. Help us win a world war.
so that democracies may survive.
We, the women of America tell you that America is not a democracy.
Twenty million American Women are denied the right to vote. President
Wilson is the chief opponent of their national enfranchisement.
Help us make this nation really free. Tell our government that if
must liberate its people before it can claim free Russia as an ally

This is the banner
that greeted the Russian
envoys on June 20.

> "THE POINT
> IS FIRST,
> WHO IS OUR
> ENEMY AND
> THEN, HOW
> SHALL THAT
> ENEMY BE
> ATTACKED?"
>
> —
>
> *Alice Paul, proposal to the*
> *Congressional Union,*
> *1914*

National Woman's Party pickets vulnerable to new attacks from opponents who branded them dangerous radicals. While criticism rained down upon them, the pickets kept their heads high, steadfastly maintaining their allegiance to American ideals of civil liberty.

The disapproval came not only from war enthusiasts and opponents of suffrage but even from nonmilitant suffragists. NAWSA president Carrie Chapman Catt was certain that such unpatriotic activity during wartime was undercutting congressional support for the suffrage cause. In May 1917, she wrote to Alice Paul urging her forcefully (and vainly) to call off the vigil because it was embarrassing President Wilson (which was, of course, precisely its point).

RATHER THAN CAPITULATE, Paul's group intensified and finetuned its protests, paying particular attention to the visit of the Russian envoys set for June 20. The National Woman's Party considered this visit a singular opportunity because the new Russian government, in one of its first official acts, had enfranchised women. The banner that the pickets unfurled on June 20, however, elicited furor from onlookers who did not appreciate the unflattering comparison being made between U.S. and Russian policies. "Treason!" came the shout. "Traitors!" soon followed. And as the Russian delegation passed through the White House gates, the offending banner was ripped down and ruined.

The next day, June 21, two thousand people swarmed to the scene at the White House, and when a new banner was unfurled, bearing the same message, a small riot broke out. The mob charged the pickets and shredded their entire display. Within a few moments, though, four more women emerged from National Woman's Party headquarters (just across Lafayette Park from the White House), holding purple, white, and gold streamers on high. The tense crowd fell back, and police reserves escorted the new pickets to their places. Quiet reigned during the rest of the day. The following morning, the *Washington Post* dryly reported that the National Woman's Party had again "endeavored to demonstrate the fitness of women for the ballot by displaying unpatriotic banners at the gates of the White House." The article also quoted former NAWSA president Anna Howard Shaw saying that the picketing was "the greatest obstacle now existing to the passage of the federal woman suffrage amendment in Congress."

Late on June 21, the police superintendent for the District of Columbia called on Alice Paul and told her that if the pickets appeared again at the White House, they would be arrested. ("Has the law been changed? Has picketing suddenly become illegal?" she recalled asking him.) But this threat only steeled her determination. Even when the chief repeated his intention, Paul replied that the picketing would continue.

On June 22, a crowd that had swelled to three thousand watched as the police kept their word. Two of the pickets were arrested, taken to court, and charged with obstructing traffic. When more women assembled at the White House the next day, the arrests continued. Warning them of their "almost treasonable behavior," the judge was chagrined when he realized that the protesters' banner had simply displayed President Wilson's war message: "We shall fight for the things we have always held nearest our hearts, for democracy, for the right of those who submit to authority to have a voice in their own government." When the arrested women refused to pay their fines, they were sent to jail for terms ranging from several days to several weeks. While they served their jail time, pickets continued to appear on the sidewalks around the White House with new banners bearing Wilson's words: "Mr. President, you say 'Liberty is a fundamental demand of the human spirit.'"

SUFFRAGISTS IN THE National American Woman Suffrage Association didn't proceed this way. Catt and her associates believed it was counterproductive to besiege and harangue the president and his party. They sought the liberty of self-representation as devotedly as the militants but opposed and deplored their tactic of picketing as well as their policy of targeting Democrats. President Wilson had to be coaxed along, they felt, and Democratic congressmen and senators persuaded as individuals.

CARRIE CHAPMAN CATT

1859 – 1947

Carrie Lane first became involved with the cause of suffrage for women during the 1880s, when she was superintendent of schools in Mason City, Iowa—an unusually lofty position for a woman of her time. Two marriages (to newspaper editor Leo Chapman and engineer George Catt) later, she became a close associate of Susan B. Anthony, who chose Catt to succeed her as the leader of the National American Woman Suffrage Assoction. Catt (shown here in a 1905 photograph) was twice president of NAWSA: from 1900 to 1904 and again from 1915 until the ratification of the Nineteenth Amendment in 1920. That same year, she founded the League of Women Voters.

This issue of Frank Leslie's Illustrated Newspaper *from November 24, 1888, shows women voting at the polls in Cheyenne, Wyoming. In 1869, the Wyoming legislature had granted women the right to vote in order to shift political power from the new territory's transient population of cowboys, miners, and railroad workers to the families who had settled there permanently.*

These disparities in judgment reflected the two organizations' differing political personalities and styles more than anything calculable. Militant and mainstream suffragists did not differ noticeably in socioeconomic status, ethnic background, marital status, or age. In both groups, despite some efforts to recruit among wage earners and immigrants, most members were white, American born, and either middle or upper class. (African-American women, who at times experienced open discrimination in both groups, generally worked for voting rights through their own organizations.) In NAWSA, middle-aged matrons perhaps had slightly more presence; and in the National Woman's Party, socialists certainly had a stronger presence; but these differences were slight, while the two groups' political styles differed markedly.

Since 1890, NAWSA had campaigned state by state to enfranchise women. This had reaped important rewards—success in eight states between 1910 and 1914—but the process was laborious and slow and there were frequent disappointments. In 1915, the major northeastern industrial states of Massachusetts, New York, New Jersey, and Pennsylvania all held popular referenda on the question of enfranchisement, and in all four states enfranchisement was defeated. Legislators and voters found many reasons for opposition. Saloon regulars thought that women voters would enact prohibition; industrialists who depended on child labor feared that women voters would ban the practice; white Democrats in the South, who had effectively disenfranchised black men, assumed that women voters would fracture the racial status quo; urban bosses were leery of the damage that women's vaunted morality might do to their well-oiled political machines. More generally, the prospect of women taking part in politics confronted many long- and firmly held assumptions concerning the proper place of women in society, and alarmists predicted that giving women the right to vote would disrupt families and put at risk the entire social order.

Although NAWSA's leadership maintained its style of patient persuasion, the setbacks of 1915 converted Catt and her colleagues to the NWP's constitutional approach. They knew a constitutional amendment would be difficult to achieve, but now they saw the advantages of this "once-and-for-all" strategy. Beginning in early 1916, NAWSA embarked on a new plan to lobby Congress for an amendment while still campaigning for suffrage in key states. (Continuing these state-level campaigns would further the constitutional goal, it was believed, because congressmen from states

This February 1915 cartoon shows the western states that had already enfranchised women.

where women voted would be more likely to support a suffrage amendment.) With feminine sweetness and sometimes tears disguising their political acumen, NAWSA's activists began what they called a "Front Door Lobby" campaign, appealing to selected national legislators and the president on the issue dear to their hearts.

N
AWSA THUS SHOWED ITSELF willing to use pressure-group tactics, as all disenfranchised groups must do sooner or later; yet even so, it didn't use them in the same way as the National Woman's Party. Throughout 1917, NAWSA cajoled legislators while the National Woman's Party, choosing to shock the nation, picketed. The more hypocritical the militants judged President Wilson's rhetoric of democracy to be, the more they used his own words against him. On July 4, 1917, pickets held overhead the words "Governments derive their just power from the consent of the governed." This banner, torn down by police as they overpowered the resisting women, was brought into court at the defendants' insistence and suspended, ironically, from the judge's bench during their trial. As July wore on, new signs insisted that the president "make America safe for democracy before he asks the mothers of America to throw their sons to the support of democracy in Europe."

This February 1916 photograph shows Carrie Chapman Catt at the Harris Theater in New York City seated between the wife of the New York governor and the chair of the New York State Suffrage party. Known as "the General" to her many dedicated followers, Catt directed what she called her "Winning Plan" much as any general would conduct a military campaign. The metaphor described her organizational strengths well, yet she never wavered from her ladylike demeanor.

Having resolved to face down arrests, the National Woman's Party protesters became even bolder. On August 14, they raised a new banner addressed to "Kaiser Wilson," asking, "Have you forgotten your sympathy with the poor Germans because they were not self-governed? Twenty million American women are not self-governed." This likening of President Wilson to the demonized Kaiser Wilhelm II was too scandalous for the crowd of observers, whose numbers had increased along with the pickets' arrests. Members of the crowd pelted the offending words with eggs and tomatoes and then wrested away dozens of banners, flags, and sashes, knocking some women down and dragging others along the street until the police intervened. The following day, the police themselves turned on the marchers. As soon as the women unfurled their banners, officers took them away. Relief corps from the nearby National Woman's Party headquarters tried repeatedly (and unsuccessfully) to outwit their uniformed opponents. If only for moments before the police swept them up, new statements fluttered aloft: "The Government orders our banners destroyed because they tell the truth." "Mr. President, how long must women be denied a voice in a government which is conscripting their sons?" Meanwhile, jail sentences were lengthening, and those arrested were being sent to an outdated and ill-maintained prison workhouse in Occuquan, Virginia, with sentences of thirty to sixty days.

These tactics had the desired effect of keeping national attention focused on the cause of woman suffrage when the issue might have otherwise been buried in the war news. Suffragists who had been in prison—where they went on hunger strikes to protest the conditions and were painfully force fed by authorities—traveled around the country, telling excited audiences that they had only been trying to realize at home the same democratic ideals that the war was intended to assure abroad. The National Woman's Party called the women in jail "political prisoners," characterizing their arrests and rough prison treatment as civil liberties violations akin to the prosecution of anarchists and socialists under new wartime sedition laws. These claims to martyrdom brought the group new recruits from among pacifists, civil libertarians, labor radicals, and socialists—but there was a cost to pay as well. The shock of the Bolshevik uprising that fall (the October Revolution that overturned Russia's fragile constitutional democracy) fired the emotions and rhetoric of conservative antisuffragists, who more than ever insisted that female enfranchisement was allied to Communism, tyranny, and world disorder.

Wilhelm II, emperor (kaiser) of Germany from 1888 until the end of World War I, was known internationally for his militaristic and arrogant manner. Although his imperial powers were limited by the German constitution of 1871, he often claimed bombastically to be the person who made all the important decisions.

DURING THIS TUMULTUOUS PERIOD, the National American Woman Suffrage Association had hardly been standing on the sidelines. Counting on legislators' appreciation, Carrie Chapman Catt had pledged her organization's support to the war effort. Since then, NAWSA suffragists (along with millions of unaffiliated American women) had been spending energetic days, weeks, and months supporting the troops abroad and replacing men's labor at home. Most mainstream suffragists were horrified by the National Woman's Party's attack on the government during wartime. They saw it as political suicide and complained vociferously among themselves about having to answer to legislators for the NWP's scandalous behavior. Although NAWSA leaders tried hard to quarantine their own public image from contamination, they found this was not an easy task. They were further exasperated when the National Woman's Party took credit for a favorable report issued by the Senate Committee on Woman Suffrage in mid-September, shortly after committee chairman Andreius Jones of New Mexico had visited the suffrage prisoners in Occuquan. Next, the House voted to create a Woman Suffrage Committee of its own—a proposal it had bypassed the previous four years.

NAWSA leaders were certain that these advances came not from the pickets' hounding of the president but from their own patient behind-the-scenes work with Wilson and national legislators. They believed, with much justification, that their patriotic defense of the country's war aims and their cultivation of the administration's esteem lay behind Wilson's crucial support for the creation of a Woman Suffrage Committee in the House. Wilson was also persuaded by Catt's chief lieutenant, Helen Hunt Gardener, to endorse woman suffrage in New York, the nation's most populous state (and the one with the largest congressional delegation), just before another referendum was held there in November 1917. This time, New York women won the right to vote, as they did in five other states during 1917, doubling the number of women enfranchised and lining up the congressmen of those states behind the proposed constitutional amendment.

When the House of Representatives passed the woman suffrage amendment on January 10, 1918—the first anniversary of the pickets' appearance outside the White House—members of the National Woman's Party hailed it as their own vindication (adding to Catt's fury) and ceased picketing. Yet when the Senate refused to follow the House's

Police arrest a suffrage demonstrator outside the White House on July 14, 1917. Once escorted into the waiting car, she was driven to the station house.

This November 1917 photograph shows National Woman's Party pickets recently released from jail demanding a new hearing for their imprisoned leader, Alice Paul. Lucy Burns is the second woman from the left.

OVERLEAF:

This photograph, printed from the original glass negative, shows the pickets on one of the less eventful days in 1917.

On January 21, 1918, *Montana congresswoman Jeanette Rankin was presented with the flag that flew over the Capitol on January 10, the day that the House voted to approve the suffrage amendment.*

This 1920 *Life cover congratulating women on their enfranchisement was drawn by Charles Dana Gibson, creator of the eponymous Gibson girl, whose fashionable elegance became the popular ideal for American women of the 1890s.*

lead, the picketing resumed, this time at the Capitol rather than at the White House. While NAWSA's state-level campaigns made voters of women in ten more states, the Prison Special, a carload of former suffrage prisoners wearing facsimiles of their workhouse garb, toured the country giving sensational speeches. Back in D.C., NWP leaders invented newly outrageous demonstrations. During the winter of 1918–1919, after the armistice and while Wilson was away at the peace conference in Versailles, the militants burned "watch-fires" in front of the White House, setting aflame Wilson's pronouncements on democracy as soon as they were transmitted from abroad. These and other protests continued until June 4, 1919, when the Senate finally passed the woman suffrage amendment. At that point, both organizations quickly switched gears to pursue ratification of the Nineteenth Amendment by the necessary three-quarters of the states. Their exhausting political labors came to a happy end on August 26, 1920, when the thirty-sixth state, Tennessee, squeaked through. Suffragists from both groups claimed credit for overcoming the hostility or indifference of the governors and legislators who had been holding out.

THE TWO SUFFRAGE ORGANIZATIONS' divergent strategies, hammered out on the forge of the Great War, created lifelong antipathies between NWP and NAWSA leaders. Yet the war also advanced their shared goal. American women served the war effort so effectively—as nurses, as auxiliaries to the armed forces, as a "Land Army" substituting for farmer-soldiers, as housewives conserving resources, as volunteers at home and abroad sending comforts to the front—that full citizenship for them came to seem undeniable. Sympathetic legislators could now contend that women had earned the right to vote because of their war service (just as Reconstruction congressmen, seeking the vote for freedmen, had emphasized the valor of the former slaves who had served as Union army volunteers). This argument converted many legislators at both the state and national levels.

Even so, the war was not the cause of the Nineteenth Amendment. To suggest as much robs seven previous decades of their significance and makes the 1920 outcome seem foreseeable and fixed in 1917, which it was not. Women's service in the Great War alone, without the previous decades of struggle, would never have attained the suffrage goal—

This 1917 New York Evening Post *cartoon of a nurse ministering to a wounded soldier bore the caption, "Would the soldier give her the ballot?"*

"THE RIGHT OF CITIZENS OF THE UNITED STATES TO VOTE SHALL NOT BE DENIED OR ABRIDGED BY THE UNITED STATES OR BY ANY STATE ON ACCOUNT OF SEX."

—*Nineteenth Amendment to the U.S. Constitution*—

whereas, if the war had not intervened, suffragists would still have succeeded, though perhaps not so quickly. Generations of suffragists worked to bring both women's and men's views around, and it was this work that made the difference. During the culminating decade of the 1910s, neither the shocking militancy of the National Woman's Party nor the ladylike moderation of NAWSA was so solely responsible for victory as each group publicly claimed of itself—and neither was as counterproductive as each group privately complained of the other. In retrospect, it's clear that the two organizations complemented each other, although they believed they worked at cross purposes. The outlaw tactics of the National Woman's Party forced the government and the nation to confront the exclusion of women from "the people," and they kept this issue in the headlines despite the world war. Even critics who condemned their behavior had to marvel at the pickets' courage and persistence. At the same time, years of precisely calculated lobbying by NAWSA, along with the war work performed by NAWSA members and millions of other women, earned the admiration of the legislators who eventually passed the Nineteenth Amendment.

During World War I, women took over many of the jobs vacated by men sent overseas. These two women were photographed in September 1918 delivering the huge blocks of ice that were used to chill food in the days before electric refrigerators.

OPPOSITE:

On November 2, 1920, Carrie Chapman Catt and millions of other women cast their first votes for president of the United States. Catt is shown here voting at 111th Street and Broadway in New York City.

Broadcasting from the U.S. Capitol on April 21, 1922, Alice Paul announces plans for a new National Woman's Party headquarters in Washington, D.C.

FURTHER READING

★ Nancy F. Cott, *The Grounding of Modern Feminism* (1997)

★ Marjorie Spruill Wheeler (ed.), *One Woman, One Vote: Rediscovering the Woman Suffrage Movement* (1995)

NEVERTHELESS, THE SHARP ANTAGONISMS between mainstream and militant suffrage groups resounded into the 1920s and 1930s. Not long after ratification of the Nineteenth Amendment, leaders of the National Woman's Party proposed an Equal Rights Amendment to the U.S. Constitution, guaranteeing that "equality of rights shall not be abridged on account of sex." Although other women's organizations—including NAWSA's successor, the League of Women Voters—thought the Equal Rights Amendment wrongheaded, heavy handed, and too blunt an instrument to be useful in gaining parity between the sexes, the National Woman's Party pursued it doggedly, alienating many potential supporters. (Most women who fought the new amendment believed it would threaten sex-specific labor laws, allowed by the Supreme Court's 1908 decision in *Muller v. Oregon*.) The debilitating conflict over the Equal Rights Amendment differed in character from the earlier suffragist divergence over tactics; but the single-mindedness of Alice Paul's organization, and the furious animus it evoked in women outside its circle, echoed the recent past.

The ballot had been a singular goal, deceptive in its apparent simplicity. It had enclosed a capacious range of associations that various individuals and groups brought into play as different emotions and needs warranted. It was a symbol of political liberty and also its substance. To suffragists, the ballot represented power itself, and it opened a path toward rights and privileges previously unattainable. Suffragists linked its achievement to an all-promising freedom of action, which they felt women had been denied. New employment opportunities, wifely independence, educational advancement, personal respectability, moral heft—all were considered benefits of the ballot, along with political representation. For decades after the ratification of the Nineteenth Amendment, however, public memory shrank these meanings to their minimum and rarely probed what had led ordinary women to undertake such extraordinary methods in dedication to their cause. Why had the pickets outside the White House gates in 1917—on June 20 and August 14 and so many other days—exposed themselves to insults, physical attacks, arrests, and imprisonment? What had they hoped to gain? Not simply the right to elect this Democrat or that Republican to local or national office. These suffrage champions had broader goals in mind, yet not until the era of feminist resurgence in the 1960s and 1970s were they rediscovered, released from their dour image, and revived as forerunners of modern women's understanding of emancipation.

★ ★ ★

JULY 20, 1925

THE SCOPES TRIAL: DARROW V. BRYAN

BY ALAN BRINKLEY

I T WAS SWELTERINGLY HOT in Dayton, Tennessee, on the afternoon of July 20, 1925. Ordinarily, most people would have preferred to retreat from the sun, but this was no ordinary afternoon. It was, by almost any measure, the most unusual one in the small town's history, a few hours during which the eyes of the nation (and, indeed, the eyes of history) were fixed on a large crowd packed into the town square watching a legal proceeding in which a few men were debating the meaning of the Bible.

The trial was being held to determine whether John T. Scopes, a high school biology teacher in Dayton, had violated a new Tennes-see state law banning the teaching of Charles Darwin's theory of evolution in the public schools. Actually, Scopes's guilt was not in question. At the urging of the American Civil Liberties Union, he

had deliberately defied the law so as to generate a test case that the ACLU might use to force a ruling on the statute's constitutionality. Among the attorneys the ACLU recruited to help defend Scopes was Clarence Darrow, probably the most famous trial lawyer in America and a personification of the skeptical modern sensibility that deplored the anti-evolution law. The local prosecutors meanwhile accepted rather reluctantly the help of three-time Democratic presidential candidate William Jennings Bryan, now a leading evangelical Christian and anti-evolutionist. Bryan's presence, many interested parties hoped, would demonstrate that the anti-evolution law was not a provincial peculiarity but a cause supported by one of the century's great public figures.

B ARRED BY JUDGE JOHN T. RAULSTON from calling expert witnesses to affirm the scientific validity of evolution (the trial, Raulston insisted, was only to establish whether Scopes had broken the law, not whether the law was just), Darrow hit upon the idea of calling Bryan himself to the stand as an "expert on the Bible," a suggestion to which the publicity-seeking district court judge readily agreed. Because Raulston had earlier moved the afternoon session into the town square, all who wished to—townspeople, journalists, visitors—could see for themselves this unprecedented cross-examination, for which Darrow had carefully rehearsed with surrogates the night before. And so under trees drooping with the weight of young boys, in the terrible heat, amid the rustle of hundreds of fans, Darrow and Bryan—both in shirtsleeves, sweating—confronted each other over the foundations of Bryan's religious faith.

"I DO NOT PRETEND TO KNOW WHERE MANY IGNORANT MEN ARE SURE."

—*Clarence Darrow, speaking at trial, July 13, 1925*—

For a while, the two men sparred inconclusively. Darrow asked Bryan to explain how Jonah could have been literally swallowed by a whale, and Bryan responded simply that "one miracle is just as easy to believe as another." Darrow next turned to the Great Flood. According to the Bible, he said, the Great Flood had occurred in 4004 B.C., and Bryan agreed that this was the estimate. But how, Darrow followed up, could such an estimate be made? "I never made a calculation," Bryan replied edgily.

> Darrow: *A calculation from what?*
> Bryan: *I could not say.*
> Darrow: *From the generations of man?*
> Bryan: *I would not want to say that.*
> Darrow: *What do you think?*
> Bryan: *I do not think about things I don't think about.*
> Darrow: *Do you think about things you do think about?*
> Bryan: *Well, sometimes.*

By now, members of the audience, most of them sympathetic to Bryan's views, were beginning to laugh at his scattered and defensive replies, further shaking his confidence. Later, Darrow maneuvered Bryan into conceding that the biblical account of God's creation of the world in six days might have entailed days of any length, even days "millions of years" long. Because the sun (by which days are measured) was not

CLARENCE DARROW

1857 – 1938

For decades, Clarence Darrow was considered the country's foremost criminal lawyer. His practice in the years before World War I focused on defending union leaders in their often-violent struggles against the barons of capital. In 1911, though, labor abandoned him after he advised two of his clients, the McNamara brothers, to plead guilty to bombing the offices of the antiunion Los Angeles Times. After the war, Darrow worked hard to rebuild his practice, taking on a number of desperate yet highly publicized cases and succeeding in enough of them to make himself a national figure. He thereafter used his personal clout often to address many of his wide-ranging concerns about inequities in American life.

created until the fourth day, Darrow forced Bryan to admit that there was no way of knowing how long the first three days had lasted. "I do not think they were twenty-four-hour days," Bryan finally admitted. That statement outraged many fundamentalists, who realized—as Bryan seemed not to do—that such an admission undermined their literal interpretation of the Creation.

Soon after this, the cross-examination petered out as Darrow became more aggressive and Bryan increasingly rattled. When Bryan accused Darrow of casting a slur upon religion, Darrow lashed back, "I am examining you on your fool ideas that no intelligent Christian believes." At this point, the judge ordered an adjournment.

A few days later, the trial ended anticlimactically when Scopes was found guilty and ordered to pay a small fine. A few months after that, his conviction was overturned on a technicality—a finding that conveniently dismissed the case and barred the ACLU from filing an appeal of the original verdict. The Tennessee anti-evolution law remained on the books (although rarely enforced) for half a century. But the enduring legacy of the Scopes trial was not the verdict itself. It was, rather, the tremendous reverberations that followed from Darrow's humiliation of Bryan on the stand, a moment that even today stands as a central episode in the modern history of American Christianity.

This is Market Street in Dayton, Tennessee, as it appeared on June 15 and most other days in 1925. For two weeks in July, though, Market Street was clogged with hot dog and lemonade stands, hawkers of biological and religious texts, and hundreds of newsmen, evangelists, and Holy Rollers. H. L. Mencken, who covered the trial, described Dayton as "full of charm and even some beauty," though suffocatingly moral.

DARROW BEFORE SCOPES

Darrow's most famous trial prior to Scopes involved the sensational 1924 Leopold and Loeb murder case. Nathan Leopold and Richard Loeb, both Chicago teenagers, had kidnapped and killed a young boy simply for the thrill of it. Darrow's defense made use of psychiatric evidence, then a novelty, and it ended with a spellbinding two-day plea for mercy that persuaded the jury to give his clients life imprisonment, rather than the death penalty most people expected.

The Scopes trial jury poses for a newspaper photograph on July 12, shortly after being impaneled.

"IT SHALL BE UNLAWFUL... TO TEACH ANY THEORY THAT DENIES THE STORY OF THE DIVINE CREATION OF MAN AS TAUGHT IN THE BIBLE."

—

*House Bill No. 185,
State of Tennessee
General Assembly,
enacted March 13, 1925*

THE SCOPES TRIAL, and the Tennessee anti-evolution law that precipitated it, were both products of a great schism in American Protestantism that had begun in the mid–nineteenth century and come to a head during the early twentieth—a schism that had emerged partly in response to the growing acceptance of Darwin's theory of evolution and partly in response to other changes in American culture and intellectual life.

Many late-nineteenth-century Protestants, persuaded of the truth of evolution, had come to terms with its challenge to the biblical story of the Creation by discarding from their theology those elements of religion that were incompatible with the teachings of science—the literal interpretation of the Bible, above all. Later, during the first years of the twentieth century, this new "liberal Protestantism" underwent a further transformation when the rising popularity of Freudian psychology brought new attention to the internal psychic origins of human behavior. Modern psychology suggested that an individual's mental health and spiritual well-being depended on personal fulfillment within society as it existed— in other words, on the individual's relationship to this world, not to God. The psychologist G. Stanley Hall, one of the principal early exponents of Freudian ideas in America, argued that the true Christianity stressed what he called "the cult of condition"—the cult of feeling "alive, well, young, strong, buoyant, and exuberant, with animal spirits at the top notch," the cult of "the universal hunger for more life." The Kingdom of

This photograph was taken during Sigmund Freud's 1909 visit to the United States. It shows him visiting Clark University, where G. Stanley Hall was president from 1889 until 1920. Seated (left to right) are Freud, Hall, and Carl Jung; behind them stand A. A. Brill, Ernest Jones, and Sandor Ferenczi.

God, he said, exalted man in the "here and now." Preoccupation with the next world was merely a diversion from man's proper preoccupation with his present condition.

Increasingly during the 1920s, these pressures for a new, more secular view of religion spread to Protestant ministers and theologians themselves. The most influential spokesman for liberal Protestantism in the 1920s was Harry Emerson Fosdick, the pastor of Riverside Church in New York City. The basis of Christian religion, he claimed, was not unexamined faith but a fully developed personality: "Not an outward temple, but the inward shrine of man's personality, with all its possibilities and powers, is…infinitely sacred." Christianity, he said in his 1926 book *Adventurous Religion*, should "furnish an inward spiritual dynamic for radiant and triumphant living."

The advertising executive Bruce Barton made an even more direct connection between Christianity and personal fulfillment in *The Man Nobody Knows*, which was published in the same year as the Scopes trial and quickly became one of the best-selling books of the decade. Barton's book told the story of the life of Christ in a startlingly unorthodox way. It described Jesus as "a young man glowing with physical strength and the joy of living," a man who had "our bounding pulses, our hot desires," a man who had "perfect teeth." According to Barton, "If there were a world's championship series in town, we might look for Him there." Jesus was also attractive to women and the most popular dinner guest in Jerusalem. "He did not come to establish a theology, but to lead a life," to live one that was more healthful and fulfilling than those of his contemporaries, and to show them how to do the same. This was, in fact, Jesus' most important service to the world: He was a salesman, an advertiser for a healthy and abundant life and for the values that made such a life possible. "He picked up twelve men from the bottom ranks of business," Barton wrote, "and forged them into an organization that conquered the world." The parables, he said, were "the most powerful advertisements of all time," and liberal Protestantism was, in short, a form of religion wholly compatible with the new, urban, secular, consumer-driven society of which much of the American middle class was becoming a part.

From 1929 until 1946, the reach of Harry Emerson Fosdick was considerably extended by the National Vespers radio program, which aired nationwide. Fosdick was also an early advocate of the church's cooperation with psychiatry.

Bruce Barton's The Man Nobody Knows *sold 750,000 copies during its first two years of publication. Later, Barton tried to match its success with* The Book Nobody Knows *(about the Bible), but that title flopped, as did two more books on religious themes.*

**WILLIAM
JENNINGS BRYAN**

1860 – 1925

*In 1890, riding the
insurgent Populist wing
of the Democratic party,
William Jennings Bryan
won election to Congress
from Nebraska, where
the voters appreciated
his passionate commit-
ment to the free coinage
of silver. Six years later,
his magnificent "Cross of
Gold" convention speech
earned him his first
presidential nomination.
The Boy Orator of the
Platte traveled eighteen
thousand miles that
summer, while William
McKinley never left his
Ohio front porch. Yet
McKinley won, kicking
off two generations of
Republican ascendancy,
interrupted only by
Woodrow Wilson's
curious victory in 1912.
Bryan served as Wilson's
first secretary of state but
resigned in 1915 when
he thought the president
might be leading the
country into war.*

B UT MANY OTHER PROTESTANTS, both rural provincial people and
urban educated people, found liberal Protestantism unfulfilling
and threatening. During the last years of the nineteenth century,
they coalesced into a movement that quickly became known as fundamentalism. The fundamentalists were dedicated to protecting the
traditional precepts of Protestant faith, especially its belief in a personal
God directly connected to the world. They opposed the secularization of
religion and what they considered the modern deification of man. Above
all, they believed in a literal interpretation of the Bible, including the
story of the Creation. Most fundamentalists also embraced the idea of
"pre-millennialism," the belief that the wicked world would soon be
redeemed by the second coming of Christ, who would usher in a
thousand years of peace and justice for those who believed in Him.

The path of the believer, many
fundamentalists insisted, was
not to focus on the temporal
world but to pray, to evangelize,
and to wait for Christ's coming.
And so they strenuously
opposed the drift toward
secularism they saw in those
denominations that had strayed
from the traditional truths.

For several decades,
fundamentalism remained a
purely theological phenomenon and not a particularly
belligerent one. But beginning
in 1917, the movement entered

This illustration *appeared in Bryan's
brief 1924 theological work* Seven
Questions in Dispute.

a second, more aggressive phase, in large part because of World War I
and the contrasting liberal and fundamentalist interpretations of that
cataclysmic event.

Liberal Protestants considered the war to be a struggle between the
forces of darkness and ignorance, represented by Germany, and the
modern, enlightened, progressive forces of the United States and its
allies. It was, as Pres. Woodrow Wilson maintained, a crusade for world
betterment, a battle to dispel ignorance and superstition and to enshrine
democratic civilization in its most progressive form. The urgency of this
crusade persuaded some modernists to lash out at the fundamentalists for
being, like the Germans, antiprogressive and antimodern. The pre-
millennial belief that the world was irredeemably wicked and that only

the second coming of Christ could save it denied the possibility of the war being an occasion for the advancement of democracy and the betterment of the world.

The University of Chicago Divinity School, a center of Protestant modernism, launched a strong attack on pre-millennialism beginning in 1917. Pre-millennialism, the modernists argued, was not only backward but also possibly subversive. "Two thousand dollars a week is being spent to spread the doctrine," one divinity professor wrote. "Where the money comes from is unknown, but there is a strong suspicion *that it emanates from German sources. In my belief the fund would be a profitable field of governmental investigation.*"

The fundamentalists were stunned by the ferocity of such attacks—stunned in particular by the portrayal of them as unpatriotic, because most supported the war with at least as much fervor as did the modernists. Evangelist Billy Sunday, for example, was far more pro-war and anti-German than all but the most rabid modernists. In a prayer he delivered before the House of Representatives in 1918, he called the Germans "a great pack of wolfish Huns whose fangs drip with blood and gore." (He was also fond of saying, "If you turn hell upside down, you will find 'Made in Germany' stamped on the bottom.") Yet what truly shocked most fundamentalists was the modernist assumption that they represented a faith that was somehow aberrant and alien, that their views were outside the American mainstream, that they were an obsolete minority. They believed, rather, that fundamentalism represented the true America and that the modernists were the alien subversives. So they launched a strong counterattack, which carried them into a new phase of political activism.

THE FUNDAMENTALISTS adopted the same tactic the modernists had used—identifying their opponents with America's enemy, Germany. However, the Germany to which they linked the modernists was a very different country from the one the liberal Protestants had described. To the fundamentalists, German militarism and brutality were not a result of ignorance or backwardness. They were, rather, a result of German rationalism and modernism, of Germany's infatuation with new secular philosophies that subordinated God to man; a result of the influence of Nietzsche and his idea of the secular "superman"; above all, a result of the German acceptance of the doctrine

Before embracing evangelism in 1896, Billy Sunday was a professional baseball player known for his flamboyance. During his much more successful preaching career, Sunday held three hundred revivals attended by an estimated one hundred million believers. He claimed to have more than a million converts to his credit and was prominent during the late 1910s in the campaign to enact Prohibition.

The Anti-Evolution League *was one of many advocacy groups peddling its wares outside the Scopes trial.*

of evolution, with its teachings that "might is right" and that man exists apart from God. (This may not have been an entirely accurate picture of Germany, but it was certainly no more inaccurate than the modernist portrait of a nation of savages and barbarians and was one that many liberal and secular Americans would take seriously during World War II.) According to the fundamentalists, Germany's modern secular culture, based on despotism and militarism, demonstrated what could happen to a society when it abandoned traditional faith. And thus World War I, they believed, was not only a battle to save America from conquest by Germany but also a battle to prevent the United States from becoming what Germany had become.

In 1918, the fundamentalists formed their first official organization, the World's Christian Fundamentals Association, which called for a militant crusade to roll back the tide of modernism. The tone of its appeal suggested how desperate, in the minds of the new organization's members, the crisis brought on by Darwinism was:

> *The Great Apostasy [is] spreading like a plague through Christendom. Thousands of false teachers, many of them occupying high ecclesiastical positions, are bringing in damnable heresies, even denying the Lord that brought them, and [they] bring upon themselves swift destruction.*

After the war, the fundamentalists remained active. No longer content to wait passively for the millennium while leading Christian lives, they became energetically engaged in preventing American society from following the German path to godlessness. And they fought this holy war on two fronts.

They fought, first, to rid the Protestant denominations of those modernists who were, the fundamentalists believed, denying the basic teachings of the faith. Beginning in 1918, for example, the fundamentalists launched strong and continuing efforts to purge modernist clergy from the Northern Baptist Church and the Northern Presbyterian Church, while also targeting elements of the Methodist, Episcopal, Southern Baptist, and Southern Presbyterian denominations.

The fundamentalists' second goal was to rescue American education from those who would pervert schooling into an instrument of modernism and godlessness—to rescue education, that is, from those who were using the schools to promote the theory of evolution, which in the fundamentalist canon was the doctrine that posed the greatest threat to traditional faith. During the 1920s, this included winning passage of legislation to ban the teaching of evolution in the public schools. Early in that decade, the fundamentalists managed to get anti-evolution laws passed in one house (but not both) of the state legislatures of five southern states. And then, in 1925, an anti-evolution measure actually became law in Tennessee. The measure's principle sponsor—John Washington Butler, head of the Association of Primitive Baptists in the small town of Round Lick—had been elected to the legislature in 1922 on the basis of his opposition to evolution. The statute he helped push through the state legislature made it illegal "for any teacher in any of the universities, normal, and all other public schools of the state, to teach any theory that denies the story of the divine creation of man as taught in the Bible and to teach instead that man has descended from a lower order of animals." This was the law that precipitated the Scopes trial and helped change the face of American religion.

FURTHER READING

★ Ray Ginger, *Six Days or Forever?: Tennessee v. John Thomas Scopes* (1958)

★ Edward J. Larson, *Summer for the Gods: The Scopes Trial and America's Continuing Debate Over Science and Religion* (1997)

Judge John Raulston *on July 15, the sixth day of the twelve-day trial. "A popular local attorney of no special competence," according to one press report, Raulston was a quite religious man whose deference to Bryan was obvious. He relished the attention that came with the trial and seemed obsessed with having his picture taken as many times as possible.*

JOHN T. SCOPES

1900 – 1970

John T. Scopes began teaching science in the Rhea County schools in 1924, the year of his graduation from the University of Kentucky, where he was taught Darwin's theory of evolution. Only twenty-four at the time of his trial, Scopes looked notably boyish with light red hair and a wide, easy smile. Trial observers described him as friendly, helpful, modest, and shy. After the trial, he was offered his old job back, but he declined and instead accepted a scholarship, offered as a gift by scientists and newsmen, to attend the University of Chicago. After two years there studying geology, Scopes got a job with Gulf Oil and spent the rest of his working life in the oil-and-gas business.

THE SCOPES TRIAL WAS, IN FACT, A DISASTER for the fundamentalists. It transformed the popular image of the movement, exposed it to savage ridicule, and made it possible for much of the public to identify all of fundamentalism with its most provincial and dogmatic elements. In reality, fundamentalism was a primarily urban and northern phenomenon; the Scopes trial made it seem the possession of rural southerners. In reality, fundamentalism attracted many highly educated men and women; the Scopes trial, and the Darrow cross-examination of Bryan in particular, made it seem an expression of ignorance and obscurantism. The fallout from the trial destroyed the cohesiveness and political strength of fundamentalism as its moderates, intimidated by the ridicule, allowed control of the movement to fall into the hands of extremists (including the Ku Klux Klan), who attracted even more ridicule and lost it still more influence.

In the aftermath of the Scopes trial, the public, activist efforts of the fundamentalists quickly fell apart. The anti-evolution crusade crumbled altogether, and no more states passed laws banning the teaching of Darwinism. After his humiliation in Dayton, Bryan traveled around rural Tennessee trying to revive interest in the anti-evolution crusade; however, in the midst of this effort, he took a nap in his Dayton hotel room one afternoon (after an enormous lunch) and died in his sleep. The manner and location of Bryan's death inspired a classic vitriolic obituary from H. L. Mencken that suggested (and somewhat exaggerated) the contemptuous way in which modernists were then portraying the religious ideas Bryan had defended:

> *His career brought him into contact with the first men of his time; he preferred the company of rustic ignoramuses. It was hard to believe, watching him at Dayton, that he had traveled, that he had been received in civilized societies, that he had been a high officer of state. He seemed only a poor clod, full of an almost pathological hatred of all learning, all human dignity, all beauty, all fine and noble things. He was a peasant come home to the barnyard. Think of a gentleman, and you have imagined everything that he was not.*

The effort to purge the denominations also failed completely, as the fundamentalists began squabbling among themselves over tactics while the modernists coalesced and fought back effectively. By mid-1926, it was possible for the modernist *Christian Century* to write:

Looking at it as an event now passed, anybody should be able to see that the whole fundamentalist movement was hollow and artificial.... If we may use a biological term, fundamentalism has been a spore (a mutant growth), an accidental phenomenon making its sudden appearance in our ecclesiastical order, but wholly lacking the qualities of constructive achievement or survival.... It is henceforth to be a disappearing quantity in American religious life, while our churches go on to larger issues.

In early June *before the Scopes trial began, Darrow took a trip to New York City, where he was interviewed by reporters looking for new angles on the impending "monkey trial."*

SUCH VIEWS DOMINATED both popular and scholarly understanding of fundamentalism for nearly fifty years. They inspired the famous Jerome Lawrence and Robert E. Lee play *Inherit the Wind,* a dramatization of the Scopes trial that opened to great acclaim on Broadway in 1955 and five years later became a feature film. *Inherit the Wind* portrayed fundamentalism as part of a long tradition of threats to intellectual freedom from backward, bigoted, uneducated people. (The trial, the playwrights noted, "might have been yesterday. It could be tomorrow.") Fundamentalism flourished, according to this view, among people who hadn't yet caught up with the modern world—rural, provincial, unsophisticated people. But the story had a happy ending: Like all antimodernist forces in a modernizing society, fundamentalism

FIVE MONTHS AGO

TODAY

EVOLUTION IN TENNESSEE

This Clifford Berryman cartoon, published about the time of the Scopes trial, contributed to the popular stereotype that all fundamentalists were attention-seeking yokels.

OPPOSITE:

William Jennings Bryan prepares to deliver a guest sermon not long before the opening of the Scopes trial.

gradually withered, becoming the refuge of a dwindling band of yahoos and playing an ever-smaller role in American life.

That interpretation has not fared so well in recent decades in the face of the remarkable resurgence of fundamentalist strength. In the years after the Scopes trial, fundamentalists indeed faded from the view of mainstream culture; yet they succeeded brilliantly in creating an alternative culture of their own. Having lost the battle for the existing denominations, they created new denominations committed to a more traditional view of Christian faith. Having lost the battle for control of mainstream education, they built schools, colleges, and universities whose teachings were compatible with the fundamentalist faith. Facing the scorn of the established press, they started their own newspapers, magazines, publishing companies, and eventually television and radio networks. By 1960, the Southern Baptist Convention, a fundamentalist federation, had become the largest Protestant denomination in the United States, with other fundamentalist groups not far behind. And by the late 1970s, fundamentalists had emerged again as an important political force, crusading once more against modernism in theology and culture, this time denouncing it as "secular humanism." At times, they even renewed the assault on evolution and promoted legislation to bar its teaching from the schools. Fundamentalist leaders such as Jerry Falwell conferred with presidents and established themselves as respectable (if controversial) commentators on public affairs in the mainstream media. Important new scholarship on the history of the movement by George Marsden, Edward Larson, and others forced intellectuals to reconsider the movement's origins and social basis.

IN 1965, *Time* published a famous cover story examining what many secular Americans believed to be the virtual disappearance of religious belief from any significant place in American life. The cover art consisted of a shocking question, posed in bright red letters on a stark black background: "Is God Dead?" A decade later, few people could doubt that the answer to that question was no. Few could deny that religious belief in America, and fundamentalist belief in particular, was not only alive but growing. The Scopes trial was thus not the end of the battle between fundamentalism and modernism in American religious life. It was only an interruption.

★ ★ ★

MAY 22, 1933

HARRY HOPKINS BRINGS RELIEF

BY LINDA GORDON

HARRY HOPKINS SITS AT HIS desk in the middle of a hallway in the Federal Security Building. The day is May 22, 1933. Heating pipes are banging, paint is peeling, footsteps are echoing on the uncarpeted floors. The building smells of antiseptic soap, mildew, and stale tobacco. His feet on the old scratched-up desk, cigarette ash beginning to accumulate on the floor beneath him, Hopkins is writing a steady stream of telegrams and handing them to messengers to run to the Western Union office. He is giving away money.

When FDR arrived in Washington on March 3, the night before his first inauguration, "terror held the country in its grip," his adviser Raymond Moley wrote. Vast numbers of Americans were clinging desperately to subsistence. One-third of the population was in "dire poverty,"

AT LEFT: *Public Works Administration employees put up the steel frame for a new state office building in Madison, Wisconsin. Construction jobs were what federal work relief mainly provided.*

ABOVE: *An Agriculture Department photographer recorded this farm foreclosure sale notice in 1933.*

reported the *New York Times.* One-quarter of the labor force was out of work entirely, and in some cities one-half was unemployed; black unemployment was 30 to 60 percent higher than white. Sixty percent of families earned less than the minimum poverty line. The suicide rate was climbing rapidly.

Existing sources of aid—or relief, as it was called at the time—had dried up after three years of depression. Private charity donations plunged just as demand soared. (In 1931, Detroit's Emergency Relief Fund aimed to collect $3.5 million but took in only $645,000.) The only public relief came from town, county, or state governments, whose tax income had also plummeted. (In Boston, only one in four jobless families was getting aid.) Conservatives panicked because the economic disaster was swelling a Communist movement. Liberals urged government action. From all across the political spectrum came calls for the president to assume dictatorial powers. In Germany and Italy, economic disasters had in fact led to fascist governments, and reactionary populist movements were growing in the United States.

HELPING THE IMPOVERISHED to cope was nothing new to social worker Harry Hopkins. A man in a female-dominated profession, he had formed strong alliances with pioneering women advocates of government aid to the poor. His network included Lillian Wald, Sophie Loeb, Mary Van Kleeck, Mary Dreier, and Frances Perkins, and he had learned to respect women's commitment, activism, and intelligence. (These women reformers were glad to have male support, although they might be forgiven some resentment that, typically, more junior and less experienced men were promoted over senior women.) In 1930, as head of the New York Tuberculosis and Health Association, Hopkins joined others in raising $30 million for an Emergency Work Bureau to help the growing numbers of the unemployed. Although the bureau's funds were never adequate, the experience convinced Hopkins that government should create public jobs to counter economic depressions.

This red-paint graffiti *appeared on a church wall in New York City in October 1930, just a few weeks before the midterm congressional elections. Until the Great Depression, the Communist Party USA had been a tiny, isolated sect. During the 1930s, though, it gained popularity advocating unemployment relief and labor organization.*

In 1931, Franklin Roosevelt, then governor of New York, hired Hopkins to run the state's emergency relief and public jobs program. Immediately after FDR's election as president in 1932, Hopkins began to lobby for a similar post at the federal level. But getting Roosevelt's attention proved difficult. For the first two months after the inauguration, banking, agriculture, and a special session of Congress occupied the president. On March 5, he declared a four-day national bank holiday, suspending all transactions. Four days later, he forced through Congress the Emergency Banking Relief Act, which gave him emergency powers and allowed solvent banks to reopen. A week after that, he sent to Congress the Agricultural Adjustment Act, which paid farmers to restrict the crops they raised. Direct aid to the impoverished was not at the top of FDR's agenda, but at least one cabinet member was trying to put it there.

Secretary of Labor Frances Perkins, repeating for the federal government the job she had done for New York State, had two thousand proposed relief plans on her desk—some crackpot, some impractical, some sound. Americans of all sorts were trying to think of solutions. She was used to citizens' pressure because she had been a reform activist outside of government most of her career. Since 1904 she had worked for one or another advocacy organization, most recently the National Consumers' League, on whose behalf she had become a skilled lobbyist. Now she was the first woman cabinet member, a position in which her responsibility extended not only to labor relations but also to the welfare of women, children, and the poor in general.

Anxious depositors mill about outside during this March 1933 run on a bank.

KNOWING THAT PERKINS was a crucial ally, Hopkins sought her out immediately after the inauguration to pitch his ideas. Unable to get an appointment, he managed to corner her at the Women's University Club, where she lived, and persuaded her to take his ambitious plan for universal relief to Roosevelt. At her urging, FDR agreed to see Hopkins and Hopkins's ally, William Hodson of the Russell Sage Foundation. Although the president remained extremely reluctant to engage in deficit spending, Hopkins doggedly nudged him closer to accepting the necessity of emergency measures. FDR then wanted to substitute for Hopkins's plan his own pet idea—rural conservation projects that would employ about 250,000 men. Perkins and Hopkins knew, however, that they needed help for millions of men and women.

So Perkins ambushed FDR by recruiting three powerful senators—Robert Wagner of New York (Democrat), "Fighting Bob" LaFollette of Wisconsin (Republican/Progressive), and Edward Costigan of Colorado (Democrat)—to turn the Hopkins plan into a bill, the $500-million Federal Emergency Relief Act. It passed on May 12, and on May 19, FDR sent for Hopkins to run the Federal Emergency Relief Administration (FERA). Confirmed by the Senate without debate on May 20, Hopkins quit his job running emergency relief for the state of New York on one day's notice—infuriating Herbert Lehman, Roosevelt's successor

THE BANKING CRISIS

On March 4, 1933, the day that Franklin Roosevelt took office, the U.S. financial system was on the verge of collapse. Because nervous depositors around the country were increasingly liquidating their accounts, governors had closed banks in thirty-eight states, and even in the remaining ten, financial institutions were operating on a limited basis. During the national bank holiday, however, FDR sent in teams of federal auditors to look over banks' records and assess the solvency of each. The public confidence generated by this review helped prevent further runs.

HARRY HOPKINS

1890 – 1946

*Harry Hopkins was not
your typical social
worker. A thin and
unhealthy-looking man,
he chain-smoked
cigarettes (leaving him
with perpetually stained
fingers) and chain-drank
cups of black coffee.
Both habits no doubt
sustained his innate
drive but also con-
tributed to the stomach
cancer diagnosed in
1939. Nor was Hopkins
your typical politician.
He had no interest in
money and was paid just
a pittance—only eight
thousand dollars a year,
or half of what he'd been
earning at the TB
association and four
thousand dollars less
than New York State had
been paying him.
Hopkins also had no
regard for status—
refusing, for example, to
have his office carpeted.
His only ambition was
to end the depression
the only way possible:
through massive federal
intervention.*

as governor—and arrived in Washington on May 21. The next day, after spending just five minutes with the president, he launched a bold pioneering program.

Harry Hopkins was not charming: He was unkempt, sarcastic, and foulmouthed, and Secretary Perkins was not alone in considering him arrogant and self-centered. However, she had seen his single-minded commitment to helping the poor and his energy at work. Equally important, FDR knew that Hopkins was invulnerable to corruption, invincible to opposition, and unwaveringly loyal. At the beginning of 1933 no one outside New York State and the profession of social work had heard of him, but by the end of the year he was a recognized power in Washington.

IN HIS FIRST TWO HOURS on the job, he spent $5.3 million ($65 million in 2001 dollars). By the time he left work that night, he had hired a staff, instructed forty-eight governors what they needed to do to get emergency relief, and sent out relief checks to Colorado, Georgia, Illinois, Iowa, Michigan, Mississippi, Ohio, and Texas. Next morning, the *Washington Post* headlined, MONEY FLIES.

The press, unaccustomed to such governmental activism, immediately began to badger Hopkins, searching for corruption and/or boondoggling. Hopkins snarled back, "I'm not going to last six months here, so I'll do as I please." In fact, Hopkins's own operation was run on the smallest possible budget. At year's end, when $1.5 billion had been distributed to 17 million people, the FERA's 121-person payroll was still just $22,000 a month.

Of the FERA's initial $500 million, half was set aside to match state contributions and half to be given outright to states on the basis of need. Hopkins disliked having to rely on state and local governments for distribution of the aid, but he saw no other option because the federal government lacked the administrative capacity to initiate a relief program speedily. So he fretted constantly about the bias, fraud, and corruption that were almost inevitable when funds were dispensed by local politicians.

Despite the best efforts of Hopkins and his staff, race and sex prejudice permeated the distribution of FERA aid. Direct grants went disproportionately to southern and western states, because they were poorer but also because they were more tightfisted than midwestern and northeastern states when it came to helping the poor. (Some, like Virginia, never contributed a single dollar to relief programs.) These states regularly excluded or shortchanged people of color, principally African Americans, Mexican Americans, American Indians, and Asian Americans.

Everywhere, relief discriminated against women. Everywhere, politicians, Democrats as much as Republicans, used the money to enhance their own political power through patronage. So the FERA "feds," led by the squeaky-clean Hopkins, were continually clashing with the state relief administrations, sometimes winning, often losing.

At the same time, the FERA had to battle a conservative social work establishment convinced that the poor needed moral supervision and surveillance lest welfare encourage them in laziness and dependence. By contrast, Hopkins's logic, and that of the group of administrators he was rapidly recruiting, was that the moral character of aid recipients was no more suspect than that of the rich or of those lucky enough to have employment. FERA policy was to distribute aid without humiliating and infantilizing surveillance. Why was it the FERA's business if an aid recipient had a boyfriend or drank beer in a saloon?

Despite political battles, corruption, and injustice, FERA money was reaching many of the needy, and millions were being fed and sheltered. But the quick recovery predicted by FDR's planners was not materializing, and by October 1933, with no end to the depression in sight, the winter loomed ominously. Hopkins worried that FERA funds would be inadequate to meet the need.

The **Washington Post** *reported Hopkins's first day of work at the FERA on its front page.*

Washington, D.C., police *break up a demonstration for relief staged by hundreds of unemployed workers on March 6, 1933. This photograph shows a rioter carrying a child in his arms being led away by police.*

Besides, Hopkins and FDR believed that providing jobs was preferable to straight relief, and most relief recipients agreed. The evidence was overwhelming that, even for the same stipend, people preferred work to nonwork relief. The discrimination being practiced in dispensing relief only confirmed this: Southern officials often reserved jobs for whites and gave straight relief to blacks, and officials everywhere gave jobs to men and straight relief to women, because straight relief was cheaper and more stigmatized.

Displaying his typical resourcefulness, Hopkins got FDR to issue an executive order on November 9, 1933, establishing the Civil Works Administration (CWA) to provide public jobs. Then he got $400 million out of Congress for the program. Again he initiated it with great speed, ignoring accusations of hurried, slapdash decision making. "People don't eat in the long run," Hopkins snapped at critics, "they eat every day." Almost immediately two million FERA relief recipients became CWA wage earners. By Christmas 1933, 3.5 million were employed, 4.3 million by the program's peak in mid-January 1934. Many workers were at first skeptical of what the CWA seemed to be offering. So unprecedented was this federal aid that some employees feared that their federal paychecks would not be honored at banks. Relief was popular, but the CWA was cause for celebration among the unemployed: It eventually assisted eight million households with twenty-eight million people, or 22 percent of the population.

As part of a 1934 work relief project, FERA *employees widened Merrimon Avenue in Asheville, North Carolina.*

Only Hopkins's determination brought us the CWA. Despite the president's ability to project confidence and decisiveness, in fact he was indecisive and ambivalent about how to attack the depression. Sometimes he was persuaded by progressives like Hopkins that public spending was needed not only to help people survive and to head off right- and left-wing radicalism but also to rev up the economy; at other times, budget-balancing advisers held sway. At the end of 1933, FDR's mercurial political leanings were captured by the budget balancers, notably Lewis Douglas, the conservative director of the budget. So in

January 1934, Roosevelt announced the winding down of the CWA. Although Hopkins loyally accepted the decision, the public didn't, and there were howls of protest. More than fifty thousand letters and seven thousand telegrams protested the abolition of the CWA, but with no success. The CWA passed out of existence on May 1, 1934, and the relief burden returned to the FERA.

THE STUBBORN BUT FLEXIBLE HOPKINS, still convinced that jobs were superior to straight relief, responded by creating jobs within the FERA. By the end of 1934, approximately 5 million people were on the FERA rolls, of whom 2.3 million were receiving "work relief." Unlike contemporary "workfare," FERA work relief offered jobs that paid prevailing wages for work on public projects.

In fact, FERA leaders wanted to promote jobs in preference to relief *permanently.* They wanted to install such a policy not only on an emergency basis during this depression but also in the future to *prevent* further depressions or recessions. Along with the policy planners already at work on Social Security in 1934, Hopkins advocated an unemployment system that primed the economic pump by creating government employment whenever private-sector unemployment rose above a set figure. Emergency relief, in this view, merely treated symptoms; a permanent jobs program could *prevent* impoverishment.

Hopkins's preference for public employment to fight the depression contained, of course, limitations and biases. It discriminated against women, who were not then considered entitled to jobs in the way that men were, and ignored the many mothers and children who did not have a man to "depend" on. Besides, many women already had a job—child raising and husband tending and housekeeping—and although this "job" drew no wages, it made it harder for women to take on paying employment. Furthermore, a policy of aid through work would certainly have favored whites, who were widely preferred over people of color in hiring for the better jobs. Nevertheless, the federal injection of money and useful work into the economy boosted incomes and spending and buoyed people's spirits in a way that did help people of color and white women, if not as much as white men.

> "WITH THE SLOW MENACE OF A GLACIER, DEPRESSION CAME ON. NO ONE HAD ANY MEASURE OF ITS PROGRESS; NO ONE HAD ANY PLAN FOR STOPPING IT. EVERYONE TRIED TO GET OUT OF ITS WAY."
>
> —
>
> *Frances Perkins,*
> People at Work, *1934*

By September 1938, *Hopkins and FDR had become much more close. As a result, Hopkins often accompanied the president on personal trips such as this one to the Mayo Clinic, where Roosevelt's son James had recently undergone surgery.*

BUT MORE NEEDED TO BE DONE; and despite the overwhelming endorsement of the New Deal in the 1934 elections, in which many of FDR's vociferous opponents were defeated, the Social Security Act of 1935 offered only short-term unemployment assistance. Hopkins and his allies, failing to get a permanent jobs program, once again compromised and accepted another temporary fix: the Works Progress Administration (WPA).

This time, however, the size of the fix was audaciously large. Funded in May 1935 with $4.8 billion (the largest peacetime appropriation in U.S. history to that time), the WPA proposed to employ 3.5 million people, more than one-quarter of the 11–12 million unemployed. Because most of its projects involved large constructions, the WPA became the most visible and popular New Deal program. WPA employees put up more than 40,000 buildings, including courthouses, firehouses, hospitals, and schools; they built 350 airfields, 78,000 bridges, 800 parks, 1,400 athletic fields, 1,800 public swimming pools, and 40,000 miles of roadway. Their contribution to conservation and public health included 20,000 acres reforested, 20,000,000 trees and bushes planted, 500 water treatment plants, 1,500 sewage treatment plants, and 24,000 miles of sewers. (The largest structures—such as the Golden Gate and Triborough Bridges, the Queens-Midtown Tunnel, and the Grand Coulee and Bonneville Dams—were built by the Public Works Administration under Harold Ickes.) In 1938, when disastrous floods hit the Northeast, washing out railroad bridges, highways, and power lines, Hopkins sent fifty thousand WPAers to work around the clock evacuating endangered people, diking the waters, providing temporary drinking water and power, and then cleaning up the massive expanses of mud that coated the streets and buildings—a federal helping hand never before possible.

Providing jobs, however, produced more controversy than providing straight assistance had. Despite their avowed commitment to the work ethic, conservatives tended to prefer relief, in part because it was less expensive: Providing

This truck took part in a December 6, 1938, parade celebrating completion of the University Avenue project in Des Moines, Iowa. After the parade, the sign was placed at one of University Avenue's major intersections.

This Is Another of Many
WPA PROJECTS
Made Possible by the Cooperation of
The FEDERAL GOVERNMENT
With The
CITY of DES MOINES
1796 Men Assigned to work during peak
Operations in Oct. 600 Men have been
working at one time. Project opened
June 3rd 1938 – Will Close Dec.15 1938
WPA $380.000 CITY $300.000

The Civilian Conservation Corps, *known as FDR's "forest army," was designed to employ young men in vigorous outdoor labor. This April 1933 photo shows the first group of CCC recruits outside their tents in Virginia's George Washington National Forest.*

jobs required considerable expenditures for tools, supplies, planning, and supervision. Low-wage employers also lobbied to keep government wages down, because they feared being unable to hire cheap farmhands and domestic servants if workers could get higher wages from the WPA. Unions, of course, insisted that public-job wages match prevailing private-sector wages, lest substandard pay in the public sector make private employers unwilling to pay a living wage.

Rocky Neck, Connecticut, *was one of many northeastern towns that suffered heavy damage during the floods of September and October 1938.*

A<small>T THE SAME TIME</small>, the federal administrators supervising the jobs programs were dismayed with what they learned about low standards of living, especially in the South and Southwest. Although federal wage rates varied according to geographic zones, the FERA had established a national minimum of thirty cents an hour. Administrators in Washington believed this marked a bottom subsistence level, but they discovered that many prevailing wage rates were lower still—for example, twenty cents an hour in Colorado, often as low as five cents an hour in the South. The federal goal was to rehabilitate the economy, not just provide relief, and these below-subsistence wages would do nothing to increase purchasing power. (Indeed, federal administrators were seeing in these sub-subsistence wages the long-term causes of the depression: Many workers had too little buying power.)

Moreover, compared to private employers, the federal government offered not only better wages but also job security, better working conditions, and less discriminatory employment practices. So public jobs increased the bargaining power of workers, who had lost, due to the depression, nearly all the gains they had made during the century's first two decades. The fact that work relief did not have the contemporary stigma of "welfare" further reduced the pressure on workers to accept any job offered, no matter how terrible the terms.

Employers of low-wage labor fought back, of course. FERA straight relief had actually been facilitating the payment of beneath-subsistence wages by providing supplementary aid to workers. Relief also allowed private employers to treat their workers like temps, laying them off in slack times and letting the FERA support them until they were rehired. FERA relief thus functioned in some industries as unemployment insurance with no cost to the employer. After 1935, employers tried to use WPA jobs in the same way. Southern planters in particular persuaded

O<small>VERLEAF</small>:

Dorothea Lange, *working as a photographer for the Farm Security Administration, recorded these Texas drought refugees in November 1936 at a migrant camp near Exeter, California.*

This poster from the late 1930s was created by the Federal Arts Project, itself a WPA program.

local relief administrators to lay off workers during planting or harvest or other times of peak labor demand. Throughout the South but also in some northern locations, it became standard practice to fire women from WPA jobs so they would be forced to accept domestic service or seasonal agricultural jobs paying less than half as much.

Sometimes relief administrators refused such employers' requests—just often enough to enrage them further, as when a 1935 NAACP protest stopped the WPA from closing several projects in order to increase the supply of cotton pickers. But employer pressure, notably southern, did force the "feds" to rescind the thirty-cents-an-hour minimum wage, a move that the Urban League denounced as a capitulation "to those whose conception of decent living standards for Negro workers is little above that of lower animals." Throughout the life of the WPA, Hopkins and other public works and relief administrators found themselves constantly calculating whether it was best to resist, dodge, compromise with, or capitulate to these complaints.

One WPA program for African-American women in the South was the Savannah Spanish moss mattress project. The women shown here are taking the moss out of the cooking chamber (where it has been steamed to kill the plant life) and hanging it on lines to dry in the sun.

CRITICISMS CAME ALSO from those who saw WPA employment of professionals, human service workers, and artists as frivolous. In 1934, for example, one-quarter of New York City's relief jobs went to white-collar or service workers: They cataloged in libraries, inventoried historical records, produced historical roadside markers, promoted public health, supervised playgrounds, helped teachers by working with special-needs children. In fact, had there been a higher proportion of such jobs and less emphasis on construction, discrimination against women would have been reduced. The CWA had initiated the first programs to employ artists (government subsidization of the arts was common in Europe but previously unknown in the United States), and the WPA continued the practice, paying unemployed arts workers not only to produce art but also to teach. In new community art centers and settlement houses, an estimated eight million people received free or low-cost art lessons. The WPA hired Nelson Algren, John Cheever, Kenneth Patchen, Kenneth Rexroth, Muriel Rukeyser, Studs Terkel, and hundreds of other writers. It gave a substantial boost to African-American artists, hiring, for example, writers Arna Bontemps, Ralph Ellison, Zora Neale Hurston, Claude McKay, Margaret Walker, and Richard Wright; artist Jacob Lawrence; dancer Katherine Dunham; and scholars Horace Cayton and St. Clair Drake.

The most successful attacks on New Deal relief called on anti-Communism, and the arts programs were favorite targets. Along with light operas, puppet shows, and foreign-language plays, federal theater projects in several large cities produced controversial and explicitly left-wing drama. Sinclair Lewis's antifascist novel *It Can't Happen Here* was dramatized and presented in eighteen cities in 1936. Congressional committees

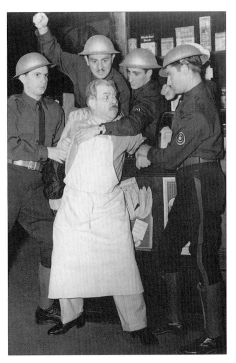

A scene from a 1936 Federal Theater Project performance of It Can't Happen Here, *staged in New York City. Sinclair Lewis's novel tells the story of a president-turned-dictator who takes over the over the country (including Congress and the Supreme Court) through use of force.*

> ## "NOT ONLY OUR FUTURE ECONOMIC SOUNDNESS BUT THE VERY SOUNDNESS OF OUR DEMOCRATIC INSTITUTIONS DEPENDS ON THE DETERMINATION OF OUR GOVERNMENT TO GIVE EMPLOYMENT TO IDLE MEN."
>
> —*Franklin D. Roosevelt, fireside chat, April 1938*—

investigating "un-American activities" (the House Un-American Activities Committee was not formed until 1938) charged that these theater groups were dominated by Communists. The charge had a grain of truth, but it was a truth that should have made no difference in evaluating the worthiness of the projects. Nevertheless, in 1939 Congress prohibited further federal expenditure on theater.

Notwithstanding the inevitable political attacks and in spite of discriminatory administration, the positive impact of public jobs and relief was undeniable. At its peak in November 1938, the WPA

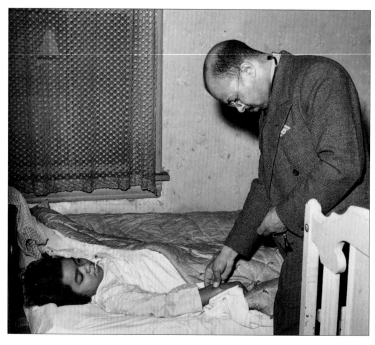

Emergency relief offered medical care to those who might otherwise not have been able to afford it. This Farm Security Administration photograph records a black physician making a house call in Chicago.

FURTHER READING

★ Linda Gordon,
*Pitied But Not Entitled:
Single Mothers and the
History of Welfare,
1890–1935*
(1994)

★ June Hopkins,
*Harry Hopkins: Sudden
Hero, Brash Reformer*
(1999)

employed 3.2 million people and produced 2 percent of the gross national product. This was more than the wage forces of American Telephone & Telegraph, General Electric, and Westinghouse; U.S., Bethlehem, and Republic Steel; and the Baltimore & Ohio, New York Central, Pennsylvania, and Union Pacific Railroads *combined.* By the WPA's end in 1943, over eight million Americans had been on its payroll at least once. Average weekly earnings were double the weekly FERA stipends. A large minority of WPA workers received higher wages than they had ever previously earned. In fact, one of the most under-recognized aspects of New Deal emergency aid was the way in which it lifted predepression standards of living among those at the very bottom. This effect was strongest among rural workers, especially in the South. A Hopkins investigator reported that the coal-mining people of Scott's Run, West Virginia, were "doing immeasurably better": Children who had never before had milk or adequate food, clothing, or shoes were now well nourished and well clad. Retail stores there were also doing better than ever.

Even in northern industrial cities, relief raised predepression standards of living among the poor. In New York City, a Visiting Housekeepers Project, initiated by the Urban League under the CWA, offered to many women the best-paying jobs they had ever had; the project was so successful that it was used later by the WPA in numerous towns and cities. In Boston, families that never had what investigators called a "decent standard," possibly one-eighth of all the cases, gained from even the least federal offerings. In Michigan, New York, and New Jersey, medical care became better than ever thanks to FERA provision. In Harlem, nine of ten relief clients gained access to clinical services never before available to them. In Providence, children's deaths from tuberculosis dropped from thirty to three per year, an improvement that the local TB society attributed to better diet and weight gain as a result of New Deal welfare programs.

NEVERTHELESS, RELIEF RECEIVED some bad press. Accusations of favoritism were widespread, and some were true because Hopkins's administration had been able only to begin the task of removing government spending programs from local politicians' patronage. By contrast, accusations of corruption or fraud were rare in proportion to the size of the programs or in comparison to the stigmatizing of welfare that began in the 1960s. The most common complaints were against "boondoggling" workers—one popular wisecrack was that WPA stood for "We Poke Along"—but most of these charges, even when investigated by anti-Roosevelt officials, proved to be unfounded. The director of public relief in Virginia, a state government hostile to the New Deal, claimed that the real problem was that WPA workers were "too darned efficient" and completed work so quickly that they worked themselves out of jobs.

The occasional bad press, though, had little effect on the popularity of federal relief. We know this from two measures: White House correspondence with the public and public opinion polls. President Roosevelt invited and received an unprecedented quantity of mail—450,000 letters in the first week of his presidency and an average of 8,000 a day after that (compared to Herbert Hoover's average of 600 a day). Some were appeals for individual help, but more contained proposals for ambitious programs from citizens who took their citizenly responsibilities seriously and who did not think government should be left to professional politicians. Among these proposals, the single most common was for a relief program. (Others expressed, in descending frequency, demands for inflation and hostility to "money interests," monopolies, and "big boys.")

Modern public opinion polling did not develop until 1935, but the data collected thereafter demonstrated widespread public approval for government aid to the victims of economic downturn. A July 1935 poll showed that 76.8 percent of respondents believed government should see that every man had a job. An October 1936 poll showed

FRANCES PERKINS
1882 – 1965

After her graduation from Mount Holyoke in 1902, Frances Perkins taught school and performed some church-related social work before earning in 1910 a master's degree from Columbia University in social economics. Because she was regarded as a social reformer (and probably also because she was a woman), both business and union groups responded to Roosevelt's appointment of Perkins as his labor secretary rather coolly. During her twelve years in office, however, she effectively pushed for Social Security and for minimum-wage and maximum-workweek legislation, as well as for limits on the employment of children under sixteen. Perkins is shown here with a foreman and a riveter surveying construction of the north tower of the Golden Gate Bridge in March 1935.

OUT IN THE FIELD

By the mid-1930s, more and more, Hopkins's field investigators were uncovering aspects of American poverty rarely seen even by social workers. One of his investigators, Lorena Hickok, concluded after a visit to Puerto Rico that no one there qualified for "emergency relief" because the traditional poverty of many Puerto Ricans was so extreme that she couldn't imagine the depression having worsened it. Other reports written by FERA and WPA investigators documented just how prevalent below-subsistence wages had been even before the Great Depression began.

that 54.2 percent of respondents believed that the WPA was doing useful work (13.5 percent didn't think so). An August 1937 poll found that 68 percent of respondents disagreed with the statement that WPA workers should be dropped after a fixed period even if they had not found private-sector jobs (46 percent believed they should be able to refuse to leave the WPA until they found jobs just as good).

E VEN SO, THOSE WHO OPPOSED public relief and jobs, particularly those who depended on low-wage labor or who resented giving up traditional political patronage, vilified Hopkins and his allies, including Secretary of Labor Perkins. In 1937, conservatives in Congress cut Hopkins's salary from twelve thousand dollars a year to ten thousand, thus expressing their fury (and compensating for their political impotence) through petty revenge. By contrast, those who supported relief tended to credit the president, not Hopkins, who never inspired mass affection.

Yet it was Hopkins who deserved much of the credit for this innovative extension of government responsibility. True, during a crisis as severe as the depression of the 1930s, in an advanced industrial economy, greater government regulation of the economy and the provision of social welfare were likely in any event, and had Hopkins not led the way, someone else probably would have. But Hopkins put his singular energy, determination, selflessness, and combativeness—even his rudeness—at the service of the country.

No one can say what would have happened if Hopkins had not demonstrated that red

Social realist Reginald Marsh,
who believed that the press often understated the ravages of the depression, created this early 1930s lithograph of men waiting in a long bread line.

tape could be cut and billions of dollars spent without significant corruption, but we do know what happened because he did.

Many saw Hopkins as a stereotypical liberal, a sucker for the underdog, a man with a soft heart beneath a crusty exterior—a positive or negative stereotype, depending on one's perspective. But Hopkins's vision was actually more ambitious than a simple desire to feed the hungry. It constituted as well a new vision of citizenship, what Europeans came a decade later to call "social citizenship." Hopkins's ideas prefigured and tried to implement two of the Four Freedoms that President Roosevelt later conceptualized as his goals for World War II: freedom from want and freedom from fear.

Time **profiled** the chain-smoking WPA director in its July 18, 1938, issue.

T HE GREAT DEPRESSION made it unambiguously clear that most unemployment and poverty arose not from personal failings but from economic dynamics far beyond the control of individuals. The old litany of blaming poverty on male irresponsibility, female immorality, and inbred "depravity" lost its hold on social policy experts. The emergency relief programs Hopkins began on May 22, 1933, shifted American political culture, transforming expectations in the direction of a welfare state, government responsibility to regulate the markets, and a positive valuation of the public sector. The political debates that surround us today at the century's turn focus to a substantial degree on whether these principles should be preserved or rejected.

★ ★ ★

THE BREAD LINE · Reginald Marsh

C-3

NAME _____
      (Last)   (First)   (Middle)

R E S T R I C T E D

ARMY-NAVY COLLEGE QUALIFYING TEST

A-12, V-12

INSTRUCTIONS: This test consists of three parts. You will be allowed two hours (120 minutes) for the three sections. Work as rapidly as is consistent with accuracy. Attempt every item. You are advised to divide your time according to the following schedule, but if you finish any section in less time than that suggested you may go on to the next section or go back to a section you did not finish. Time will be announced in accordance with the following suggested schedule:

Section I, starting on page 2	30 minutes
Section II, starting on page 5	30 minutes
Section III, starting on page 8	60 minutes

You are to indicate the answers to all questions on the separate answer sheet enclosed in this booklet. NO CREDIT WILL BE ALLOWED FOR ANYTHING WRITTEN IN THIS BOOKLET. For each question, several numbered or lettered answers are given, from which you are to choose the <u>one</u> you think is the best. On the answer sheet, the numbers or letters are repeated, and under each is a small square box. When you decide which answer is best for a given question, make a cross (X) in the box under the number or letter which corresponds to that answer. Make a heavy black cross. For example:

The <u>opposite</u> of:

A. GOOD: 1-beautiful 2-homely 3-bad 4-dull 5-pretty

<u>Bad</u> (numbered 3) is most nearly opposite in meaning to GOOD; therefore, number <u>3</u> would be marked in line A.

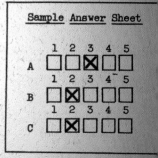

B. ADMIRAL is to NAVY as: 1-secretary is to president 2-general is to army 3-fleet is to cruiser 4-general is to captain 5-army is to air force

Of the five answers, number 2 (general is to army) corresponds most closely to the relationship between ADMIRAL and NAVY. Therefore, number <u>2</u> would be marked on the answer sheet in line B.

Which pair of words best completes the following definition when the first word in the pair is inserted in the first blank and the second word in the second blank?

C. A --- is a place for keeping --- articles: 1-closet..clean 2-safe..valuable 3-cellar..damp 4-closet..valuable 5-bin..lost

A <u>safe</u> is a place for keeping <u>valuable</u> articles; therefore, number <u>2</u>, which corresponds to the pair of words <u>safe..valuable</u>, is marked on the answer sheet in line C.

DO NOT TURN THE PAGE UNTIL TOLD TO DO SO. WAIT FOR FURTHER INSTRUCTIONS.

APRIL 2, 1943

TESTING AMERICA

BY NICHOLAS LEMANN

ARS, IN PROPORTION to their magnitude, always wind up rearranging the societies that fight them; and because this is so obviously the case, people who want to rearrange societies seize upon wars as opportunities. In the United States during World War II, the main, obvious project was to defeat the Axis powers, but it was possible to pursue that goal wholeheartedly and still, on a second front, be trying to influence the form the nation would take after the war.

Two prime practitioners of this two-front strategy were James Bryant Conant, the president of Harvard University, and a lieutenant of his, Henry Chauncey, an assistant dean at Harvard. During the war, Conant was almost never at Harvard, because he was so caught up with important matters in Washington—mainly the Manhattan Project, which developed the first

AT LEFT: *The Army-Navy College Qualifying Test was used to select individuals for the army A-12 and navy V-12 special training programs. Among those chosen for the army program was author Kurt Vonnegut.*

ABOVE: *SAT preparation has grown, by some estimates, into a two-hundred-million-dollar-a-year industry.*

atomic bomb. Chauncey—who was in his late thirties and had a wife and small children, so he couldn't serve at the front—managed to get himself appointed a consultant to the U.S. Navy in the area that was his professional specialty, mental testing. Simultaneously, Conant produced a series of astonishingly ambitious manifestos delineating his preferred future for the United States, while Chauncey pursued his lifelong dream of creating a national testing regime. Their maneuvers were, understandably, not much noticed at the time—we had a war to win. But now these moves look like the birth of a new order, one whose coming into being was quite a near thing and not at all inevitable.

April 2, 1943, was the day on which Henry Chauncey supervised the administration of something called the Army-Navy College Qualifying Test to 316,000 high school seniors all over the United States (about half of all the male seniors in the country), most of whom had never taken a standardized test before. It was not an obviously dramatic event; indeed, the lack of drama was the whole point. What was being demonstrated on that day was that, in practice, the entire youth of the United States could be tested, sorted, and routed from a localized public education system into a nationalized university system, and from there to their individual socioeconomic destinies.

Why did that matter? Because you could then create what we'd now call a "meritocracy" (the word didn't exist in 1943)—a system for establishing a new national elite without explicit regard to social or economic background, on the basis of mental test scores alone. Chauncey's test, therefore, had to meet two tests of its own: It had to be administratively practicable, and it had to be noncontroversial. An uneventful and unnoticed administration was exactly what he and Conant wanted and what made the test such an important historical event.

THE IMMEDIATE PURPOSE of the Army-Navy College Qualifying Test was to pick out the most academically promising high school seniors and send them on to college to be trained for special military functions, rather than directly to the front. The test was an adapted version of the now-ubiquitous SAT, the college admissions test—which meant that it had an impressive lineage, dating back to the earliest days of mental testing. In 1905, French psychologist Alfred Binet had administered the first IQ test in Paris, and Binet's test had led directly to the Army Alpha, the first mass IQ test, which was given to U.S. Army inductees during World War I. The SAT was, in turn, an adaptation of the army test, created by Carl Brigham, a member of the team that had administered the Army Alpha.

From its unveiling in 1926 until the start of World War II, the SAT was, despite the energetic efforts of Conant and Chauncey to promote its use, a small test, given annually to a few thousand high school students who aspired to be awarded scholarships to Ivy League universities. Conant had selected the SAT for this purpose because he believed that it measured pure brainpower, rather than acquired education, and would therefore enable Harvard to identify extraordinary public school boys from outside the eastern seaboard.

Part of what was at stake on April 2, 1943, was the question of whether the SAT (or a test just like it) could be given to an exponentially larger group than had ever taken it before. Could enough test sites and test supervisors be found all over country? Could the test booklets be printed and delivered to all the sites on time without anybody getting an advance peek? Could the answer sheets be shipped to a central location and scored quickly and accurately? Chauncey spent the entire month of March 1943 living in a Chicago hotel room near the test printer, making

HENRY CHAUNCEY

1905 –

Henry Chauncey's route to Harvard was unusual for a member of the Episcopacy, or WASP elite. He attended Groton, founded by Endicott Peabody in 1884 to turn rich boys into leaders (rather than pantywaists). But Chauncey's minister father was far from rich and had to beg subventions from wealthy relatives to pay Groton's tuition. Henry was then enrolled at Ohio State University (Egisto Chauncey was serving as a rector in Columbus), but Grotonians of that era did not attend public universities, and Henry was soon rescued. Peabody himself intervened and persuaded financier Clarence Dillon (father of JFK treasury secretary Douglas Dillon) to fund Henry's education at Harvard.

The army was certainly
no stranger to testing.
In this 1942 photograph,
members of the air corps
take a test designed to
identify those best suited
to the roles of pilot,
navigator, and
bombardier.

sure that the answers to all these questions would be yes. And when the administration of the test went off successfully, he and Conant achieved successes on both their fronts: Beyond accomplishing their military mission, they had shown that it was now indeed possible to perform a simultaneous IQ scan of all the high school seniors in America. But to what end?

THE MAY 1943 ISSUE of the *Atlantic Monthly,* which came out only a few days after the first administration of the Army-Navy College Qualifying Test, carried an article by Conant entitled "Wanted: American Radicals." Without mentioning standardized testing per se, it proposed a social vision that, at least to Conant's mind, would accompany the big test. Demonstrating a sweep and a boldness unimaginable in a university president today, Conant proclaimed the entire American experiment in democracy to be in deep peril, and for reasons having nothing to do with the Nazis. Conant's view of the country strongly bore the stamp of Frederick Jackson Turner, the historian of the American frontier who had been a prominent member of the Harvard faculty during Conant's undergraduate days. Like Turner, Conant believed that the distinctive greatness of the United States lay in its being a classless society

Alfred Binet thought
his tests could be used to
identify slow learners in
school so that they could
be given special help.
Almost immediately,
however, Stanford
psychologist
Lewis Terman
began promoting
IQ tests for a
different purpose:
to identify the most
gifted students.

JAMES B. CONANT

1893 – 1978

In November 1932, Abbott Lawrence Lowell, president of Harvard since 1909, announced his retirement, having successfully checked the trend toward cosmopolitanism and scholarship begun by his predecessor Charles William Eliot. Lowell's successor, chemistry professor James Bryant Conant, took office in the fall of 1933. Although Conant was, like previous Harvard presidents, a Boston Puritan and Harvard graduate, he was most definitely not upper crust. Born in middle-class Dorchester to an engraver and his wife, Conant burned with a fierce disapproval for the old privileged ways at Harvard; his first goal as president was to open things up.

built around the idea that each citizen should have an equal opportunity to rise in the world. Also like Turner, Conant believed that the availability of open land of the western frontier had historically been the chief means by which this end was achieved. Since the closing of the frontier, Conant argued, the country had begun to move in the ominous direction of the old nation-states of Western Europe, with their rigid class systems. The advent of industrial capitalism had generated plutocrats who were trying to transform themselves into a hereditary aristocracy that would run the country in the future. Heavy unrestricted immigration (another by-product of capitalism) had meanwhile brought to the big cities millions of poor foreign workers who were inclined to embrace socialism or even communism. Our national creed, it seemed, might soon disappear.

The "American radical" that Conant wanted to oppose these forces was a generic, superheroic version of himself, a figure who was so steeped in our great national traditions that he would "rack his brains to find the equivalent of those magic lands of the old frontier" in the new industrial economy. And what new social system would he develop? Conant touched lightly on the idea of allowing people to make high incomes and then imposing a 100 percent inheritance tax—thus using

> ## "THE WHOLE EDUCATIONAL SYSTEM HAS BECOME ONE MASSIVE QUIZ PROGRAM, WITH THE PRIZE GOING TO THE... MOST REPULSIVELY WELL-INFORMED PERSON."
>
> —*Sarah Lawrence president Harold Taylor, conference, 1947*—

"the powers of government to reorder the 'haves and have-nots' every generation." But the main means of national restoration he proposed was universal public education—the American radical, he wrote, "will be little concerned with the future of private education"—because it came closest to the supposed function of the frontier during the nineteenth century.

It is important to remember that public education through high school was still quite new at the time Conant was writing. At the outset of the twentieth century, only 6 percent of eighteen-year-olds had a high school diploma, and by midcentury we were just nudging up against the landmark of most teenagers completing high school. Other countries, if they had universal public education at all, usually ended the universal aspect of their systems after the eighth grade. This helps explain why in his writings Conant consistently presented the public school, especially the public high school, as a thrilling new social instrument. Yet it is also important to understand that beneath Conant's billowing clouds of democratic and egalitarian rhetoric lay a set of steelier ideas. Although he was a champion of the comprehensive high school—one that concentrated in a single new, large, modern, central facility thousands of students who had previously attended small rural high schools—Conant also believed that IQ tests should be administered to all entering students in order to identify the highest scorers among them and ensure that they received special instruction—leaving the great majority, of course, to a non-college preparatory course of study. In the realm of higher education, Conant never favored—in fact, he opposed—what we now think of as the great breakthrough of his era: the dramatic expansion of the college-going population. Even when only one American in twenty was getting a bachelor's degree, Conant was for sending *different* people to college, not more people. He was perhaps the leading opponent of the GI Bill of Rights, because it failed to differentiate veterans who deserved a college education from those who didn't. (Even after the GI Bill was passed in 1944, he dreamed of getting it repealed.) Conant believed in staging a truly open and democratic contest for a strictly limited number of slots in a new, educationally derived elite. This he considered to be a radically egalitarian idea; most people today would not.

Along with Conant's lead essay, the May 1943 Atlantic Monthly *contained articles about slum schools, the fighting in North Africa, and being a German American, as well as a short story by Vladimir Nabokov entitled "The Assistant Producer."*

ONANT MAY HAVE HAD HUBRIS, but he was not a hypocrite or a cynic. The reason that he believed an elaborate exercise in elite selection would promote democracy and classlessness was that he was sure his new elite would be selflessly devoted to public service and that the rest of the country would see this and regard with admiration his new "natural aristocracy" (a term of Thomas Jefferson's that Conant loved to quote). He also conceived of membership in the new elite as a single-generation phenomenon: Its members would rise out of decent obscurity, and their children would return to it. In an unpublished manuscript written during the war, he justified the creation of such an elite in this way: "If we are to continue to have an essentially free and classless society in this country, we must proceed from the premise that

there are no educational privileges, even at the most advanced levels of instruction. We must endeavor to sort out at each stage in the educational process those boys and girls who can profit from one type of advanced education, and those who can profit by another. There must be a variety of educational channels leading toward different walks in life. As far as possible there should be no hierarchy of educational discipline, no one channel should have a social standing above the other."

In hindsight, this seems terminally naive. How could Conant not see that people would regard such a system as a means to broad socioeconomic success and madly endeavor to pass their positions on to their children? But he didn't. One reason is that, elsewhere in the world, similar testing systems had led only to public service—and Conant's underlying idea, if one factors out the rhetorical flourishes and IQ testing, wasn't all that new or distinctively American. China had been using tests to identify future mandarins for centuries, and, more recently, Western European countries had put testing regimes into place. In every case, these procedures were used to select supergrade academics, technocrats, and government administrators. Why couldn't that be the case here, too?

Chauncey (shown here as a Harvard assistant dean in 1942) lacked the sort of detailed social vision that motivated Conant. Instead, he believed simply in standardized testing and its nearly miraculous power to improve the lot of humanity. He pushed tirelessly for the development and administration of as many new tests as possible and wasn't wedded to the idea that they be IQ tests. For his part, Conant wasn't much interested in tests unless they were IQ tests.

B Y NOW WE HAVE GOTTEN SO COMPLETELY used to the system Conant and Chauncey set up that it takes a real effort to see that its creation was not foreordained. When the war ended, Harry Truman, the last American president without a college degree, set up a blue-ribbon commission on the future of higher education, headed by George Zook, the president of the American Council on Education, an association dominated by large state universities. The commission's report—a stirring, expansive liberal document—called for an end to racial segregation in southern universities and a tremendous expansion of the American university system to the point at which most young people would go to college. (The first of these two ideas Conant didn't mention in his writings at the time, and the second he ardently rejected.) At the same time, the report completely ignored Conant's own cause, the institution of mass mental testing in order to select a small gifted group of students to attend these universities. Truman's commission assumed that relatively open admission to college, then standard practice at the state universities, would continue in the future. Apparently, it didn't find the private universities of the Ivy League or their admissions practices worth mentioning.

Nonetheless, Conant and Chauncey—through a deft series of bureaucratic maneuvers, including a timely palm greasing of Zook that got him to stop resisting—were able to create during the late 1940s the Educational Testing Service, a private agency with a quasi-public monopoly on the testing of applicants to colleges and graduate schools. This development, which affected the lives of millions of people (and initiated a highly consequential national IQ test, something no other country in the world had adopted), occurred with no public debate, no governmental assent, no oversight, and no press coverage. It represented quite a different path for the country than the one suggested in the Truman commission's report.

THE FOUNDING OF THE ETS after the war required a merger of all the leading educational testing programs in the country into a single national agency, which would hold what Chauncey called "a bread-and-butter monopoly" in testing and thus function as a kind of national personnel office. Conant had been pushing this idea for at least a decade without success. Now, though, his main roadblock was gone—SAT creator Carl Brigham, who had opposed the creation of a big national testing agency, had died in 1943—and he had a powerful new ally in the rich and influential Carnegie philanthropies. He also

During World War II, James B. Conant (shown here in 1946) was arguably the most influential private citizen in America.

THE HARVARD NATIONAL SCHOLARSHIPS

At the start of the 1933–1934 academic year, Conant's first as president of Harvard, he asked Chauncey to set up a scholarship program that would diversify the school, then fed predominantly by private schools in New England and New York. Conant particularly wanted to recruit academically promising students from mid-western public high schools. Chauncey's job was to figure out how to identify these students, who were not expected to score well on achievement tests because of deficient instruction. The solution that he and colleague Wilbur J. Bender devised (in consultation with Carl Brigham at Princeton) turned out to be the basic technique now used to sort the entire national population.

had the record of Henry Chauncey's testing success during the war. The Carnegie people set up a commission on the future of testing, with Conant at its head, and it soon issued a report recommending the creation of a unified testing agency. To make this agency big and national, however, the American Council on Education would have to participate, and the ACE was loath to yield any of its authority to the elite College Board, whose testing operation (now being run by Chauncey) would serve as the kernel of the new agency. After a seemingly endless couple of years, during which Conant somewhat grandly set the broad outlines and Chauncey shuttled back and forth between the equally suspicious state university and Ivy League camps, the ETS was chartered. It opened for business on January 1, 1948, in Princeton, New Jersey, the site of the College Board testing office established decades earlier by Brigham.

The ETS got an initial grant from the Carnegie Foundation; after that money ran out, it would have to sustain itself financially through fees paid by test takers. This meant that it had a powerful incentive to persuade as many universities as possible to require its tests of all applicants. Under the presidency of Henry Chauncey, who was a gifted and an enthusiastic administrator, the ETS energetically marketed its tests to hundreds of schools all over the country, public as well as private. The result was an odd hybrid of Conant's ideas and the ideas of his enemies: Higher education did expand enormously after the war, but as it did, many universities began to use ETS tests to admit students more selectively. The country wound up with a mass higher education system that was also tracked, or organized by ability as measured by the SAT. And the ETS itself boomed. During the 1950s, Chauncey bought a four-hundred-acre farm outside Princeton and built an elaborate new ETS headquarters campus with extensive grounds and buildings named after Conant, Brigham, and other testing pioneers. Chauncey also began ambitiously planning for more, newer, better tests of everything from personality to persistence to sense of humor. All this was the direct result of Chauncey's having demonstrated in April 1943 that he could test the entire nation.

T HE RAMIFICATIONS OF THIS SYSTEM have been practically endless. It pervades American life so thoroughly that we can hardly recognize that it *is* a system, constructed by people and not occurring naturally. For a large segment of the population, the trajectory of life is profoundly linked to performance on the SAT and its companion tests. Public schools are judged on their average SAT scores, even though Conant chose the SAT as the big test precisely because he

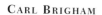

CARL BRIGHAM

1890 – 1943

Like many early IQ experts, Carl Brigham was a eugenicist who felt that immigration was disastrously diluting the country's "native stocks." During World War I, he worked with Robert Yerkes, who had persuaded the army to let him test nearly two million recruits. The army thought Yerkes's IQ tests would help it select officer candidates, but Yerkes had another goal: building a statistical record. At first, Brigham interpreted the results— people of Northern European descent scored highest—as proof of his eugenicist views. But in 1928, he recanted. "The more I work in this field," he wrote, "the more I am convinced that psychologists have sinned greatly in sliding easily from the name of the [intelligence] test to the function or trait measured."

believed it did *not* measure school quality (but rather native intelligence). In many towns, real estate prices vary with each school system's average SAT scores, affecting a typical family's net worth. Nationally, average scores are seen as an indicator of the health of our educational system, and even the health of our nation itself.

Every university that requires applicants to submit SAT scores insists that it does not make admissions decisions based on these scores alone. But students and their parents believe that SAT scores have a disproportionate effect on college admission. That belief has created a substantial, and growing, market for test-prep courses that teach tricks for beating the test, and practically every American high school now offers SAT prep as well. For a certain segment of American society—upper-middle-class people who live in big metropolitan areas—the SAT has become the most visible manifestation of a strange, obsessive, quasi-open competition for designation (via university admission) as a lifelong member of a new American elite. Because Conant never imagined that his test would play as an opportunity to gain financial rewards (he thought it would determine who would govern), he also failed to foresee how intense the competition over admissions slots would be—or that the attempt by universities to depart from strict adherence to test scores, in the interest of racial integration, would result in legal and political challenges.

> " LIBERTY LIKE CHARITY MUST BEGIN AT HOME. "
>
> —
>
> *James Bryant Conant,*
> *Harvard College address,*
> *June 30, 1942*

Two generations of children of the SAT have now grown to adulthood, and they indeed form a distinct new sociological category: an American mandarinate. They are bright, well educated, prosperous, and strongly invested in the idea that their early, educationally attained success was both earned and deserved, rather than conferred by birth or chance. They are more likely to be private professionals than public servants, and, despite Conant's intent, they are not regarded by the rest of the country as its rightful leaders. In an election campaign, coming across

In the second century B.C., *Confucian China developed the mandarin system to train its future high officials. In the sixth century, competitive examinations were added to aid in the selection of appropriate candidates. Beginning in the late eighteenth century, several European nations developed similar systems for selecting and training high-level civil servants that were remarkable for their lack of concern with family background.*

FURTHER READING

★ Nicholas Lemann, *The Big Test: The Secret History of the American Meritocracy* (1999)

★ Michael Young, *The Rise of the Meritocracy, 1870–2033: The New Elite of Our Social Revolution* (1959)

OPPOSITE:

Teenagers take the SAT in 1953. Although widely considered an "intelligence" test, the modern SAT is actually designed to predict how well students will perform during their first year in college. (The test's predictive validity falls off markedly after that.)

as a mandarin is a minus—just think of Al Gore, who did, and George W. Bush, who didn't. The mandarins may regard themselves as self-made, but they don't appear that way to outsiders. Nonetheless, the big test and its attendant assumptions and rituals have profoundly shaped them, as well as the institutions where they work, the schools at which they were educated, and the communities in which they live. Out of a large test administration on April 2, 1943, a routine-seeming event, has come a minor social revolution.

THE TROUBLE, THOUGH, with describing merely what has happened is that it leaves out what didn't happen, which is often just as important. In this case, the United States developed a means of operating a Cinderella-style national search for people of unusually high academic promise, who would then be specially trained at the best universities. Because the rhetoric associated with this system has always been unusually broad, we associate its creation with developments that are actually unrelated. The system didn't represent the advent of equal opportunity, either as an ideal (because that ideal long predated the SAT) or as a reality (because there still isn't equal opportunity in our society). It didn't represent the restoration, or even the strengthening, of American democracy. It hasn't had any statistically detectable effect on social mobility or classlessness, partly because there simply aren't enough people admitted to selective colleges to affect national averages. Even if the SAT democratized the Ivy League, that doesn't mean it democratized the country generally—the Ivy League is only one small subculture.

The main point is that the SAT's goal of elite selection just isn't the same thing as pro-

¹**merit** *vt* (1526) : to be worthy of or entitled or liable to : EARN ~ *vi*
1 *obs* : to be entitled to reward or honor   **2** : DESERVE
mer·i·toc·ra·cy \ˌmer-ə-ˈtä-krə-sē\ *n, pl* **-cies** [¹*merit* + *-o-* + *-cracy*] (1958)   **1** : a system in which the talented are chosen and moved ahead on the basis of their achievement   **2** : leadership selected on the basis of intellectual criteria — **mer·it·o·crat·ic** \ˌmer-ə-tə-ˈkra-tik\ *adj*
mer·it·o·crat \ˈmer-ə-tə-ˌkrat\ *n* (1960) *chiefly Brit* : a person who advances through a meritocratic system
mer·i·to·ri·ous \ˌmer-ə-ˈtōr-ē-əs, -ˈtȯr-\ *adj* (15c) : deserving of honor or esteem — **mer·i·to·ri·**

The term meritocracy *was invented by English socialist Michael Young in 1958 to describe a social order that he personally considered abhorrent. Young explicitly rejected the idea that giving rewards to the deserving few could serve as the basis for an admirable society.*

moting the good of the many. Even if we agree with the most generous interpretation, that the American elite has been dramatically democratized, we must realize that the mass of people has not been. Conant's system was never designed to achieve the educational goals that would have had the broadest salutary effects—improving the quality of public schools or expanding access to higher education. The country has made significant progress toward these goals during the past half century, and it is poised to make considerably more during the next half century—but not because of the advent of the SAT.

★ ★ ★

JULY 25, 1945

"THE MOST TERRIBLE BOMB IN THE HISTORY OF THE WORLD"

BY JOHN W. DOWER

I N 1945, AFTER LONG AND terrible struggle, World War II came to a sudden, shocking end with the nuclear destruction of Hiroshima on August 6 and Nagasaki on August 9, followed by Japan's capitulation five days later.

Was it necessary to use the atomic bombs, at such great cost in civilian lives, to bring about Japan's surrender? To this day, most Americans would answer yes, arguing that simple chronology bears them out. The bombs were dropped, and the surrender of a hitherto fanatical enemy followed almost immediately. One can only (this familiar argument continues) "thank God for the atomic bomb" that saved untold thousands of American lives by making invasion of the Japanese homeland unnecessary. What more need be said?

In fact, a great deal more needs to be said about the decision to drop the bombs. Ever since the moment the enormity of their human toll became known soon after the war's end, more than a few conservative as well as liberal American critics have questioned the morality of using the bombs. With the passage of time, moreover, many hitherto secret or neglected documentary materials pertaining to the atomic-bomb decision have been disclosed. Although we still have gaps in the available record, it has become increasingly clear that there were indeed not one but several "roads not taken" available to Pres. Harry S. Truman and his top advisers at the time.

The issues that arise here—moral and strategic alike—were, and remain, enormously complicated. They involve not only feasible alternatives *to* using the atomic bomb to bring about Japan's surrender but also alternative ways *of* using the new weapon that would not have involved such wholesale killing of civilians. Far-reaching questions concerning relations between the United States and the Soviet Union also came into play in these internal wartime deliberations. Some concerned participants at the time, particularly within the scientific community, warned that the very

AT LEFT: *A three-year-old Japanese girl, her head bandaged to cover burns she suffered in the atomic explosion, wanders in the ruins of her house in Nagasaki.*

ABOVE: *The safety plug from the plutonium bomb, known as Fat Man, that was dropped on Nagasaki.*

HENRY L. STIMSON

1867 – 1950

Henry Stimson began serving presidents in 1906, when his friend Theodore Roosevelt appointed him U.S. attorney for the Southern District of New York. In 1911, William Howard Taft gave him a cabinet post (as secretary of war), and in 1929, Herbert Hoover made him secretary of state. During the late 1930s, Stimson became an outspoken interventionist and a leader of the Committee to Defend America by Aiding the Allies. In 1940, Franklin Roosevelt, a Democrat, asked Stimson to return to government as his secretary of war—judging correctly that nominating Stimson, a lifelong Republican, would increase bipartisan support for his foreign policy.

manner in which the bombs were developed and used made postwar mistrust and a nuclear arms race virtually inevitable.

President Truman and his advisers operated under enormous pressure (whereas we, of course, have the luxury of hindsight). Even at the time, however, there were clearly articulated options that rarely come through in most reminiscences and ex post facto accounts of the decision to drop the bombs. There was no single date on which all of these issues and options came together on the table for Truman to decide. We can, however, point to a moment—around July 25—when things came to a head, options and alternatives resurfaced, and irrevocable decisions were made. There are few episodes more tangled and controversial in modern American history. This is, it seems fair to say, the story that will never go away.

As FRANKLIN ROOSEVELT'S VICE PRESIDENT, Truman had been out of the loop where knowledge of the atomic-bomb project was concerned. He received his first formal briefing from Secretary of War Henry L. Stimson on April 25, 1945, thirteen days after President Roosevelt's death. At this time, even *before* the top-secret bomb had been assembled and tested, Stimson took care to emphasize that the new weapon differed transcendently from all that had gone before. "Within four months," the secretary's report began, "we shall in all probability have completed the most terrible weapon ever known in human history, one bomb of which could destroy a whole city." Great Britain had assisted

The Big Three *pose for photographers on July 25, 1945, in the garden of the Cecilienhof Palace in Potsdam, a suburb on the outskirts of Berlin.*

in developing the bomb, he continued, but "probably the only nation which could enter production within the next few years is Russia." Stimson, then seventy-seven years old, was shaken by the prospect of what might lie ahead. "Modern civilization," he told the new president, "might be completely destroyed."

Stimson's estimate of when the terrible weapon would be completed was off by a month, but his fearsome vision was widely shared. On July 16, President Truman received terse notification that the bomb had been successfully tested in the desert of New Mexico. The first detailed report to reach him, which arrived on July 21, included a vivid firsthand description by Brig. Gen. Thomas F. Farrell that spoke of an "awesome roar which warned of doomsday and made us feel that we puny things were blasphemous to dare tamper with the forces heretofore reserved to The Almighty."

The test bomb Jumbo being hoisted into position at Alamogordo, New Mexico.

Other Americans close to these developments also pondered the morality of tampering with such forces. J. Robert Oppenheimer, the charismatic chief scientist of the Manhattan Project that designed the bomb, later observed sorrowfully and famously that "in some crude sense, which no vulgarity, no humor, no overstatement can quite extinguish, the physicists have known sin." Fleet Adm. William D. Leahy, one of Truman's most intimate military aides, lamented in his memoirs that by using such a weapon the United States "had adopted an ethical standard common to the barbarians of the Dark Ages."

President Truman was abroad at the time of the New Mexico test, attending the famous Big Three conference that took place at Potsdam from July 17 through August 1. It was the president's first meeting with British prime minister Winston Churchill and Soviet premier Joseph Stalin; and he recorded various events in a handwritten loose-leaf diary that he kept during this period. This extraordinary, though vexingly incomplete, diary remained buried in an archive until scholars uncovered it in 1979. It is a fascinating document, of the sort

FARRELL'S REPORT

"The effects could well be called unprecedented, magnificent, beautiful, stupendous and terrifying. No man-made phenomenon of such tremendous power had ever occurred before. The lighting effects beggared description. The whole country was lighted by a searing light with the intensity many times that of the mid-day sun. It was golden, purple, violet, gray and blue. It lighted every peak, crevasse and ridge of the nearby mountain range with a clarity and beauty that cannot be described but must be seen to be imagined."

Even before the attacks on Hiroshima and Nagasaki, the United States had adopted a policy that included the bombing of civilians. The March 9–10 fire-bombing of Tokyo, for instance, had killed eighty-five thousand Japanese. The B-29 air raids went on for five months and caused the sort of devastation shown in this low-level aerial reconnaissance photo.

historians treasure, for it captures the president's most intimate and immediate thoughts as he made decisions of the greatest consequence. There is no reason to believe he was shading his words or writing "for the record" in these hastily scribbled pages. The president's entry for July 25 included these passages:

> *We have discovered the most terrible bomb in the history of the world. It may be the fire destruction prophesied in the Euphrates Valley Era, after Noah and his fabulous Ark.*
>
> *This weapon is to be used against Japan between now and August 10th [apparently a vague reference to estimates of how long it would take to ready a bomb for use against Japan]. I have told the Sec. of War, Mr. Stimson, to use it so that military objectives and soldiers and sailors are the target and not women and children. Even if the Japs are savages, ruthless, merciless and fanatic, we as the leader of the world for the common welfare cannot drop this terrible bomb on the old capital [Kyoto] or the new [Tokyo].*

He & I are in accord. The target will be a purely military one and we will issue a warning statement asking the Japs to surrender and save lives. I'm sure they will not do that, but we will have given them the chance. It is certainly a good thing for the world that Hitler's crowd or Stalin's did not discover this atomic bomb. It seems to be the most terrible thing ever discovered, but it can be made the most useful.

Stimson's doomsday voice rings like an echo here—though muffled, in conclusion, by the president's more sanguine hope that terror might be rendered useful. There are also curious, truly puzzling remarks. "Soldiers and sailors are the target," the president noted, "and not women and children." This was not true. On May 31, the top-secret Interim Committee that advised the president on the bomb had agreed that "the most desirable target would be a vital war plant employing a large number of workers and closely surrounded by workers' houses." Isolated or purely military targets, not to mention "a purely technical demonstration," had been explicitly *rejected* by the committee on the grounds that "we should seek to make a profound psychological impression on as many inhabitants as possible." A small number of major Japanese cities had been spared the U.S. air raids that had been devastating Japan since March 1945 to ensure that there would still be relatively unscathed urban centers left to demonstrate the awesome power of the new weapon. The president knew all this—and knew from Stimson's April 25 briefing that one bomb "could destroy a whole city." Had he somehow persuaded himself to think otherwise? (This is not at all implausible. Men engaged in mass destruction often find it expedient to deflect full acknowledgment of their actions through evasive and euphemistic language. Psychological blocking of this nature pervades the documentary record of the decision to drop the bomb on heavily populated urban "targets.")

Also provocative is the president's certainty that the Japanese government would not surrender in response to a "warning statement." The real question here—which had been intensively discussed at the highest levels since late May—was precisely what such a warning should convey concerning the nature of the new weapon and what Japan might expect from the victors if it did surrender.

Acting Secretary of State Joseph Grew delivers a radio address on V-E Day (May 8, 1945) announcing the surrender of Germany but also stressing the nation's "unfinished business" in the Pacific. As undersecretary of state, Grew became acting secretary whenever the secretary of state was out of town. In this case, Secretary of State Edward R. Stettinius Jr. was attending the United Nations conference in San Francisco. Stettinius had replaced the ailing Cordell Hull in December 1944 and was himself replaced by James F. Byrnes in July 1945.

CLARIFYING THE TERMS OF SURRENDER was a knotty issue indeed, involving both imperial politics and the curious state of Japanese-Soviet relations. Despite a long history of animosity, in April 1941 Japan and the Soviet Union had found it mutually expedient to sign a five-year neutrality pact. Beginning in June 1945, top Japanese leaders had grasped at this fragile relationship and begun soliciting Soviet help in mediating an end to their hopeless war with the other Allied powers. Although these overtures were intended to be secret, American cryptographers had broken the Japanese diplomatic code. President Truman was actually reading intercepts of cables from Foreign Minister Tōgō Shigenori to his ambassador in Moscow while en route to Potsdam as well as while the conference was in session.

Secretary of War Stimson and others took particular care to call the president's attention to a July 12 cable stating that Emperor Hirohito personally desired to send a special envoy to solicit Soviet help. "We are now secretly giving consideration to the termination of the war because of the pressing situation which confronts Japan both at home and abroad," Tōgō had written. At the same time, he went on to emphasize that "so long as England and the United States insist upon unconditional surrender the Japanese Empire has no alternative but to fight on with all its strength for the honor and the existence of the Motherland." Subsequent cable intercepts similarly revealed Tōgō's desperate desire to enlist Moscow's support (and, simultaneously, to keep the Soviet Union from repudiating the neutrality pact and entering the war against Japan now that its struggle against Germany had come to an end).

There was no confusion on the American side concerning what made "unconditional surrender" anathema to the Japanese. On May 28, for example, Acting Secretary of State Joseph C. Grew, who had served as ambassador to Japan from 1932 until the attack on Pearl Harbor, had personally conveyed this advice to the president:

The greatest obstacle to unconditional surrender by the Japanese is their belief that this would entail the destruction or permanent removal of the emperor and the institution of the Throne. If some indication can now be given the Japanese that they themselves...will be permitted to determine their own future political structure, they will be afforded a method of saving face without which surrender will be highly unlikely.

An excellent moment to present such modification of the surrender terms, Grew argued, would arise as soon as the battle of Okinawa (which had begun in early April) ended in the inevitable U.S. victory.

D URING THE WEEKS THAT FOLLOWED, a considerable range of civilian and military advisers followed Grew's lead in broaching the possibility of offering some sort of guarantee concerning the future security of the emperor and the imperial institution. They included, among others, Secretary of War Stimson, Admiral Leahy, Secretary of the Navy James V. Forrestal, Assistant Secretary of War John J. McCloy, Undersecretary of the Navy Ralph A. Bard, Consul to the President Samuel I. Rosenman, and U.S. Army Chief of Staff George C. Marshall. Similar proposals came to the Americans from the British side, even at the Potsdam conference. On the eve of the president's departure for Europe, a joint committee of the state, war, and navy departments worked out a draft declaration that responded to these concerns by including the following key "paragraph 12":

The occupying forces of the Allies shall be withdrawn from Japan as soon as our objectives are accomplished and there has been established beyond doubt a peacefully inclined, responsible government of a character representative of the Japanese people. This may include a constitutional monarchy under the present dynasty if it be shown to the complete satisfaction of the world that such a government will never again aspire to aggression.

Why, then—given the desperation that Foreign Minister Tōgō's cables revealed, together with the willingness of many top U.S. and British planners to offer assurances concerning the imperial dynasty—was President Truman so sure that the Japanese would not respond to the "warning statement" mentioned in his diary? The answer is that— primarily on the advice of his most influential confidant, Secretary of State James F. Byrnes— the president had approved deletion of the key

Truman and Byrnes talk privately on July 11, 1945,
aboard the Augusta, *the ship that carried them across the
Atlantic to Antwerp on their way to Potsdam.*

Secretary of War Stimson *walks from his plane soon after arriving at Berlin's Gatow Airport on July 15, 1945, to attend the Potsdam conference. Stimson was not alone in urging the president to consider softer policies toward Japan. Joseph Grew, John McCloy, Generals Marshall and Eisenhower, and Admiral Leahy all favored some degree of leniency, but Byrnes, an unapologetic hard-liner, had the president's ear.*

sentence (underlined above) from the state-war-navy draft. The secretary of state's rationale has never been entirely clear. Byrnes was notoriously secretive and took particular care not to leave a paper record of his conversations with the president, but it can be conjectured that he had many considerations in mind. He may have deemed it domestically risky for the untested neophyte president to repudiate Roosevelt's frequently reiterated commitment to "unconditional surrender," especially because these were the terms under which Germany had surrendered. Additionally, Byrnes probably saw little to be gained from compromising the conditions of U.S. postsurrender control over Japan. It is also possible—and this is the most cynical reading of the decision—that he wished to make the bomb known to the world in the most dramatic fashion and thus deliberately chose to render the warning statement unacceptable to the Japanese leadership. Be this as it may, it was clear to everyone on the American side that the Japanese would never respond positively to the demand for surrender without some kind of clarification concerning the emperor and his dynasty.

In this regard, the president's July 25 diary entry was also misleading, for he and Stimson were not really "in accord" on this extremely sensitive issue—which Stimson's own personal diary makes clear. At Potsdam, the secretary of war learned, first from Byrnes and then from the president himself, that the critical "paragraph 12" qualifying sentence had been deleted. On July 24, the president informed him that the final draft of the call for Japan's surrender had been sent to Chiang Kai-shek, China's head of state, for approval. Stimson recorded this as follows:

> *I then spoke of the importance which I attributed to the reassurance of the Japanese on the continuance of their dynasty, and [how] I felt that the insertion of that in the formal warning was important and might be just the thing that would make or mar their acceptance, but that I had heard from Byrnes that they preferred not to put it in, and that now such a change was made impossible by the sending of the message to Chiang.*

Chiang Kai-shek approved the draft, and this became the famous Potsdam Proclamation issued through the print and broadcast media on July 26 over the names of the leaders of the United States, China, and Great Britain. The proclamation, consisting of thirteen paragraphs, declared that "there must be eliminated for all time the authority and

influence of those who have deceived and misled the people of Japan into embarking on world conquest." It also stated that "we do not intend that the Japanese shall be enslaved as a race or destroyed as a nation, but stern justice shall be meted out to all war criminals, including those who have visited cruelties upon our prisoners." The Japanese government would be expected to support "democratic tendencies" and "fundamental human rights." The defeated country would, in return, be permitted to maintain a peaceful economy, with access to necessary raw materials and eventual participation in global trade. The often-quoted final paragraphs read as follows:

(12) The occupying forces of the Allies shall be withdrawn from Japan as soon as these objectives have been accomplished and there has been established in accordance with the freely expressed will of the Japanese people a peacefully inclined and responsible government.

(13) We call upon the Government of Japan to proclaim now the unconditional surrender of all the Japanese armed forces, and to provide proper and adequate assurances of their good faith in such action. The alternative for Japan is prompt and utter destruction.

This photograph shows the last meeting at Potsdam. Stalin is at the top of the table in a white uniform. Seated to his left is Soviet foreign minister Vyacheslav Molotov. Truman is on the right side of the table, with Byrnes seated to his right and Admiral Leahy seated to Byrnes's right. At the bottom left (with his chair slightly pushed back) is British prime minister Clement Attlee, who took over for Churchill at Potsdam after his Labour party routed Churchill's Conservatives in Britain's July 26 general election.

JOSEPH STALIN

1879 – 1953

Joseph Stalin became general secretary of the Communist party of the Soviet Union in 1922, though he didn't consolidate his control over the country until 1927, when he finally succeeded in expelling Leon Trotsky, his chief rival, from the party. The next year, Stalin began an industrialization program that reorganized Soviet society, often brutally (as with the forced collectivization of Russian agriculture). Although he signed a nonaggression pact with the Nazis in 1939 (agreeing secretly with Germany to divide the independent Baltic states between them), Hitler's 1941 invasion of the Soviet Union forced Stalin into an uncomfortable wartime alliance with Britain and, later, the United States.

THE SOVIET UNION WAS NEITHER CONSULTED about the ultimatum nor invited to join in issuing it. This, too, was by no means an inevitable decision—and here a whole new dimension of politics and policy making at Potsdam enters the picture. Despite the neutrality pact, Stalin's animosity toward Japan was an open secret, and no one was under any delusions about his fastidiousness concerning treaty obligations. Ever since the latter part of 1943, U.S. and British military planners had been looking forward to the Soviet Union's promised entry into the war against Japan within roughly three months of the defeat of Germany—this being the amount of time Stalin had estimated would be required to move his forces from Eastern Europe to the Asian front. In military circles, it was widely believed that the shock of a Soviet declaration of war might well prove decisive. An "Estimate of the Enemy Situation" prepared within the U.S. Department of War on the eve of the Potsdam conference (dated June 30, 1945) expressed this in fairly typical terms:

> *It is believed that many Japanese consider defeat to be probable. The increasing effects of sea blockade and the cumulative devastation wrought by strategic bombing should make this realization increasingly general. The entry of the Soviet Union into the war would finally convince the Japanese of the inevitability of defeat.*

The issue of Soviet entry into the war came up again on the first day of the Potsdam conference, when Stalin disclosed the secret overtures coming to him from the Japanese (he had no way of knowing that the Americans had broken the Japanese diplomatic code and were reading Tokyo's cables). Brushing these aside—as Truman and Churchill agreed was appropriate—he stated that Soviet forces would be ready to join battle against Japan within a week of the long-anticipated "three months" timetable. Here again, the president's Potsdam diary is terse and tantalizing. On July 17, his brief summary of the initial meeting with Stalin included these sentences: "He'll be in the Jap War on August 15th. Fini Japs when that comes about." The diary entry for the following day elaborated on these matters, but with a striking twist. Recapitulating his conversations with Prime Minister Churchill, the president recorded:

> *P.M. & I ate alone. Discussed Manhattan (it is a success). Decided to tell Stalin about it. Stalin had told P.M. of telegram from Jap Emperor asking for peace. Stalin also read his answer to me. It was satisfactory.*

Believe Japs will fold up before Russia comes in. I am sure they will when Manhattan appears over their homeland. I shall inform Stalin about it at an opportune time.

The turn of thought here is quite startling. One moment President Truman is envisioning Japan capitulating as soon as the Soviet Union enters the war. Twenty-four hours later, we find him expressing confidence that dropping the bomb will bring about Japan's defeat *before* the Russians get in on the kill. Something had clearly intervened to change his mind—but what? The most probable explanation would appear to be a cryptic message that Truman received on the morning of July 18, indicating that the bomb tested in New Mexico had been far more devastating than initially imagined. Decoded, this two-sentence cable stated that the flash of the explosion had been visible 250 miles away and the sound had carried 50 miles. Suddenly it seemed possible to end the war without Soviet involvement.

President Truman did not find an "opportune time" to inform the Soviet leader about the atomic bomb until the end of the plenary session on July 24. Even then, his approach was informal to a fault. As he later noted in his memoirs, he "casually mentioned to Stalin that we had a new weapon of unusual destructive force. The Russian Premier showed no special interest. All he said was that he was glad to hear it and hoped we would make 'good use of it against the Japanese.'" Although the president left Potsdam convinced that Stalin had no idea what he was talking about, he was mistaken. As was revealed years later, Soviet spies had penetrated the Manhattan Project, prompting Stalin to initiate his own secret atomic-bomb program.

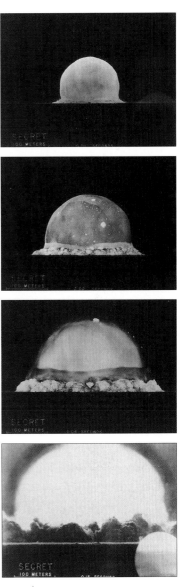

These photographs, *taken from six miles away, document the New Mexico bomb from 0.01 to 0.15 seconds after its ground-level detonation. They show a highly radioactive dust skirt, which scientists later concluded weakened the bomb's destructive force. Planners compensated for this by setting the August 6 bomb to detonate 1,870 feet above Hiroshima.*

THESE COMMENTS AND EXCHANGES give some inkling of the complexity with which thinking about the bomb had become entangled with considerations concerning the Soviet Union. The Soviets had confirmed that they planned to enter the war around August 15 ("Fini Japs when that comes about"). Exhilarated by incoming reports of the phenomenal success of the New Mexico test, however, the president had become sanguine that, by using the bomb quickly, the Japanese "will fold up before Russia comes in." The bomb, that is, had suddenly emerged as a compelling means of *preventing* Soviet entry into the war in Asia. At the same time, the Potsdam Proclamation itself had been weakened (or strengthened, depending on one's objectives) not

James Franck *was one
of several eminent refugees
(including Enrico Fermi
and Leo Szilard) who
worked on the University
of Chicago branch of the
Manhattan Project, which
in December 1942
produced the first self-
sustaining nuclear
chain reaction.*

merely by deletion of the "dynasty" guarantee but also by the exclusion of the Soviet Union from any direct participation, or even symbolic involvement, in the ultimatum.

This latter decision often passes sotto voce in discussions of the decision to drop the bomb. As early as September 1944, Churchill had commented on the growing "sense of hopelessness" in Japan in a personal cable to Stalin. "I believe," he observed, "it might well be that once the Nazis are shattered a triple summons to Japan to surrender, coming from our three Great Powers, might be decisive." The British prime minister returned to this notion of a "triple" or "four-power" (including China) ultimatum on later occasions; but at Potsdam, bomb in hand, neither he nor President Truman deemed it desirable to strengthen the impact of the demand for Japan's surrender in this manner. Here was yet another road considered but in the end not taken.

The relationship between the bomb and U.S. policy toward the Soviet Union was, in fact, an issue of major debate long before Harry Truman assumed the presidency. Here one encounters a highly contro-versial question: Did U.S. and British wartime policy concerning the secret development (and not just *use*) of the new weapon exacerbate Soviet mistrust and help precipitate the postwar nuclear arms race?

During the war, there were a number of confidential warn-ings that this would be the case—the most famous of which came from the great theoretical physicist Niels Bohr, who had escaped Nazi-occupied Denmark and knew about the Manhattan Project. As early as July 1944, Bohr urged Roose-velt and Churchill to recognize that "quite apart from the question of how soon the weapon will be ready for use and what role it may play in the present war," it was essential to inform Stalin about the existence (though not the details) of the Manhattan Project. The future security of the world, in his view, depended on the issue of postwar international controls being seriously addressed *before* the bomb was used.

These words fell like water on stone. In a secret *aide-memoire* of September 1944, President Roosevelt and Prime Minister Churchill explicitly rejected Bohr's suggestion that other powers be informed of the project to develop an atomic bomb "with a view to an international agreement regarding its control and use." To the contrary, they agreed that "full collaboration" between their two countries in developing nuclear technology "for military and commercial purposes should continue after the defeat of Japan unless and until terminated by joint agreement."

Both Oppenheimer and General Marshall touched on this issue in passing during the Interim Committee's important May 31 meeting. Oppenheimer ventured, rather vaguely, that "if we were to offer to exchange information before the bomb was actually used, our moral position would be greatly strengthened." Marshall went so far as to raise the question of "whether it might be desirable to invite two prominent Russian scientists to witness the test." But the committee—led by Byrnes, who strongly believed in the Roosevelt-Churchill policy of operating from a position of demonstrated strength—dismissed any such ideas. On several occasions, scientists connected with the Manhattan Project issued detailed impromptu reports warning, as Bohr had done, of the futility and peril of attempting to monopolize nuclear knowledge and power—and they met similar abrupt rejection. One such report, submitted to the secretary of war on June 11 by a committee headed by Nobel laureate James Franck, succinctly summarized the scientists' apprehensions: "We cannot hope to avoid a nuclear armament race, either by keeping secret from the competing nations the basic scientific facts of nuclear power or by cornering the raw materials required for such a race." Here was yet another road not taken.

O N JULY 24, TWO DAYS BEFORE the Potsdam Proclamation was released, President Truman ordered the U.S. military to prepare for deployment of the available nuclear bombs "as soon as weather will permit visual bombing after about 3 August." (Only two bombs were ready at the time, and they differed in manufacture—one utilizing plutonium, the other enriched uranium.) On July 28, as the president had anticipated, Prime Minister Suzuki Kantarō was quoted in the Japanese press as stating that the proclamation offered nothing new and that Japan intended to ignore it. Even as he spoke, U.S. aircraft were dropping huge numbers of leaflets carrying the Potsdam terms to the Japanese populace in translation.

Things moved swiftly thereafter. President Truman gave the final go-ahead for the fatal missions on July 31. The first bomb was dropped on Hiroshima on August 6. The Soviet Union hastily declared war on Japan two days later. On August 9, the United States dropped the second bomb on Nagasaki. On August 10, the Japanese government announced its readiness to accept the Potsdam terms of surrender "with the understanding that the said declaration does not comprise any demand which prejudices the prerogatives of His Majesty as a Sovereign Ruler."

OVERLEAF:

A train proceeds toward Nagasaki on the main trunk line. The pole in the center foreground of the photograph marks ground zero. The number of fatalities in Nagasaki would have been much higher had the bomb not landed almost two miles off target.

The secret nuclear facility at Oak Ridge, Tennessee, was just part of the vast industrial foundation that supported the bomb project. To some extent, the army's enormous investment in this infrastructure ensured that nuclear weapons development would continue after the war.

The following day, the United States issued a carefully phrased response drafted by Secretary of State Byrnes and approved by Britain, China, and the Soviet Union. The key sentence was this:

From the moment of surrender the authority of the Emperor and the Japanese Government to rule the state shall be subject to the Supreme Commander of the Allied powers who will take such steps as he deems proper to effectuate the surrender terms.

This photograph of Gen. Douglas MacArthur signing the Japanese surrender belonged to Gen. Jonathan M. Wainwright, who had succeeded MacArthur in the Philippines, defending Bataan and Corregidor until forced to surrender in 1942.

Although this response adroitly circumvented the Japanese demand, Foreign Minister Tōgō managed to persuade the emperor and enough of his colleagues that the imperial prerogatives had been guaranteed. On August 14, by way of a previously recorded radio broadcast, Emperor Hirohito spoke directly to his subjects for the first time ever. "After pondering deeply the general trends of the world and the actual conditions obtaining in Our Empire today," he began, "We have decided to effect a settlement of the present situation by resorting to an extraordinary measure." He had ordered the government to accept the provisions of the "joint declaration."

This Waterman desk pen was the first of several used to sign the Japanese surrender documents during a ceremony that took place on September 2, 1945, aboard the USS Missouri in Tokyo Bay.

EVEN BEFORE JAPAN CAPITULATED, President Truman agonized over the devastation he had unleashed. On August 9, in a personal letter to a senator who had urged him to continue bombing the Japanese unrelentingly, the president wrote that "my object is to save as many American lives as possible but I also have a human feeling for the women and children of Japan." The following day, he informed his cabinet of the initial Japanese response and ordered that there be no more nuclear attacks without his explicit approval (a third bomb had become imminently available). As recorded in the diary of Commerce Secretary Henry Wallace, "Truman said he had given orders to stop atomic bombing. He said the thought of wiping out another 100,000 people was too horrible. He didn't like the idea of killing as he said, 'all those kids.'"

Four months after the war ended, Truman explained his decision to use the bombs in simple terms that, for most Americans, have essentially defined the issue ever since: "It occurred to me that a quarter of a million of the flower of our young manhood was worth a couple of Japanese cities, and I still think they were and are." The numbers vary, even in official accounts, but the basic argument is clear: Had the Allied powers been forced to bring about Japan's surrender by invading its home islands, the number of Americans killed and wounded would have been huge. That is why, before the bombs were in hand, U.S. civilian and military planners were so eager to secure Soviet entry into the war.

On this, there can be no doubt. Japan's top military leaders were, as the president declared, fanatics. The Japanese populace was being mobilized to fight to the bitter end should an invasion take place. Official military plans for defense of the homeland—code-named *Ketsu-go* (literally, "Operation Decisive") and distributed to field commanders on April 8, 1945—called for suicide attacks on the enemy fleet by planes and midget submarines, followed by suicidal resistance on the beaches and unrelenting guerrilla resistance throughout the land. Every man, woman, and adolescent was being exhorted to prepare to die "like a shattered jewel," as one popular

Japanese prisoners of war held on Guam bow their heads as they listen to Emperor Hirohito announce Japan's unconditional surrender.

slogan went, should the diabolical enemy set foot on Japan's sacred soil. While Americans were perfecting the atomic bomb, Japanese civilians were being drilled in wielding bamboo spears and Japanese fighting men (and civilians as well, as in Okinawa) were dying in appalling numbers in utterly futile battles of resistance.

President Truman went to Potsdam with Okinawa fresh in his mind, for that ferocious struggle had ended only on June 21. The emperor's loyal forces, close to one hundred thousand strong, had fought virtually to the last man. About one third of the island's civilian population—another hundred thousand individuals, possibly many more—had perished. U.S. fatalities numbered some seven thousand soldiers and marines and five thousand sailors. Suicidal "kamikaze" attacks had caused serious trauma as well as material damage among the attacking U.S. naval forces. Beyond any doubt, an all-out invasion of Japan would have been a bloodbath, even more so for the Japanese than for the invaders. (The Japanese-to-American "kill ratio" during the

A marine rifleman crouches in June 1945 near the entrance to one of the many caves honeycombing the hills of Okinawa. His mission was to pick off enemy snipers on the opposing ridge. In addition to the heavy American casualties, the three-month struggle for Okinawa took over two hundred thousand Japanese lives, less than half of them soldiers, proving that the emperor was indeed willing to sacrifice civilians in large numbers.

just-concluded Philippines campaign, which planners used before full data from Okinawa became available, had been 22:1.)

As became publicly known soon after the war, however, there was no invasion of Japan in the immediate offing when President Truman made the decision to use the bombs without delay. The U.S. war plan, code-named DOWNFALL and prepared within the command of Gen. Douglas MacArthur, who would have led the invasion, was addressed at a major White House meeting on June 18. The first stage of this invasion (OLYMPIC) would have entailed an assault on Kyushu, the southernmost of Japan's four main islands, commencing on November 1. The second major assault (CORONET), directed against the main island of Honshu, was not scheduled to begin until March 1946.

This timetable has obvious bearing on the questions of whether and how to use the bombs. It can be argued that the president's primary obligation, no matter what the circumstances, was to end the war as quickly as possible. Even if only hundreds (rather than hundreds of thousands) of "the flower of our young manhood" could be spared death, it was his duty to save these men.

It is misleading, however, to argue simply that the bombs saved huge numbers of lives and that there were no reasonable options to using them as they were, in fact, used. On the contrary, there were a number of options, or "roads not taken"—some considered at the time and rejected, others clearer to us now with the benefit of hindsight. Indeed, hindsight entered the picture quickly to cast the use of the bombs into question at official levels as early as 1946. Immediately after the war, the new role of air power was subjected to intense scrutiny by the high-powered (and lavishly staffed) U.S. Strategic Bombing Survey, which produced a cornucopia of technical reports concerning the effects of bombing on Germany and Japan. The most often-quoted conclusion here is surely a single sentence that appeared in its summary report on the Pacific war: "It is the Survey's opinion that certainly prior to December 31, 1945, and in all probability prior to November 1, 1945, Japan would have

surrendered even if the atomic bombs had not been dropped, even if
Russia had not entered the war, and even if no invasion had been planned
or contemplated." This was, as the survey itself noted, just "opinion."
It was a conclusion reached by able technocrats who had descended on a
defeated and occupied land and relied on a potpourri of Japanese inform-
ants who had their own agendas to promote. The survey may have been
incorrect. But it raised the question that has never gone away: Was it
really necessary to kill all those "women and children"?

T HERE ARE NO CERTAIN ANSWERS here, but there are certainly
provocative and troubling questions. As the preceding narrative
suggests, it has become increasingly clear that serious alternatives
to bringing about Japan's surrender were considered at the time; and even
after it was agreed that the
bombs should be used, the
manner in which this was
done might still have been less
barbaric, less morally damaging
to the United States, perhaps
even more conducive to
ameliorating the Cold War
tensions and nuclear terror
that followed. The "roads not
taken" were these:

1. *Modifying or clarifying*
"unconditional surrender" in
order to assure the Japanese
that this would not imperil
the emperor or the imperial
institution. This is the "Joseph

One of the most
destructive *Japanese*
suicide attacks took
place on May 11, 1945,
when two kamikaze dive
bombers struck the
aircraft carrier Bunker
Hill *off Okinawa. The*
resulting fire, fed by all
the aircraft fuel, killed
372 crewmen and
wounded 264.

Grew argument" that was shunted aside in May 1945 and again during
the "paragraph 12" disagreement on the eve of the Potsdam Proclamation.

Such modification clearly carried political liabilities within the
United States, where Americans expected their despised Japanese enemy,
already on the ropes, to submit to the same surrender terms that the
Germans had been forced to accept. It is highly unlikely, moreover, that
the "dynasty" guarantee in itself would have persuaded Japan's die-hard
militarists to capitulate. (The "roads not taken" on the Japanese side is a
profoundly depressing story in itself.) At best, they might have asked for
further, harder guarantees—but even this would have opened the door
to some kind of exchange. The great challenge for the Americans would

HIROHITO

1901 – 1989

Hirohito became regent for his mentally declining father in 1921 and formally acceded to the throne in 1926. As emperor, he generally ratified the policies of the militarists, whose merciless invasion of Manchuria in 1931 began the pattern of brutal expansion that led to the Pacific war. Few historians blame Hirohito for starting the war, but more than a few hold him responsible for continuing it. Even after Japan's defeat became obvious in late 1944, the emperor urged his generals and admirals to win one last victory so that he might prevent an invasion of Japan's main islands and secure a conditional surrender. While they tried, more than 1.5 million Japanese were killed.

have been to frame any further "clarification" in persuasive terms—comparable to those of the Byrnes note of August 11—which gave Japan's top leaders hope and some semblance of honor without actually turning the surrender into a conditional one. Had the surrender been conditional, or "contractual," the United States would not have been able to introduce the sweeping agenda of demilitarization and democratization that it subsequently promoted in a defeated and occupied Japan.

2. Delaying the use of the bombs until the impact of the impending Soviet entry into the war could be assessed. Until the bombs were in hand, U.S. and British leaders had expressed great hope that the shock of a Soviet declaration of war would persuade even Japanese hard-liners of the inevitability of defeat. It was obvious that the imperial high command's plans for the defense of the home islands would be thrown into chaos by the need to divert resources to a massive new front in continental Asia. By mid-July, it also was obvious that the emperor's desperate "peace" overtures to Moscow would be shattered by Soviet entry into the war. There would be nowhere else to turn.

It is not difficult to trace how and why this option was abandoned. Most of the Potsdam conference was devoted to European issues and futile attempts to resolve mounting U.S. and British concern over the oppressive nature of Soviet policies in Eastern Europe. In his 1947 memoirs, Byrnes frankly acknowledged that he had come to hope that "the atomic bomb would be successful and would force the Japanese to accept surrender on our terms. I feared what would happen when the Red Army entered Manchuria."

This was a reasonable concern. The Soviet army's actions in Manchuria were indeed inhumane vis-à-vis both civilians and prisoners of war. But this urgency to use the atomic bombs "before Russia comes in" (as Truman put it in his diary on July 18) undercuts the simplistic argument that the bombs were used simply "to save our boys." It also evades the more subtle issue of whether the Potsdam ultimatum could and should have been made far more forceful by adding the Soviet Union's endorsement. Had President Truman elected to combine some form of this "Soviet option" with some sort of ambiguous "dynasty" reference as mentioned above, the Japanese leadership would have found it impossible to dismiss the Potsdam Proclamation as nothing new.

3. Laying the ground for the international control of nuclear weapons before the bombs were actually used. Consistent with the policy laid down by Roosevelt and Churchill, Truman and his top advisers rejected the arguments advanced by Niels Bohr and others that scientific knowledge could not be monopolized and that prevention of a nuclear arms race depended on trust building with the Soviets. This reflected the triumph, one might say, of "hard" over "soft" realism. Flaunting the finished bomb (rather than trying to use its development as a basis for promoting postwar cooperation), it was argued, would be the most effective way of ensuring its usefulness as a weapon of postwar policy—and, indeed, as an inducement to postwar international arms control.

Perhaps Soviet policy would have proved intractable on this point no matter what the United States did. At the same time, however, the Soviet position was at least partly rooted in deep and not entirely unfounded suspicion of Anglo-American intentions. We know now what Roosevelt and Truman did not know: that, through spies in the Manhattan Project, Stalin was already aware that his erstwhile American and British allies were withholding knowledge of momentous import. The policy pursued by the U.S. and British leadership at Potsdam—discussing imminent Soviet entry into the war with Stalin and his military commanders, while at the same time preparing to preempt this very eventuality with nuclear strikes—could only have confirmed the Soviet leader's deepest fear: that the bomb was being developed for use not merely against the Axis powers but against the Soviet Union as well. As the Franck Report anticipated, this hard-line nuclear policy did precipitate a wasteful and terrifying nuclear arms race. What would have been lost had President Truman ventured to disclose the nature of the new weapon (*not* the details of its manufacture) more frankly, even as late as Potsdam?

4. *Demonstrating the bomb at a test site, dropping it on a target other than a predominantly civilian population, or dropping it with adequate prior warning.* Many of the scientists who had reservations about trying to intimidate the Soviet Union with the new secret weapon coupled their proposals concerning early trust building with recommendations that the bomb be "first revealed to the world by a demonstration in an appropriately selected uninhabited area," such as a desert or barren island, with representatives of all the Allied powers present as observers (the quotation is from the June 11 Franck Report). A poll conducted in July 1945 among 150 Chicago-based scientists working on the bombs found 46 percent in support of a "military demonstration" in Japan prior to "full use" of the weapon and 26 percent favoring "an experimental demonstration in this

On the morning of August 10, 1945, *the day after the bombing of Nagasaki, a mother and son hold boiled rice balls given them by an emergency relief party. This photograph was taken one mile southeast of ground zero.*

J. ROBERT OPPENHEIMER

1904 – 1967

In late 1942, the army assigned Robert Oppenheimer the task of setting up the Manhattan Project bomb laboratory. For its site, Oppenheimer, who had attended a boarding school nearby, chose Los Alamos, New Mexico. His often-quoted reaction to the Alamogordo test blast was a line from the Bhagavad Gita: "Now I am become Death, the Destroyer of worlds." Many historians believe that Oppenheimer became caught up in the momentum to finish the bomb so that it could be used before war's end. This was an outcome that he later regretted. "Mr. President, I have blood on my hands," an anguished Oppenheimer told Truman in March 1946. "It'll all come out in the wash," Truman replied.

country, with representatives of Japan present; followed by a new opportunity for surrender before full use of the weapon is employed." Only 15 percent favored using the new weapon "in the manner that is from the military point of view most effective in bringing about prompt Japanese surrender at minimum human cost to our armed forces."

The possibility of inviting outsiders to witness the initial bomb test was never seriously considered by the top planners. Perhaps more surprising, the argument that the first bomb used should be dropped on a genuinely military target also received short shrift. General Marshall captured the gist of the latter option when he suggested at an early point (May 29) that the first bomb be dropped on an isolated military target, such as a large naval installation. If that failed, he continued, the United States "ought to designate a number of large manufacturing areas from which the people would be warned to leave—telling the Japanese that we intend to destroy such centers."

The rebuttal to such arguments was short and swift, as reflected in the Interim Committee's emphasis on the need "to make a profound psychological impression on as many inhabitants as possible." Other arguments were also advanced against giving the Japanese any clear warning of an impending nuclear attack. Byrnes, for example, was persuaded that the Japanese might bring American prisoners of war into the announced demonstration site (something they had not, for unexplained reasons, previously ventured to do in the scores of major cities already subjected to U.S. air raids). Moreover, as he later put it, if the bomb failed to explode, it would simply give "aid and comfort to the Japanese militarists."

The ultimate rationale for targeting densely populated cities actually turned the notions of "demonstration" and "warning" in directions almost completely antithetical to those advocated by the concerned scientists. Thus, for example, Arthur Compton, one of the several influential scientists on the

***A small-scale model** of the Fat Man bomb.*

Interim Committee, took issue with the Franck Report on the grounds that it "did not mention the probable net saving of lives, nor that if the bomb were not used in the present war the world would have no adequate warning as to what was to be expected if war should break out again."

Whatever else Compton may have had in mind, his comment revealed the grander global framework in which the decision to drop the bombs was made. The demonstration U.S. policy makers desired was one that would shock not just Japan's militarist leaders but also "the world" in general—thereby reducing, they hoped, the chance of future conflict and certainly of future nuclear war. Although no one put it precisely this way, the import of such early deterrence thinking was clear: The higher cause of idealism required an initial exemplary slaughter.

What this meant in concrete human terms was that the designated targets of "the most terrible bomb in the history of the world" were major urban areas with civilian populations numbering in the hundreds of thousands. Five such cities comprised the original list of targets, a number subsequently reduced to four when Kyoto was eliminated at the last moment. The total dead in Hiroshima by the end of 1945 is estimated to have been around 140,000, and in Nagasaki around 70,000—together, more than twice as many civilian dead as the total number of U.S. combat fatalities in the entire Pacific war. Tens of thousands of additional victims died lingering deaths in the years that followed.

"Military objectives and soldiers and sailors are the target and not women and children," President Truman had written in his diary on July 25. One hears in this sentence the ring of an old-fashioned morality that, by the end of the war, no belligerent still took seriously. Incendiary bombing of urban centers had become standard U.S. practice, and Hiroshima and Nagasaki were available as unscathed targets in August 1945 only because they had not been deemed critical military sites earlier. The president had been told that the light of the New Mexico blast was visible 250 miles away. He knew that "ground zero" was the center of every city on the target list and that the notion of explicit prior warning had been rejected.

And yet, at the same time, there is no reason to believe that President Truman was writing his hasty little Potsdam diary with the thought of future readers in mind. Was he, then, deluding himself concerning the true nature and implication of his decision—trying to reaffirm a precious old morality, even as he participated in its horrendous repudiation? Very possibly, he was. That would help explain why, when the enormous human consequences of his decision did sink in, he put a hold on the use of a third bomb. But why did this troubled morality not, at least, delay the use of the second bomb?

5. *Delaying the second bomb.* Plain hatred of a "ruthless, merciless and fanatic" enemy certainly helps explain the bombing of Nagasaki so quickly after that of Hiroshima; but more than this was at play. An almost

This is the July 25 page from the Truman Potsdam diary. Although a number of scholars knew of the diary's existence, having come across references to it, none was able to track it down until 1979.

OPPOSITE:

Emperor Hirohito in 1945 riding the white horse that symbolized his place at the center of Japan's formidable military culture. After the war, to promote a peaceful occupation, MacArthur spared Hirohito the war crimes tribunal that sentenced Prime Minister Tōjō Hideki to death.

irresistible momentum propelled the development and use of the atomic bomb. The weapon was possible, and therefore it would be made; the weapon was made, and therefore it would be used. The United States possessed two bombs as of July 24, and the go-ahead was given to ready them both for deployment in quick succession. Technological imperative was melded with bureaucratic momentum. One decision governed the bombing of the two cities. No serious consideration was ever given to the fact that the Japanese leadership would need time to absorb the nature and effects of the first bomb before responding.

Among Americans, Nagasaki tends to be the forgotten bomb, and for an obvious reason. The ostensible rationale for using the second bomb without delay—namely, that Japan had to be persuaded that the United States had more than one bomb—is morally troubling, even to some of those who defend the bombing of Hiroshima. The physicist Victor Weisskopf, who worked on the Manhattan Project, conveyed this widely held sentiment succinctly in his memoirs when he observed that "the first bomb might have been justifiable, but the second was a crime." Had President Truman opted to delay the second bomb (as he did the third), it is difficult to imagine that the political outcome of the war would have been any different.

HARRY TRUMAN LATER BELITTLED second-guessers, as did James Byrnes. "Monday-morning quarterbacking is a very pleasant pastime," Byrnes commented in a 1960 interview on the anniversary of Japan's capitulation, "but it is not a fruitful one."

Where the decision to use the most terrible weapon in the history of the world is concerned, it would seem more appropriate to say that hindsight is painful rather than "pleasant." We can only hope that it is fruitful as well, for to reconsider the decision to destroy Hiroshima and Nagasaki is to ask whether hundreds of thousands of civilians really needed to be killed to end the war. It is to ask—in the critical words of Annapolis graduate and *New York Times* military editor Hanson Baldwin, looking back on the war in 1950—whether Americans actually had to "become identified, rightfully or wrongly, as inheritors of the mantle of Genghis Khan and all those of past history who have justified the use of utter ruthlessness in war." It is to ask whether it might have been possible to avoid triggering the nuclear arms race that followed.

It is to ask, as well, whether there are not political and moral lessons here that are still pertinent to our own lives in the age of terror these bombs have bequeathed.

FURTHER READING

★ Gar Alperovitz, *The Decision to Use the Atomic Bomb and the Architecture of an American Myth* (1995)

★ Martin J. Sherwin, *A World Destroyed: Hiroshima and the Origins of the Arms Race* (1975)

★ ★ ★

SEPTEMEBER 19, 1946

THE PRESIDENT LEARNS ABOUT CIVIL RIGHTS

BY WILLIAM E. LEUCHTENBURG

O N SEPTEMBER 19, 1946, a delegation from the National Emergency Committee Against Mob Violence called on President Harry Truman to inform him of outrages being committed against black citizens in the United States. In one Georgia county, he was told, the only black man who had dared to vote had been gunned down by four whites in his own front yard. In another, two blacks, one of them a Bronze Star air corps veteran, had been murdered by a white mob—and when one of the victims' wives recognized one of her husband's assailants, both women were killed as well.

The president was especially shocked by the report of an incident that had taken place in South Carolina. The victim was Isaac Woodard, a black sergeant who had earned a battle star in the South Pacific. Just three hours after receiving his honorable discharge, Woodard was within sixty miles of his home—and the joy of finally seeing his wife and child again—when he was arrested after a minor fracas with a white bus driver and hauled off to jail. There police blackjacked his eyes so severely that Woodard was blinded. On hearing this awful account, Truman, hands clenched and face registering horror, got up from his chair in the Oval Office and said, "My God! I had no idea it was as terrible as that! We've got to do something!"

The head of the visiting delegation, NAACP secretary Walter White, warned the president that racists in Congress would forestall any general civil rights inquiry. "I'll create it by executive order," Truman replied, "and pay for it out of the president's contingent fund." Later, Truman told minority affairs adviser David Niles, "I am very much in earnest on this thing, and I'd like very much to have you push it with everything you have." The very next day, he notified Attorney General Tom Clark that the time had come for a national commission on civil rights. "I know you have been looking into the…lynchings," Truman wrote, "but…it is going to take something more than the handling of each individual

AT LEFT: *After their September 19 meeting, President Truman poses with members of the National Emergency Committee Against Mob Violence. On Truman's left is delegation head Walter White.*

ABOVE: *A 1948 presidential campaign button distributed by Dixiecrat candidate Strom Thurmond, who ran in opposition to the Truman administration's civil rights policy.*

American Red Cross
*field director David
Edwards helps Isaac
Woodard complete an
application for disability
benefits on July 22, 1946.
Behind them stand
NAACP public relations
director Oliver Harrington,
American Red Cross
assistant field director
Edward Nottage, and
Woodard's mother.*

THE BLINDING OF ISAAC WOODARD

*When members of the
staff of the American
Red Cross heard the
news reports of Isaac
Woodard's beating and
blinding at the hands of
South Carolina police,
they invited Woodard to
New York City and
personally escorted him
to the offices of the
Veterans Administration,
where they helped him
apply for disability
benefits. When the VA
proved reluctant to grant
the benefits, veterans
groups organized a
petition drive to pressure
the War Department.*

case after it happens—it is going to require the inauguration of some sort of policy to prevent such happenings."

On December 5, 1946, Truman announced the creation of a President's Committee on Civil Rights under the chairmanship of Charles E. Wilson, the public-spirited president of General Electric. The committee's membership, it was remarked, constituted a "Noah's Ark" of appointees: There were two southerners (both known to be liberal on race), two African Americans, two women, two Catholics, two Protestants, two Jews, two college presidents, two corporation heads, and two labor leaders. "I want our Bill of Rights implemented in fact as well as on paper," Truman instructed the group. And though the president acknowledged the importance of local sovereignty, he made it clear that there were "certain rights under the Constitution of the United States which I think the federal government has a right to protect, and I want to find out just how far we can go."

Truman could still have had second thoughts. After all, civil rights was an extremely divisive issue, and few believed Truman could afford to alienate the South with a presidential election just two years away. Even after naming a committee that was "tilted to civil rights," in the words of one historian, the president could have intimated subtly (or not so subtly) that the committee should undertake nothing that would be politically injurious to him. "You can't legislate morals," the attorney general warned the committee; and Robert Cushman of Cornell University, one of the country's most highly regarded scholars, urged its members not to disregard the "constitutional limits upon the federal government." Truman, though, never made any such request and instead kept up his strong encouragement of the committee's work, doing nothing that would temper its recommendations even though he knew they would be explosive. Harry Truman thus acted as Franklin D. Roosevelt, confronted with the bloody race riots of World War II, had not.

> "NO DEMOCRACY CAN LONG SURVIVE WHICH DOES NOT ACCEPT AS FUNDAMENTAL... THE RIGHTS OF MINORITIES."
>
> —
>
> *Franklin D. Roosevelt, letter to the NAACP, June 1938*

Truman's initiative stunned and angered southern whites, who had been confident that the new president, a native of Missouri, shared their racial outlook. "I was raised amidst some violently prejudiced southerners," Truman once acknowledged. His grandparents, in fact, had received slaves as a wedding gift, and his parents were "Lincoln haters." He recalled that his mother had once flung Harriet Beecher Stowe's *Uncle Tom's Cabin* on the floor and kicked it about. In Independence, where Truman was raised, blacks could not even use the town library. With such an upbringing, Truman did acquire an abiding belief in white supremacy, and to the end of his days he indulged in racial epithets. It therefore seemed quite reasonable for southerners to support his vice-presidential nomination in 1944 and for Democratic senator Burnet Maybank of South Carolina to assure a friend as they traveled together on the funeral train carrying Franklin Roosevelt's body, "Everything's going to be all right—the new president knows how to handle the niggers."

In this 1946 drawing *by African-American artist Charles Wilbert White, a policeman, backed by a Klansman holding a whip, points his gun at three black soldiers coming home from World War II. One reason for the terrible violence against returning black servicemen was the determination of returning white southerners to keep the old system of racial segregation firmly in place.*

W HY, THEN, DID TRUMAN become so committed to civil rights? According to one theory of social change, elites act only when compelled to do so by the masses. That conception, though, falls short in Truman's case. It's certainly true that black veterans returned from World War II in a more militant mood. "Throughout the Pacific," Walter White informed a Senate committee, "I was told with grim pessimism by Negro troops that 'we know that our fight for democracy will really begin when we reach San Francisco on our way home.'" But during the 1940s, the civil rights movement was not

In an improvised shelter *on the Anzio beachhead, Sgt. Charles Glasco (left) of West Chester, Pennsylvania, and Sgt. Audrey Barnes of Chicago read some mail from home during a lull in the enemy shelling on April 16, 1944.*

Lynching disfigured the 1930s and 1940s—and not merely in the South. This photograph from August 1930 shows the gruesome fate of two African Americans accused in Marion, Indiana, of murdering a white youth and assaulting his girlfriend. A mob took nineteen-year-old Abram Smith (left) and eighteen-year-old Thomas Shipp out of the Grant County Jail and lynched them in a public square.

A protester marches in a 1922 anti-lynching parade in Washington, D.C.

nearly so well mobilized as it later became. Hence, Truman felt no coercion to act, either because of mass demonstrations or because of ghetto rioting. Moreover, Truman knew that white southerners were determined to preserve the racial status quo. The war, indeed, had reinforced among white southern troops the belief that they were fighting to defend their traditional way of life, which included white supremacy.

There is more substance to the suggestion that Truman acted for political reasons. Before World War II, most African Americans lived in the South. During the war, however, more than a million migrated north and west to take factory jobs in electorally important states such as Michigan and California. The black population of Detroit grew 40 percent during the 1940s, while the number of African Americans in San Francisco jumped 227 percent and the number in the greater Portland area 437 percent. In the 1946 midterm election returns, the Democrats had noticed a disturbing trend: Black voters, dismayed by southern demagogues (nearly all of whom were Democrats), had begun drifting away from the party—most conspicuously in New York, the home state of Gov. Thomas E. Dewey, the likely 1948 Republican nominee. Truman may conceivably have had stabilization of the black vote in mind when he created his committee on civil rights, but he had to weigh that consideration against the substantial risk of provoking white southerners into bolting the Democratic party, which they had already been threatening to do.

Foreign policy concerns appear to have played a more significant role in motivating Truman. In the incipient Cold War, discrimination against people of color put the United States at a disadvantage in its struggle with the Soviet Union for the allegiance of the third world. One NAACP official had already noted with some irony that Secretary of State James F. Byrnes was demanding "free and unfettered elections" for Rumanians, Bulgars, and Poles while millions of southern blacks, including those in Byrnes's home state of South Carolina, were still being denied their right to vote. "The top dog in a world which is over half colored ought to clean his own house," Truman concluded.

Even more important was Truman's personal indignation. He abhorred the denial to blacks of their fundamental rights as American citizens and found especially intolerable the gross mistreatment of men in uniform. The World War I veteran who had once been known as Captain Harry of Battery D was especially moved by Isaac Woodard's gouging because Woodard had been a soldier and anyone wearing a uniform, in Captain Harry's view, merited respect. The executive order creating the civil rights committee made a point of noting that "ex-servicemen" had been "killed, maimed, or intimidated."

And once Truman set out on this course, he would not relent. When Democratic leaders asked him to back off, he replied:

> My forebears were Confederates.... Every factor and influence in my background—and in my wife's for that matter—would foster the personal belief that you are right. But my very stomach turned over when I learned that Negro soldiers, just back from overseas, were being dumped out of Army trucks in Mississippi and beaten. Whatever my inclinations as a native of Missouri might have been, as President I know this is bad. I shall fight to end evils like this.

When the committee members returned to the White House on October 29, 1947, prepared to present nearly three dozen far-reaching proposals, Truman greeted them by saying, "I have stolen a march on you. I have already read the report, and I want you to know that not only have you done a good job but you have done what I wanted you to." That same day, he asked every American citizen to read the report as well, calling it "an American charter of human freedom in our time." He expected the document to be, he said, "a guide for action."

> "ONE OF THE THINGS THAT MAKES A NEGRO UNPLEASANT TO WHITE FOLK IS THE FACT THAT HE SUFFERS FROM THEIR INJUSTICE."
>
> —
>
> *H. L. Mencken,*
> Notebooks (1930)

President Truman *accepts the report of his Committee on Civil Rights on October 29, 1947. Handing the report to Truman is GE president Charles E. Wilson.*

A New York City policeman *hauls a bleeding African American into a police station during the August 3, 1943, Harlem race riot, in which 5 people were killed and 410 wounded.*

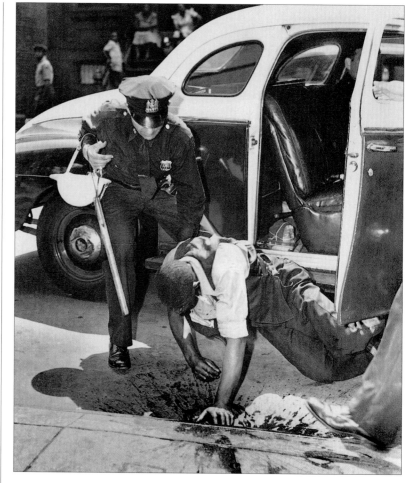

WORLD WAR II RACE RIOTS

During 1943, as many as forty people were killed in race riots across the country. Troops were dispatched to put down civil disturbances in Mobile and in Detroit, where the worst rioting occurred. Twenty-nine people were killed in the June 22 Detroit riot, hundreds more were injured, and thirteen hundred blacks were arrested. The cause was the resistance of white auto plant workers to the hiring and promotion of blacks. The August 3 Harlem race riot began when the rumored murder of a black man exacerbated similar underlying tensions.

THE COMMITTEE'S HISTORIC REPORT, entitled *To Secure These Rights*, continued work begun by Swedish sociologist Gunnar Myrdal, who published his findings in *An American Dilemma* (1944). As Myrdal had, the committee discovered a gaping disparity between the American ideal of equality and the country's actual behavior, especially its treatment of blacks. This grievous shortcoming, the report continued, had produced "a kind of moral dry rot which eats away at the emotional and rational bases of democratic beliefs." Furthermore, with an eye toward the Cold War, the committee concluded that the United States "is not so strong, the final triumph of the democratic ideal is not so inevitable, that we can ignore what the world thinks of us or our record."

The report's recommendations included expanding the Justice Department's civil rights division, creating a permanent civil rights commission, enacting laws punishing lynching and police brutality, broadening African-American suffrage (by abolishing the poll tax and safeguarding the right to cast ballots), and outlawing discrimination in private employment. The committee also endorsed "renewed court attack, with intervention by the Department of Justice," on restrictive covenants in housing and, most controversially, an end "immediately" to both discrimination and segregation in the armed forces and federal agencies. It advocated making the District of Columbia a model for the nation by integrating all of its facilities (including its school system) and further recommended the denial of federal money to any public or private program that persisted in Jim Crow practices. "I do not believe," declared Dorothy Tilly, the only white southern woman on the committee, "that there is anyone in the United States who, had he been with us and seen the things we did, would have signed his name to any less strong a report."

The white South—both rank-and-file citizens and prominent Democratic politicians—responded predictably. "These recommendations, aimed directly at the South," a North Carolinian protested, "even exceed in fervor the preachings of the murder-minded old John Brown…who,

for his butcherings of southern sympathizers and other outrages, was justly hanged." One Greensboro, North Carolina, man told the president, "This stand of yours will cost you hundreds of thousands of white votes. I shall take great pleasure in voting against you in 1948." The Democratic town chairman in Danville, Virginia, wired Truman, "I really believe that you have ruined the Democratic Party in the South," and a Baptist minister from Jacksonville, Florida, informed him, "The report of your civil liberty committee today put you in bad south of the Mason and Dixon line. If that report is carried out, you won't be elected dogcatcher in 1948. The South today is the South of 1861."

> # "FREEDOM IS NEVER GIVEN; IT IS WON."
>
> —
>
> *A. Philip Randolph, keynote speech at the Second National Negro Congress, 1937*

On February 2, 1948, the president, undaunted by these and other threats, sent a special message to Congress asking for enactment of a number of the committee's recommendations. He called for an anti–poll tax statute, a fair employment practices commission, an antilynching law, and a permanent Commission on Civil Rights. To end intimidation at the polls, he also asked for voting rights legislation that would specifically ban governmental and private interference with the free exercise of suffrage. Two features of his message struck directly at Jim Crow: Truman asked Congress to outlaw segregation in interstate travel, and he

African Americans, led by A. Philip Randolph (left), picket the 1948 Democratic national convention hall in Philadelphia. The most important civil rights activist of the 1940s, Randolph presided over the Brotherhood of Sleeping Car Porters and was the person most responsible for pressuring FDR into issuing Executive Order 8802, which banned discrimination in U.S. defense industries.

Minneapolis mayor (and future vice president) Hubert H. Humphrey, shown here exhorting his fellow convention delegates, figured prominently in the effort to add a strong civil rights plank to the 1948 Democratic party platform.

promised to issue an executive order desegregating the armed forces. "As a Presidential paper," one historian has written, "it was remarkable for its scope and audacity."

Truman's message aroused even more anger than had the release of the committee's report three months earlier. Mississippi congressman John Bell Williams, who turned to the wall one of the portraits of Truman in his office and draped the other in black, declared, "The people of the South are directly responsible for Mr. Truman's ascendancy to the presidency; yet…he has seen fit to run a political dagger into our backs and now he is trying to drink our blood." At the same time, his fellow Mississippian, Sen. James O. Eastland, charged Truman with seeking "to secure political favor from Red mongrels in the slums of the great cities of the East and Middle West." As the 1948 Democratic national convention approached, one of the state's leading newspapers, the *Jackson Daily News*, warned, "Insofar as Mississippi is concerned, Truman is through, finished, washed up, blotted out. And we don't mean maybe either."

At the Philadelphia convention that July, southerners worked hard to nominate Sen. Richard B. Russell of Georgia, but the insurgency failed; and when the platform committee approved a plank strongly endorsing civil rights for blacks, rebellious Alabama and Mississippi delegates walked out. Forming their own States' Rights party, the Dixiecrats (as they were more familiarly called) nominated South Carolina governor J. Strom Thurmond for president. Earlier, Thurmond had declared, "Not all the laws of Washington, or all the bayonets of the Army, can force the Negro into our homes, our churches, and our schools, or into our places of recreation and amusement." Later, from a balcony of the Dixiecrat headquarters in Birmingham, demonstrators hanged the president in effigy, with the chest of the dummy bearing the sign, "Truman killed by civil rights."

Still, the president would not budge. He had signaled his determination in February, shortly after he sent his message to Congress. At a White House banquet for the Democratic National Committee, a committeewoman from Alabama had lectured him, "I want to take a message back to the South. Can I tell them you're not ramming miscegenation down our throats? That you're not for tearing up our social structure? That you're for all the people, not just the North?" In response, Truman had shown his defiance and contempt by reaching into his pocket, whipping out a copy of the Constitution, and reciting to this woman the Bill of Rights. "I stand on the Constitution," he said. "I take back nothing of what I proposed and make no excuses for it." So overwrought did a black waiter become listening to this exchange that he accidentally knocked a cup of coffee out of Truman's hands.

No amount of verbal abuse and no number of personal appeals, even from old army buddies, could shake the president's commitment to uphold the constitutional rights of blacks. In a crudely typed letter from a Salt Lake City hotel, one former corporal, addressing the president as "Dear friend Harry" and calling himself "your silent pardner," wrote:

FURTHER READING

★ Donald R. McCoy and Richard T. Ruetten, *Quest and Response: Minority Rights and the Truman Administration* (1973)

★ John Frederick Martin, *Civil Rights and the Crisis of Liberalism: The Democratic Party, 1945–1976* (1979)

Oh Harry, you are a fine man but you are a poor salesman so listen to me. You can win the South without the "Equal Rights Bill," but you cannot win the South with it. Just why? Well you, Bess and Margaret, and shall I say myself, are all Southerners and we have been raised with the Negroes and we know the term "Equal Rights." Harry, let us let the South take care of the Niggers, which they have done, and if the Niggers do not like the southern treatment, let them come to Mrs. Roosevelt.

Harry, you are a Southerner and a D— good one so listen to me. I can see you do not talk domestic problems over with Bess.... You put equal rights in Independence and Bess will not live with you, will you Bess.

Democratic delegates *from Alabama wave and shout to get the attention of convention chairman Sam Rayburn so that they can announce their intention to walk out. But, rather than recognize them, the Texas congressman ignored their commotion and ordered a recess. In the end, of course, this tactic only delayed the Alabamans' leave-taking.*

The president replied, "I am going to send you a copy of the report of my Commission on Civil Rights and then if you still have that antebellum proslavery outlook, I'll be thoroughly disappointed in you."

Two weeks after the Philadelphia convention, Truman demonstrated his determination to carry out the committee's recommendations by issuing, on July 26, two executive orders. The first, drawing on his authority as commander in chief, affirmed the principle of equality of treatment in the armed forces and ordered their desegregation "as rapidly as possible." (That goal took a while to achieve, but the pace was quickened after the Korean War broke out in 1950.) The other directive forbade discrimination within the federal civil service and established a Fair Employment Board to monitor hiring. Later that summer, after telling his sister how a mob had gotten away with brazenly murdering four people, Truman declared, "I can't approve of such goings on, and…I am going to try to remedy it and if that ends up in my failure to be reelected, that failure will be in a good cause."

At the Democratic convention *in July, a reporter asked Strom Thurmond to clarify his position on the southerners' walkout. "President Truman is only following the platform that Roosevelt advocated," the reporter prompted, noting that every Democratic platform since 1932 had included a civil rights plank. "I agree," Thurmond replied, "but Truman really means it."*

ALTHOUGH TRUMAN DID WIN REELECTION in November 1948, his boldness earlier that year with regard to civil rights opened a great divide in American political culture that has never been repaired. Since the removal of federal troops from the South in 1877, Democrats had been able to count on the electoral support of the states of the former Confederacy almost without fail. Yet in 1948—as a result of that September 19, 1946, meeting and its aftermath—the phenomenon of the Solid South came to an end. Strom Thurmond and the Dixiecrats carried four Deep South states—Louisiana, Mississippi, Alabama, and South Carolina—that hadn't gone any way other than Democratic since 1876 (when Louisiana and South Carolina allegedly went for Rutherford B. Hayes). After 1948, however, the South was never "solid" for the Democrats again.

That September 19 meeting also produced another shift, one of far greater consequence. It helped make the quest for racial justice a truly national cause. The social forces necessary for change had been gathering for some time, yet it was Truman who paused to listen, and it was Truman's determination between 1946 and 1948 that finally placed civil rights high on the national agenda for years to come. It's unlikely that Walter White and the other delegation members, as they left the White House on September 19, could have imagined what soon lay ahead: the 1954 *Brown* decision desegregating public schools, the Civil Rights Act of 1964, the Voting Rights Act of 1965. Certainly they could not have foreseen that within twenty years Congress, the same recalcitrant institution that had refused to pass Truman's civil rights bill, would declare the old order at an end and Jim Crow stone-cold dead. The South, and the nation, would never be the same again.

★ ★ ★

MAY 3, 1948

HOLLYWOOD AT THE CROSSROADS

BY ANN DOUGLAS

I N EARLY MAY 1948, HOLLYWOOD'S studio moguls were worried, very worried. They had political problems with the House Un-American Activities Committee. They had revenue problems with falling foreign and domestic profits. Most important, though, were their legal problems. In 1944, at the urging of a group of independent theater owners, the Justice Department had renewed an antitrust suit filed six years earlier against the eight most powerful studios. From February 9 to 11, 1948, the Supreme Court had heard oral arguments in *U.S. v. Paramount,* the most important case in the film industry's history. On May 3, the justices handed down their decision, finding that the studios were indeed a "monopoly" and ordering them to divest themselves of the bulk of their theater holdings.

The Court's ruling reshaped the film industry, transforming not only its business arrangements but also the content and style of the movies it made. Before May 3, 1948, Hollywood had been dominated by the "studio system," an arrangement under which the major studios controlled in the smallest detail the manufacture, distribution, and exhibition of their chief product, the feature film. After *U.S. v. Paramount,* the system seemed to collapse.

S ELLING OFF THEIR THEATER CHAINS was especially difficult for the Jewish immi- grants who had built the film industry because most had gotten their start as exhibitors. Before the Johnson-Reed Act of 1924 virtually suspended immigration to the United States for forty years, men such as Adolph Zukor and Louis B. Mayer benefited from the open-door policy the United States maintained at the turn of the twentieth century, becoming Horatio Alger success stories on an improbable scale. In a sense, Hollywood's notorious penchant for happy endings comprised their collective auto- biography. As Jack Warner explained, he and his brothers were "examples of what this country does for its citizens. There were no silver spoons in our

AT LEFT: *The entrance to the Paramount lot in its heyday. While starting on the East Coast in the 1900s, the film industry had by the 1920s moved the bulk of its operations to Hollywood. Much of radio and television, also originally based in New York City, followed during the 1950s.*

ABOVE: *Sound film was introduced in 1927.*

Adolph Zukor (left) *and Jesse L. Lasky review plans for their new Paramount film studio. In 1916, Zukor had merged his Famous Players production company with the Lasky Feature Play Company to form Players-Lasky. Zukor became president of what would later be called Paramount Pictures—with Lasky, a former vaudeville producer, serving as vice president in charge of production. Until 1914, American films shared the global market with French and Italian offerings. World War I, however, smashed the European movie industry, and Hollywood gained a lead that it has never since surrendered.*

mouths when we were born. If anything," he said, adding to the lore that the immigrant studio heads were comically clumsy manhandlers of their adopted American idiom, "they were shovels."

The Jewish moguls didn't invent the technology that made movies possible (that honor belonged to Thomas Edison and the Lumière brothers), and they didn't create the industry's basic corporate structure (that was the work of "the Trust," a group of largely Gentile producers, distributors, and theater owners who organized themselves under Edison's umbrella in 1908). But they did see possibilities that others had missed and took advantage of the fact that film was a new, open industry with no long-entrenched elite presiding over it. In the words of Harry Cohn, the founder of Columbia Pictures, "Anyone with a normal intelligence knows as much as the other fellow in six months." The relatively small capital outlay required to produce and distribute a film attracted many talented, ambitious people, but the appeal was particularly strong for recently arrived Eastern European Jews, who found more established industries barred to them.

It was these Jewish entrepreneurs who chose Hollywood as the industry's capital, and by the late 1910s, they had supplanted the Trust. During the 1920s, they created the studio system. Its main characteristics were star-genre combinations (such as Warner Brothers' association in the 1930s with James Cagney and gangster pictures), vertical integration (meaning that the major studios owned many of the theaters in which their films were shown), and global reach. The system also tended to promote monopolism

Mary Pickford in 1916.

because the studios colluded (rather than competed) with one another to keep independent filmmakers and theater owners out of the market.

The "star system" was almost as old as the industry. Roughly half of the original studios began with a star-producer partnership, and Adolph Zukor's Paramount was a frequently cited example. In 1916, Zukor gave Mary Pickford ten thousand dollars a week, her own production company, and a share of the profits to appear in vehicles that showcased her singular blend of girlish good nature and tomboy adventurousness. Zukor was not an unduly generous man; Pickford had made his studio, and he knew it. Other studio bosses followed Zukor's lead, turning their biggest stars into franchises to be skillfully packaged and promoted.

OF COURSE, MOVIES WERE a new art form as well as a new industry; in Hollywood, however, the former took its cues from the latter. If it is true, in the words of historian V. G. Kiernan, that "an economic system, like a nation or a religion, lives not by bread alone, but by beliefs, visions [and] daydreams," then capitalism lived out its fantasy life in the Hollywood movie, advertising its pleasures to the first global audience in human history. Whatever their failings, the Hollywood Jews, classic capitalists one and all, understood and expressed the desires of the largely immigrant urban masses that constituted the movies' first great audience. The films they made were the work of creative outsiders who imported new qualities into American life, if only because they had not been part of it from the beginning.

Would-be immigrants were also part of Hollywood's audience from the start. Even after the passage of the Johnson-Reed Act, Hollywood offered those who might have immigrated a chance to imitate instead by keeping up with American fashions and buying American products. As William Fox, founder of the Fox Film Corporation, remarked, "American trade follows American pictures...not the American flag." And movies themselves quickly became one of the country's most successful exports: By the late 1920s, 50 percent of Hollywood's profits came from overseas. The film industry was a glittering emblem of the new-style American imperialism that disdained geographic empire in favor of trade dominance. Although Hollywood films masqueraded as "universal," they always bore the unmistakable stamp of their country of origin. "The world is being Americanized by the photoplay," one English observer lamented as early as 1921.

Even a series of scandals in the early 1920s ultimately served the industry's greater purpose. When the excesses of several stars provoked national outrage and calls for outside regulation, the studios moved to protect their creative autonomy by censoring themselves. Many aspects of what eventually became known as the Production Code seemed ludicrous even then—neither toilets nor ladies' rooms could be mentioned on screen, and condemnations of big business and public institutions were prohibited. Yet rigorous enforcement of the code had at least one positive

THE CODE SCANDALS

At the center of the Hollywood scandals of the early 1920s was Roscoe "Fatty" Arbuckle (above), who became a star for Mack Sennett during the silent-film era. In 1921, at the height of his popularity, Arbuckle was accused of sexually assaulting a starlet who subsequently died from complications related to the alleged attack. At trial, Arbuckle was acquitted of manslaughter, but his films were banned nonetheless. Moreover, Arbuckle's trial exposed a hedonistic Hollywood lifestyle that exacerbated public concerns about overly licentious films (Their Mutual Child, Plaything of Broadway) and spurred development of the Production Code.

effect: It helped Hollywood reach not the relatively small "adult" market that innovation attracts but *everyone*. Only by pitching its films to the broadest possible common denominator could Hollywood produce what one studio head called "universal entertainment for the universe."

THOUGH SUBJECT TO TEMPORARY profit declines—caused by the conversion of theaters to sound in the late 1920s, the Great Depression in the early 1930s, and the closing of European markets in the late 1930s as Hitler began his rampage—Hollywood entered the 1940s prosperous and exuberant. Even under the Production Code, movies remained as they had begun: "pure, raw, private enterprise," in the words of one Hollywood producer. Because Hollywood (unlike the European film industry) sought and received no direct government subsidies, it ran its business, by and large, free of federal oversight.

In the fall of 1941, though, Republican senator Gerald Nye of North Dakota publicly accused Hollywood of making movies that advocated U.S. entry into the European war. Hitler hated Jews, and most Hollywood studio bosses were Jews; therefore, Nye reasoned, the bosses hated Hitler only because they were Jews. The Hollywood moguls in question, ever fearful of having their empires stolen from them by a prejudiced WASP elite and always careful not to alienate any portion of their market, seldom acknowledged, much less defied, the anti-Semitism of their critics. On September 9, 1941, however, appearing before a Senate sub-committee with his counsel, Wendell Willkie, to answer Nye's charges, Harry Warner boldly asserted that his studio and its movies did indeed oppose the principles espoused by Hitler and his Third Reich. In doing so, Warner said, he was merely joining "the world's struggle for freedom…in its final phase."

The bombing of Pearl Harbor three months later effectively ended the Nye affair but not Hollywood's involvement with the war effort. Fending off domestic isolationists on the brink of World War II, Pres.

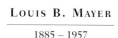

LOUIS B. MAYER

1885 – 1957

Born in Russia, Louis B. Mayer immigrated with his parents to Canada in the late 1880s. Working in his father's scrap-iron business, he put together enough money to open a nickelodeon in Haverhill, Massachusetts, in 1907. By 1918, Mayer controlled the largest chain of movie theaters in New England. To increase his supply of films, he founded a production company in 1917, which merged with two other companies in 1924 to form MGM, the largest and most prestigious of the studios. From 1937 to 1946, the lavish, autocratic Mayer was America's highest-paid citizen. He was also well connected in politics: A staunch Republican, he was Herbert Hoover's first weekend guest at the White House.

"IT WAS THE KIND OF WORLD THAT TODAY ONLY EXISTS… FOR THE SONS OF A FEW LATIN AMERICAN DICTATORS."

—

Groucho Marx,
Groucho and Me, *1959*

Franklin D. Roosevelt found important allies in Hollywood. Later, through its Office of War Information (OWI), FDR's administration closely supervised studio production, ensuring that Hollywood's movies conformed to the needs of war propaganda. Among the most controversial were those films, fostered and applauded by the OWI, that portrayed the Soviet Union, America's wartime ally, as a democracy in disguise bearing striking similarities to the United States. In *Mission to Moscow* (1943), a Warner Brothers project recommended to Hollywood by FDR himself, Stalin's purges were presented as mere variations on FDR's quarantine policy. Mrs. Molotov, wife of the Soviet foreign minister, reported that the cosmetics industry was booming in Russia because the women there had discovered what their American counterparts already knew: that "feminine beauty was *not* a luxury." In *Song of Russia* (1943), even conservative MGM portrayed the Soviet Union as a patriotic land whose townsfolk listened to Jerome Kern tunes in their clubs at night.

In exchange for this cooperation, Hollywood benefited a great deal. For one thing, the Justice Department allowed the studios to settle the outstanding 1938 antitrust suit by signing consent decrees that left their vertical integration (their control of distribution and exhibition as well as production) intact.

OWNERSHIP OF KEY THEATERS in important urban areas was the cornerstone of the distribution system that kept big studios in control of the movie market. Another important element was block booking: Theater owners who wanted a Clark Gable or Betty Grable picture had to take up to a season's worth of other films from the same studio, often sight unseen. Meanwhile, studios staggered release dates to create a price-tiered system of "runs." The studio-owned theaters got the best pictures during their first (and most profitable) run, while smaller, unaffiliated theaters were stuck with later runs, when ticket prices (and profits) were substantially lower. Before 1948, the theater chains accounted for up to 90 percent of the major studios' assets and profits.

In 1946, Hollywood profits exceeded $1.5 billion. Americans, flush with postwar cash and facing a shortage of goods and services on which to spend their money, attended on average more than two movies per

OVERLEAF:

Hollywood's emergence in the mid-1910s coincided with Henry Ford's installation of the mass assembly line in his Detroit factories, a move that revolutionized American industry. By the 1940s, Hollywood sets, such as this one on the Paramount lot, had come to resemble what film critic Otis Ferguson called "fairyland on a production line."

The moguls used income from their theater chains to bankroll their early productions. Since 1932, of course, when this Eddie Cantor film premiered, Warner has itself become a subsidiary, first of Time and then of AOL.

week. Yet by early 1948, Hollywood stood at the brink of disaster. Foreign markets had long been an important source of profits to the industry, but England and France, critical markets for Hollywood now caught up in postwar balance-of-payments crises, had dramatically reduced the amount of currency Hollywood could export. Even worse, ticket sales

This photograph was taken on October 21, 1947, the second day of the House Un-American Activities Committee's film industry hearings. Chairman Parnell Thomas can be seen standing at right, his hand raised, with committee member Richard M. Nixon of California seated to his left. The first witnesses called were generally friendly. They included Eric Johnston, president of the Motion Picture Association of America, who testified that Hollywood's ability to advertise the "American way of life" was "propaganda for capitalism" and as important to the struggle against Communism as it had been to the war against fascism. Four years later, HUAC began a second, more extensive round of hearings, after which it gave Hollywood a clean bill of health.

at home were starting to fall as the marketing of television sets, postponed by the war, picked up speed. In 1947, American bought fourteen thousand televisions; in 1949, they purchased one million. During the next ten years, television penetrated nearly 90 percent of American households—still the fastest conquest of the domestic market by any medium, including the Internet. By 1960, the audience for movies would be cut in half.

Politically, too, the picture had darkened dramatically. The Soviet Union was no longer an ally, and the House Un-American Activities Committee (HUAC) was determined—in the words of its chairman, J. Parnell Thomas—"to expose the New Deal as a Communist project and New Dealers as subversive per se." Given Hollywood's close collaboration with the Roosevelt administration, the film industry was an obvious target. The committee opened formal hearings on October 20, 1947. One HUAC member, the openly anti-Semitic John Rankin of Mississippi, called the film colony "the greatest hotbed of subversive activities in the U.S."

Over the years, various Hollywood representatives seeking to win First Amendment protection for films had argued that movies were not "merely" entertainment but vehicles of ideas and information, just as theatrical productions and newspaper articles were. Now HUAC turned these arguments against Hollywood with a vengeance. By its own account, wartime Hollywood had worked with the OWI to create films of ideas that carried an avowedly pro-American message. What was to stop the studios, Thomas asked pointedly, from producing movies full of "flagrant Communist propaganda"?

THINGS DIDN'T LOOK PROMISING for the film industry on May 3, 1948, the day that the *Paramount* decision was handed down. The ruling was historic, constituting even today the only successful antitrust action ever brought against a branch of the entertainment industry. It specifically dismantled the studio's distribution system, barring such practices as tiered runs and block booking and making it possible for unaffiliated theater owners to rent films one at a time, screen by screen. Faced with the forced sale of its theater assets, under investigation by HUAC, and worried about the loss of its market share to television, the film industry entered a period of turmoil. Movies survived, of course, but the studio system in its old form did not. What finally emerged twenty years later was a Hollywood financially and artistically transformed.

The political threat, serious as it was, proved to be the most transitory. During the October 1947 HUAC hearings, Rankin pointedly identified several prominent liberal-left stars as Jews, including Danny Kaye (né David Daniel Kaminsky) and Edward G. Robinson (né Emmanuel Goldenberg); several former and present Communist party members were exposed. But HUAC's primary victims, a group of largely Jewish left-wing screenwriters, ridiculed the notion that they could have subverted movies tightly controlled by their supremely capitalist bosses. After all, Louis B. Mayer had refused to let the word *community* be uttered in *Song of Russia* because it sounded to him suspiciously like *Communist*.

Nonetheless, Congress eventually censured the Hollywood Ten, as the group of witnesses who refused to cooperate with the committee came to be known, and the studios abandoned them. The studio heads, hopelessly out of their depth, were certain that the long-feared WASP reprisal was finally upon them, but they were also not entirely averse to purging their industry of the troublemakers who had unionized Hollywood's creative personnel during the 1930s. The informal blacklist that they instituted took hundreds of jobs before it came to an end in the early 1960s.

HUAC chairman Parnell Thomas (right) *examines film prints as part of his investigation into Communist infiltration of the motion-picture industry. "Jesus," Jack Warner complained after his HUAC testimony, "I couldn't even get a laugh out of them."*

Seven members of the Hollywood Ten walk up the steps of a federal courthouse in Washington, D.C., to face contempt-of-Congress charges relating to their defiance of HUAC.

T ELEVISION'S RISE STRUCK at the very foundations of the movie business. A half century earlier, movies had displaced vaudeville as America's primary source of entertainment because movies came, as vaudeville could not, to people in their own neighborhoods and to many neighborhoods simultaneously. Sweeping economies of scale also permitted movies a drop in ticket prices that theatrical producers couldn't match. Television simply took this process one giant step farther. Now millions of Americans could watch the same show at the same time without leaving their living rooms or paying a cent.

Hollywood's profits did not recover until the late 1960s, and the industry has never regained the audience share it enjoyed before television's arrival. Yet Hollywood soon learned that it didn't have to compete with television: Cooperation proved a much more successful strategy. In the mid-1950s, the studios began renting their old films to television and producing new shows for the networks. The business grew rapidly. By 1960, Hollywood accounted for 80 percent of all television production. Rental income also took off: In 1966, ABC paid Columbia Pictures two million dollars to air *The Bridge on the River Kwai*; in 1978, viewing rights to *Gone with the Wind* cost CBS thirty-five million. Hollywood studios became irresistible takeover targets in the late 1960s, in large part because of their film libraries. Studio income from global television rights reached seven billion dollars in 1998, and analysts expect it to realize eleven billion dollars by 2002.

In addition, as media historian Christopher Anderson has pointed out, TV gave Hollywood access to the suburban home, the new ideological and cultural center of American consumption and leisure, while at the same time putting the studios' large lots and expensive equipment, underutilized with the downturn of the industry's fortunes, back in full gear. Thanks to reruns on television, old Hollywood films came to be seen as a national archive. For the first time, movies could be revisited and reappraised as art, shedding their status as ephemeral entertainment even as their long-term rental value soared. The pattern Hollywood established with television—resistance followed by cooperation, even co-optation—held in the reception the movie industry gave to later technological rivals: Hollywood has benefited from VCRs and

VIDEO

The pattern that Hollywood established with television (resistance followed by cooperation) held in the reception that the movie industry later gave videocassette technology. Hollywood battled alleged VCR copyright infringement right up to the Supreme Court (where it lost in 1984). Afterward, it relented, and videos today bring Hollywood as much revenue as the box office. Moreover, the market penetration of videos has allowed Hollywood to resurrect its old price-tiered system of runs. The venues are different, but the distribution dynamic is the same: Movies go first to the theaters, then to pay-per-view, video stores, and television, with progressively more modest fees for the viewers.

television—as, in the long run, it probably will from the Internet. Each new medium has increased the pie from which it takes a slice.

The *Paramount* decision, along with the advent of television, as the film historian Janet Staiger has demonstrated, accelerated trends toward diversification of market, product, and talent that were already present in the later stages of the studio system. By the late 1940s, Warner Brothers had 108 subsidiaries, including holdings in every field of the entertainment business from music publishing and recording to radio and television, as well as several real estate companies. Even Harry Cohn's much smaller and poorer Columbia Pictures boasted 28 subsidiaries—one of which, Screen Gems, became an early leader in television production.

Between the 1940s and the 1970s, Hollywood unbundled its large centralized production units into smaller, more highly individuated and fluid ones. No longer acting as auteurs associated with particular star-genre combinations, the studios released their personnel from the long-term contracts that were the studio system norm and instead worked closely with independent producers, providing facilities and financial backing for single- or multipicture deals. Harry Cohn had pioneered such arrangements during the late 1930s with his Outside Productions division, but the pace of change picked up significantly after the *Paramount* decision: There were 40 independent producers in 1945 and 165 by 1956. Big stars, including Burt Lancaster and Jimmy Stewart, teamed up with agents (who took over the producer's role) to form some of the most successful new independent companies—a pairing that, with modifications, still dominates moviemaking today. Following this strategy, by the early 1970s, as in the 1930s, the major studios accounted for 90 percent of domestic movie profits and the lion's share of the global market.

M EANWHILE, FROM THE 1950s ON, Hollywood movies emphasized what they could do that television could not. Frequently they were filmed on location—often faraway, glamorous locations. The studios also stressed popular genres that didn't adapt well to television, epics and musicals in particular. And new wide-screen processes—Cinerama in 1952, CinemaScope in 1953—further promoted Hollywood's visual superiority to "the Box."

In more subtle ways, too, Hollywood pressed its advantage. Because Hollywood was no longer the dominant medium of family entertainment, censorship's custodians made television the focus of their activities.

RUNAWAY PRODUCTIONS

Another factor promoting the 1950s trend toward location shooting was the problem Hollywood had exporting currency from Europe. Hollywood was making a great deal of money overseas, but postwar restrictions on currency flow kept the funds on the Continent. Needing to make some use of those profits, the U.S. film industry began producing movies in the countries where its money was trapped. The 1957 Burt Lancaster vehicle Trapeze, *for instance, made use of circus acts from fifteen different nations. Exemplifying Hollywood's new Global Look, the film (one of whose many European sets is pictured above) was actually eligible for European film subsidies covering up to 80 percent of its production cost.*

> **"I NEVER GO OUTSIDE UNLESS I LOOK LIKE JOAN CRAWFORD THE MOVIE STAR. IF YOU WANT TO SEE THE GIRL NEXT DOOR, GO NEXT DOOR."**
>
> —*Joan Crawford*—

Filmmakers and actors had learned decades earlier how to get around the Production Code—"They can't censor the gleam in my eye," Charles Laughton, playing an incest-minded father in *The Barretts of Wimpole Street* (1934), assured his MGM producer, Irving Thalberg—and they cannily exploited the latitude interpretation allowed. Film noir, the last major genre of the studio system, in which the lawless glitter while the law-abiding are often ignored, peaked between 1946 and the early 1950s. Then, in 1952, the Supreme Court finally extended to movies the same First Amendment protection enjoyed by other media. (It would be years before television received such protection.) The Production Code wasn't scrapped right away, but from the early 1950s onward, amid its blockbusters, Hollywood also produced smaller films dealing more or less openly with such controversial social problems as racism (1950's *No Way Out*) and juvenile delinquency (1955's *Blackboard Jungle*).

Hollywood's relationship with its stars also changed dramatically with the dismantling of the studio system. Bound by morals clauses in their contracts not to disgrace themselves and consciously, sometimes proudly personifying their corporate employers, the studio-system stars had a magnificence, a glamour, not seen in their descendants. When Joan Crawford, a megastar first at MGM and then at Warner, left a nightspot during the 1930s, the first thing she did upon entering her chauffeured limousine was turn on the passenger light so that her fans could see her. Touring in 1964 to promote one of her last movies, *Strait Jacket,* Crawford sent ahead to her destinations a booklet of detailed instructions for her reception—stipulating, among other things, how her fifteen pieces of luggage should be handled and that her chauffeurs not smoke (though the brand and quantity of cigarettes she required were carefully spelled out). Above all, no one was ever to forget that "Miss Crawford is a star in every sense of the word; and everyone knows that she is a star."

By the 1960s, *because of Hollywood's modernization, old-style female stardom, such as that enjoyed by Joan Crawford (above), became strictly camp.*

The guard changed in September 1949, when Marlon Brando arrived in Hollywood—outfitted, as legend has it, in jeans and a soiled sweatshirt, intent on keeping his private life private and representing no one but himself. Eager not to be typecast, during the first five years of his movie career Brando played a paraplegic veteran, the conflicted leader of a motorcycle gang, a failed boxer, Shakespeare's Brutus, a Damon Runyon song-and-dance man, and a Japanese prankster-philosopher. In each of these incarnations, he remained as stubbornly Marlon Brando as Cary Grant stayed suave, impeccable Cary Grant, whether starring in a George Cukor comedy or an Alfred Hitchcock thriller. Yet Brando's ideas of stardom and acting were a world apart from Grant's, not to speak of Crawford's. On the screen, Brando didn't seem to be playing a part but living the moment, a moment actually happening, right here and now to real bodies in real space.

A LTHOUGH THE STUDIO SYSTEM existed in fully realized form for only two decades of the movies' century-long span, its greatest contribution, the star-genre combination, has proved extraordinarily tenacious. Megastars like Tom Cruise and Julia Roberts still constitute franchises, and not one of Hollywood's staple genres, from horror to the epic, has disappeared. Today, Hollywood has fulfilled its founders' most imperial ambitions, claiming more than 75 percent of the world's film market, while non-English-language films reach less than 1 percent of the U.S. market. America is the only nation to exercise the dubious privilege of never seeing the world, or itself, through anyone's eyes but its own.

The story with which Hollywood has conquered the world is a narrative bred on the adrenaline of the first moguls' rise. Even severe critics of Hollywood's transparent imperialism acknowledge that foreign audiences turn out for American movies not only because it's exciting to be in on a superpower's chosen mode of self-congratulation but also because they find something in American films that they need: a charismatic optimism, sustained by hope as well as by lies. During the next few decades, as instantaneous digital transmission replaces time-bound analog delivery and movies move to screens still smaller than TV's, we will learn whether, and in what form, Hollywood's core story will survive. But no one who has known them in their glory is likely to stop watching Hollywood's classic movies—the chance to multiply the imagination's life and be alone, as the critic David Thomson puts it, in the dark with the light.

The star on the set of one of Warner Brothers' signature James Cagney gangster pictures. With the demise of the studio system, Hollywood, once a prototypically Fordist industry, remade itself into a more flexible, specialized post-Fordist one.

FURTHER READING

★ Ann Douglas, *Entertaining the Universe: Hollywood* (2002)

★ Robert Sklar, *Movie-Made America: A Social History of American Movies* (1994)

★ ★ ★

JANUARY 17, 1961

A FAREWELL TO ARMS

BY DOUGLAS BRINKLEY

O N THE NIGHT OF January 17, 1961, three days before John F. Kennedy would declare in his inaugural address that "the torch has been passed to a new generation of Americans," tens of millions of those Americans gathered around their still-newfangled television sets to watch Dwight D. Eisenhower, the outgoing president, deliver a few parting words to the nation. Ike's speech began at 8:30 P.M., broadcast from the Oval Office, but it wasn't the set of "farewell pleasantries" that, according to his memoirs, most people expected him to deliver. Rather, the talk the president gave turned out to be the most memorable farewell by a chief executive since another old soldier, George Washington, published his own famous good-bye in 1796.

Eisenhower certainly had Washington's text in mind as he prepared his farewell address.

In the fall of 1958, White House speechwriter Malcolm C. Moos had given his boss a book of notable presidential declarations that included Washington's farewell address. Although Eisenhower's second term wouldn't end for another two years, the president's reading of Washington's message, according to Moos, set him to musing. "I hope you'll be thinking about this," Ike told his aide.

The speech that Moos and his White House colleague Ralph F. Williams eventually prepared sounded many of the first president's 1796 themes because, like Washington and virtually every other combat veteran, Eisenhower had concluded that making the soldier's profession obsolete should be the goal of humankind. "I hate war," the former Allied commander told John Gunther, author of Ike's 1952 campaign biography, "as only a soldier who has lived it can, as only one who has seen its brutality, its futility, its *stupidity*." But Eisenhower's farewell was much more than a simple appeal to humanity's better nature. It was a warning as well.

Lives mattered a great deal to Eisenhower. In fact, it was the unnecessary sacrifice of lives in the Korean War that had brought Dwight D. Eisenhower to the White House in the first place. "I will go to Korea," he had promised during the 1952 presidential campaign, and twenty-four days after his November 5 victory, he did just that. During his three-day visit, the president-elect worked to revive stalled peace talks; and on July 27, 1953, just six months into Ike's first term, United Nations and North Korean officials signed an armistice ending three years of fighting that had killed more than a million Chinese and Korean soldiers, along with fifty-four thousand Americans. Afterward, Eisenhower resolved that under his stewardship the United States would fight no more land wars (including the one the French were then losing in Vietnam).

President-elect Eisenhower *leaves the headquarters of the Fifth Field Artillery Group on December 4, 1952. During his three days in Korea, Ike spent most of his time visiting front-line units. His trip persuaded him that the war, begun in June 1950, had to be ended as soon as possible on the best terms he could get.*

The president further believed that the cost of being prepared to intervene militarily anywhere in the world at any time was more than Americans should have to bear. "There must be a balance between minimum requirements in the costly implements of war and the health of our economy," he wrote to a friend shortly after the signing of the Korean armistice, echoing a sentiment he had expressed in an April 1953 address to the American Society of Newspaper Editors—dubbed the "Chance for Peace" speech. In that speech, Eisenhower had explained, "Every gun that is made, every warship launched, every rocket fired signifies, in the final sense, a theft from those who are not fed, those who are cold and not clothed." Proving that his words weren't just hollow rhetoric, the commander in chief soon unveiled a new defense strategy that, among other things, included a ban on new military procurement programs for 1954.

The New Look, as Pentagon public relations personnel called the administration's policy (after Christian Dior's acclaimed 1947 fashion style), committed the United States to nuclear weapons as the centerpiece of its defense strategy. With atomic bombs as a deterrent, the president was able to reduce substantially the nation's conventional forces and cut the federal budget during each of his first three years in office while still funding fully many nonmilitary programs. By nature a fiscal conservative, Ike had no patience for the self-interested claims of corporate contractors who wanted him to believe that the United States needed more and newer weapons systems. As a career soldier who understood how the Pentagon worked, Eisenhower knew better.

CHARLES E. WILSON, WHO LEFT the presidency of General Motors to become Eisenhower's first defense secretary, should have known better as well. Yet he infuriated Ike when he suggested during his confirmation hearings that he would be a shill for the arms industry. "For years I thought what was good for our country was good for General Motors and vice versa," Wilson told the Senate Armed Service Committee on January 15, 1953. Once in office, the defense secretary further irritated the president by submitting huge Pentagon budget requests. It was with some relief, then, that Ike accepted Wilson's resignation in 1956.

In the meantime, the Eisenhower administration was beset by charges that the New Look wasn't stopping the Soviet Union from taking a substantial lead in high-tech weaponry. The critical drumbeat began in August 1953, after the Soviets detonated their first hydrogen bomb, and it reached a fever pitch in October 1957, when Sputnik became the world's first artificial satellite. In the aftermath of Sputnik, Eisenhower appointed a panel of military, scientific, and business leaders to review U.S. defense readiness. On November 7, the Gaither Committee—named for its chairman, H. Rowan Gaither Jr. of the Ford Foundation—issued a top-secret report, though much of it was soon leaked to the press. Among its alarmist recommendations were a whopping increase in military spending, especially for missile production, and the appropriation of thirty billion dollars for the construction of a nationwide network of fallout shelters. Even worse, the suggestion, implicit throughout the report, that the administration's defense-budget penny pinching had put America at grave risk made the president's position even more difficult, at least as far as his relations with the public and Congress were concerned.

Certain concessions would have to be made. "On the domestic front, the first signs of the 1958 economic recession were becoming obvious," Vice Pres. Richard M. Nixon noted in his 1962 book, *Six Crises.* "At the same time it

H. Rowan Gaither Jr. was a prominent San Francisco lawyer before becoming president and then chairman of the board of the Ford Foundation.

Newspapers around the world headlined the October 4, 1957, launch of Sputnik. These show the British press's reaction.

was equally apparent that we would have to find more money to bolster our missile program. We were having serious budget problems: The fiscal 1958 budget was $71.8 billion, the highest in peacetime history; the government had borrowed up to its legal debt limit; and we had to prepare the fiscal 1959 budget with still higher defense spending." Yet, by and large, Eisenhower stuck to his fiscal conservatism. He increased funding for ICBM production and enhanced some civil defense programs, but otherwise he ignored the Gaither Report's recommendations. This saved billions of dollars but gave the Democrats an opening.

I N AUGUST 1958, DEMOCRATIC SENATOR J. William Fulbright of Arkansas warned Americans of the country's "drift to disaster," claiming that U.S. defense funds had been "impounded, sunk, and hidden" by the Republican administration. Making matters worse, Eisenhower's second secretary of defense, Neil H. McElroy, had speculated openly that the Soviet Union *might* have as much as a three-to-one advantage in nuclear warheads. Congressional Democrats were quick to seize upon this supposed "missile gap" as a partisan issue, with Missouri senator Stuart Symington leading the charge. As chairman of an armed forces subcommittee, Symington issued a report in which he pronounced, "It is now clear that the U.S....may have lost control of the air" because of Eisenhower's insistence on placing fiscal concerns above the nation's security. The Eisenhower administration, Symington's report continued, had a worrisome "tendency to either ignore or underestimate Soviet military progress." Publicly and loudly, Symington insisted that only a massive increase in U.S. defense spending, leading to the creation of a much larger air force with nuclear capabilities, could return America to military parity with the Soviets.

It rankled the president how willing the former air force secretary was to inflame Cold War hysteria over a trumped-up "bomber gap" simply to further his own presidential hopes and push the interests of the big defense contractors backing him. After all, Eisenhower had himself initiated funding for the three main weapons systems that together formed the basis of America's Cold War defenses: the Minuteman

> "THE TRUE SECURITY PROBLEM IS NOT MERELY MAN AGAINST MAN OR NATION AGAINST NATION. IT IS MAN AGAINST WAR."
>
> — *Dwight D. Eisenhower, letter, 1956*

STUART SYMINGTON

1901 – 1988

A World War I veteran, Stuart Symington attended Yale (1919–1923) and then went to work for his uncle at an iron works in Rochester, New York. Several jobs and fifteen years later, he became president of Emerson Electric Manufacturing, based in St. Louis. During World War II, under Symington's direction, Emerson built the world's largest aircraft armaments plant, producing gun turrets for U.S. bombers. Symington became the first air force secretary in 1947 (when the National Security Act reorganized the armed forces) and won election to the Senate from Missouri in 1952. He was later a vocal critic of the U.S. presence in Vietnam, which he considered irrelevant to national security.

intercontinental nuclear missile, the Polaris nuclear-missile-firing submarine, and the nuclear-bomb-carrying B-52 bomber. What's more, to ensure future technological advancement, Eisenhower had even approved creation of the National Aeronautics and Space Administration in October 1958.

That same year, though, when Congress tried to appropriate $137 million for production of the dubious Nike Zeus anti-missile missile, Eisenhower blocked the funds, insisting that production be delayed "until development tests are satisfactorily completed." Fighting back, lead contractor Western Electric (along with eight of its subcontractors) immediately launched an expensive public relations campaign to promote the Nike Zeus, taking out full-page ads in newspapers around the country to show where the $137 million would be spent. Congressmen whose districts stood to benefit took the hint and began warning the public about Soviet military superiority. House majority leader John McCormack, a Massachusetts Democrat, pleaded for the United States to "close the gap in our missile posture, muzzle the mad-dog missile threat of the Soviet Union, and loose the Zeus through America's magnificent production line." Still, the president refused to buckle, and he scoffed at the preference of the "loose the Zeus" crowd for pork-barrel spending above the nation's economic and security interests.

The Nike Ajax was the first operational guided surface-to-air missile. It was deployed in large numbers across the United States to counter what was then believed (incorrectly) to be the threat posed by Soviet strategic bombers. The Nike Zeus (shown here at a California test range) was later developed in response to another illusory threat— that posed by Soviet ICBMs—but the Zeus was never deployed.

IT'S DIFFICULT TO IMAGINE TODAY the genuine panic that swept over America in the wake of Sputnik and how lonely Eisenhower's voice of reason was. Yet Ike ignored the provocations directed at him by the supposed "wise men" of the eastern political establishment and continued to maintain that America's defenses were more than adequate. He knew, but couldn't say, that secret U-2 reconnaissance photographs, provided by the CIA, showed that the Soviet Union had built and deployed very few ICBMs. "Everyone knows," air force general Nathan Twining privately told the president, "[that] we already have a [nuclear] stockpile large enough to obliterate the Soviet Union."

On January 19, 1960, still beset by the "missile gap" issue and post-Sputnik fears of Soviet technological superiority, Eisenhower's third defense secretary, Thomas S. Gates Jr., presented to the House Defense

President Eisenhower *looks on in September 1958 as Malcolm Moos is sworn in as his new administrative assistant. Moos was a tall, demure political scientist on loan to the White House from Johns Hopkins.*

WASHINGTON'S FAREWELL

Unlike Eisenhower's, Washington's address was never actually spoken. Rather, it was written in the form of a letter to the American people. The text was released to the Daily American Advertiser *in Philadelphia (then the nation's capital) and published on September 17, 1796, six weeks before the presidential election and nearly six months before Washington left office. The president's parting words warned the public against foreign alliances, too much federal debt, a large standing army, and the influence of any "small, but artful and enterprising minority."*

Appropriations Committee revised intelligence estimates indicating that earlier estimates of Soviet military strength had been mistaken. According to Gates, the new information showed, in fact, "a clear balance in our favor." Democrats—including Massachusetts senator John F. Kennedy, another presidential hopeful—countered with accusations that the administration was unfairly manipulating the statistics. It was thus within a White House beleaguered by presidential politics and phony defense-gap allegations that Malcolm Moos and Ralph Williams set to brainstorming how best the current occupant of the Oval Office might respond to the military establishment, the defense contractors, and their patrons in Congress.

The speechwriters began by reviewing a disturbing congressional report stating that the nation's top one hundred defense contracts currently employed some 1,400 retired U.S. military officers above the rank of major, including 261 generals and admirals. After a long conversation about this with Moos, Williams offered in an October 31, 1961, memo what would become the foundation of Eisenhower's January 17, 1961, address. "For the first time in its history, the United States has a permanent war-based industry," Williams wrote about "the problem" of militarism. "Not only that, but flag and general officers retiring at an early age take positions in the war-based industrial complex, shaping its decisions and guiding the direction of its tremendous thrust. This creates a danger that what the Communists have always said about us may become true. We must be very careful to ensure that the 'merchants of death' do not come to dictate national policy."

EISENHOWER HIMSELF HADN'T GIVEN much thought to a farewell address since his musings on George Washington's effort two years earlier. But that changed after *Saturday Review* editor and arms control advocate Norman Cousins called the White House on December 14 and left this message (recorded by Eisenhower's secretary, Ann Whitman): "Norman Cousins called. His suggestion: that you give a 'farewell' address to the country…reviewing your Administration, telling of your hopes for the future. A great, sweeping document." Already so inclined, Eisenhower requested a draft, into which Moos incorporated the basic propositions of Williams's October 31 memo, especially the passage warning against the growth of a "war-based industrial complex."

Shortly before Christmas, Moos handed the finished draft to the president, who "liked the speech," Moos recalled. "He said, 'I think you have got something here, Malcolm. Let me sleep on it.'" Later, with the help of his brother Milton, then president of Johns Hopkins, Ike made a few changes, rewriting a couple of passages and excising some dozen lines. The only other significant change was made at the urging of James Killian, Eisenhower's science adviser, who persuaded the president to shorten Moos's original caution against a "military-industrial-scientific complex" to the now-famous phrase.

Eisenhower's bald pate and wire-rimmed glasses flickered on television screens across the nation as he prepared to deliver the speech. Sitting behind a pair of those old paper-clip-shaped radio microphones, he cleared his throat, shuffled his papers, and began with a few opening formalities, wishing the president-elect well and thanking Congress for having "cooperated" with the administration in serving "the national good."

Next, Eisenhower recounted the current state of the Cold War. In his forceful but flat Great Plains monotone, the president declared, "We face a hostile ideology, global in scope, atheistic in character, ruthless in purpose, and insidious in method. Unhappily the danger it poses promises to be of infinite duration. To meet it successfully, there is called for, not so much the emotional and transitory sacrifices of crises, but rather those which enable us to carry forward steadily, surely, and without complaint the burdens of a prolonged and complex struggle—with liberty at stake."

Ike visits the nuclear submarine Seawolf *in September 1957. Future president Jimmy Carter served briefly aboard the* Seawolf, *the navy's third nuclear-powered sub, as an engineering officer.*

Defense Secretary Thomas S. Gates *testifies in 1960 before the defense subcommittee of the Senate Committee on Appropriations. Seated next to him is Gen. Nathan Twining.*

THE MISSILE GAP

The alleged U.S.-Soviet "missile gap" sprang in part from the erroneous assumption that the Soviets had the greater capability to manufacture new missiles. In fact, the Soviet Union never undertook a substantial increase in missile production—and probably couldn't have for lack of resources. Spy satellites deployed during the Kennedy administration revealed that CIA estimates of Soviet strength had been much too high, as Eisenhower had always insisted. Studies completed in 1963 indicated that Soviet ICBM strength in 1961 had been only 3.5 percent of the official U.S. estimate.

The departing chief executive then went on to explain the great irony of the Cold War: that to maintain some freedoms, we had to sustain a megalithic military establishment threatening to others. "Until the latest of our world conflicts, the United States had no armaments industry. American makers of plowshares could, with time and as required, make swords as well. But now we can no longer risk emergency improvisation of national defense; we have been compelled to create a permanent armaments industry of vast proportions.

"This conjunction of an immense military establishment and a large arms industry is new in the American experience," Eisenhower continued. "The total influence—economic, political, even spiritual—is felt in every city, every statehouse, every office of the federal government." Then came the kicker: "In the councils of government, we must guard against the acquisition of unwarranted influence, whether sought or unsought, by the military-industrial complex. The potential for the disastrous rise of misplaced power exists and will persist."

LIKE ABRAHAM LINCOLN'S Gettysburg Address, which the *New York Times* initially called "dull and commonplace," Eisenhower's farewell sparked little public fire at the time of its delivery. A cursory survey of coverage in the next day's national newspapers—the *Washington Post, New York Times, Baltimore Sun,* and the like—shows that the "military-industrial complex" warning was downplayed, as was Eisenhower's concept of "disarmament with honor." Instead, the press generally treated the president's tocsin as just one more old-fashioned anti-Communist bromide.

Two months later, though, the message of Eisenhower's farewell address began to come into focus. On March 17, 1961, former presidential aide Bryce Harlow sent this note to his old boss:

There is an interesting development, Mr. President, involving your Farewell Address. At least two vigorous young Republicans in the House (Bob Michel of Illinois and Brad Morse of Massachusetts) have interested themselves in your warning to America against excessive power being accumulated by the military-industrial complex and are girding their loins to raise a rumpus through the Congressional investigation route. Nation *magazine, of all things, has suddenly interested itself in the same thing and has run a column on the subject written by Jerry Greene, one of the most conservative correspondents in Washington.* Congressional Quarterly,

The scene in Gettysburg, Pennsylvania, on November 19, 1863, just before President Lincoln delivered his brief address.

widely read, will run a whole spread on this in its next issue. The point is, this part of the Address turns out to be curiously yeasty, and one can expect some fall-out from it in the Congressional-political arena over the coming months. All of the interested parties (except Nation, of course!) have been in touch with me about this; I have quietly, without attribution, sought to add fuel to this still small flame.

A few years later, Ike's farewell would also be embraced by the anti–Vietnam War left, which interpreted the speech as a prophetic clarion call from a reformed old warhorse. Phrases such as "We must never let the weight of this combination endanger our liberties or democratic processes" appealed to those who most feared the power of "the Establishment," and left-leaning intellectuals—among them Noam Chomsky, Eugene McCarthy, and William Appleman Williams—wrote books and articles transforming Eisenhower's dire warning of an arms industry run amok into familiar liberal boilerplate. As journalist Murray Kempton put it in 1967, Eisenhower was "the great tortoise upon whose back the world sat for eight years. We laughed at him; we talked wistfully about moving; and all the while we never knew the cunning beneath the shell."

For their part, conservatives tended to dismiss this interpretation of the farewell address as unfair, suggesting that Eisenhower was being quoted out of context. For example, soon after his January 1969

Ike greets Vice Pres. Richard Nixon and his family in May 1958 on their return from a trip to South America. During the 1960 presidential campaign, Kennedy hit Nixon hard with charges that the Eisenhower administration had been "soft" on defense.

President Kennedy *watches a navy submarine test-launch a Polaris missile off the Florida coast on November 16, 1963.*

OPPOSITE:

Eisenhower waves to the crowd during a New York City parade in late 1945, shortly after his return home from Europe. As the Boston Globe *later noted, had any other political figure uttered the sentiments expressed in Ike's January 1961 farewell address, his words would surely have been dismissed as Leninist claptrap.*

FURTHER READING

★ Stephen E. Ambrose,
Eisenhower:
The President (1984)

★ Geoffrey Perret,
Eisenhower
(1999)

inauguration as the thirty-seventh president, Richard Nixon labeled the military-industrial complex a "straw man issue" in dismissing the charge that America's defense budget was bloated. If he were to err with regard to military spending, Nixon declared, it would be "on the side of too much, and not too little. If we do too much it will cost us our money. If we do too little, it may cost us our lives."

IN FACT, EISENHOWER HAD BELIEVED quite the opposite: that too much defense spending could cost lives. "Peace is what matters; peace is the end game," the retired president told Moos during a 1964 visit that the former speechwriter made to Eisenhower's dairy farm outside Gettysburg, Pennsylvania. "And the more bombs and bombers built, the more difficult it will be to disarm with honor, to negotiate away their demise." Eisenhower's insight was an extension of his plain old midwestern common sense, which made it seem obvious to him that, in a nuclear age, it was sufficiency and not superiority that mattered most. Had we heeded him more closely, perhaps the military escalations of the 1960s, particularly in Vietnam, could have been avoided.

As Stephen E. Ambrose has pointed out, Ike understood, as few other men on the planet could have, how much the nature of warfare had changed since D-Day. Back in June 1944, if General Eisenhower had sent a hundred planes to bomb Germany and ninety had come back, the mission would have been a failure, even if the target had been destroyed, because the Allies couldn't have afforded losses of even 10 percent. By 1961, however, if President Eisenhower had sent a hundred B-52s over Soviet territory and only one had gotten through, the mission would have been a triumph "so long as the one [had] dropped its bomb on Red Square," as Ambrose has written.

Eisenhower considered it his duty, as he "lay down the responsibilities of office," to warn his fellow citizens that they must scrutinize the motives of every politician and military leader who calls for another new, expensive weapons system. Honoring his frugal Main Street values, the retiring president simply wanted to remind his countrymen, gathered around their television sets and radios, that the nation's resources were limited: that a single fighter plane was paid for with a half-million bushels of wheat, that every new destroyer meant thousands of poor people would remain homeless. His farewell address, as Washington's had been, was fundamentally a call for prudence and compassion at the dawn of an epoch that put the fate of the world at the touch of a button on one man's phone. We fail to heed its message at our own peril.

★ ★ ★

THE STRUCTURE
OF SCIENTIFIC
REVOLUTIONS *by*
THOMAS S. KUHN

JUNE 21, 1961

THE DECISION TO PUBLISH KUHN

BY DAVID A. HOLLINGER

"ON WEDNESDAY THE 21ST of June the phone rang as I was leaving my home," historian-philosopher Thomas S. Kuhn recalled many years later. The call, which Kuhn described as "transforming," came from Carroll G. Bowen. Its purpose was to inform Kuhn that the University of Chicago Press had decided to publish *The Structure of Scientific Revolutions,* destined to become one of the most important American books of the second half of the twentieth century. Now translated into two dozen languages and cited in countless articles and books spanning virtually all social scientific and humanistic disciplines, Kuhn's book is today one of the few modern works that all college graduates are expected to recognize, if not to have read.

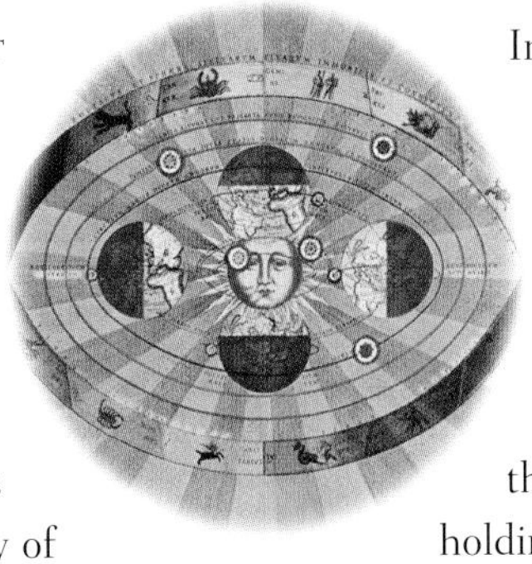

AT LEFT: *This is the copy of the first hardcover edition of* Structure *that Kuhn inscribed to his daughter Sarah.*

ABOVE: *In* The Copernican Revolution (1957), *Kuhn used Nicolaus Copernicus's model of the universe (shown here in a 1661 illustration) to explore ideas he worked out more fully in* Structure.

In later years, Kuhn often used melodramatic language to describe the circumstances under which *Structure* came to be published. He had been anxious about his manuscript that June, and with good reason. He often liked to tell the story of "crossing my fingers and holding my breath" as the package containing his submission "slid down the mail slot" of the box at the corner of Webster Street and College Avenue in the bucolic Elmwood section of Berkeley, California, where he lived.

Why had Thomas Kuhn been so nervous? In what context did Bowen, the press's associate director, make the decision to publish *The Structure of Scientific Revolutions*? What did Kuhn's book say, and why is it now regarded as having such historical significance? Why, in other words, is June 21, 1961, a day of destiny in intellectual history?

KUHN WAS ANXIOUS for a number of reasons. His manuscript was several times the prescribed length of the monograph he had been commissioned to write

This is the original correspondence between *Kuhn and Bowen. The letter (top) that Kuhn sent on June 18, 1961, begins, "You undoubtedly know, though you may have properly suppressed, my name as the author of one of the two still outstanding monographs in the* Encyclopedia of Unified Science. *Since the manuscript which accompanies this letter will indicate that I have not been totally unconscious of the obligation, I shall not bother you with explanations of my prolonged delinquency." Bowen's reply (bottom) is tinted blue because it's the carbon copy that he kept for his files.*

for an ongoing multivolume series being published by Chicago. Worse, he was late by more than a dozen years, and what he had prepared was radically out of step, in both style and theoretical outlook, with the rest of *The International Encyclopedia of Unified Science.* Publishers must reserve "a special circle of Hell" for authors such as himself, Kuhn wrote in his submission letter to the press, expecting the worst from Bowen, whom he had never met and about whose tolerance for authorial idiosyncrasy he had no clue.

KUHN HAD ALL THE MORE REASON to worry because his submission came in the wake of a disquieting and altogether unexpected rebuke that he had suffered only a few weeks earlier. His philosopher colleagues at the Berkeley campus of the University of California, after reading the bulk of his manuscript, had decided to throw him out of the philosophy department. Concluding that Kuhn did not amount to much as a philosopher, the senior members of the department had asked the dean to move him entirely into the department of history. (Kuhn's appointment as an associate professor with tenure had been divided equally between the two departments since his hiring in 1956.) During a routine review of Kuhn's qualifications for promotion to the rank of professor, the philosophers had balked; and instead of joining their history colleagues in recommending Kuhn's promotion, they requested his transfer, explicitly asking that he be prevented from ever again taking part in the deliberations of the philosophy department. So contemptuous were Berkeley's senior philosophers that they never even discussed with Kuhn a possible transfer to history, nor did they inform him of their decision to be rid of him. Kuhn got the word instead from the campus administration in May, six months after the department meeting at which the decision was made.

Kuhn was crushed. Appreciative as he was for the enthusiasm with which Berkeley's historians then welcomed him, he had a strong sense of identity as a philosopher, even though his Ph.D. was neither in philosophy nor in history but in physics. His uncertainty about his professional location was also part of a larger uncertainty in academia as a whole about the history of science and its status as a discipline. Did this field belong in science departments or in history departments, or should it properly be considered auxiliary to the philosophy of science and thus taught in philosophy departments?

Kuhn had developed his interest in the field while assisting Harvard president James B. Conant in the development of a course on the history of science. Conant's goal was to familiarize undergraduates with what he considered the foundation for modern civilization; and the essence of science, Conant believed, could be more effectively conveyed by historical episode than by lab work or philosophical analysis of the scientific method. Thus the physicist Kuhn got into philosophy and history through a back door, and never was he altogether comfortable in either field, because he worked on the basis of a belief that most philosophers and even most historians found implausible: that the study of the history of science had serious implications for the philosophical analysis of science.

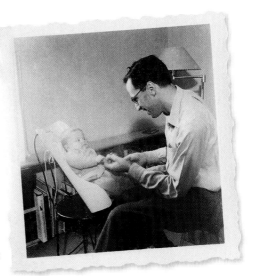

Kuhn plays with his three-month-old daughter Sarah in the family's Cambridge, Massachusetts, apartment during the fall of 1952. The son of an industrial engineer, Kuhn was graduated summa cum laude from Harvard in 1943 and worked as a civilian employee of the federal government's Office of Scientific Research and Development before returning to Harvard at the end of World War II.

THE DAY THAT HE LEARNED he had been "evicted" from philosophy, as the action was later described in a private memorandum written by Berkeley chancellor Edward Strong, was dreadful for Kuhn. Thirty years later, he confessed to a friend that it was "the worst day of my life." It should not be surprising, then, that a few weeks later, as he sent off his manuscript and contemplated its reception by the University of Chicago Press, Kuhn's mood was somber, chastened, and uncertain. He believed that his manuscript had important things to say, yet he suffered from more than the standard authorial nervousness. He knew that it might be some time before Chicago got back to him, but only three days passed before the phone rang. It was Bowen, calling to say he had read the manuscript straight though at one sitting and loved it.

Bowen was not alone in his embrace of *Structure*. Many readers during the 1960s and thereafter have found Kuhn's book downright exciting. What most caught the attention of readers in 1962 was the idea that scientific knowledge, rather than being objective (as was commonly believed), was in fact highly dependent on assumptions about the world brought to scientific study by human beings. Scientific truth, Kuhn argued, was *not* absolute and immutable; and in saying so, he spoke not only to a

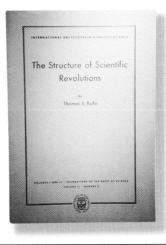

This is the edition of Structure *that was* published as part of The International Encyclopedia of Unified Science.

THOMAS S. KUHN

1922 – 1996

Thomas Kuhn once traced the origin of his inspiration for Structure *to a moment in 1947 when he was working toward his doctorate in physics at Harvard. It was just after James Conant had asked him to teach a class on the history of science for undergraduates majoring in the humanities. Until then, Kuhn said later, "I'd never read an old document in science." But looking through Aristotle's* Physics, *he realized that Aristotle wasn't "bad Newton" but simply "different." After the publication of* Structure, *Kuhn moved his academic home twice, shifting first in 1964 to Princeton, where he was welcomed by both philosophers and historians, and then in 1979 to the Massachusetts Institute of Technology, where he taught until his retirement in 1992.*

relatively unsophisticated public who needed this correction but also to scholars who understood that science was indeed more complicated.

Before Kuhn, even most scholars understood the progress of science in terms of a series of heroic individual discoveries. These contributed, in turn, to an accumulating body of knowledge warranted, ultimately, by nature itself. In 1960, while Kuhn was writing his book, Charles Gillispie enunciated this traditional view with great force in *The Edge of Objectivity,* one of the most accessible and elegant histories of science ever written. Kuhn countered that tightly organized communities of specialists, not individual minds, were the central actors in scientific development. Figures such as Isaac Newton and Charles Darwin were, of course, important; but the significance of these giants—true scientific revolutionaries—depended on the communities with which they interacted.

THESE COMMUNITIES made progress in two distinctive modes: In "normal science," researchers did narrow, technical work guided by a "paradigm," a picture of the field that functioned as a set of predictions for what the investigators would find. When these researchers observed, instead, phenomena that did not match their expectations, the community of which they were a part entered a period of "revolutionary science." In this mode, the community debated the utility of various alternative paradigms and eventually selected one that explained a greater range of relevant phenomena, making it more suitable to guide the next phase of normal science. The transition from one paradigm to another was, Kuhn wrote, a "scientific revolution."

For example, as long as astronomers continued to believe, with Aristotle and the ancients, that the sun revolved around the earth, they found many movements of the planets and the stars confusing. When Nicolaus Copernicus proposed a heliocentric model of the universe, however, these observations suddenly made sense. Indeed, it was while studying the process by which scientists became persuaded of the soundness of the Copernican view that Kuhn himself developed his basic ideas about scientific change. His 1957 book, *The Copernican Revolution,* explored some of the territory he later mapped more extensively in *The Structure of Scientific Revolutions.*

In his overall view of the process by which scientific truth is warranted, Kuhn diminished the role of nature and emphasized the role played by communities of specific human beings. He suggested that scientific development is best seen not as movement toward a fixed goal set by nature but as progress from existing knowledge toward more fully confirmed answers to questions put to nature by scientific communities. And because the questions themselves sometimes change, the progress of science is sometimes discontinuous.

Kuhn compared the growth of knowledge to the evolution of living things as conceptualized by Darwin— who, according to Kuhn, "recognized no goal set either by God or nature." Kuhn wrote that just as natural selection "was responsible for the gradual but steady emergence of more elaborate, further articulated, and vastly more specialized organisms," so, too, did "selection by conflict within the scientific community" determine the "fittest way to practice future science." Both kinds of selection had no pre-established goal but, rather, responded as best they could to opportunities and obstacles in their respective environments.

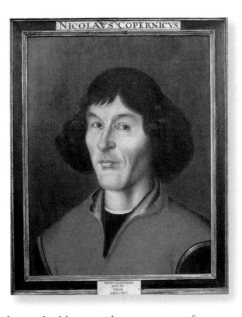

Nicolaus Copernicus *began observing the orbits of the heavenly bodies in 1497. Gradually, he abandoned accepted Ptolemaic astronomy, according to which the sun and the planets revolved around the earth, and instead developed the modern heliocentric system. Fearing reprisals, he kept his theories largely to himself until 1543, the year of his death, when he finally published* De revolutionibus orbium coelestium *at the urging of a student.*

K UHN WAS QUICK TO INSIST that he did not mean the world had no shape. He never denied that phenomena present patterns of resistance when scientists test their hypotheses experimentally. Science would not work as well as it did if the world that scientists studied did not possess what Kuhn described (albeit vaguely) as "quite special characteristics." As to what those characteristics were, he was firmly agnostic. He refused to say, for example, that science works because nature fits our hypotheses. Instead, he transferred the chief responsibility for warranting scientific truth from the natural order—whose character, Kuhn was at pains to emphasize, could be discerned only through the testimony of fallible human witnesses—to the communities of human beings who studied that natural order.

What most distinguished science from other human activities, according to this view, was not the character of the objects being studied but the

With a paradigm shift, *Kuhn wrote, "one conceptual world view is replaced by another." Thus, Einsteinian relativity swept away Newton's concept of physics, and the theory of natural selection put forth by Darwin (shown here about 1855) overthrew earlier visions of a world governed by design.*

According to Kuhn, there is, of course, something "out there" that scientists uncover. (These particular scientists are shown at work in the George Washington University School of Medicine histology lab in October 1963.) What they uncover, though, is not as "true" as it may sometimes seem.

KUHN'S LIFE AFTER 1962

Was Thomas Kuhn himself a Kuhnian? This question dogged him from the earliest controversies over Structure. *What made the issue so persistent was his habit of quarreling with readers, notably the influential philosopher Richard Rorty, who carried his basic insight about the social construction of scientific knowledge to what Kuhn considered an untenable extreme. (Kuhn often said that he liked many of his critics better than his fans.) Like many protean thinkers, Kuhn began a conversation that developed beyond his control, during which he sometimes found himself soberly instructed on the meaning of his own work.*

extent to which scientific communities agreed on what they were doing (as a community) and retained for themselves control over what would count as truth within their specialized areas of inquiry. The fact that sociologists and political scientists were less able to do this than were chemists and physicists no doubt had something to do with those "quite special characteristics" of the phenomena studied by chemists and physicists; yet, despite this vagueness, Kuhn can still be credited with resisting the easy conclusion that social scientists only *interpreted* the character of their objects of study, while natural scientists *discovered* the character of theirs.

This tilt from the "objective" to the "subjective" was even more pronounced in Kuhn's account of the social psychology of scientists, in which he emphasized the power of preconceived ideas to control the observations of researchers. Kuhn insisted that without the focusing effect of paradigms, investigators would not even *see* the contradictory phenomena whose explanation was essential to the creation of new knowledge. Scientists were traditionally understood to be open minded, but Kuhn argued that a fully "open" mind could not focus on the relevant particulars. If scientists didn't wear blinders, that is, they'd lose sight of the track.

Using language calculated to challenge traditional ideologies of science, Kuhn wrote that the everyday practice of science in a particular field required the unquestioning acceptance of the "dogmas" of that field. Normal scientists confirmed and extended inherited doctrines; yet in doing so, they also generated findings that did not fit their theoretical models—"anomalies," Kuhn called them. In this way, normal scientists amassed the inventory of genuinely new things indispensable to revolutionary science and the creation of new paradigms. Hence, for Kuhn, the wearing of blinders served the much larger, genuinely critical process by which scientists devised more comprehensive theories.

ALL OF THIS WAS RECEIVED within a number of different, sometimes overlapping contexts following the book's publication on October 2, 1962. Science, five years after Sputnik, had become a more prodigious presence in American life than ever before, and the market for interpretations of this vast, apparently mysterious field was unprecedented. Programs in the history, philosophy, and sociology of science were launched on campus after campus, and popular books on the relationship between science and society proliferated. Kuhn's own contribution was at once austere and accessible. The book had strong scholarly bona fides but at the same time could be engaged by readers with no more science than high school physics and chemistry and no more philosophy than an introductory college course.

Within academia, *The Structure of Scientific Revolutions* became the central item in a science studies renaissance that flowered throughout the Anglophone world. This remarkable mid-1960s moment saw the critical discussion of works by Warren Hagestrom, Norwood Russell Hansen, Fritz Machlup, Robert K. Merton, Michael Polanyi, Karl Popper, Don K. Price, and Stephen Toulmin, among others. Some of Kuhn's emphases were not unique to him. The philosophers Hansen and Toulmin, for example, had vividly demonstrated the role of preconceived ideas in the psychology of science; and a long tradition of pragmatist philosophy, from Charles Peirce in the 1870s to W. V. O. Quine in the 1950s, had prepared many American readers to appreciate Kuhn's point about the power of an intellectual tradition. Yet no one had put together in a single package all of the ideas that constituted *The Structure of Scientific Revolutions*, and Kuhn's book caught people's imagination because it was uniquely suited to answer questions then surfacing about science within and across many academic disciplines. It was also uniquely suited to serve as a grindstone for several axes then waiting to be sharpened. In fact, to understand more fully the role played by *Structure* in our intellectual history, we must first attend to the ax grinding that Kuhn facilitated.

FURTHER READING

★ Thomas S. Kuhn, James Conant (ed.), and John Haugeland (ed.), *The Road Since Structure: Philosophical Essays, 1970–1993* (2000)

★ Alexander Bird, *Thomas Kuhn* (2001)

Kuhn is shown here *conversing in 1983 with Lorenz Krüger (left) at Krüger's home in Bielefeld, Germany. In 1977, Krüger had edited a collection of Kuhn's papers entitled* Die Entstehung des Neuen [The Creation of the New].

ONE AX PROMPTLY THRUST UP against Kuhn's book was carried by social scientists who resented the tendency of both natural scientists and the public to doubt that the social sciences were sciences at all. Nearly three hundred years had passed since Newton had organized the field of physics into a coherent whole; but the social sciences, skeptics were quick to point out, remained so badly divided that only the arbitrary exclusion of certain points of view allowed practitioners to claim the kind of consensus and intellectual autonomy that Kuhn saw in the more developed sciences. With the publication of *Structure*, though, Kuhn brought the practice of science down to behavioral earth and made it possible for people to see many "nonscientific" activities as similar to science, and vice versa. Seizing this opportunity to refute their critics, social scientists swung their Kuhn-sharpened ax early and often, giving rapid and widespread visibility to Kuhn's work.

Kuhn chats in 1986 with philosophers Paul Hoyningen-Huene, who authored Reconstructing Scientific Revolutions: Thomas S. Kuhn's Philosophy of Science *(1993), and Paul Feyerabend, Kuhn's colleague at Berkeley from 1958 until Kuhn left in 1964. "I gave [Feyerabend] this draft manuscript that I'd sent out to Chicago," Kuhn recalled. "I think he liked it in one sense, but he was terribly upset by this whole business of dogma, rigidity, which of course is exactly counter to what he believed himself."*

A second ax was brought to the grindstone by those resentful of science's standing in the culture. In Kuhn's apparent fuzzing of the line between science and nonscience, this faction saw confirmation that science's standing was illegitimate—that scientific ideas were no more objective than any others and just as relative to time and place. They asked: How are physics and chemistry all that different from the arts and the humanities? Kuhn himself was certainly no muckraker—he wrote with a rather complacent confidence in the value and stability of the scientific enterprise as practiced in his own time—yet he soon found his work taken up with enthusiasm by critics of science, including some who spoke on behalf of religious perspectives on the world.

Defenders of the natural sciences responded that neither ax cut too deeply because, even in Kuhn's account, their disciplines delivered goods that other fields did not. Still, the swinging of this antiscience ax did spread the word that Kuhn's demystification of the scientific enterprise had opened up some deep and portentous questions.

EVEN PEOPLE WITHOUT AN AX to grind found those questions engaging because Kuhn was addressing a widespread honest curiosity about the ways in which science related to and was different from other human endeavors. *The Structure of Scientific Revolutions* called attention to the dependence of scientific progress on communities of specialists at exactly the time—the age of Sputnik and the growth of the National Science Foundation—that the old, heroic-individualist model of science was receding before the obvious enmeshing of scientists into huge organizations, even bureaucracies. Kuhn showed, in other words, that scientists, like so many other contemporary workers, were "organization men."

Although Kuhn acknowledged (and even offered an account of) the distinctiveness of the most technically developed natural sciences, he simultaneously brought the behavior of scientific communities down to a level at which popularly understood theories of group dynamics could be applied. He did this most dramatically by applying to science a vocabulary normally used to describe political actors—especially revolutionaries, such as those of 1776, 1789, and 1917—in the society at large. Like political communities, Kuhn wrote, communities of scientists were organized according to recognized traditions that periodically came under strain. Revisions were sometimes sweeping; and in both cases, community leaders wielded genuine power, which they used to bring their constituencies into line.

According to Kuhn, though, the behaviorally visible mark of a truly scientific community—what made it unique—was its high degree of autonomy—that is, its ability to exercise authority over its own intellectual affairs by persuading other elements in society, including government, that it would succeed if only left alone. Kuhn thus confirmed the popular instinct that the natural sciences were truly "different" and that this difference had something to do with the interaction between technically expert groups of specialists and metaphysically mysterious natural phenomena—even while he demonstrated that within their own domain scientists were driven by needs and impulses very much like those experienced by the rest of us.

Kuhn showed that scientific truth, although derived indirectly from nature, came to us only through the actions of historically specific communities. In this way, he historicized science yet insisted at the same

"Sweeney, if I'm going to take credit for this paradigm shift, you had damn well better tell me what it means."

During the 1960s, the pervasiveness of Structure *was such that some people first learned of the book in courses on art history and others when they overheard it being mentioned at a cocktail party by an intellectually ambitious lawyer or doctor. Even today, Kuhn's ideas are being transmitted through unusual channels, as this cartoon drawn in 2000 attests.*

OPPOSITE:

This photograph of Kuhn *was taken by his second wife, Jehane, sometime during the early 1980s. Before* Structure, *science was often mystified in the sense that people, especially scientists and journalists, rendered it an awesome mystery.*

time that recognition of its historicity did not undermine science's validity. Science works, and no less so for the reality of the circumstances that have facilitated its success. Kuhn thus demystified science without degrading it.

NOT THAT KUHN GOT everything right. Indeed, there is no better index of Kuhn's creativity than his ability to transform discussions of science even while making several specific arguments that most philosophers, historians, and sociologists of science have ruefully concluded are misleading, if not mistaken. Kuhn's distinction between normal and revolutionary science has been exceedingly difficult to sustain as scholars study more and more closely the behavior of scientific communities, only to find that many of the great revolutions in the history of science resist being shoehorned into Kuhn's model. In addition, Kuhn's signature concept of the paradigm has proven frustratingly vague and his formulations about the relativity of knowledge too ambiguous to play more than a heuristic role in the animated technical debates over relativism that his work has inspired.

The Structure of Scientific Revolutions *has sold more than one million copies and been published in at least two dozen languages. Twenty of those translation editions are shown here.*

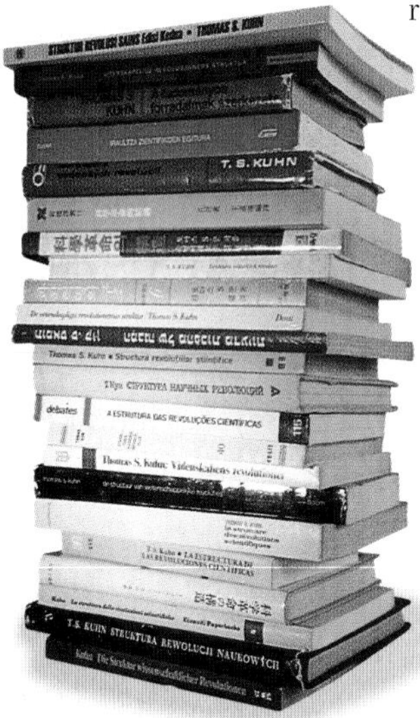

Yet for all the limitations of his analysis, Kuhn changed the way we see and analyze science. Before Kuhn, we did not have remotely the sense we do now that valid scientific knowledge depends upon the action of historically contingent communities of scientists, whose behavior is as subject to sociological and political analysis as is the behavior of any other people.

This great act of conception won Kuhn enduring praise, but it remains an irony of his unusual career that the recognition he received turned out to be rather different from the sort he most coveted. It was as a rigorous philosopher that he most wanted to be remembered—an aspiration he must have brooded over while awaiting the response from Chicago in June 1961. Yet, even during his lifetime, he was considered much more commanding as a visionary than as a rigorist. In his seminal work, Kuhn "drew the portrait of science in the manner of the Impressionists," his leading student, J. L. Heilbron, has written. "Close in, where historians and philosophers stare, it looks sketchy, puzzling, and richly challenging," Heilbron continued, but at a distance, "where most viewers stand, the portrait appears illuminating, persuasive, and inspiring."

* * *

END OF AN ERA, START OF A WAR

BY DAVID KAISER

A
T MIDDAY ON JULY 28, 1965, when he knew that the television audience would be smallest, Pres. Lyndon Johnson gave a press conference in the East Room of the White House to discuss U.S. policy in Southeast Asia and announce that the country was going to war. "I have asked the commanding general, General [William C.] Westmoreland, what more he needs to meet this mounting aggression," Johnson said. "He has told me. And we will meet his needs. We cannot be defeated by force of arms. We will stand in Vietnam."

The president then announced that the army's fighting strength in Vietnam would be raised immediately from 75,000 to 125,000 soldiers and that additional troops would be "sent as requested." What he did not say was that Westmoreland had already requested a total force

AT LEFT: *Although the president used his July 28 press conference to announce the appointment of his old crony Abe Fortas to the Supreme Court, this misdirection wasn't enough to overshadow the big news that day: his escalation of the war in Vietnam.*

ABOVE: *An antipersonnel mine of the sort used against American GIs by the Viet Cong.*

of 175,000 men by the end of the year and that this request would be granted. Johnson chose to withhold this information, and the enormous estimated cost of the increased commitment, because he desperately wanted to avoid any disruption of civilian life that might imperil his cherished Great Society programs and also because he sensed that neither Congress nor the public was ready for a war on the scale that his advisers anticipated. Nevertheless, the decision to go to war had been made, and within three years it destroyed not only Johnson's presidency but also the national consensus that had hitherto seemed likely to carry him to the loftiest heights of national leadership.

J
OHNSON MADE HIS announcement at a triumphal moment in American life. A new generation of leaders, having come of age during the Great Depression and the New Deal, believed that it had finally found lasting solutions to the problems of economic security, social justice, and world peace. In the immediate aftermath of the Second World War, many

As Martin Luther King Jr. looks on with others, the president signs the Civil Rights Act of 1964. Three weeks later, the Senate passed another Johnson-initiated bill appropriating nearly one billion dollars for illiteracy, job training, and other antipoverty measures.

Americans had feared the return of overproduction and unemployment, but the enormous postwar demand for houses, schools, automobiles, appliances, and new military technology produced instead an era of unprecedented growth. In 1965, as the economy entered its fifth consecutive year of expansion, even the brief recessions of the 1940s and 1950s seemed relics of the past, eliminated by sound government policy. Unemployment had fallen to just above 4 percent (4 percent being the operational definition of full employment), and even inflation, a serious problem during the 1950s, had been reduced to just 1 percent per year.

In part as a reward for this prosperity, voters in November 1964 gave Lyndon Johnson the largest percentage of the popular vote ever recorded in a presidential election, and his Democratic party won two-thirds majorities in *both* the House and the Senate. Johnson used this overwhelming mandate during the first six months of 1965 to persuade a receptive Congress to enact major elements of his Great Society program, which he had designed to solve lingering problems in education, housing, and health care as well as combat poverty and racial discrimination. In March 1965, Johnson signed the Appalachian Regional Development Act, aimed at one of the nation's poorest regions and a centerpiece of the president's War on Poverty. In April came the Elementary and Secondary Education Act, providing billions of federal

In early 1965, when whites Alabamans blocked efforts to register black voters in the city of Selma, civil rights leaders responded with a protest march from Selma to the state capitol in Montgomery. This photograph was taken on March 25 on the outskirts of Montgomery.

dollars for school construction and teachers' salaries, spending that Democratic lawmakers had first proposed in 1947 but had for two decades been unable to secure. Johnson even went where his hero, Franklin Roosevelt, had feared to tread (and where two subsequent Democratic presidents had tried and failed), introducing a new health insurance program for the elderly (Medicare), which he planned to sign into law just two days after the July 28 press conference.

These youths *repainting a community center in Baltimore were taking part in one of the president's many urban redevelopment programs.*

The president's ambitions for the nation and the world had, literally, no limits. His generation, having overcome the hardships of both depression and war, had no doubt that it held the future of the world in its hands. It was a spirit that pervaded Johnson's rhetoric, including this speech that he gave at Johns Hopkins University on April 7, just a few months earlier:

> *Our generation has a dream. It is a very old dream. But we have the power and now we have the opportunity to make that dream come true.*
>
> *For centuries nations have struggled among each other. But we dream of a world where disputes are settled by law and reason. And we will try to make it so.*
>
> *For most of history men have hated and killed one another in battle. But we dream of an end to war. And we will try to make it so.*
>
> *For all existence men have lived in poverty, threatened by hunger. But we dream of a world where all are fed and charged with hope. And we will help to make it so.*

Most Americans accepted these magnificent goals as real possibilities. The worst of the Cold War was now over, and national prosperity had reached unprecedented heights. The huge baby boom generation of scrubbed, obedient, high-achieving, patriotic youngsters that swelled the ranks of America's colleges seemed to want nothing more than to follow in their elders' footsteps and continue the work of progressive social change.

Most impressive of all, perhaps, were Johnson's recent steps to address the problems of segregation and civil rights. John F. Kennedy's proposed civil rights bill, which guaranteed equal access to public accommodations, was inching its way through the House when, in

THE WAR ON POVERTY

The president's War on Poverty, funded with three billion dollars by 1966, was part of his Great Society plan to bring New Deal–style relief to the most intractable pockets of urban and rural poverty. The money paid for such new programs as the Job Corps, which taught disadvantaged youth marketable skills; VISTA, a domestic version of the Peace Corps; food stamps; and Head Start, which offered preschool education to needy children. Johnson wanted to outdo his hero, Franklin Roosevelt, in promoting the general welfare, and he thought the country could afford it. But even so, Americans certainly couldn't afford a shooting war in Asia at the same time.

Before a joint session of Congress on March 12, 1947, Harry Truman makes a personal appeal for four hundred million dollars in aid to Greece and Turkey, whose governments were being threatened by Communist undergrounds. His reasoning, that the spread of Communism needed to be contained, was later formalized as the Truman Doctrine.

November 1963, the president was assassinated. During the seven months that followed, Lyndon Johnson used the country's grief to his advantage, moving Kennedy's stalled civil rights bill masterfully through Congress by transforming it into a tribute to the fallen president. At a ceremony attended by Martin Luther King Jr. and other prominent black leaders, Johnson signed the landmark Civil Rights Act of 1964 on July 2 of that year. A southerner himself, Johnson took special pride in completing the work of the Civil War, and he stunned Congress and the nation in February 1965 when he concluded his address on a proposed voting rights bill with the movement slogan "We shall overcome." That bill, which Johnson introduced after white Alabamans had responded violently to black voter registration efforts in Selma, permitted federal officials to register directly disenfranchised African-American voters in the South, and the Voting Rights Act of 1965 was on the verge of passing Congress when Johnson stepped before the cameras and microphones on July 28 to announce that he was embarking on a full-scale war in Vietnam.

In support of his decision to make a new and rather large commitment of troops to Vietnam—exactly how large, he didn't say—Johnson invoked the wisdom of his predecessors. "Three times in my lifetime," he read in his opening statement, "in two world wars and in Korea, Americans have gone to far lands to fight for freedom. We have learned at a terrible and a brutal cost that retreat does not bring safety and weakness does not bring peace." The assumption underlying this bold statement— one that Johnson shared with most of his countrymen—was that Communist success in one country would lead to Communist success in others. Because this so-called domino theory had become American conventional wisdom during the

Ike welcomes South Vietnamese president Ngo Dinh Diem to Washington in May 1957.

Eisenhower years, Johnson knew that the American public would, in principle at least, support the new war. But, at some level, he must also have known that Congress and the public would not accept a commitment on the scale that he privately anticipated. Therefore, having

concealed his plans for Vietnam for well over a year, he simply continued this strategy of implementing the escalation piecemeal and telling the American people as little as possible.

IT HAD BEEN EIGHTEEN YEARS since Harry Truman had enunciated, before a March 1947 joint session of Congress, the nation's fundamental Cold War policy: Communism had to be contained throughout the postwar world. Gradually Americans had become used to the idea that the Truman Doctrine committed them to an active role in world affairs. Yet they did not know how far their government planned to go. Few knew, for instance, that the Eisenhower administration had decided internally to commit the United States to defend the neutral nations of Southeast Asia should they be threatened by Communist insurgencies—whether America's allies agreed to help or not.

Later, President Kennedy quietly changed some of those plans, and when a political crisis threatened Laos's weak pro-American government in early 1961, he rejected advice from top military and civilian advisers that he go to war on its behalf. Kennedy also rejected similar proposals that he send a substantial number of American combat troops to South Vietnam, sending only more advisers instead. Although Ngo Dinh Diem's

Lt. Col. C. G. Kaigler, one of the early U.S. military advisers in Vietnam, and Maj. Li Van Than inspect a recently captured Viet Cong rifle in this wire-service photograph taken July 30, 1963. Some of the weapons captured in a brief but violent July 20 battle reportedly bore markings that identified them as Russian carbines made in 1960.

THE FIRST VIETNAM WAR

The first Vietnam War was fought immediately after World War II, when France tried to reinstate its colonial hegemony in Indochina. That war ended on May 7, 1954, when Communist Viet Minh troops captured the French stronghold of Dien Bien Phu. A cease-fire signed two months later in Geneva established a temporary demilitarized zone along the Seventeenth Parallel. The territory north of this line was occupied by the Viet Minh pending reunification elections, to be held within two years. In October, though, President Eisenhower offered Ngo Dinh Diem, leader of the heavily Catholic community living in the south, direct military aid. A year later, backed by the CIA, Diem declared himself president of an independent South Vietnam. Once he refused to hold the Geneva-mandated reunification elections, the North Vietnamese began making plans to unseat him.

These instructions, *captured along with a Soviet sniper's rifle, directed the Vietnamese who carried it to fire the highly prized weapon only at American officers.*

South Vietnamese government was indeed having a hard time suppressing the Viet Cong guerrillas, simultaneous events in Berlin, Cuba, Algeria, and even the Congo kept Vietnam decidedly secondary throughout 1961 and 1962.

During the summer of 1963, however, Kennedy administration claims that the war in South Vietnam was going well were undermined by dramatic television reports of Buddhist demonstrations (some including self-immolation) against the corrupt and brutal Diem regime. Amid many rumors of planned coups against Diem, Kennedy began an intense internal policy debate and ordered several emergency missions to South Vietnam. Finally, he concluded that the United States should not block a coup. Diem's subsequent overthrow and assassination on November 1, 1963—undertaken by the South Vietnamese military with the tacit consent of the Kennedy administration—was welcomed by the American press, which predicted significant improvements in the South Vietnamese war effort. Nevertheless, during 1964, the political and military situation in South Vietnam continued to deteriorate.

LYNDON JOHNSON, WHO REACTED angrily to Diem's overthrow, shared the view that Communism had to be stopped, and after becoming president he immediately put Vietnam at the top of his foreign policy agenda. In March 1964, just four months after Kennedy's assassination, Johnson indicated for the first time to his advisers a willingness to accept their recommendation that he go to war with North Vietnam. He added, however, that he needed the mandate of his own election before he could take such a step. In August 1964, he used the excuse of two North Vietnamese patrol boat attacks on U.S. destroyers in the Gulf of Tonkin—one of which had not actually taken place—to order retaliatory air strikes and ask Congress for its authorization to pursue further military action as necessary. In December 1964, just one month after his convincing electoral victory, Johnson secretly authorized planning for the sustained bombing of North Vietnam and the deployment to South Vietnam of several divisions of American troops within a very short period of time, possibly as little as a month.

Although Johnson sincerely believed that the United States had to save South Vietnam from Communism in order to preserve world peace, he also knew that his country wasn't yet ready for a military commitment

A young monk sets himself on fire in October 1963 in the central market of Saigon, the South Vietnamese capital. His death brought to six the number of ritual suicides carried out to protest Ngo Dinh Diem's brutal anti-Buddhist policies. Observers nearby heard no outcry from the stoic monk as the flames engulfed him. The three American newsmen who witnessed the suicide, including the one who took this photograph, were later attacked by Vietnamese secret police.

on such a scale. Therefore, he rejected the advice of National Security Adviser McGeorge Bundy that he fully explain his decision to the public. Instead, without much fanfare in February 1965, he approved the start of Operation Rolling Thunder, the code name given to the air force's bombing campaign, and in March he sent in the first U.S. combat troops, the Ninth Marine Expeditionary Brigade, whose official mission was to protect the U.S. air base at Da Nang from which some Rolling Thunder strikes were being launched. Meanwhile, hoping to protect the approval and financing of his Great Society programs, Johnson insisted publicly that American policy had not changed.

The marine landing was only the first step in a much larger series of planned deployments, but Johnson wanted to conceal their scope for as long as possible. In April, Secretary of State Dean Rusk explained this to former Joint Chiefs chairman Maxwell Taylor, now Johnson's ambassador to South Vietnam: "The President felt," Rusk recalled, "that he must not force the pace too fast or the Congress and public opinion, which had been held in line up to now through the President's strenuous efforts, would no longer support our actions in Vietnam."

WILLIAM C. WESTMORELAND

1914 –

On June 20, 1964, Gen. William C. Westmoreland replaced Gen. Paul Harkins as chief of the Military Assistance Command, Vietnam (MACV). A West Point graduate, Westmoreland had commanded artillery battalions during World War II and the 107th Infantry Regiment in Korea. As the top U.S. soldier in Vietnam, he became a media star. Time even named him its Man of the Year for 1965, but Westmoreland's popularity lasted only so long as the public believed his assurances that he was winning the war. Once the massive January 1968 Tet Offensive gave the lie to such statements, Westmoreland was replaced, and the Nixon administration began the slow and agonizing process of withdrawal.

Initially, General Westmoreland had believed that merely the deployment of U.S. combat troops would force the North Vietnamese to reevaluate their goals. Yet by early June he knew that he was in for a tough fight, and on June 7 he requested additional U.S. and third-country (mostly South Korean) deployments that would raise the number of men serving under his command from 82,000 to 175,000 by the end of the year—with more possibly to follow in 1966. Knowing that such an increase would have to be made public, Johnson delayed action on the request and instead sent Secretary of Defense Robert McNamara to South Vietnam in mid-July to gather information before making a final recommendation.

Upon McNamara's return to Washington on July 21, Johnson convened a series of high-level daily meetings to discuss the defense secretary's recommendation that Westmoreland's request be granted. Working carefully to maintain an internal administration consensus (and hoping to avoid leaks), the president listened to the polite dissent of Undersecretary of State George Ball and questioned his military advisers intensively regarding the possibility that the Chinese might intervene, as they had in Korea. (Their response indicated that the Pentagon clearly intended to meet any such intervention with nuclear weapons.) Johnson's posturing was successful enough to persuade some of those close to him that he was indeed undecided, yet according to a cable sent to McNamara in Saigon by Deputy Secretary of Defense Cyrus Vance, the president had already decided to approve the new troop levels—which, of course, is exactly what he did on July 27.

KNOWING THAT HE WOULD HAVE to make a public announcement of this change in policy, Johnson called his midday press conference on July 28. Yet the president still withheld much of what he had decided: He announced only half of the reinforcements he had approved, omitting mention of the other fifty thousand troops Westmoreland would be getting because they would not be available until later in the year. He also remained silent regarding what McNamara had estimated to be the ten-billion-dollar cost of the war in fiscal year 1966. Instead, his statements on the scope and

One of the fatigue shirts that General Westmoreland wore in Vietnam.

objectives of the conflict, the likely course of events, and the possibilities for peace enhanced the "credibility gap" that would play such a large part in undermining the existing national consensus and ensuring America's eventual defeat in Vietnam.

Asked by a correspondent whether the war might last "five, or six, or seven years," Johnson admitted that it could last "months, years, or decades" but added that "our cause is just." As a practical matter, though, he knew that he had to achieve his goals by 1968, when the next presidential election would be held. He believed this was possible, even though he'd been given no such assurance, because, like Westmoreland and the Joint Chiefs, he assumed that American firepower would eventually prove too much for the North Vietnamese and the Viet Cong troops to withstand. Unfortunately, this assumption was not borne out by the facts. Only a few weeks earlier, U.S. forces had encountered unforeseen difficulties when the first army unit deployed in South Vietnam made a sweep through War Zone D, a Viet Cong stronghold northwest of Saigon. Burdened by heavy clothing and equipment in the tropical heat, the soldiers of the 173rd Airborne lost ten men killed and another forty-two wounded. The mission was deemed a success because

South Vietnamese children wave at a marine truck entering the Da Nang air base in March 1965. A South Vietnamese flag flies above the banner welcoming the U.S. soldiers to Vietnam.

OVERLEAF:

Lyndon Johnson watches a squadron of helicopters perform maneuvers during a July 1966 visit to Fort Campbell, Kentucky.

of the estimated one hundred enemy killed, yet this count was speculative, being far more than the number of enemy corpses actually seen.

Four months later, the First Air Cavalry Division, whose deployment Johnson announced at the press conference, engaged North Vietnamese regulars in the Ia Drang Valley. The result was a much larger battle that demonstrated North Vietnam's willingness to sacrifice heavy casualties in order to inflict much smaller losses on the Americans. Ironically, this engagement persuaded *both* sides that the war could be won through a series of such engagements. The North Vietnamese, of course, were the ones who proved to be right on this count.

Meanwhile, in an equally critical attempt to reassure public and world opinion, Johnson reiterated at the press conference his willingness, first enunciated in the April 7 Johns Hopkins speech, to enter immediately into "unconditional discussions" with the North Vietnamese. As usual, he avoided using the word *negotiations*, because a willingness to negotiate implied the possibility of a cease-fire and an international peace conference to discuss a new political settlement. Johnson had no intention of allowing this because the position of the South Vietnamese government was much too weak. Rather, the president was merely willing to have his representatives meet with those of North Vietnam to inform the North Vietnamese that what they were doing was wrong and that they should stop it. This guise did in the short term persuade many Americans, and even a few friendly governments, that President Johnson truly desired a quick peace on reasonable terms. However, when no talks began and the United States escalated its bombing and raised its in-country troop strength during 1966 and 1967 to nearly half a million soldiers, Americans began to realize that peace was not at hand. With

ROBERT S. MacNAMARA

1916 –

Robert McNamara had poor eyesight that kept him out of combat in World War II. But he did work for the army air corps' Statistical Control Office, focusing (as he had at the Harvard Business School) on ways to improve productivity. After the war, he joined Ford and in 1960 became the first person outside the Ford family to serve as the auto giant's president. Later that year, he agreed to become John F. Kennedy's secretary of defense. McNamara masterminded the shift from Eisenhower's New Look emphasis on nuclear weapons to a more expensive "flexible response" policy that included conventional options. Yet he also pursued at the Pentagon his career-long goals of efficiency and cost control.

"JOHNSON CONDEMNED HIS OFFICIALS...TO THE EXCRUCIATING MENTAL TASK OF HOLDING REALITY AND THE OFFICIAL VERSION OF REALITY TOGETHER AS THEY MOVED FARTHER AND FARTHER APART."

—

Frances FitzGerald,
Fire in the Lake *(1972)*

extraordinary speed, this widening of the credibility gap—working in tandem with other emerging political, racial, and social strains—shattered the postwar consensus that Johnson had seemed in 1965 to be riding to greatness.

In retrospect, signs of the coming turmoil were already apparent in July 1965. Despite the passage of two major civil rights acts, young black activists were already expressing their impatience with the country's progress toward racial equality. Just two weeks after LBJ's Vietnam press conference, rioting broke out in the Watts neighborhood of Los Angeles among residents angered by routine police brutality and their difficult urban lives. At the same time, white college students, once prized as a new generation of national leaders, began rebelling against the new educational establishment created to train them. During the 1964–1965 academic year, the University of California at Berkeley had been rocked by the Free Speech Movement, as well-to-do students angrily refused to take up their preordained roles in the American socioeconomic hierarchy. Another emerging problem surfaced on the front page of the January 4, 1965, *New York Times* in a long story entitled "Narcotics a Growing Problem Among Affluent Youth."

Because the Vietnam War went so wrong, it exacerbated these social trends and others, bringing the postwar consensus crashing down. Black Americans, who initially suffered a disproportionate number of combat deaths in Vietnam (until an embarrassed army juggled assignments to make sure this didn't continue), lost faith in gradualism and the political process. Their aggressive protests between 1965 and 1969 in turn caused many white Americans to become fearful, resentful, and less sympathetic to the cause of civil rights (as well as more sympathetic to the law-and-order candidacies of Richard Nixon and Alabama governor George Wallace, whose American Independent party line took 13.5 percent of the popular vote in 1968). The Democratic vote fell from Johnson's 61.1 percent in 1964 to Hubert Humphrey's losing 42.7 percent in 1968.

These protesters *gathered in Washington, D.C., on October 21, 1967, for the March on the Pentagon, which Norman Mailer reported in his* Armies of the Night *(1968).*

FURTHER READING

★ David Kaiser, *American Tragedy: Kennedy, Johnson, and the Origins of the Vietnam War* (2000)

★ Robert Dallek, *Flawed Giant: Lyndon Johnson and His Times, 1961–1973* (1998)

Lyndon Johnson scans a newspaper the day after his October 31, 1968, announcement of a halt to Operation Rolling Thunder, the code name given in 1965 to the U.S. bombing of North Vietnam. He said the move was intended to break the stalemate at the Paris peace talks. It took four more years to reach an agreement.

Although college students were largely sheltered from the war by draft deferments, the conflict in Vietnam nevertheless made them increasingly skeptical of the direction the United States was taking. By 1969, protests directed at ending university involvement with the war effort, from ROTC training to military research programs, had become commonplace, often shutting down institutions for lengthy periods. In November 1969, hundreds of thousands of young Americans marched on Washington in the largest antiwar rally yet held in this country. Of course, in addition to protesting the war, many adopted radically different standards of dress, hair length, and sexual behavior and turned increasingly to new and illegal drugs. Much of this social upheaval was no doubt inevitable, yet the Vietnam War—and the loss of faith in American values and institutions it engendered, especially within the American academy— magnified the consequences, which continue to be felt to this day.

A DECADE AFTER LYNDON JOHNSON'S press conference— following years of mass demonstrations, two new presidential administrations, and a slow American withdrawal culminating in an equivocal 1973 peace agreement— South Vietnam finally fell to the Communists, as did the two smaller and more remote dominoes of Laos and Cambodia. Yet these events did not produce the broader international consequences that Johnson had so feared in 1965. The United States eventually prevailed in the Cold War, but its decade-long involvement in Vietnam deepened a host of political, racial, economic, and social divisions and began a long decline in Americans' faith in all their institutions. Unlike the Jeffersonian vision of America, which gradually faded away as new

In August 1965, during a search-and-clear operation just west of Da Nang, a marine leads a Viet Cong suspect to the rear. The Viet Cong were South Vietnamese guerrillas supported by the Communist North.

controversies over slavery occupied the national attention, and the Gilded Age, which succumbed slowly to the twin forces of populism and progressivism, the optimistic and confident postwar consensus ended abruptly and violently. Such was the consequence of the decisions that President Johnson announced to the American people on July 28, 1965.

★ ★ ★

JANUARY 14, 1967

THE HUMAN BE-IN

BY DAVID FARBER

CULTURES DO NOT TURN ON a dime. But sometimes a moment in time can encapsulate a profound change in societal values and normative behaviors that has been growing beneath the surface—largely invisible, like an iceberg, until it suddenly crashes into the ship of state, changing everything. One of those crashes—to all appearances, just a gentle bump—took place on January 14, 1967, when twenty thousand people—most of them under thirty, dressed in exotic garb, and under the influence of illegal substances—gathered peacefully on a sunny Saturday afternoon in San Francisco's Golden Gate Park for a "human be-in."

They had come to the Polo Field not to protest the war in Vietnam nor to confront "Establishment" authorities over some injustice. Instead they came, according to the psychedelic

posters advertising the event, simply to take part in "a gathering of the tribes." In declaring the Human Be-In's purpose, the men and women who had organized it used a utopian language the likes of which had rarely been heard before in American public life:

Now in the evolving generation of America's young the humanization of the American man and woman can begin in joy and embrace without fear, dogma, suspicion, or dialectical righteousness. A new concept of human relations being developed within the youthful underground must emerge, become conscious, and be shared so that a revolution of form can be filled with a Renaissance of compassion, awareness, and love in the Revelation of the unity of all mankind. The Human Be-In is the joyful face-to-face beginning of the new epoch.

Few Americans in 1967 could take such a declaration, or the Be-In itself, seriously. On the surface, the event seemed but a well-publicized diversion, another extravagant example of faddish

AT LEFT: *The widespread ingestion of White Lightning LSD was a critical factor in expanding the possibilities that so many people pondered at the Human Be-In.*

ABOVE: *Michael Bowen, a Be-In organizer, designed this poster, one of five created to publicize the event.*

John Muir poses in 1906 with Pres. Theodore Roosevelt atop Glacier Point in Yosemite National Park. Muir was largely responsible for the establishment of Yosemite, whose spectacular rock formations he attributed to glacial erosion (a theory now widely accepted). Muir first traveled to Yosemite in 1868, after leaving his home in Wisconsin and walking all the way to the Gulf of Mexico. His journal of that trip was published posthumously in 1916.

young Californians at play. From a historian's perspective, though, the Human Be-In takes on a much larger significance because one can see now that the day's gentle bump reverberated throughout the rest of the twentieth century. The Be-In turned out to be the first mass public manifestation of a set of cultural premises about freedom, lifestyle, equality, spirituality, aesthetics, and morality that largely redirected American life for the next several decades.

ALTHOUGH THE NEW YOUTH CULTURE seemed to most Americans at the time an overnight efflorescence, the Be-In was hardly that. Its alchemical stew of radical politics and alternative culture had been simmering for some time before being served up for mass consumption in January 1967. Since the 1950s, the ideas that inspired the Be-In had been maturing in bohemian enclaves, avant-garde lairs, subterranean urban refuges, and even in many a white, suburban, middle-class basement.

During the early 1950s, even while network television insisted that *Father Knows Best* and the nation's mainline Protestant denominations experienced their largest recorded surge in membership, an underground "Beat" culture busily challenged everything that most middle-class whites professed to hold dear. A loosely affiliated group of self-proclaimed outsiders, the Beats championed avant-garde jazz, ingested an array of illegal drugs (as well as copious amounts of alcohol), looked to Eastern philosophies and religions for spiritual guidance, embraced nonmarital sexuality (including homosexuality), and generally rejected the workaday, family-oriented, home-owning way of life that most Americans took for granted as the ideal. The Beats were, self-consciously, part of a long American (though essentially white male) underground tradition that had its roots in Henry David Thoreau's Great Refusal, Walt Whitman's democratic poesy, John Muir's solo journeys across the wild American West, and Mezz

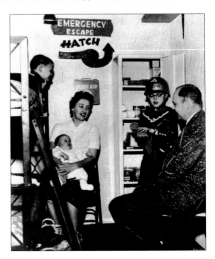

This civil defense photo shows a 1950s family enjoying a night out in its backyard bomb shelter.

Mezzrow's marijuana-laced jazz adventures. By the early 1960s, a few literary Beats had gained a great deal of public attention—most famously, Allen Ginsberg and Jack Kerouac—but the subculture's rank and file, dressing nearly exclusively in blacks and grays, lived mainly in the urban shadows. In 1958, *Time* dismissed the movement as a "pack of oddballs who celebrate booze, dope, sex, and despair." Yet the Beats' role as godparents to the hippies soon became apparent, even to those who had once refused to take the Beats' own cultural influence seriously.

The hippies *were not the first visionaries to settle in San Francisco looking for new ways to make their dreams reality. During the 1950s, San Francisco's North Beach neighborhood was the center of the Beat world. This scene at a "beatnik" coffeehouse was photographed in April 1958.*

Of course, the Beats were far from the only group stirring the nation's cultural pot during the 1950s. African-American writers and musicians (Ralph Ellison, Charlie Parker), dissident scholars (C. Wright Mills, Norman O. Brown), and—with the greatest reach—the creators of Hollywood's "rebel" movies (*Blackboard Jungle, The Wild One, Rebel Without a Cause*) pricked the nation's consciousness and pointed out a profound (and marketable) dissatisfaction with Eisenhower's America.

T HE INFLUENCE THAT THE BEATS and other cultural rebels of the 1950s had on the hippies of the 1960s was important, but in order to understand the Be-In and explain the larger impact the hippies had on American history, it's just as important to consider several other, more mainstream influences. In the years immediately after World War II, for example, affordable new media exploded onto the American scene. The most important of these were the paperback book, durable vinyl recordings, and television. Each in its own way, these media brought into people's homes radically different forms of artistic expression—from Elvis Presley's rock 'n' roll to D. H. Lawrence's *Lady Chatterley's Lover*. Also, the federal government began construction of a massive new interstate highway system just as the growth of nationally managed chain stores accelerated. Amplified by the new media technologies, these

THE HIPPIES AND THE BEATS

Some Beat luminaries, such as Allen Ginsberg and Neal Cassady, provided a measure of continuity between the two subcultures, but even the earliest hippies could never have been taken for Beats. The hippies didn't dress in black, didn't rely on alcohol for intoxication, and didn't listen to jazz. Furthermore, for the Beats, simple opposition was enough; for the hippies, there also had to be a vision of the good.

THE HAIGHT-ASHBURY COMMUNITY

Before accepting the label "hippie," a term widely promoted by the media during the spring of 1967, the bohemian residents of the Haight referred to themselves, and one another, as "freaks." The distinction was significant because of the self-image each word implied: A freak is an isolated social anomaly, a loner; whereas a hippie is part of a group defined by a common hipness.

developments in transportation and retailing hastened the breakdown of local community marketplace controls. Community control of what the local youth read, saw, and heard had been a political battleground since the 1920s. Not until the 1950s, though, did forbidden fruit such as "men's" magazines like *Playboy* and "race" music by performers like Little Richard become widely available.

Finally, none of these new technological and consumer opportunities would have meant anything had it not been for the tidal wave of affluence that swept over America during the post–World War II years. By 1959, the average American teenager was spending $555 (more than $3,200 in current dollars) annually on goods and services. Putting that kind of disposable income in the hands of teenagers produced, for the first time, a youth culture determined by the consumer choices of young people themselves. To the degree that this new consumer landscape was given up to the free-market principle of supply and demand—a very great degree, in fact—it had no clear moral boundaries, and the resulting mainstream consumermania played no

Haight Street *as it appeared during the 1967 Summer of Love.*

small role in nurturing the anything-goes, do-your-own-thing attitude of the 1960s counterculture. The Be-In was no surprise attack on mainstream culture. It was born of many influences, but the most important ones came directly from the heart of America's mid-twentieth-century experiences with unprecedented affluence.

By 1967, all these forces and influences had combined with the maturing demographic bubble of the baby boom generation and the social challenges posed by the civil rights and antiwar movements to create a decidedly dissident youth culture. This "counterculture" manifested itself most powerfully in urban enclaves—"paisley ghettos," they were called—and no big city or university town was without one. To describe the young people who inhabited these neighborhoods, the mass media eventually settled on the label "hippies." The most visible hippie community developed in the Haight-Ashbury neighborhood of San Francisco, a city famous for its live-and-let-live moral code, written a century earlier by the sailors, gold seekers, and itinerant gamblers who had turned the place upside down after 1849 as they searched exuberantly for the main chance.

FOR THE COUNTERCULTURE in the Bay Area, the Human Be-In was a coming-out party. Its purpose was to bring together the various elements that made up the dissident youth culture and demonstrate to the world the viability of its alternative lifestyles. Its two main "tribes" had not always gotten along; the Berkeley students who had launched the Free Speech Movement and now actively opposed the war in Vietnam did not see the point in waving peacock feathers and tinkling tiny silver bells. Nevertheless, the Haight-Ashbury organizers invited their more politically oriented East Bay cousins to the Be-In so they could all explore their common ground in a collective spirit of rebellion against the traditional verities of American culture.

Mario Savio, a leader of the Free Speech Movement, addresses a November 1966 rally at the University of California at Berkeley. The movement began in September 1964 to protest the university's decision to prohibit the distribution of political literature (mostly civil rights movement leaflets) on campus.

The Be-In's prime movers were Allen Cohen and Michael Bowen, editors of the *Oracle,* the local psychedelic underground newspaper. In planning the celebration, rather than consulting meteorologists or city planners, Bowen and Cohen asked a local astrologer to work out the most auspicious date. "The old control system," one countercultural enthusiast explained, with its "cunning logic…and proportion and consistency," had no hold on the minds of the hippies as they plotted their new reality. In general, mysticism and magic were their guides; and, as it happened, the astrologer made a shrewd choice: Saturday, January 14, turned out to be a beautiful day. After several weeks of

Oracle *editor Allen Cohen in August 1967.*

Rick Griffin was a surfer-cartoonist only recently arrived in town when he designed this poster for the Human Be-In. He soon became one of the leading psychedelic poster artists in San Francisco, creating some of the first underground comix, several Grateful Dead album covers, and the script masthead that Rolling Stone *used during its first ten years in business.*

typically miserable and blustery San Francisco weather, the wind died down, the clouds finally parted, and the sun came out.

To open the gathering, the organizers invited two senior statesmen of the Beat generation, the poets Allen Ginsberg and Gary Snyder, who blessed the grounds by performing the Hindu rite of *pradakshina,* walking around the Polo Field chanting prayers. This ceremony, ancient in India yet new to the counterculture, came as no surprise to those attending the Be-In. The posters promoting the event had clued in everyone, from the most experienced underground rebel to the teenage suburban day-tripper, that the Be-In would be a spiritual adventure.

THE POSTERS HAD BEEN PUT UP everywhere, not just plastered all over the Haight but also stapled to telephone poles in suburban Marin County (across the Golden Gate Bridge from San Francisco) and taped to mailboxes and storefronts in Berkeley and Oakland. The posters were the handiwork of two extraordinary artists, Stanley Mouse and Rick Griffin, who helped develop the visual language that came to dominate the era's rock album covers and T-shirt graphics. Mouse's poster featured a sadhu, or Hindu holy mendicant, with unwashed rivulets of hair running down to his waist, a curly beard snaking across his chest, and a third eye (symboling spiritual insight) penned on his forehead. For his poster, Griffin used an analogous image: a Plains Indian wearing a buckskin suit, sitting atop a pony and clutching a guitar.

These central images made clear not only the counterculture's rejection of urban industrial civilization (with its rationality, discipline, and rat-race competitiveness) but also its uninhibited longing for the exotic, the spiritual, the antimodern. Even more specifically, both posters gave form to a core belief of the counterculture: the superior virtue of the beautiful loser. That is, Mouse and Griffin's stereotypical Indians, Eastern and Western, were considered more admirable than the whites, British and American, who had conquered them.

The American Indian, in particular, as imagined by the Be-In's higher lights, exemplified a paleolithic "other way," a path not taken: the way of living gently in relation to the earth, of coming together in tribes, of questing for visions, of wearing beads and hand-tooled animal skins. That this romanticized vision of the Native American was so ignorant as to be deeply insulting to actual native peoples was irrelevant. The important point was that the young white men and women of the counterculture did not want to play the cowboy, the cavalry, the rancher, the gold miner, or even the settler—and certainly not the sheriff; they wanted to be Indians. Such a desire turned mainstream American values on their head, because the heritage of the tame-the-West cowboy, whether mythic or real, had long been the standard by which winners were judged in America's victory culture. Yet these young white people wanted to be the losers, the beautiful losers. From personal experience, they knew that American society was the richest and most powerful on the planet, yet they still believed that it had much to learn from the native peoples who had—wrongly, they insisted—been swept into history's dustbin.

FURTHER READING

★ Gene Anthony, *Summer of Love: Haight-Ashbury at Its Highest* (1980)

★ David Farber, *The Age of Great Dreams: America in the 1960s* (1994)

"THE YOUNG HIPPIES SEE THEMSELVES AS A NEW BREED."

—*Hunter S. Thompson,* New York Times Magazine, *May 1967*—

THIS GENTLE AND SOMEWHAT NAIVE turning away from the supremacy of Western culture was one piece of the utopian vision that inspired the Human Be-In. Another also appeared on Mouse's poster: It was the simple word *free*. Meaning more than literally "no admission charge," *free* was the password of the Haight—coined by the community's most influential activists, the Diggers. These energetic men and women had, as much as anybody, given purpose to the emerging alternative world that the Be-In meant to celebrate. For months in Golden Gate Park's eastern Panhandle (a blockwide swath of grass running parallel to Haight Street), they had staffed and supplied a yellow wooden structure, called the Free Frame of Reference, at which the Diggers every day gave away food. They wanted to demonstrate the feasibility of the anarcho-utopian system of exchange to which they adhered, and they meant to show that the young people arriving daily in Haight-Ashbury could sustain themselves through the communal code of "free."

Diggers dispense free food in the Panhandle during the summer of 1967.

Everything at the Be-in was free. The Grateful Dead, the Jefferson Airplane, Big Brother and the Holding Company, Quicksilver Messenger Service, and other local bands played without charge; Diggers handed out thousands of turkey sandwiches; and throughout the day, a small group of the inner circle, shrouded in druidic robes, passed out LSD tabs manufactured by the Bay Area's leading underground chemist, Augustus Owsley Stanley III. Three months earlier, California had banned LSD, but the drug's criminalization had done little to persuade its many Bay Area advocates that the hallucinatory visions it induced were any the less compelling or desirable. LSD was still considered by those in the Haight among the most powerful tools one could employ in the search for spiritual growth—a shortcut to personal understanding and cultural insight. Yet the results of LSD use were completely unpredictable—which is why the remarkable paucity of "bad trips" at the Be-In only reinforced the participants' faith in the power of the drug experience to change one's life for the better. Those tripping at the Be-In tended to float about as though propelled by a gentle breeze, soaking in the "vibe" of "free" and seeing all manner of wonders.

Although tangential, politics was not absent that afternoon. Some of the Haight intelligentsia believed that merging the radicals' insights into the workings of power with the hippies' forays into higher consciousness might produce a potent alternative to the war-torn, racist, materialist, earth-ravaging behemoth that America had become. The *Oracle* proclaimed that the Be-In would be "a union of love and activism." What actually happened, though, was that Jerry Rubin—then a rather short-haired, plain-dressing student radical—gave a short speech reminding the crowd that the Vietnam War was going on even as the generally apolitical spiritual adventurers who were the affair's main constituency drifted happily through their day.

ALLEN GINSBERG

1926 – 1997

Allen Ginsberg grew up in Paterson, New Jersey, where his father taught English and his mother was for years confined in a mental hospital. His work as a poet was influenced by another Paterson resident, William Carlos Williams, and Ginsberg's 1956 poem Howl *is considered perhaps the major literary work of the Beat generation (along with his friend Jack Kerouac's 1957 novel* On the Road*). Ginsberg is shown here at the Be-In with Gary Snyder, whose blowing of a conch shell signaled the beginning of the event. Like Snyder, Ginsberg had traveled through Asia, learned the disciplines of Eastern spirituality, ingested psychedelics, and rejected the sexual mores of his parents.*

A street peddler *hawks the* Oracle *in August 1967.*

At other times between the various band performances, speakers offered benedictions and salutations, but the events on stage were really not the point. Most of those who were ambulatory simply took pleasure in one another's presence. Circles were formed, and joints passed from hand to hand. People hadn't come to be entertained; rather, they'd come to participate in their own celebration.

As day turned to night, the Be-In closed with more haunting notes blown through a conch shell. A few hundred people cleaned up whatever litter remained; and after the park was restored, those who cared to continue the proceedings made their way across town to the edge of the Pacific Ocean, where they spent the night grouped around bonfires, chanting until the sun rose.

AFTER THE BE-IN, THE HAIGHT-ASHBURY community became a lodestar for many young Americans. During the nationally publicized Summer of Love that followed, tens of thousands of youths poured into San Francisco, seeking to join the counterculture. Dozens of other urban centers saw similar migrations during the late 1960s and early 1970s, as young people by the hundreds of thousands attempted to find meaning, solace, or just hard kicks in the nation's countercultural enclaves. Then, in the early 1970s, when many of those urban communities became overrun with witless teenage runaways and criminals come to prey on them (most infamously, Charles Manson), many original hippies moved out to rural communes as part of a "back to the land" movement that also attracted national attention. The "bible" of this movement, Stewart Brand's *Whole Earth Catalog,* sold more than two million copies between 1968 and 1970 and won a National Book Award in 1971.

Of course, only a tiny percentage of Americans lived out their countercultural dreams, but millions more were touched by aspects of the counterculture's ideals, which had already begun to win respectability and influence in the mainstream culture. Many countercultural attitudes, too, began to gain sway, even though they challenged and often offended what most Americans believed to be proper. These attitudes included casual and more experimental approaches to sexual behavior and recreational drug use, which was embraced for its "mind-expanding" possibilities; a fascination with non-Western religious and philosophical traditions; and an intense interest in alternative, nonscientific medicines, diets, and exercise. The counterculture's chief advocates asserted that American life

Jerry Rubin sits between *Gary Snyder (left) and Allen Cohen (right) at the January 11 press conference held at the Print Mint to announce the Human Be-In. Rubin's presence was important to Be-In organizers, who wanted to introduce the political radicals based in Berkeley to the alternative consciousness being nurtured in the Haight. The combining of these two rebel forces was a piece of what was meant by the "gathering of the tribes."*

OVERLEAF:

LSD guru Timothy Leary *(foreground) scans the audience as the Quicksilver Messenger Service, one of the Haight's homegrown bands, performs on the Be-In's truck-bed stage.*

The word *used most often to describe the drug-induced music and art of the Haight was psychedelic.*

had become too focused on individualistic competition and corporate consumer culture and too alienated from the natural environment, spiritual pursuits, and creative self-expression. That critique struck home with many Americans who never wore bell-bottoms, never listened to the Grateful Dead, and never attended a "be-in." As these ideals and concerns percolated through American life, they produced profound changes that have since led to what some have called the nation's "culture wars."

On a more practical level, the most obvious turn in American life produced, at least in a general sense, by the counterculture was the widespread increase in illegal drug use. Before the 1960s, few middle-class Americans saw any reason to question the claims made by medical and legal authorities that marijuana, hashish, LSD, peyote, and a variety of other drugs were dangerous and immoral. At the Be-In, though, young people celebrated the power of marijuana and LSD to free their minds and open their bodies to new experiences, and the message spread. By the mid-1970s, studies showed that a majority of high school seniors had smoked marijuana at least once. A quarter of a century later, an estimated one in three Americans has used at least one illegal drug. While one cannot attribute to the Be-In direct responsibility for

The Grateful Dead *performing during one of its many free concerts in Golden Gate Park. "I didn't need Timothy Leary or LSD," lead guitarist Jerry Garcia once declared. "I would have been a member of some weird society wherever I went."*

today's booming market in recreational drugs, the event did encapsulate a rapid and radical shift in cultural authority that made drug use seem appropriate and acceptable, even as it remained criminal.

THE METEORIC RISE IN drug use remains the most controversial reminder of the counterculture's heyday, but it's actually just one piece of a much larger cultural turn that took place in the wake of the Be-In. Millions of Americans set aside a great many moral, spiritual, and aesthetic conventions in favor of a much more tolerant, multicultural, morally relativistic (and chaotic) society. The consensus of the 1950s no longer exists. Instead, from the 1960s onward, Americans of all sorts have eagerly sought out new, adventurous, and exotic lifestyles. Although not many have chosen to follow rigorously the Hindu ways demonstrated at the Be-In, tens of

Leary lectures a San Francisco audience one week before the Be-In. His faith in the power of drug experiences to change one's life intrigued Americans but didn't fit well with their belief systems.

"ALL THAT SEPARATED THE PERFORMER FROM THE AUDIENCE WAS THE PHYSICAL FACT OF THE STAGE."

—*Jefferson Airplane vocalist Grace Slick, interview, 1979*—

millions of people have selectively adopted Eastern religious and philosophical practices that they believe promote better health and increased peace of mind. (Twelve million Americans currently practice yoga, and Eastern-style meditation techniques are taught matter-of-factly in corporate workshops and at university health centers throughout the United States.) Other non-Christian forms of spiritually have also become widely accepted.

Americans have, in general, become far more intrigued by and respectful of non-Western cultures, especially those of the Native American peoples. School textbooks no longer dismiss, as they did prior to the 1960s, American Indians as uncivilized and dangerous barbarians

LEARY AT THE BE-IN

When Timothy Leary finally made his way to the microphone, he could barely be heard over the inadequate loudspeakers chanting his new mantra, "Turn on, tune in, drop out." He told the crowd to "activate your neural and genetic equipment... interact harmoniously with the world around you...[pursue] an active, elective, and graceful process of detachment from involuntary or unconscious commitments." The mass media interpreted this as: "Get stoned and abandon all constructive activity."

***Stewart
Brand**
helped stage
the Trips
Festival,
where this
photograph
was taken, years
before creating
the* Whole
Earth Catalog.

who stood briefly in the way of American progress. Instead, Native Americans are now given a place of prominence in American history, and their violent conquest is often mourned. Likewise, American ethnocentrism, once prevalent in our mass media and educational materials, has given way to a celebration, albeit often naive and non-analytical, of cultural diversity at home and abroad. Again, the counterculture was not solely responsible for this rethinking of the superiority of the traditional American way of life. Social movements led by people of color, new scholarly understandings, the widespread availability of international travel, and the globalization of the economy all contributed profoundly to the new cultural relativism. Still, the counterculture's abiding respect for nondominant cultures provided a useful lens for seeing others, and it contributed impor-tantly to the opening up of attitudes about ways of life outside the mainstream culture, which Americans of the 1950s had refused to tolerate.

In addition, the counterculture pointed the way to a transformed understanding of the relationship between society and nature. Before 1967, few mainstream Americans had ever heard of health food stores, organic produce, or herbal remedies; even fewer employed holistic healing or practiced vegetarianism. Yet today millions of Americans worry about pesticides and hormones in their food and believe there are ways other than those prescribed by Western medicine to care for their bodies.

The countercultural emphasis on living in greater harmony with other aspects of nature has also become part of the conventional wisdom. The hippies' disgust at the willful destruction of wild places in the name of rampant materialism is now ecological common sense (even if it's embraced today more as an ideal than in practice). The strong hippie preferences for clothing

made from all-natural fibers, handcrafted furnishings, and houses built of natural materials have all contributed to the development of an earth-friendly aesthetic that now widely defines sophisticated living in the United States. The counterculture was not the first or only force to energize the environmentalist movement, but it was an important one.

AMERICANS DID NOT GATHER INTO one big hippie tribe after the Human Be-In, but many of the cultural alternatives championed that day did become critical, if not always welcome, aspects of mainstream American life. In ways both tragic and benign, life affirming and destructive, the afterglow of the Human Be-In still illuminates many important paths in the American adventure.

★ ★ ★

The clothing of the world's dispossessed—ponchos, embroidered peasant blouses, djellabas, serapes—was de rigueur at the Be-In, and few people arrived without some outward expression of their commitment to the creation of something new.

DAYS OF RAGE: THE LIFE AND DEATH OF NEWARK

BY KENNETH T. JACKSON

JOHN WILLIAM SMITH was having a hard day. The weather was hot and sticky, his cab lacked air-conditioning, and passengers were few and far between. He'd scarcely made enough money to pay for his dinner, let alone for anything extra; and in that sense at least, July 12, 1967, was a typical day in Smith's hard and unsuccessful life. Born in a small Georgia town in 1927 and raised in North Carolina, the dark-skinned Smith had served in the army before heading north to pursue his dream of becoming a trumpet player in the Big Apple. Smith's talent, though, proved insufficient even for Newark's downtrodden clubs, and he worked as an unskilled factory hand before taking his present job as a taxi driver in 1963.

His hack career hadn't gone any better than his musical career. In his fortieth year, Smith lived alone in the dilapidated Esquire Hotel on South Street, an area known mostly for its heroin dealers and prostitutes. He had no wife, no woman, no children, no money, and no close friends. He wasn't even a competent driver. Repeatedly ticketed for moving violations, he had had eight reported accidents during his first four years as a cab driver. Not surprisingly, the state of New Jersey had revoked his license.

Ignoring the license suspension, Smith continued to drive for the Safety Taxi Company—and on this particular evening, just as dusk gave way to darkness, with a female passenger in his backseat, Smith came up behind a police car on Fifteenth Avenue. The squad car, he later asserted, was double parked, leaving him no choice but to drive around it. The police officers in the car saw the incident differently. According to John DeSimone and Vito Pontrelli, Smith passed them at a high rate of speed and then drove the wrong way down a one-way street. Whatever the actual circumstances, DeSimone and Pontrelli certainly pursued Smith and forced him to stop. (With the taxi at the curb and the police officers interrogating Smith, the female passenger opened her door, departed the scene, and was never heard from again.) Smith later

AT LEFT: *A National Guardsman stands his post in Newark outside police headquarters on Saturday, July 15, 1967.*

ABOVE: *This 1910 postcard shows a view along Newark's Mount Pleasant Avenue.*

alleged that DeSimone and Pontrelli were abusive and violent; the arresting officers said the same thing about the cabbie. In any event, the slightly built Smith was soon in the backseat of the squad car on his way to the Fourth Precinct station house at the corner of Seventeenth Avenue and Livingston Street in the Central Ward.

Once at their destination, the officers again struggled with Smith before dragging him into the station house. According to the police, their 150-pound prisoner had refused to cooperate. According to Smith, the officers began pummeling him as soon as they took him into custody and kept attacking him intermittently for hours. Unfortunately for the police, just across the street from the Fourth Precinct was the Hayes Homes, a 1950s-style high-rise public housing complex, and on a sweltering night such as this one, dozens of residents were outside talking with friends, sitting on benches, and strolling along the sidewalks. More than a few watched closely as police dragged the injured Smith into the precinct house.

Accompanied by attorney Oliver Lofton, in whose custody he has just been released, cab driver John Smith talks to reporters on Friday, July 14, outside the Newark courthouse.

WITHIN MINUTES, the neighborhood was alive with rumors that the prisoner had died—yet another victim of white racism and official brutality. By 10 P.M., approximately an hour after Smith had disappeared into the station, dozens of angry black men were hurling stones and bottles at the now-besieged building. When Police Director Dominick Spina arrived at the scene, he immediately called for reinforcements. However, as carloads of police officers, some arriving for the 10:45 P.M. shift change, reached the precinct, the crowd only grew larger and more agitated. Bottles, cans, rocks, and bricks flew through the night air, crashing against the brick walls of the station house. Around midnight, two Molotov cocktails slammed against upper floors, igniting brief fires. Next, twenty-five policemen, replete with riot helmets and nightsticks, charged out of the precinct, clubbing anyone who stood his ground. The crowd gave way and dispersed, but some of the demonstrators regrouped and moved on to Belmont Avenue, where some liquor and furniture stores were looted.

Meanwhile, John Smith was in a holding cell, writhing in pain. In an attempt to restore calm, the police had allowed a delegation of civil rights leaders—including Robert Curvin, the local director of the Congress of Racial Equality, and Oliver Lofton, the administrative director of the Newark Legal Services Project—to visit the prisoner.

Horrified by Smith's obviously battered condition, they insisted that he receive immediate medical attention. Spina agreed, and a squad car was assigned to take Smith to Beth Israel Hospital, where he was diagnosed with three broken ribs, numerous bruises, and a groin injury. Outside the precinct house, Curvin and Lofton urged the demonstrators to march peacefully on City Hall to express their outrage at the municipal administration and especially its abusive police department. A few dozen protesters fell into line, but the nascent march broke up in confusion as rocks and bottles continued to fly. Finally, by 3 A.M., the streets of Newark were quiet. The next afternoon, Mayor Hugh J. Addonizio suggested to reporters that a few broken ribs, a bit of broken glass, and a few looted stores represented nothing more than "isolated incidents" and should not be a cause for alarm.

O NE MIGHT HAVE EXCUSED the mayor his optimism on the grounds that Newark had long been an American success story: an avenue for upward mobility, a place of promise as well as achievement. Founded in 1666 on the banks of the Passaic River by Puritans from Connecticut, Newark was, after New York and Boston, the third oldest major city in the United States. During the eighteenth century, its business had been largely agricultural (it was cut off from Manhattan and other population centers by salt marshes and rivers); in 1831, however, the Morris Canal linking Newark to Phillipsburg opened, and in 1845, the Morris & Essex Railroad began service between Newark

"A RIOT IS AT BOTTOM THE LANGUAGE OF THE UNHEARD."

—

Martin Luther King Jr., Where Do We Go From Here?, *1967*

This view *of the Hayes Homes, looking west from Belmont Avenue, was taken during the early 1950s.*

Skyscrapers of Newark, N. J.

In this 1915 postcard view of the Newark skyline, the Prudential building can be seen second from the left.

and Dover. Improved transportation brought industrial opportunities, and master shoemakers in Newark were soon hiring underemployed farmers to make shoes during their idle winter months.

Newark boomed after the Civil War, becoming the largest city in New Jersey and one of the dozen largest in the United States. By 1900, more than 90 percent of the country's patent leather was being produced in Newark, and the city had become a national leader in the manufacture of trunks, drugs and chemicals, electrical machinery, jewelry, and paints and varnishes. It also attracted banking, insurance, legal, and government services. The giant Prudential Insurance Company began in Newark in 1875 as the Widows and Orphans Friendly Society.

During the early twentieth century, Newark continued to prosper. Port Newark opened in 1915, Newark Airport in 1928, and Newark's Pennsylvania Station in 1935. By 1931, both the airport and the downtown intersection of Broad and Market Streets were touted as the busiest in the world, and the thriving central business district featured big department stores, elegant movie theaters, and prestigious

An American Airlines plane unloads its passengers at Newark Airport during the late 1930s or early 1940s.

hotels. Local nightclubs were legendary, and Newark's sports teams of the 1930s, especially the all-white Newark Bears and the all-black Newark Eagles, are still regarded as among the finest minor league baseball operations of all time.

Newark during the 1930s was beautiful as well. As World War II began, the cherry blossoms and shade trees of Branch Brook Park were more numerous than those along the Tidal Basin in Washington, D.C., and the houses along High Street near Military and Washington Parks were as attractive as those anywhere. Not surprisingly, local boosters repeatedly predicted national prominence for their city, and some boldly proclaimed that Newark would one day rival New York City as a world capital. In 1930, Princeton University economist James G. Smith opined that Newark had potential "comparable to the phenomenal growth of Los Angeles."

O F COURSE, NEWARK did not fulfill such prophecies. Indeed, even before the arrest of John William Smith, the city was well on its way to becoming a symbol more of pathology than of promise. With hindsight, we can see that five distinct public policies, most predating the 1967 riots by decades, combined to make it impossible for New Jersey's largest city to keep pace with its competition elsewhere in the state and in the nation.

The first of these was Newark's failure early in the twentieth century to annex its outlying suburbs. Throughout American history, the adjustment of local boundaries has been the dominant method by which the population of every city of consequence has grown. Philadelphia took in the formerly independent suburbs of Spring Garden, Northern Liberties, Kensington, and Southwark in 1854; Chicago annexed Hyde Park and most of what is now the far South Side in 1889; New York combined its five boroughs into one enormous metropolis in 1898; Baltimore tripled in size in 1917; and Dallas grew in area by 507 percent between 1940 and 1960. Newark wanted to do the same thing, and its mayor in 1900 said as much when he remarked, "East Orange, Vailsburg, Harrison, Kearny, and Belleville would be desirable acquisitions."

But Newark did not acquire these suburbs (Vailsburg's annexation in 1906 being the notable exception), and it failed to secure the open spaces it needed to sustain future growth. Instead, Newark remained stuck at just twenty-three square miles, much of it marshland. Even St. Louis and San Francisco, the smallest of America's other major cities, had twice the municipal area of Newark. As a result, Newark's leading businessmen were unable to expand their companies and build the luxury homes that they wanted for their families. Although little mention was made of it at the time, by 1930 more than half of the members of the elite Newark Chamber of Commerce had moved to the suburbs.

A second cause of Newark's long decline was weak land-use control. Unlike its affluent suburbs and many other U.S. cities, which either excluded industries altogether or required vigorous cleanup policies

The Newark Eagles played in the Negro National League from 1936 until 1948, the year the league folded. In 1946, the team won the Negro World Series. The next season, it won the first-half pennant but slumped during the second half after star outfielder Larry Doby left the Eagles to become only the second African American to cross the color line and play in the white major leagues.

OVERLEAF:

This 1874 bird's-eye view of Newark shows the Passaic River in the foreground. A futuristic 1925 description of Newark predicted that by 1975 the city's central business district would rival Manhattan's.

This 1923 photograph shows the industrial pollution
of the Passaic River already well underway.

of polluting factories, Newark allowed obnoxious enterprises to exist in close proximity to residential neighborhoods, making nearby residences much less attractive. One of the worst polluters was the Diamond Alkali Company, which made pesticides along the Passaic River from 1951 until 1969. During the Vietnam War, when the firm was operating twenty-four hours a day making ingredients for the chemical defoliant Agent Orange, Diamond Alkali and other companies released into the water such large amounts of cancer-causing dioxin that the Environmental Protection Agency had to put the Passaic River on its list of the nation's most endangered waterways.

These two factors contributed enormously to the shift of wealthy (mostly white) residents from the city to the suburbs, and an important part of the city's tax base went with them. As Newark businessman Frank Kingdon noted gloomily as early as 1936, "The more people with money move into residential areas outside the city, the less money will be available from highly assessed properties and for privately maintained social agencies. Either the city will have to maintain such agencies or else it will pay a heavier bill for crime. In either case taxes will rise. As taxes rise business will move out to avoid them."

Kingdon was right: Because Newark had nowhere to expand, middle-class families seeking to build dream homes had to move out to the suburbs, and the city subsequently had to raise property taxes to make up for the loss—eventually to the point of diminishing return. By 1967, Newark's taxes were

In 1917, this impoverished
woman paid nine dollars
a month for two rooms at
148 Broome Street, one
of which was dark.

about twice as high as those in surrounding counties. Few families could afford to buy homes, and few landlords saw any point in paying for necessary repairs. Even with the high taxes, revenues were still down, leaving less money to spend on education and giving middle-class families even more reason to flee.

Athird cause of the Newark crisis was the Home Owners Loan Corporation (HOLC) and its successor, the Federal Housing Administration (FHA). Together, these federal agencies initiated the policy of residential "redlining." When HOLC appraisers looked at Newark in 1939, not a single neighborhood was considered worthy of a First Grade, or "green," rating. The so-called "high-class" Jewish sections of Weequahic and Clinton Hill received Second Grade, or "blue," ratings, as did such upscale non-Jewish areas as Vailsburg and Forest Hill. Typical Newark neighborhoods—such as the well-maintained and attractive working-class sections of Roseville, Woodside, and East Vailsburg—were tagged with Third Grade, or "yellow," ratings; and the rest of the city, including immigrant Ironbound and every predominantly African-American neighborhood, was marked Fourth Grade, or "red," and labeled "hazardous." As a result, HOLC and FHA mortgage commitments typically went to the suburbs, not to Newark, and the redlining influenced private lenders to abandon the city as well. This made ordinary residential loans difficult to secure in Newark, while suburban areas were treated generously.

A fourth cause was Newark's decision to build more than thirteen thousand public housing units, more per capita than any other city in the United States. According to the 1937 federal legislation under which the units were funded, each community had to decide for itself whether it needed low-income housing. This decentralization was crucial because it invariably reinforced racial segregation. Newark's exclusive suburbs kept public housing projects out simply by not asking for them. Meanwhile, Newark—perhaps to house people, perhaps to generate lucrative cement contracts—built more and more monolithic projects, reshaping large parts of the city. Even by the degraded standards that obtain in America, they were a disaster.

The final reason for Newark's peculiar dilemma was its long-standing tolerance of public corruption. In 1953, for example, a grand jury indicted Ralph Vilani, the city's first Italian-American mayor, for taking part in a shakedown racket. Three years after the riots, Mayor Addonizio was himself convicted, along with several other high city administrators, on charges of extortion and income tax evasion.

The Hayes Homes, *shown here as they were being built, were part of Newark's sweeping postwar slum-clearance program. As longtime director of the Newark Redevelopment and Housing Authority, slum-clearance boss Louis Danzig ruled his domain with an iron fist and an iron brain. He ruthlessly razed entire neighborhoods, some of them healthy, in a vain effort to "modernize" his city.*

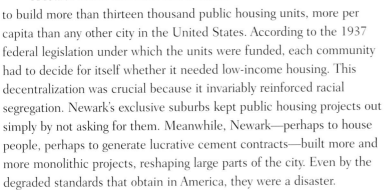

HUGH J. ADDONIZIO

1914 – 1981

Hugh Addonizio was born and raised in Newark. A month after the Japanese bombed Pearl Harbor, he left his job at Newark's A & C Clothing Co. to join the army. Although he enlisted as a private, he was transferred to Officers Candidate School at Fort Benning and then sent overseas as a second lieutenant. A Democrat, Addonizio was elected to Congress in 1948 and served seven terms in the House of Representatives before resigning in June 1962 after winning his first Newark mayoral election. Long suspected of corruption and involvement with organized crime, he was convicted in 1970 on charges of racketeering. Addonizio (shown here at his City Hall desk in September 1963) eventually served five years in a federal prison.

B Y THE MID-1960s, Newark was suffering as much as any city in America from changing public policies and personal preferences that favored new construction over old, curvilinear streets over the gridiron plan, restrictive residential zoning over mixed uses, homogeneity over ethnic and racial diversity, private automobiles over public transportation, and suburbs over cities. In January 1967, a group of business and community leaders announced that Newark's problems were "more grave and pressing than those of perhaps any other American city." Municipal officials were equally pessimistic. Later that spring, in its application for planning funds under the Model Cities Act, the city government noted that Newark had the nation's highest crime rate, its heaviest property tax burden, its largest percentage of slum housing, and its most elevated levels of venereal disease and tuberculosis. In drug addiction, infant mortality, and automobile theft, Newark wasn't first but ranked in the top five.

Moreover, in late 1966, the problems of race and class had been exacerbated in Newark when the New Jersey College of Medicine and Dentistry announced its plans to build a new campus in the Central Ward. This might have been a joyful prospect—world-class medicine in a minority setting—but the medical school, which had preferred a suburban location, wanted to make room by clearing dozens of acres of tightly built-up ghetto, destroying hundreds of structures and evicting thousands of low-income tenants. In place of these homes would go parking lots, doctors' offices, and research structures. What the community wanted were recreational facilities and affordable housing. A local activist named James Walker gave voice to the community's anger when he proclaimed that, if the medical school was built instead of housing, "blood will run down the streets of Newark—your blood and my blood."

The proposed medical school was not the only point of conflict. Early in 1967, the white secretary of the Newark Board of Education announced his intent to retire. Because public school enrollment in the city was 70 percent minority, the African-American community promoted the candidacy of one of its own: the city's budget director, who held a master's degree. Mayor Addonizio, though, had promised the post to a white man with only a high school education. Infuriated black activists proceeded to disrupt and prolong regular board of education meetings. One such gathering began at 5 P.M. and lasted for more than eight hours. In the end, the incumbent secretary decided to stay on, which satisfied no one.

Finally, the United States as a whole was far from tranquil in July 1967. The nation was in turmoil, in part because of opposing views about the Vietnam War, in part because of the mounting frustration of people on both sides of the civil rights revolution, and in part because a cultural revolution was alienating one generation from another. Such was the situation on July 13, when Mayor Addonizio suggested that the disturbances of the previous evening had been simply "isolated incidents."

Y ET THE MAYOR WAS WORRIED enough to meet that afternoon with local civil rights leaders, who made three demands: that DeSimone and Pontrelli be suspended; that Lt. Edward Williams, the highest-ranking African American on the police force, be promoted to captain; and that the mayor appoint a special panel to investigate the violence in the Fourth Precinct. Addonizio agreed to all three. But the situation in Newark on July 13 was not under the control of either the city administration or the civil rights leadership. As radical organizer Tom Hayden later wrote, "The authorities had been indifferent to the community's demand for justice; now the community was going to be indifferent to the authorities' demand for order." Indeed, even as civil rights negotiators were meeting with the mayor at City Hall, inflammatory leaflets were circulating throughout the Central Ward: "Stop Police Brutality. Come Out and Join Us at the Mass Rally Tonight, 7:30 P.M., Fourth Precinct." Several news organizations picked up on the story and sent reporters and cameramen to the Fourth Precinct station house.

Aware of the leafleting and the potential for violence, Police Director Spina decided at 4:45 P.M. to extend officers' shifts that night from eight to twelve hours. He also ordered half the force out on patrol and notified off-duty officers to be prepared for emergency assignments. As it turned out, Spina needed every available cop that night, and then some. By 6:30 P.M., a crowd had already begun to gather outside the Fourth Precinct; by 7:30, it numbered in the hundreds; by 8:30, a full-scale riot was underway; by 9:30, Newark was a shopkeeper's nightmare.

The situation was especially bad along Springfield Avenue, the major commercial artery connecting affluent Short Hills, Milburn, and Maplewood to the city's central business district. Roving gangs of looters smashed the windows of all manner of retail stores, helping themselves to radios, televisions, mattresses, sofas, shoes, clothing, toasters, and tools. Twenty-four rifles disappeared from a Sears store. The rioters then fanned out toward other shopping areas within the Central Ward. As yet, however, only a few shots had been fired, and no one had been killed.

"THERE'S NO MONEY IN WASHINGTON, BUT YOU CAN MAKE A MILLION BUCKS AS MAYOR OF NEWARK."

—

Hugh J. Addonizio, answering a reporter's question as to why he was leaving Congress, 1962

Protesters gather outside the Fourth Precinct station house in the early evening on Thursday, July 13.

Among those killed on Saturday night was a forty-one-year-old fire department captain, who was shot while working to contain a fire, one of 250 that raged over the four days of rioting. He left behind a wife and seven children, one of them not yet born. This fire burned Friday night near the corner of Broad and Branford Streets.

Meanwhile at City Hall, even as the looting continued with relative impunity, both the mayor and the police director resisted admitting that they could no longer maintain order. During a lull in the violence that occurred about midnight, a considerably relieved Addonizio told reporters that the city had turned the corner. Then more reports of looting and burning came over the police radios. Finally, at 2:20 A.M., Addonizio placed an urgent telephone call to Gov. Richard J. Hughes, requesting that Hughes declare Newark a disaster area and that he order out the state police and the New Jersey National Guard. The governor responded immediately, and Col. David B. Kelly of the state police arrived at City Hall within the hour. "It's all gone, the whole town is gone," the mayor told Kelly, and when Kelly asked Addonizio to identify the worst problem areas, the mayor said, "It's all over."

AT DAYBREAK ON JULY 14, 1967, the first state troopers began to arrive in Newark; and by 9 A.M., nine battalions of the National Guard were rolling into the city. By noon, the forces of order numbered more than fifteen thousand, and Newark was an armed camp, with military sectors and roadblocks at 137 critical intersections. Governor Hughes ordered his men to restore order immediately and take a "hard line" against criminals. Presumably, the riot was already history.

Not so. For one thing, the three elements occupying Newark—the local police, the National Guard, and the state police—didn't trust one another, and they weren't even operating on the same radio frequencies. Literally and figuratively, they couldn't communicate. Colonel Kelly of the state police, who'd been preparing for the possibility of a major civil disorder, had overall command of the operation, but he didn't know Newark well (and didn't even have a good map of the city). Maj. Gen. James F. Cantwell of the National Guard, who commanded the largest contingent of "peacekeeping" forces, thought that he should be in charge.

More important, with television and radio stations bombarding the public with news of the looting, burning, and violence, the rumor mill began operating in the other direction—that is, exaggerating the extent of the damage and danger. The young National Guard soldiers—98 percent of whom were white, and most of whom had just hours earlier been leading ordinary civilian lives—rode into Newark wearing full combat gear, carrying loaded rifles, and facing what they perceived to be a mortal threat for the first time in their lives. These were not Korean or Vietnam War veterans, accustomed to hostile gunfire and disciplined in the face of uncertainty. They were ordinary kids, and when reports began to spread through the ranks of "scattered sniper fire," they reacted, understandably, with fear.

Thus, there were essentially two riots in Newark that weekend. The first featured young black men throwing bottles and rocks, starting fires, and stealing from vulnerable businesses. The second featured the state police and the National Guard firing guns, sometimes indiscriminately, and ultimately killing nearly two dozen people. The first riot had essentially ended by the time the second riot began.

Mayor Addonizio and *Governor Hughes conduct a hurried press conference at the Roseville Armory on Friday, July 14.*

T HE LOOTING HAD STOPPED by Friday afternoon, but the gunfire had become only more intense. Later, investigators learned that 13,319 rounds of ammunition were fired by the National Guard and the state troopers (compared to fewer than 100 rounds even allegedly fired by snipers). At the time, though, no one knew who was doing the shooting, and the soldiers and the state police each assumed that the gunfire was coming from the rifle barrels of revolutionaries and criminals. They were scared of being picked off from darkened windows, and many became trigger happy, inclined to shoot first and ask questions later. State police killed thirty-four-year-old James Snead as he worked on his car in front of his house and seventeen-year-old Karl Green as he stood on his sister's porch. Ten-year-old Eddie Moss was in his family's car—coming back from a restaurant with his parents, three brothers, and an uncle—when his father approached a National Guard checkpoint. Hearing a gunshot, Eddie's father swerved and stepped on the gas. "I thought it was just a street repair site," he said later. Not until the family began piling out of the car at home did they realize that Eddie was dead, the victim of a bullet to the head.

On Friday night, National Guardsmen detain some African Americans suspected of looting stores on Springfield Avenue.

Tom Hayden, *one of the founders of Students for a Democratic Society, went to Newark in 1964 to prove that white working stiffs could join with blacks to build a more egalitarian polity. Hayden's attempt at interracial politics failed to achieve any electoral success, but it did make him aware of the many problems demoralizing Newark's African-American community.*

The horror continued Saturday night. At 6 P.M., a National Guard platoon supported by state police began firing into the Hayes Homes at the corner of Springfield Avenue and Hunterdon Street. Several middle-aged black women were killed, gunned down because they happened to live in a dark and crowded public housing project. Eloise Spellman, a mother of seven, took a bullet in the neck as she stood in her own apartment. Hattie Gainer, a grandmother, was standing with a group of spectators when several state troopers suddenly turned and fired into the crowd. Rebecca Brown was killed by National Guard fire as she reached to pull her two-year-old daughter away from a window. Later, General Cantwell testified before the House Armed Services Committee that "there was too much firing against snipers" and that a large part of the problem was "our thinking [that our mission] was a military action."

By Sunday afternoon, there was a new problem: the shortage of food. Families in the most riot-torn sections of the city had lain low for days, but now their provisions were running out. As hunger overcame their fear, they ventured outside only to find that local groceries had been burned or looted or left padlocked by their owners. Fortunately, the National Guard began distributing emergency rations. But the violence had still not ended. At 11 P.M., Lucille Pugh looked out of her window to see whether the streets were clear. Satisfied that they were, she asked her eleven-year-old son to take out the garbage. As he reached the street, a single shot, presumably fired by a police officer, ended his life.

On Monday, July 17, the National Guard and the state police began to leave Newark. The second riot was over. Twenty-three people were dead who had not been so Friday morning—two of them white and the rest black. Hundreds more were wounded. Businesses and individuals had suffered millions of dollars in property damage. The once-prosperous stores of Springfield Avenue were mostly smashed or still-smoking ruins. Newark's dazed populace stumbled back onto its streets.

Springfield Avenue before: *Its three-way intersection with Belmont and Fifteenth Avenues in 1957. Springfield Avenue after: Near West Kennedy Street in March 1969.*

THE POSTMORTEMS began even before the embers had cooled as a wide variety of investigating commissions and independent scholars attempted to assess blame. The first out of the gate was Tom Hayden, whose *Rebellion in Newark: Official Violence and Ghetto Response* was published within months of the tragedy. Portraying the riot as a justifiable revolt against intolerable conditions and military suppression, Hayden blamed civil authorities not only for creating the crisis but also for overreacting to the violence once it began. Governor Hughes appointed his own commission to investigate both the riot and its causes in detail. The Hughes Commission report, released in February 1968, was especially critical of the police and the National Guard, concluding that they had used "excessive and unjustified force." The commissioners obviously believed that state troopers and guardsmen had been responsible for most of the unexplained deaths. (They even accused the state police of vandalizing black-owned stores, "for which there is no possible justification.") Later in 1968, the state police union published the results of its own investigation. Predictably, the union concluded that the uniformed services were largely blameless, with outside agitators and violent revolutionaries being the guilty parties.

LeRoi Jones was already an acclaimed poet and dramatist when the Newark riots broke out. That weekend, Jones and two other blacks were stopped by Newark police and charged with carrying unlawful firearms and resisting arrest. According to Jones, who was beaten while in custody, the guns were planted.

Anthony Imperiale later became a Republican state assemblyman and then a state senator.

At the same time, racial and ethnic lines in Newark began to harden dramatically. On one side was Anthony Imperiale, a stocky former marine sergeant who became president of the heavily Italian North Ward Citizens Committee. Fiery and confrontational, the thirty-seven-year-old karate expert and part owner of a construction company waved a rifle in front of television cameras and warned Newark's black population not to "come into the North Ward and try anything." The leader of the opposition, playwright LeRoi Jones, made up in demeanor what he lacked in physical stature. The slight, skinny Jones tried to bring African Americans together, organizing the United Brothers, calling for a boycott of the white-owned *Newark Evening News,* and telling his followers to "think, talk, act, and love black." Meanwhile, he grew a beard, became a Muslim (changing his name to Amiri Baraka), and argued that "Newark is a city where black people are in the majority, and we mean to be masters of our own space."

OVERLEAF:

A National Guardsman patrols a nearly abandoned Newark on Sunday, July 16.

Kenneth Gibson, *shown here on the night of his 1974 reelection, served four terms as mayor of Newark. In 1986, running for a fifth term, he suffered an upset loss to city councilman Sharpe James. Although never accused of corruption while in office, Gibson was indicted in July 2000 on charges of defrauding the Irvington, New Jersey, school board in connection with a school construction project.*

W E GONNA WIN. My God, we gonna win," an elderly man exclaimed as he listened to the election returns in the Georgian Room of Newark's Robert Treat Hotel. "Black power," a younger group chanted, their fists raised. "Beep, beep, make way." And they had won. In the spring of 1970, thirty-seven-year-old Kenneth Gibson became the first African-American mayor of Newark and indeed the first black chief executive of a major eastern city. Unfortunately, the blacks of Newark did not win much, because the city they now controlled was nearly an empty shell. In fact, Newark had become almost synonymous with urban decline at the same time that it—along with Washington, D.C.— became the first major American city with a black-majority population. Gibson himself was widely quoted as saying, "Wherever urban America is going, Newark will get there first."

The comment was prescient. Between 1950 and 2000, Newark's population dropped by 38 percent. Of the residents who remained, a staggering one-third were on some form of public assistance. Job loss in Newark was equally stark. Some firms, including the Ballantine Brewery, simply closed their doors. Others, such as the Spring Air Mattress Company and the Barton Press, moved out of town. A few, notably Prudential Insurance, kept a nominal presence in Newark while shifting the bulk of operations elsewhere.

Poverty and unemployment were visible throughout the city. Once-bustling thoroughfares became avenues of ghostly burned-out, boarded-up buildings. Commercial districts were littered with blowing paper, used condoms, liquor bottles, and tattered plastic sheeting from the hidden dens of the homeless. Newark's residential areas were not much better off. Even in 1960, an astonishing 32.5 percent of Newark's 134,872 housing units were considered substandard; after 1967, that number only grew. Although some neighborhoods—for example, Weequahic—retained a middle-class ambience, most never recovered from the riots. On almost every block in these areas one found, like a bruise, an unkempt house with a sagging porch, a trash-filled yard, and broken windows partly boarded up. Garbage-strewn gutters became breeding grounds for roaches and rats, shifting the balance of power in the city's day-and-night war against vermin. Meanwhile, Newark's once-bustling theaters and clubs shut down, and the local schools became so bad that the state had to take them over in 1996. Of course, the city also continued to rank at or near the top in most categories of crime.

The most desperate places in Newark continued to be the public housing projects. Built during the 1940s and 1950s, these multistory red-brick complexes had become by the 1970s wretched residences of last resort. Dark and frightening stairwells, broken elevators, and grime-covered halls permeated with the stench of urine were common characteristics. Not surprisingly, the Newark Housing Authority decided during the 1980s simply to demolish them.

What part did the rage of July 1967 play in Newark's decline? Did the lootings, fires, deaths, and resulting terrible publicity condemn New Jersey's largest city to a precarious existence at the lowest levels of

BLACK FLIGHT

Not everyone who left Newark during the 1950s and 1960s was white. Black Newarkers who experienced professional success and became able to buy larger, more prestigious homes also moved to the suburbs, often to East Orange. Their departure, though, was particularly costly because it deprived the many poor African Americans left behind of a natural source of leadership.

The Christopher Columbus Homes (*shown here in 1982*) *were one of several Newark public housing projects, including the Hayes Homes, demolished during the 1990s and replaced with federally subsidized low-income town houses.*

A quarter of a century after Hugh Addonizio's conviction, the feeling remained common in Newark that everybody at City Hall was still available for the right price. In 1996, the police commissioner was indicted on thirty-seven counts of theft and fraud, and two years later, the chief aide to Mayor Sharpe James resigned in disgrace in the face of similar charges. Here, Mayor James is shown talking with Pres. Bill Clinton at Newark Airport in October 1993.

American life? The answer has to be, in part, yes. The riots didn't cause Newark's decline, and they certainly weren't responsible for the long-term difficulties the city faced even before 1967. But the negative publicity with which news coverage burdened Newark accelerated the city's collapse and hastened the departure of the middle class, both as residents and as shoppers. Before the riots, one Staten Island family with eight children routinely shopped at Bamberger's, the grand Market Street department store, to avoid New York City sales taxes. After the rioting, that family never returned to downtown Newark. More generally, middle-class families who lived in Newark left, and those who had already left decided not to go back, even for the day.

IT TOOK THREE DECADES before Newark again exhibited any strong signs of life. In 1997, the glittering $187-million state-subsidized New Jersey Performing Arts Center opened within a couple of blocks of the railroad station and the vibrant Portuguese immigrant community in Ironbound. It was an immediate success, managing to attract people of all races and classes to its presentations and even luring other institutions to downtown Newark. A new minor league baseball stadium helped restore the legacy of the Eagles and the Bears, and a proposed two-mile esplanade along the Passaic River promised to make the waterfront pleasing and popular again. New York City developers, too, began eyeing office and industrial sites in Newark because the city's transportation assets and modern fiber-optics infrastructure compared favorably to those of Manhattan at a fraction of Gotham's stratospheric costs.

Yet even if Newark were someday to return to the optimism of its past, the violence of 1967 would remain a touchstone of the city's three-century-plus history. Twenty-three mostly innocent men, women, and children lost their lives over that weekend, and those who loved them have found their own remaining years diminished by the loss. Dozens of store owners, many of them underinsured or uninsured, lost their livelihoods, and the looters themselves discovered soon after the riots that, with their local commercial options

In May 2000, the New York Times *declared Newark "hip" and cited the New Jersey Performing Arts Center as a main reason why.*

KAWAIDA TOWERS
READY FOR OCCUPANCY

NEW JERSEY HOUSING FINANCE AGENCY

KAWAIDA TOWERS

WE DON'T WANT SLUMS
LEON

In defiance of the Newark Housing Authority, Amiri Baraka (formerly LeRoi Jones) won interracial support in the early 1970s to build the Kawaida Towers apartment complex, billed as the beginning of a black renaissance in Newark. Instead, the North Ward project was scuttled soon after its 1972 groundbreaking, when city councilmen led by Anthony Imperiale rescinded the project's tax abatement and Newark's police chief resigned rather than protect black citizens from violently anti-Kawaida white mobs.

substantially reduced, they had to pay much higher prices for ordinary goods. Newark's image as a city out of control, a city in flames, a city of sirens and danger and fear proved nearly impossible to shake, and even yet it persists.

As Mayor Kenneth Gibson said, among American cities, Newark got there first, but it certainly didn't get there alone. After the Newark violence, there was no denying the problems that faced—and still face—urban America. President Lyndon B. Johnson had this in mind when he addressed the nation just two weeks after the July 1967 riots:

> *The only genuine, long-range solution for what has happened lies in an attack—mounted at every level—upon the conditions that breed despair and violence. All of us know what those conditions are: ignorance, discrimination, slums, poverty, disease, not enough jobs. We should attack those conditions— not because we are frightened by conflict, but because we are fired by conscience. We should attack them because there is simply no other way to achieve a decent and orderly society in America.*

★ ★ ★

FURTHER READING

★ Kenneth T. Jackson, *Crabgrass Frontier: The Suburbanization of the United States* (1985)

★ Otto Kerner et al., *Report of the National Advisory Commission on Civil Disorders* (1968)

NOVEMBER 22, 1971

SALLY REED DEMANDS EQUAL TREATMENT

BY LINDA K. KERBER

WHAT'S FAIR? The cries of the playground—"that's fair," "that's not fair"—echo throughout our adult lives. Sometimes an entire society's understanding of what's fair shifts in a decade, a year, even a single day. Children of Jehovah's Witnesses refuse to salute the flag in school. Oliver Brown thinks it's unfair that his daughter can't attend her neighborhood school. Rosa Parks refuses to give up her seat on a Montgomery bus. Sometimes you go to sleep one night, and when you wake up, the rules have changed. That happened on November 22, 1971, when the U.S. Supreme Court ruled for the first time that arbitrary discrimination on the basis of sex could be a denial of equal protection of the laws.

The case that triggered this shift was a modest one. It came from a small state (Idaho) and involved hardly any money ($930, which lawyers' fees completely consumed). To most people, the dispute seemed merely a family squabble, hardly worth the expensive attention it would get.

Yet Sally Reed's complaint was far from frivolous. It disrupted well-established rules of fairness and challenged the way that both men and women make some of the most important choices in their lives.

THE REEDS WERE A FAMILY of modest resources. Cecil Reed, a mechanic, worked for the state highway department. Sally Reed had more education; she worked white-collar jobs as a secretary or bookkeeper. When the Reeds divorced in 1958, Sally was awarded custody of their adopted son, Richard. But when Richard grew into a rambunctious teenager, breaking curfew and generally getting into trouble, the county court removed him from Sally's care, placed him briefly in the local Children's Home, and then sent him to live with Cecil. In March 1967, sixteen-year-old Richard committed suicide in the basement of his father's home using one of his father's guns.

AT LEFT: *This photograph of Sally Reed and her attorney Allen Derr was taken for the* Idaho Statesman, Boise's daily *newspaper, in July 1987.*

ABOVE: *One of Allen Derr's business cards from the time of the* Reed case.

This early photograph of Sally Reed, which Allen Derr kept in his files, is undated but probably from the 1950s. Now in her late eighties, Reed still cherishes the cornet that, along with a small savings account, made up the bulk of her late son's estate.

Richard Lynn Reed as a teenager. His nickname was Skip.

The estate Richard Reed left behind included his beloved cornet—he'd planned to study music in college—and the small savings account his mother had set up for his college education. Sally Reed began the process of administering the estate—she had, after all, established the account—and petitioned the probate court to name her its administrator. Cecil Reed also applied to the probate court to administer the estate, telling Sally that she was "too dumb" to handle it.

Under an Idaho law dating back to 1864 and never repealed, when a person died without a will, the probate court was directed to assign an administrator in the following order: surviving husband or wife; children; father or mother; brothers or sisters. (Until 1919, married women were excluded from this list.) The law also provided that "of the several persons equally entitled, males must be preferred to females"—or, as Ruth Bader Ginsburg later put it, "All people are equal, but male people are more equal than female people." Because Sally could not show that her ex-husband was incompetent, the probate court promptly appointed Cecil administrator of his son's estate. Idaho's rules were not peculiar: Similar statutes were in force in Arizona, Nevada, South Dakota, Wyoming, and the District of Columbia.

S ALLY REED WAS OUTRAGED. Hindsight makes it easy to see that the ingredients for her outrage were easily at hand. For the previous four years, women throughout the country had been naming the discrimination they faced. In 1963, Congress had decided that men and women hired for the same job should receive the same pay. (As one judge said famously when considering the differences between maids and janitors, "Dusting is dusting is dusting.") Also in 1963, the President's Commission on the Status of Women (whose honorary chair was Eleanor Roosevelt) published a stunning report, outlining the disparities in treatment men and women received throughout American law and society. And finally that year, Betty Friedan published her bestselling manifesto, *The Feminine Mystique,* which exposed as degrading to women a wide range of behaviors once seen as mere courtesy and innocent social practice. Then in 1964, after what can only be described as a quirky congressional debate, Title VII of the Civil Rights Act became law. This statute listed sex along with race as inherited characteristics that could not be used to exclude people from jobs (not even to "protect" them from overwork).

Sally Reed had never counted herself a feminist, but living in Boise she was surrounded by the sounds of the women's liberation movement.

This is the house *at 1622 Vista Avenue in Boise where Sally, Cecil, and Richard Reed lived before the Reeds' divorce and where Sally lived afterward. During the 1970s, Sally offered care to disabled veterans there.*

In Boise (as throughout the country), pregnant teachers were complaining that they were being forced to take unpaid leave as soon as their pregnancies became discernible, girls were resentful of rules that barred them from taking part in programs open only to boys, and women student-athletes were grumbling that they had to hold bake sales to raise travel money while the travel expenses of male teams were being paid for with student activity fees (to which women were required to contribute). Rules like these had long been considered fair—an aspect of the social structure that, it was believed, privileged girls and women and protected them from the competition of a "man's world." By the late 1960s, though, what most women considered fair had changed.

Sally Reed decided to get a new lawyer. Friends brought her to Allen Derr—forty-three years old, in general practice for a dozen years. Derr needed no persuading. As a young marine serving in China late in World War II, he had been troubled by the discrimination he saw practiced against African-American corpsmen. Back in civilian life, he encountered even more serving as assistant executive secretary of his college fraternity, Tau Kappa Epsilon. "We had chapters who wanted to take in colored pledges," he recalled; "we had alumni who disagreed." During the early 1950s, Derr spent four years traveling to TKE chapters around the country, working to make sure that chapters could "pledge who they wanted to pledge." In the process, he found himself fighting racism. Thinking about his eleven-year-old daughter, he remembered, it became easy for him to transfer those feelings to the cause of women's civil rights.

> "A GIRL SHOULD NOT EXPECT SPECIAL PRIVILEGES BECAUSE OF HER SEX, BUT NEITHER SHOULD SHE 'ADJUST' TO PREJUDICE AND DISCRIMINATION."
>
> —
>
> Betty Friedan,
> The Feminine Mystique,
> 1963

Arguing that the 1864 probate law violated promises of equal protection of the laws in Idaho's state constitution and also in the Fourteenth Amendment, Derr helped Sally Reed appeal to Idaho's Fourth Judicial District Court. Agreeing with Derr's argument, the judges there sent the case back to the probate court for a new determination on the merits of the issue. (The probate court would have to decide, for example, whether Sally's bookkeeping experience made her a more suitable administrator than Cecil.) But Cecil appealed the district court ruling to the Idaho Supreme Court, which ruled unanimously in his favor. "Philosophically," the judges' decision read, "it can be argued that the [statute does] discriminate against women on the basis of sex. However, *nature itself has established this distinction* [italics added].… The statute…is only designed to alleviate the problem of holding hearings.… The legislature…evidently concluded that in general men are better qualified to act as an administrator than are women."

IT WAS NOW FEBRUARY 1970. Thirty-eight-year-old Ruth Bader Ginsburg had just taken up at Columbia Law School an appointment that allowed her to spend half her time leading the American Civil Liberties Union's new Women's Rights Project. The project's basic principle was that discrimination on the basis of sex was neither benign nor harmless. When it began, Ginsburg recalled, "the possibility of getting a favorable decision seemed nil. The Supreme Court had held the line so long." But when she saw Derr's notice of appeal to the Supreme Court, she pounced. ACLU director Melvin Wulf joined in enthusiastically, and Derr agreed to accept the ACLU's help, provided that he conduct the oral argument if the Court agreed to hear the case.

"We are here today to ask you to do something that this Court has never done since the Fourteenth Amendment was adopted in 1868," Derr began on Tuesday, October 19, 1971; "and that is to declare a State statute that distinguishes between males and females as unconstitutional. We feel that this case could have a significance for women somewhat akin to what *Brown v. Board of Education* had for the Colored People." For more than a century, discrimination on the basis of sex had been respectable so

RUTH BADER GINSBURG

1933 –

Ruth Bader grew up as an only child in Brooklyn. In 1950, she received a scholarship to Cornell, where she met Martin Ginsburg, who became her husband in 1954. Five year later (after the birth of a daughter), she completed law school at Columbia, where she tied for first in her class. When she applied to Justice Felix Frankfurter for a Supreme Court clerkship, however, she was turned down without even an interview. Nor did she receive any job offers from New York City law firms. As Ginsburg (shown here in a 1977 photograph) later recalled, her status as "a woman, a Jew, and a mother to boot" was "a bit much" for employers at the time.

ACLU lawyer Mel Wulf *defended civil rights workers in Mississippi before turning his attention to women's issues.*

long as some legitimate public interest was invoked (as the protection of women's reproductive health had been invoked in the Court's landmark 1908 *Muller v. Oregon* decision). Yet *Muller* and similar cases had sustained the situation, Derr insisted, "that wherever there has been a classification on the basis of sex, anything goes."

The principal example that Derr had in mind was a case that reached the Supreme Court shortly after World War II. It concerned a Michigan law, enacted at the urging of an all-male bartender's union, that forbade women to tend bar unless they were the wife or daughter of the owner. Margaret Goesaert, the widow of a bar owner, had brought the case because she couldn't sustain the family business unless she and her daughter Valentine continued to tend bar as they had when Valentine's father was still alive. The salary they would have to pay a male bartender was more than the small tavern could afford. Yet as Associate Justice Felix Frankfurter observed in his 1948 opinion deciding the case, Michigan had a legitimate interest in keeping order in bars, and it was not irrational for the state legislature to believe that "bartending by women may…give a rise to moral and social problems" because the practice lacked "the protecting oversight" provided by a man. (Frankfurter chose to ignore a deposition submitted along with Goesaert's brief in which another woman bar owner reported that male bartenders "would drink upon the premises, and she has not had any of this difficulty with a barmaid.") This test of "rationality," Derr argued, was for women "almost as bad as the separate-but-equal test of *Plessy v. Ferguson,* holding back women…from their entitlements under the Fourteenth Amendment, the Equal Protection Clause."

This snapshot of **Allen Derr** *on the steps of the Supreme Court was taken at the time he made his oral argument before the Court in October 1971.*

D ERR WAS BACKED by a formidable eighty-eight-page brief, carefully prepared by Ginsburg and Wulf, that laid out what would become the standard line of argument against discrimination on the basis of sex. Unafraid to invoke feminism, Ginsburg and Wulf wrote that "a new appreciation of women's place has been generated in the United Sates…. Courts and legislatures have begun to recognize the claim of women to full membership in the class 'persons' entitled to due

The justices who *decided* Reed v. Reed *(from left to right):* John M. Harlan, Thurgood Marshall, Hugo L. Black, Potter Stewart, Warren Burger, Byron R. White, William O. Douglas, Harry A. Blackmun, and William J. Brennan.

FURTHER READING

★ Linda K. Kerber, *No Constitutional Right to Be Ladies: Women and the Obligations of Citizenship* (1998)

★ Sandra F. VanBurkleo, *Belonging to the World: Women's Rights and American Constitutional Culture* (2001)

process guarantees of life and liberty and equal protection of the laws." Leaning on Pauli Murray's classic essay "Jane Crow and the Law," Ginsburg emphasized the similarities between discrimination on the basis of race and on the basis of sex: Both misused "congenital and unalterable biological traits of birth" to justify prejudice. "Once thought normal, proper and ordained in the very nature of things," the brief continued, "sex discrimination may soon be seen as a sham, not unlike that perpetrated in the name of racial superiority…and based on inaccurate stereotypes of the capacities and sensibilities of women."

Ginsburg, Wulf, and Derr were hoping the Court would make a decision broad enough to overturn not only *Muller v. Oregon* and *Goesaert v. Cleary* but also the relatively recent and important opinion handed down in *Hoyt v. Florida* (1961). In that case, the Court upheld rules adopted by the state of Florida that made it far less likely for women than men to be called for jury service on the grounds that a "woman is still regarded as the center of home and family life." The Court thus denied murder defendant Gwendolyn Hoyt a jury drawn from a full cross section of the community. In doing so, the Court sustained the antique practice of defining a woman's civic obligations primarily in terms of her service to her husband.

Those decisions all reflected what most Americans believed to be the common sense of the matter. Legally, they were based on the English law of domestic relations—and the elaborate system of coverture (the legal state women entered upon marriage) that flowed from it—which men of the founding generation had adopted for the United States virtually unchanged. As a result, the new republic was committed to different systems of fairness for men and women (especially married women). Beginning with the premise that, from the moment of marriage, husbands controlled the physical bodies of their wives, the original law of domestic relations placed sharp limits on the extent to which married women could own property and make economic and social choices for themselves. Idaho's probate law, like Florida's jury service law, was in 1971 one of many remnants of this system still in force throughout the United States.

URING THE FALL OF 1971, while the justices deliberated Sally Reed's appeal, the Senate Judiciary Committee took up the Equal Rights Amendment already approved by the House. The text of the ERA was simple: "Equality of rights under the law shall not be denied or abridged by the United States or by any state on account of sex." North Carolina senator Sam Ervin's energetic efforts to rewrite it into inadequacy stirred debate over the amendment. With the ERA controversy filling many front pages, few newspapers took much notice of the amicus (friend of the court) brief filed by the New York City Human Rights Commission, noting the flood of unfairness complaints it had been receiving from women and urging the Court to declare sex discrimination unconstitutional. It argued, in other words, that what New York City women now considered fair had changed.

In fact, the Supreme Court was itself beginning to question the basic traditions of coverture that still applied to women. In 1960, it had held in *Wyatt v. U.S.* that, under certain circumstances, a wife could be compelled to testify against her husband. Lower courts, such as the Fourth Judicial District Court in Idaho that had found for Sally Reed, were also reconsidering old assumptions. A random sample: In 1968, courts in Pennsylvania and Connecticut invalidated sentences for women that were longer than those given men who had committed the same crimes; in 1969, a federal district court in Kentucky held that women could not be excluded from juries even if discussions in jury rooms were likely to embarrass them; in 1970, Faith Seidenberg and Karen DeCrow of the National Organization for Women's New York City chapter persuaded a federal district court that it was indeed unconstitutional for bars to exclude women patrons who were unaccompanied by men (a practice originally intended to keep out prostitutes, because it was believed that only a prostitute would enter a bar without a male escort). And only a few months before the Supreme Court began its consideration of *Reed,* an attorney named Wendy

Idaho was one of the first states to ratify the *Equal Rights Amendment. It was also, however, one of five states that rescinded ratification after Congress voted to extend the deadline in 1978. In this photograph from the Idaho Statesman, pro- and anti-ERA demonstrators confront one another at a 1979 protest.*

PAULI MURRAY

1910 – 1985

An orphan at twelve, Pauli Murray was raised by maternal aunts and grandparents in Durham, North Carolina. In 1933, she was graduated with honors from New York City's Hunter College but five years later was denied admission to the University of North Carolina law school because of her race. Spurred on to a life of activism, she took part in 1940s sit-ins to integrate Washington, D.C., lunch counters and was jailed briefly for refusing to sit on the broken seats at the back of a bus taking her home to North Carolina for a visit. Meanwhile, Murray (shown here in 1946) earned a law degree from Howard University and was named Woman of the Year by Mademoiselle *in 1947.*

Williams, barely thirty years old, wrote a brief that persuaded the California Supreme Court to overturn a *Goesaert*-style law forbidding women to tend bar.

Given these developments, few legal arguments remained for Cecil Reed's attorney, Charles Stout, to make. He could only splutter that Idaho women were voters (they had been since 1896), and if they didn't like the probate law, they could elect new legislators to change it:

> *The legislators in enacting this statute knew that men were as a rule more conversant with business affairs than were women…. One has but to look around and it is still a matter of common knowledge that women still are not engaged in politics, the professions, business, or industry to the extent that men are…. In all species…nature protects the female and the offspring to propagate the species and not because the female is inferior. The pill and the conception of children in a laboratory and incubation in a test tube, if this occurs, …cannot get away from this prime necessity if the race is to be continued, and there will still remain a difference and the necessity for a different treatment.*

THE FOURTEENTH AMENDMENT, ratified in 1868 in the aftermath of the Civil War, had promised "equal protection of the laws" to "all persons." But every time women had challenged disparities of treatment based solely on sex—from Myra Bradwell in 1873, challenging Illinois's exclusion of women from the practice of law, to Gwendolyn Hoyt in 1961—the Supreme Court had responded that different treatment was reasonable, based (as the Idaho Supreme Court had said) on distinctions that "nature itself has established."

On November 22, 1971, though, the Supreme Court decided differently, and the ruling was unanimous: Idaho's preference for males was arbitrary, and mere administrative convenience was not sufficient to justify the discrimination. The justices sent the case back to Idaho to be decided on the merits, but a new trial was avoided when Sally Reed agreed to be serve as a coexecutor with Cecil. More important, Ginsburg would later observe, the *Reed* decision "was the turning-point case"—the first time the Supreme Court sustained a woman's complaint that she had suffered unconstitutional gender discrimination. "This transformation," Wendy Williams has explained, "required the justices to see the world in a different way."

Yet much of what the Court thought was left to inference. In their ruling, the justices never mentioned *Goesaert* or *Hoyt*, nor did they offer broad principles for their decision. *Reed* was not the triumph for which Ginsburg and Wulf had hoped. Indeed, the California Supreme Court had already gone much farther, unanimously declaring discrimination on the basis of sex as suspect as discrimination practiced on the basis of race. After *Reed*, many disparities of treatment fell, but because *Reed* had been decided on such narrow grounds, more than three decades of often-bitter argument followed, with legislators and courts having to define what constituted sex discrimination point by point, issue by issue, case by case.

T HE *REED* DECISION DID MAKE it more difficult for states to ground their laws, and Americans to ground their social practices, in stereotypes about men's and women's differences. No longer could it be assumed that men had "a better head for numbers," that women shouldn't be police officers, or even that workmen's compensation death benefits should automatically go to surviving wives but not to surviving husbands (unless they could show they had been economically dependent on their wives). At the time *Reed* was decided, a man charged with rape in most states could defend himself by claiming that the victim

On August 26, 1970, to mark the fiftieth anniversary of the Nineteenth Amendment's ratification, American women organized parades all over the country. At least fifty thousand people attended the event in New York City, and in Washington, D.C., the women and men shown here marched from Dupont Circle to Lafayette Park, across the street from the White House. The marchers knew that men and women were governed by different sets of rules, and their public protest made visible a stunning range of ways in which Americans were then challenging the established relations between the sexes.

had dressed provocatively; no state yet believed it was possible to charge a married man with the rape of his wife; in five states, if a wife committed adultery, her husband could kill her lover and plead—it was considered a reasonable defense—that the murder had been a crime of passion.

Although it has taken decades to litigate these and similar issues, they were the easy ones. The more difficult cases have been those in which the situations of the men and women concerned were not precisely the same and the matters to be decided involved not only equality but what the law calls "equity"—that is, fairness when the circumstances of the parties differ. What is "equal protection of the laws" when reproductive rights or access to abortion is involved? Men and women have equal rights to privacy and to personal liberty; those are the terms in which claims to reproductive rights are generally argued before the courts. Is pregnancy leave a matter of vacation time? sick leave? Or is it an accommodation that makes it possible for women to be both mothers and workers (as men are unproblematically both fathers and workers)? Questions of equity have been painfully difficult to resolve, because the answer to the question "What's fair?" is rarely obvious. These issues have been and are still being argued point by point, issue by issue, case by case.

Nor did *Reed* resolve the question of what counts as equity when disparities of sexual identity are at stake. In 1996, the Supreme Court did rule that the exclusion of sexual preference from human rights ordinances could be considered a denial of equal protection of the laws, but in 2000 it sustained the Boy Scouts of America policy prohibiting gay scoutmasters. At this writing, an overwhelming majority of the states permit employment, housing, and credit discrimination on the basis of sexual preference; and eighteen states still criminalize consensual gay sex. The legal arguments used to litigate these cases are often the equal protection strategies and equity arguments used by feminists in the *Reed* case and its successors.

Reed performed no miracles. But Sally Reed, Allen Derr, and Ruth Bader Ginsburg—along with all the women and men who made the social movement we call Women's Liberation and encouraged in Sally Reed her skepticism of an unjust Idaho law—opened a door, tested a legal argument, and validated a new set of assumptions about what is reasonable. Ginsburg's brilliant *Reed* brief became a template for many more lawsuits, many more arguments, and much more complex reasoning about the elements of fairness.

DOROTHY KENYON

1888 – 1972

In early 1950, Dorothy Kenyon completed her service with the UN Commission on the Status of Women. On March 8—just a month after his famous speech charging the presence of Communists in the state department—Joseph McCarthy accused her of having ties to "at least 28 Communist front organizations." During testimony before the Senate (shown here), Kenyon denied being a "fellow traveler," later calling McCarthy "an unmitigated liar." One of the "fronts" McCarthy named was the ACLU, on whose national board Kenyon had sat since 1930. Two decades later and still a national board member, Kenyon, along with Pauli Murray, persuaded the ACLU to establish its Women's Rights Project.

INSBURG HERSELF POSSESSED a finely honed appreciation of her own historical debt. On the brief that she filed with the Supreme Court in the *Reed* case, along with her own name and those of Melvin Wulf and Allen Derr, she placed two more: Dorothy Kenyon, who had been arguing for equal treatment of women since her graduation from New York University School of Law in 1917, and Pauli Murray, the great-granddaughter of both slave and slave master who did as much as anyone of her generation to fight segregation, linking racism with sexism and making the argument early on that denial of equal treatment on the grounds of sex undermined the Fourteenth Amendment. Neither woman had written a word of the brief, yet it bore their names because Ruth Bader Ginsburg understood more clearly than almost anyone of her time the debt that the women of her generation owed to those of preceding generations. Without their efforts, she would never have been able to challenge successfully a century's worth of law and social practice—a century's misunderstanding of what fairness and equality really mean.

This photograph shows Allen Derr with Ruth Bader Ginsburg in March 2000, seven years after Ginsburg took Byron R. White's seat on the Supreme Court. The Senate voted 97–3 to confirm Ginsburg's nomination, and she took office on August 10, 1993.

★ ★ ★

JUNE 14, 1973

THE BATTLE OVER BIOTECHNOLOGY

BY DANIEL J. KEVLES

O N THE MORNING OF JUNE 14, 1973, a private conference of molecular biologists was in session at the New Hampton School in rural New Hampshire. It was Herbert Boyer's turn to speak. Some months earlier in a Honolulu delicatessen, Boyer, a faculty member at the University of California at San Francisco, and Stanley Cohen, a professor at Stanford, had mulled over a problem of high interest among molecular biologists: how to isolate genes and study their function. The methods so far developed were tedious and cumbersome. Munching their corned beef sandwiches, Cohen and Boyer hit on a simple, efficient means of accomplishing this task. Now, at the Gordon Research Conference in New Hampshire, Boyer described the method publicly for the first time, reporting that he and Cohen had managed to snip a gene from one organism and stitch it into the genetic material—the DNA—of another, the

AT LEFT: *Human insulin was one of the first commercial products derived using recombinant DNA technology.*

ABOVE: *James D. Watson and Francis Crick developed the breakthrough double-helix model for deoxyribonucleic acid (DNA) in 1953.*

laboratory workhorse *E. coli* (a bacterium commonly found in the human gut). Once in place, Boyer said, the genes became fully functional and thus analyzable.

As the day wore on, the import of Boyer's news sank in among his colleagues. Although he and Cohen had recombined *E. coli* genes with genes from a different species of microorganism, those who heard Boyer quickly realized that, in principle, his and Cohen's method of "recombinant DNA" (as it was eventually called) could be used with animal or even human genes to create more ambitious genetically engineered life. It could, in other words, facilitate the transformation of organisms—plants, animals, and possibly even humans—at the very core of their hereditary essence. "Now we can put together any DNA we want to," one of the assembled scientists remarked.

T HAT PROSPECT TROUBLED several of the conference participants. Two years before, the Stanford biologist Paul Berg had proposed inserting into *E. coli* a viral gene related to the formation of tumors in monkeys. Berg expected the experiment to yield clues to

Herbert Boyer at the 1975 Asilomar Conference. The four-day gathering, called to consider the potential hazards of recombinant DNA research, began on Monday, February 24, with a presentation by David Baltimore.

THE GORDON CONFERENCES

The Gordon Research Conferences were initiated in the early 1930s by Johns Hopkins chemist Neil E. Gordon, who recognized the difficulty in establishing open communication among scientists working in the same research field. The Gordon Conferences still bring together scientists dozens of times each year for weeklong discussions that promote the free exchange of ideas at the research frontiers of the biological, chemical, and physical sciences.

the causes of some cancers, but he was persuaded to drop the work after a few colleagues warned him that incorporating a tumor virus into a bug that normally inhabits the human intestines might provoke a cancer epidemic if it somehow escaped from Berg's laboratory. The episode also provoked among molecular biologists worried discussions of whether creating new combinations of genetic material might yield unpredictable and possibly hazardous results.

The worriers included two of the younger scientists at the New Hampshire conference, thirty-year-olds Edward Ziff and John Sedat. Both possessed deep senses of social responsibility that had been awakened by the civil rights movement (which Ziff had worked for in Mississippi) and heightened by the domestic turmoil over the war in Vietnam (which both opposed). The antiwar movement had lately been attacking scientists for their complicity in the military-industrial complex, while other critics had been calling into doubt the moral legitimacy of science by linking it to immoral consequences such as environmental degradation. (One prominent biologist recalled that at a 1972 conference in Switzerland, "[We] started off talking about biohazards, and the next thing I knew, I was discussing the American position in Vietnam.") After hearing Boyer's talk that morning, both Ziff and Sedat felt that biologists ought to pause and think before rushing ahead with this potentially transformative genetic technology.

In the lecture hall during a break later in the day, they quietly put their views to the cochairs of the meeting, Maxine Singer of the National Institutes of Health (NIH) and Dieter Söll of Yale, urging that the question of what dangers might lie in recombinant DNA be brought before the entire conference. By custom, the discussions at Gordon Conferences were limited strictly to scientific issues; and, to encourage the free exchange of ideas, the deliberations were by rule unreported. Had devotees of those standards been in charge, Ziff and Sedat would likely have been brushed aside. Indeed, Sedat recalled that Söll seemed reluctant to depart from custom and rule. (Söll, a German native, agreed later that he might well have appeared skittish and admitted that he felt uncomfortable because he was only just establishing himself as a bio-chemist and wasn't fully familiar with the discussions that Berg's proposed experiment had stimulated.) Yet Söll recognized the significance of what troubled Ziff and Sedat, and so did Maxine Singer—who, unlike Söll, was outspoken and politically aware.

During the late 1950s, she had been brought into contact with the politics of science by her husband, Daniel Singer. A lawyer, he represented the Federation of American Scientists, a group devoted to nuclear arms control, and appeared at congressional hearings on its behalf. He became increasingly involved in the social issues of science, with his range expanding beyond nuclear matters into the biomedical area. Maxine Singer had long sensed that molecular genetics was fraught with rising social implications, and along with her husband she felt that biomedical scientists had an ethical duty to address the potential dangers of their work. As Singer and Söll talked over the issues that Ziff and Sedat had raised, they found themselves to be of one mind: Recombinant DNA posed moral and technical hazards that knowledgeable scientists ought to consider.

THE MORNING AFTER BOYER'S TALK, on what happened to be the final day of the conference, Singer and Söll set aside fifteen minutes for a discussion of the socially charged topic of recombinant DNA. Then, a month later, they wrote a letter to Philip Handler, the president of the National Academy of Sciences (NAS), raising questions about the safety of recombinant research on behalf of "a majority of those attending the Conference." This step led the following year to an unprecedented action: In a letter published July 26, 1974, in the widely read periodical *Science* (and simultaneously in two other major scientific journals), eleven biologists led by Paul Berg called for a moratorium on most recombinant DNA research pending a review of its potential hazards. The signatories included Boyer; Cohen; David Baltimore, a microbiologist at the Massachusetts Institute of Technology; and James D. Watson, a codiscoverer (with Francis Crick) of the structure of DNA. Such an appraisal, they said, should take place at "an international meeting of involved scientists from all over the world...convened early in the coming year."

The call for a moratorium achieved virtually unanimous voluntary compliance, and some 140 biologists attended the

E. COLI

E. coli *has been widely used in genetics research since the 1940s because of its cheapness, genetic simplicity, and rapid rate of reproduction. In addition, part of its genetic material is carried on plasmids (loops of DNA) into which foreign genes can be inserted and their functions analyzed. Until the early 1970s, researchers inserted these genes using bacterial viruses. Lately, genes have been inserted directly using recombinant DNA techniques.*

Daniel Singer—*a lawyer with the Washington, D.C., office of Fried Frank—converses here between panels at Asilomar. The Wednesday evening panel he led was entitled "Brief Analysis of Responsibility of Research Scientists and of Risk Balancing."*

Asilomar organizers
(left to right) Maxine
Singer, Norton Zinder,
Sydney Brenner, and Paul
Berg draft the conference's
final statement.

subsequent conference held in February 1975 under the sponsorship of the NAS at the Asilomar Conference Center in Pacific Grove, California, nestled among the redwoods and pines of the Monterey Peninsula. The Asilomar Conference was suffused with a sense that molecular biologists had to embrace the kind of moral responsibility for which Ziff and Sedat had quietly agitated. Many of the biologists particularly wanted to avoid the taint that had stigmatized nuclear physicists after Hiroshima. (In a speech to a college audience in 1970, Daniel Singer had warned that if biologists "cop out on the problems they create," they might share the fate of those physicists who have "for a generation been wringing their hands and donning hair shirts to expiate their guilt.") Some years after Asilomar, DeWitt Stetten, a biologist at NIH, recalled that the conference "had many elements of a religious revival meeting," adding, "I heard several colleagues declaim against sin, I heard others admit to having sinned, and there was a general feeling that we should all go forth and sin no more."

Of course, not every scientist at Asilomar considered recombinant DNA sinful. Among the impenitents were the Nobel Prize–winning biologist Joshua Lederberg, who thought its hazards greatly exaggerated, and his fellow laureate Watson, who loudly regretted his initial support for the moratorium. But attitudes turned sharply after the presentation of an evening panel arranged by Daniel Singer. At his suggestion, several lawyers (himself included) had been invited to the conference because, as he had told the organizers, recombinant DNA

James Watson and
Sydney Brenner at
Asilomar. Brenner, a
British molecular
biologist, was at the time
associated with
Cambridge's Medical
Research Council
Laboratory and one of
two non-Americans on
the Asilomar organizing
committee.

raised not only scientific and ethical but also legal issues. In their Asilomar panel, Singer and his colleagues emphasized that if something went wrong during a recombinant experiment, the scientists conducting the experiment could be held personally liable for damages. "That got everyone's attention," Daniel Singer recalled.

In the aftermath of Singer's panel, those who considered the potential biological hazards real and those who didn't—but who worried about the legal hazards—found common ground on which to proceed. Both groups wanted to get on with recombinant research because the scientific payoffs promised to be enormous. To that end, they agreed on the need to establish rules for the conduct of recombinant research that would ensure its safety. With Berg leading the effort, a set of recommendations was produced that formed the basis of guidelines issued in June 1976 by the National Institutes of Health to govern federally sponsored recombinant work. The guidelines sought to protect public health and safety by confining research with recombinant organisms to special containment facilities and engineering them biologically so that they couldn't survive even if somehow they did escape.

NEVERTHELESS, BOTH SCIENTISTS and laypeople found a good deal to question about the leap into research with recombinant DNA. Robert Sinsheimer, a prominent molecular biologist (and John Sedat's doctoral adviser at Cal Tech), declared, "We are becoming creators, inventors of novel forms that will live on long after their makers and will evolve according to their own fates. Before we displace the first Creator we should reflect whether we are qualified to do as well." Other critics pointed out that permitting an elite of self-interested biologists to shape the guidelines under which they worked was, in the words of one MIT biologist, tantamount to "having the chairman of General Motors write the specifications for safety belts." Even NIH, according to this view, had a conflict of interest because the agency would be both regulating and, as the country's principal sponsor of basic biological research, funding the work.

The dissidents made themselves felt most dramatically in Cambridge, Massachusetts, after Harvard decided in the spring of 1976 to transform a floor of one of its science buildings into a recombinant DNA containment facility. The mayor of Cambridge, Alfred E. Vellucci, learned of the plans from an extensive article in the June 8 issue of the *Phoenix,* Boston's formerly underground alternative weekly. The article revealed not only Harvard's intentions but also the strenuous opposition of several prominent faculty members—among them the biologists Ruth Hubbard and George Wald, Hubbard's husband and another Nobel laureate. Hubbard warned that the risks of recombinant DNA were "worse than radiation danger."

Vellucci, who was known for the cranberry double-knit sports jacket he liked to wear and for his abiding loyalty to the blue-collar members of his constituency, had built a political career in large part by bashing

> "NATURE DOES NOT NEED TO BE LEGISLATED. BUT PLAYING GOD DOES."
> —
> *Anonymous biologist, remark to a reporter at the Asilomar Conference, February 1975*

This cartoon— *published in the February 9, 1977, Boston Globe—was captioned "Crack out the liquid nitrogen, dumplings…we're on our way."*

> **" I HAVE AN OBLIGATION TO A WHOLE LOT OF LAY PEOPLE IN THIS CITY WHO DO NOT UNDERSTAND THIS WHOLE GODDAMN THING. AND SO I DON'T WANT TO TAKE A CHANCE."**
>
> —
>
> *Cambridge mayor Alfred E. Vellucci, interview, January 1977*

Harvard and MIT. Now, with Hubbard and Wald on his side, he eagerly announced that the city council would hold a hearing on the issue, declaring, "We want to be damned sure the people in Cambridge won't be affected by anything that would crawl out of that laboratory."

The hearing was held on June 23, 1976—the same day that the long-awaited NIH guidelines were issued. It played to a packed city council chamber and opened with a local high school group singing "This Land Is Your Land." Vellucci then announced his intention to introduce at the council's next meeting (scheduled for July 7) a resolution banning within the Cambridge city limits all experiments relating to recombinant DNA for "at least two years." Local university biologists complained that passage of such a measure would devastate molecular research at both Harvard and MIT; and at the July 7 council meeting, which was lengthy and contentious, Vellucci's resolution was indeed voted down. But in the early-morning hours of July 8, by a vote of five to three with one abstention, the council did vote to impose a three-month "good faith" moratorium on any recombinant research requiring containment facilities. The council also established a review board to decide whether such research should proceed. Later, Mayor Vellucci told a reporter, "I have learned enough about recombinant DNA molecules in the past few weeks to take on all the Nobel Prize–winners in the city of Cambridge. Regardless of what the review board says, I'm opposed to this work."

On January 5, 1977, the six-member Cambridge Experimentation Review Board—composed entirely of laypeople, among them two physicians, a nurse, and a nun—delivered its report to the city council amid a crowd of television and magazine reporters, not to mention numerous city residents. The board proposed that recombinant research be allowed to proceed in Cambridge, although under safeguards somewhat stronger than those required by the NIH guidelines. On February 7, the council formally accepted the CERB's recommendation.

Ruth Hubbard (left), Maxine Singer (center), and Alfred E. Vellucci (right), at the Cambridge City Council's June 23, 1976, hearing on restrictions proposed for recombinant DNA research.

In the meantime, the dangers explored at Asilomar were provoking widespread lay apprehension elsewhere in the country. As Sen. Edward Kennedy of Massachusetts told a meeting of the American Medical Writers Association in September 1977, "We are entering a new era of public participation in critical policy decisions in science." By "public," of course, Kennedy meant primarily "popular government," and the U.S. Congress soon joined state and local authorities in gearing up for hearings designed to legislate tough new restrictions on DNA research. A bill in the New York State legislature, for example, proposed empowering local health commissioners to levy fines of five thousand dollars a day against scientists conducting recombinant DNA experiments that the commissioners believed to be hazardous. Keeping up the pressure in his impertinent way, Mayor Vellucci wrote to NAS president Handler on May 16, 1977, asking whether the recent sighting of a "strange, orange-eyed creature" in Dover, Massachusetts, might be "in any way connected to recombinant DNA experiments taking place in the New England area."

THESE EVENTS LEFT MANY BIOLOGISTS aghast at what their embrace of social responsibility had wrought. One complained bitterly that it had unleashed a "medieval prescription for punishing witches and sorcerers"; another, pointing to the "search and seizure provisions" in a pending congressional measure, declared, "They read like a narcotics bill." Even Paul Berg was dismayed. "This exercise in science and public policy has become nightmarish and disastrous," he wrote in January 1979 to New Mexico senator Harrison Schmitt, adding, "I now believe that Society has more to fear from the intrusions of government in the conduct of scientific research than from recombinant DNA research itself."

James Watson advised his colleagues to "head down to Washington and tell Congress that these scaremongers are an odd coalition of spaced-out environmental kooks and leftists who see genetics as a tool for enslaving the masses." They did, although the language they used was not quite so provocative. To whichever legislators and reporters would listen, molecular biologists repeatedly argued that recombinant DNA research should be left unburdened by unwarranted restrictions, not only because it was safe but also because it would yield wonderful practical benefits through genetic engineering. They predicted that recombinant DNA techniques would revolutionize medicine by replacing disease-causing genes with normal ones; that it would transform pharmaceuticals by turning bacteria into factories for the production of miracle drugs; and

PAUL BERG

1926 –

Paul Berg has been in the forefront of recombinant DNA research (and its regulation) since the early 1970s. He was born in Brooklyn and educated in New York City public schools before attending Penn State and serving in the navy during World War II. After teaching briefly at Washington University in St. Louis, he became a member of the Stanford University School of Medicine's biochemistry faculty in 1959. He was elected to the National Academy of Sciences seven years later and in 1980 won the Nobel Prize in Chemistry for his work with DNA. In 1991, Berg (shown here in April 1971) was named head of the Human Genome Project's Scientific Advisory Committee.

HERBERT BOYER

1936 –

Herbert Boyer, the son of a railroad conductor, grew up in Derry, Pennsylvania, where he played high school football. Although many young men in that hardscrabble area of western Pennsylvania ended up working for the railroad or the mines, Boyer was encouraged to study science by his football coach, who doubled as a science teacher. Later, Boyer got hooked on DNA at St. Vincent's College, a Benedictine school in nearby Latrobe. (He so loved molecular biology that he named his Siamese cats Watson and Crick.) Boyer eventually worked as vice president of Genentech from the company's founding until 1990, when he resigned and accepted a seat on the board of directors.

that it would dramatically alter agriculture by equipping plants to fix their own nitrogen from the air. Under this barrage, the threat of legislative intervention steadily diminished until by the spring of 1978 there seemed no longer much cause for concern.

AT THE SAME TIME, a growing number of biologists, including Herbert Boyer, began talking up investment bankers. Boyer, at UCSF since 1967, was a genuine Bay Area hybrid. He opposed the war in Vietnam and loved blue jeans, unbuttoned shirts, beer, and the Pittsburgh Steelers; he was also a proto-entrepreneur who had been even in his high school days eager "to become a successful businessman," according to his senior class yearbook. During 1975, bullishly optimistic, he had tried and failed to interest several backers in the commercial possibilities of recombinant DNA. On a Friday afternoon in January 1976, however, Boyer was visited by Robert A. Swanson, a twenty-eight-year-old venture capital wunderkind who was decidedly interested in its commercial prospects.

Swanson had talked to a number of academics, all of whom had predicted that the commercial application of gene splicing was ten years away. But that Friday afternoon, first in Boyer's laboratory and then over a beer at Churchill's (a local bar), he heard differently. Swanson remembered that after the meeting, "We did some thinking, him on the technology side, me on the business side, to see what was possible." Enough seemed possible that they agreed to form a company to exploit recombinant DNA for profit. The company's initial capitalization was one thousand dollars, half from Swanson and half from Boyer (who had to borrow the money). On April 7, 1976, Genentech (an acronym for "genetic engineering technology") was formally incorporated with additional capital, notably a hundred thousand dollars from Thomas Perkins of the Kleiner Perkins Caufield & Byers investment banking firm.

During the three months that passed between their first meeting and the formal establishment of Genentech, Boyer and Swanson considered the various potential markets for synthesized proteins and concluded that Genentech's first project should be the production, by recombinant techniques, of human insulin. At least five million Americans had diabetes, and of those one-quarter required a daily insulin dose. At the time, the world's supply of therapeutic insulin came from the pancreases of slaughtered cows and pigs. (Cow and pig insulin were close enough to human insulin in chemical structure to do the job, although they did sometimes provoke allergic reactions.) But the extraction process was costly and, moreover, projections at Eli Lilly & Co., which controlled 80 percent of the U.S. insulin market, indicated that the insulin needs of the U.S. diabetic population might one day outstrip the animal supply.

In early September 1978, at a press conference crowded with media, Genentech announced to the world that it had succeeded in bioengineering human insulin and that, about two weeks earlier, it had entered into an agreement with Eli Lilly to manufacture and market the hormone.

The facilities at Genentech. On the day that the company went public, its share price rose from thirty-five to eighty-nine dollars within minutes.

Nearly every major newspaper and magazine in the United States heralded the breakthrough, and as reports of dramatic technical progress multiplied, the interest of the financial markets in biotechnology grew feverish. When Genentech (assigned the stock symbol "GENE") went public in mid-October 1980, its shares were snapped up at a more than twice the thirty-five-dollar offering price. The success of its IPO astonished many Wall Street observers because Genentech's earnings in fiscal 1979 had been just two cents a share.

F EDERAL POLICY MAKERS WERE ALSO KEENLY interested in Genentech and other biotechnology start-ups, but not because they wanted to revisit the matter of research controls. Instead, they had the nation's sizable trade deficit on their minds—a deficit that would have been much larger had it not been for the country's substantial trade surplus in high-technology goods. Hoping for an expansion of the fledgling biotechnology industry, the government in 1980 gave it a triple boost: NIH, which had been easing restrictions on recombinant research, now ended them almost entirely. Congress passed the Bayh-Dole Act, which explicitly encouraged universities to privatize (and profit from) the results of federally sponsored high-technology research. And in June, the Supreme Court ruled in *Diamond v. Chakrabarty* that a genetically modified living organism could be patented. Over various legal and moral objections, the Court held that whether the invention was alive was irrelevant to deciding whether it qualified for intellectual property protection.

The molecular biologists had won the battle over biotechnology, preserving their field from unwarranted lay interference and gaining the freedom to pursue the scientific and commercial prospects of recombinant

THE HUMAN GENOME PROJECT

The government-sponsored U.S. Human Genome Project began in 1990 with the goal of identifying all hundred thousand genes in human DNA within thirteen years. That goal was met earlier than planned when project leaders announced in June 2000 that they had (along with the private biotechnology company Celera) created the first "working draft" road map of the entire human genome. Their work is expected to enhance understanding of how genetics influences disease development and speed the discovery of new therapies.

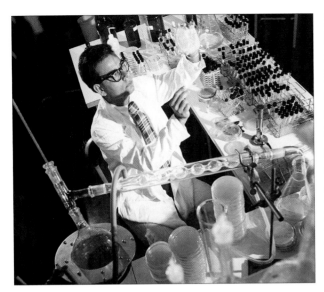

Soon after earning his Ph.D. at the University of Calcutta, microbiologist Ananda Chakrabarty went to work for General Electric in the United States, where he developed a bacterium to break down environmental pollutants (especially crude oil). This bacterium became the subject of a landmark Supreme Court decision in 1980, when five justices held that patents could be issued for "anything under the sun that is made by man." According to Chief Justice Warren Burger, the "relevant distinction" is not between living and inanimate things but between things that are naturally existing and those that are man-made.

DNA. By the mid-1980s, biotech was burgeoning with many new companies clustered around San Francisco Bay and Boston, some well equipped and financed, others operating with little more than a small technical staff and the address of the U.S. Patent Office. Most had boards of directors and advisory panels that included recombinant-savvy biologists, and a number of these academics—including Herbert Boyer, who had handsomely fulfilled his high school ambition—suddenly found themselves rich.

Some had been activists at Asilomar, and some—for example, David Baltimore— continued to speak out on biological issues of public import, such as AIDS. But with success, the willingness of many molecular biologists to confront the social questions raised by their work had substantially diminished. It had been dissipated by the fear of Vellucci-like threats to the autonomy of science; by the conviction, rooted in thousands of experiments, that recombinant DNA was safe; and by the vested interests that so many had in the scientific and commercial revolution the recombinant method was fostering.

Recombinant techniques were being used first to isolate human genes and then to insert those genes into laboratory mice, making the mice useful models for the study of human disease. They were also being exploited to engineer a broadening spectrum of diagnostic tests and pharmaceuticals, and work was being done that raised the practical possibility of substituting normal genes for defective ones—a practice called "gene therapy." At the end of the 1980s, the federal government launched a project to locate all the genes in the human genome and determine the entire structure of its DNA. Estimated to cost three billion dollars over fifteen years, the project was justified by the stunning advances occurring in human genetics and by the claim that the biotechnologies arising from it would strengthen U.S. economic competitiveness in the post–Cold War world then dawning.

In the meantime, following the Supreme Court's ruling in the *Chakrabarty* case, the Patent Office extended patent protection to genetically engineered plants and animals. By the early 1990s, the biotechnology industry was beginning to devise genetically modified plants that were, variously, resistant to cold, pests, and insecticides.

Companies were also attempting to manipulate the genes of agricultural animals to enhance their market value—engineering, for example, cows that gave more milk, sheep that provided more wool, and pigs that produced leaner meat.

Many Americans, including many investors, marveled at these developments, but a number responded to them with apprehension and alarm. Some critics attacked the patenting of plants and animals as unethical in and of itself and also because it fostered corporate control over mankind's genetic heritage. Others pointed to the conflict of interest created by university research that was increasingly funded by and furnished to biotechnology companies—noting, for example, that it had already led to hazardous gene-therapy experiments with human patients. Still others attacked the stocking of genetically modified foods in grocery stores, calling them potentially dangerous to the health of consumers.

FURTHER READING

★ Donald S. Fredrickson, *The Recombinant DNA Controversy: Science, Politics, and the Public Interest, 1974–1981* (2001)

★ Arnold Thackray, *Private Science: Biotechnology and the Rise of the Molecular Sciences* (1998)

THESE CRITICISMS PROMPTED a chorus of rebuttals from biotechnology interests and a number of leading molecular biologists. Amid the cacophony of claims and counterclaims, it became difficult for members of the lay public, and even for many scientists, to know what to believe. Several of the original Asilomar participants wondered whether it might be worthwhile to attempt a revival of the sense of social obligation that had once been prompted by such matters.

To that end, in February 2000, a group of scientists, journalists, lawyers, and historians—including Paul Berg, David Baltimore, and the Singers—convened at Asilomar on the twenty-fifth anniversary of the original conference. Over several retrospective days, they tried to devise ways to stimulate sensible public debate on such controversial issues as gene therapy and genetically modified foods. The discussions led to a gloomy conclusion: The biologists who knew the most about these issues were so commercially entangled that it would be difficult to obtain from them disinterested opinions. Many of the molecular biologists at the first Asilomar Conference may have wanted to avoid the fate of the early nuclear physicists, but their victory in the battle over biotechnology had, ironically, clouded the sense of moral responsibility with which Ziff, Sedat, Singer, and Söll had been roused to action that distant day in New Hampshire.

★ ★ ★

This demonstrator *protests the creation and distribution of genetically modified organisms at a January 2000 conference in Montreal hosted by the United Nations Convention on Biological Diversity.*

ABOUT THE CONTRIBUTORS

JOYCE APPLEBY teaches American history at the University of California—Los Angeles. Her books include *Inheriting the Revolution: The First Generation of Americans* (2000). She has been president of the Organization of American Historians and the American Historical Association.

JAMES AXTELL is William R. Kenan Jr. Professor of Humanities at the College of William and Mary. He is the author of eleven books in ethnohistory and the history of education. His most recent publications are *The Pleasures of Academe: A Celebration and Defense of Higher Education* (1998) and *Natives and Newcomers: The Cultural Origins of North America* (2001). He is at work on a history of twentieth-century Princeton University, which he did not attend.

IRA BERLIN is Distinguished University Professor at the University of Maryland. He is the author of *Many Thousands Gone: The First Two Centuries of Slavery in North America* (1998) and is the coeditor of *Remembering Slavery: African Americans Talk about Their Personal Experiences of Slavery and Freedom* (1998). He is a member of the Council of the National Endowment for the Humanities and

president-elect of the Organization of American Historians.

ALAN BRINKLEY is Allan Nevins Professor of History at Columbia University, where he has taught since 1991. His works include *Voices of Protest: Huey Long, Father Coughlin, and the Great Depression* (1982), which won the National Book Award; *The Unfinished Nation: A Concise History of the American People* (1993); *The End of Reform: New Deal Liberalism in Recession and War* (1995); and *Liberalism and Its Discontents* (1998).

DOUGLAS BRINKLEY is director of the Eisenhower Center for American Studies and Professor of History at the University of New Orleans. He is the author of biographies of Dean Acheson, James Forrestal, Jimmy Carter, FDR, and Rosa Parks.

NANCY F. COTT is Stanley Woodward Professor of History and American Studies at Yale, where she has taught U.S. history courses focusing on women and gender issues since 1975. She was among the founders of Yale's Women's Studies Program, has chaired its American Studies Program, and is currently director of the university's Division of the Humanities. Her books include

The Bonds of Womanhood: "Woman's Sphere" in New England, 1780–1835 (1977); *The Grounding of American Feminism* (1987); and, most recently, *Public Vows: A History of Marriage and the Nation* (2000).

JOHN DEMOS is Samuel Knight Professor of History at Yale University. His books include *Entertaining Satan: Witchcraft and the Culture of Early New England* (1982), winner of the Bancroft Prize, and *The Unredeemed Captive: A Family Story from Early America* (1994), winner of the Parkman and Ray Allen Billington Prizes and a finalist for the National Book Award in General Nonfiction.

ANN DOUGLAS is Parr Professor of Comparative Literature at Columbia University. She taught previously (1970–1974) at Princeton, where she was the first woman to teach in its English Department. Her works include *The Feminization of American Culture* (1977) and *Terrible Honesty: Mongrel Manhattan in the 1920s* (1995)—which received, among other honors, the Alfred J. Beveridge, Lionel Trilling, and Merle Curti Intellectual History Awards. She is currently completing *Entertaining the Universe: Hollywood, 1930–1960* and is at work on a long-term project, *If You Live, You Burn: Cold War Culture in the United States, 1939–1965.*

JOHN W. DOWER is Elting E. Morison Professor of History at the Massachusetts Institute of Technology. His numerous books include *Empire and Aftermath: Yoshida Shigeru and the Japanese Experience, 1878–1954* (1979); *War Without Mercy: Race and Power in the Pacific War* (1986), which won the National Book Critics Circle Award for Nonfiction; and *Embracing Defeat: Japan in the Wake of World War II* (1999), which won the Pulitzer Prize for General Nonfiction, the National Book Award in Nonfiction, and the Bancroft Prize.

JOSEPH J. ELLIS is Ford Foundation Professor of History at Mount Holyoke College. He is the author of six books on American history, including *American Sphinx: The Character of Thomas Jefferson* (1997), which won a National Book Award, and *Founding Brothers: The Revolutionary Generation* (2000), which won the Pulitzer Prize for History.

DAVID FARBER, a professor of history at University of New Mexico, is the author of *Chicago '68* (1988), *The Age of Great Dreams: America in the 1960s* (1994), and (with Beth Bailey) *The Columbia Guide to America in the 1960s* (2001). He has also edited *The Sixties: From Memory to History* (1994) and is currently coediting (again with Bailey) the book series *Counterculture.*

ERIC FONER is DeWitt Clinton Professor of History at Columbia University. He is the author of numerous works, including *Reconstruction: America's Unfinished Revolution, 1863–1877* (1988), which won the Parkman and Bancroft Prizes. He is also a past president of the American Historical Association.

WILLIAM H. GOETZMANN is Jack S. Blanton Sr. Chair of History and American Studies at the University of Texas in Austin. He is the author of *Exploration and Empire: The Explorer and the Scientist in the Winning of the American West* (1966), which won both the Pulitzer Prize for History and the Parkman Prize.

LINDA GORDON wrote about the New Deal in her *Pitied But Not Entitled: Single Mothers and the History of Welfare, 1890–1935* (1994). Her most recent book, *The Great Arizona Orphan Abduction* (1999) won both the Bancroft Prize and the Alfred J. Beveridge Award for the best book on the history of the Americas.

DAVID A. HOLLINGER is Chancellor's Professor of History at the University of California at Berkeley. His books include *Science, Jews, and Secular Culture: Studies in Mid-Twentieth-Century American Intellectual History* (1996) and *Postethnic America: Beyond Multiculturalism* (1995).

KENNETH T. JACKSON is Jacques Barzun Professor of History and the Social Sciences at Columbia University. His books include *Cities in American History* (1972); *Crabgrass Frontier: The Suburbanization of the United States* (1985); and, as editor, *The Encyclopedia of New York City* (1995). He is currently at work on *Gentlemen's Agreement: Race, Class, and Differential Development in Newark, White Plains, and Darien, 1840–1990.*

DAVID KAISER is a professor in the Strategy and Policy Department of the Naval War College, having also taught at Harvard and Carnegie-Mellon Universities. He is the author of *Epic Season: The 1948 American League Pennant Race* (1998), *American Tragedy: Kennedy, Johnson, and the Origins of the Vietnam War* (2000), and (with William Young) *Postmortem: New Evidence in the Case of Sacco and Vanzetti* (1985).

LINDA K. KERBER is May Brodbeck Professor in the Liberal Arts and Professor of History at the University of Iowa. Her books include the prize-winning *No Constitutional Right to Be Ladies: Women and the Obligations of Citizenship* (1998) and the essay collection *Toward an Intellectual History of Women* (1997). She is a past president of the Organization of American Historians and of the American Studies Association.

ALICE KESSLER-HARRIS is Professor of History at Columbia University. Her books include *Women Have Always Worked: A Historical Overview* (1981), *Out to Work: A History of Wage-Earning Women in the United States* (1982), and *A Woman's Wage: Historical Meanings and Social Consequence* (1990). She specializes in the history of labor and the comparative and interdisciplinary exploration of women and gender.

DANIEL J. KEVLES, a professor of history at Yale University, has written widely on the history of science and its relationship to society. His books include *In the Name of Eugenics: Genetics and the Uses of Human Heredity* (1985); *The Physicists: The History of a Scientific Community in Modern America* (1987); and, most recently, *The Baltimore Case: A Trial of Politics, Science, and Character* (1998). He is currently completing *Inventing America*, a coauthored history of the United States that integrates science and technology into the narrative of American development.

NICHOLAS LEMANN writes the *New Yorker*'s "Letter from Washington." He has been a magazine journalist for more than twenty-five years. His books include *The Promised Land: The Great Black Migration and How It Changed America* (1991); *The Big Test: The Secret History of the American Meritocracy* (1999); and *Sons* (2000), an e-book about George W. Bush and Al Gore.

WILLIAM E. LEUCHTENBURG is William Rand Kenan Jr. Professor of History at the University of North Carolina at Chapel Hill. His many books include the prize-winning *Franklin D. Roosevelt and the New Deal, 1932–1940* (1963) and *In the Shadow of FDR: From Harry Truman to Bill Clinton* (1993). He has been elected president of the American Historical Association, the Organization of American Historians, and the Society of American Historians.

DAVID LEVERING LEWIS is Martin Luther King Jr. University Professor at Rutgers. Among his publications are *King: A Biography* (1978), *When Harlem Was in Vogue* (1981), and the two-volume biography of W. E. B. Du Bois

awarded the Pulitzer Prizes for Biography in 1994 and 2001.

JAMES M. MCPHERSON is George Henry Davis '86 Professor of American History at Princeton University, where he has taught since 1962. He is the author of a dozen books, mostly on the era of the American Civil War. His *Battle Cry of Freedom: The Civil War Era* (1988) won the Pulitzer Prize for History, and his *For Cause and Comrades: Why Men Fought in the Civil War* (1997) won the Lincoln Prize.

ROBERT MIDDLEKAUFF is Preston Hotchkis Professor Emeritus at the University of California—Berkeley. Among his books are *The Mathers: Three Generations of Puritan Intellectuals, 1596–1728* (1971), *The Glorious Cause: The American Revolution, 1763–1789* (1982), and *Benjamin Franklin and His Enemies* (1996).

JACK N. RAKOVE is Coe Professor of History and American Studies and Professor of Political Science at Stanford University, where he has taught since 1980. He is the author, among other books, of *The Beginnings of National Politics: An Interpretive History of the Continental Congress* (1979) and *Original Meanings: Politics and Ideas in the Making of the Constitution* (1996), which won the Pulitzer Prize for History.

CHRISTINE STANSELL, Professor of History at Princeton University, is the author, most recently, of *American Moderns: Bohemian New York and the Creation of a New Century* (2000). She has written widely on the history of American women.

GEOFFREY C. WARD, the former editor of *American Heritage*, is the author of a dozen books, including *Jazz: A History of America's Music* (2000) and *A First-Class Temperament: The Emergence of Franklin Roosevelt* (1989), which won the Parkman Prize. He also writes historical documentaries for public television.

ELLIOTT WEST is Distinguished Professor of History at the University of Arkansas. The most recent of his five books, *The Contested Plains: Indians, Goldseekers, and the Rush to Colorado* (1998), received the Parkman Prize. He is currently writing a book on the 1876 Sioux and 1877 Nez Perce Wars.

SEAN WILENTZ is Dayton-Stockton Professor of History and director of the Program in American Studies at Princeton University, where he has taught since 1979. He is the author of five books, including *Chants Democratic: New York City and the Rise of the American Working Class, 1788–1850* (1984), which won both the Alfred J. Beveridge and Frederick Jackson Turner Awards. Wilentz is also a contributing editor at *The New Republic*.

GORDON S. WOOD is University Professor and Professor of History at Brown University. He is the author of *The Creation of the American Republic, 1776–1787* (1969), which won the Bancroft and John H. Dunning Prizes, and *The Radicalism of the American Revolution* (1992), which won the Pulitzer Prize for History as well as the Ralph Waldo Emerson Prize.

Index

Greene, Jerry, 370

Grew Joseph, 314–315, 318, 329

Grier, Robert C., 150, 151

Griffin, Rick, 408

Griffith, D. W., 237

Griswold v. Connecticut (1965), 182

Groton, 298

Gulf of Tonkin Resolution, 392

Gunther, John, 363

Güssefeld, F. L., 73

H

Hagestrom, Warren, 381

Haight-Ashbury, 406–411, 414

Hall, G. Stanley, 268–269

Hallalhotsoot, *see* Lawyer (Nez Perce chief)

Halleck, Henry W., 164

Hamilton, Alexander, 58, 62–63, 74, 77, 78–89, 94

  biography, 82

Hancock, John, 40, 45, 48

Hand, John, 216

Handler, Philip, 455, 459

Hansen, Norwood Russell, 381

Hardin, Lil, 244

Harkins, Paul, 394

Harlan, John M., 218, 446

Harlow, Bryce, 370

Harper's Weekly, 173, 175, 182, 200

Harrington, Oliver, 338

Harrison, Benjamin (Continental Congress member), 50

Harrison, Benjamin (U.S. president), 215

Hart, Gary, 100

Harvard University, 16, 214, 216–217, 226, 297, 298, 299, 300, 302, 303, 305, 377, 378, 398, 448, 457–458

  Harvard National Scholarships, 303

Hastings, Lansford, 115

Hawken rifles, 107, 108

Hayden, Tom, 429, 432, 433

Haydon, Benjamin R., 135

Hayes, Rutherford B., 346

Hayes Homes, 420, 421, 427, 432, 437

Head Start, 389

Healy, G. P. A., 145

Heilbron, J. L., 384

Heinmot Tooyalakekt, *see* Joseph (Nez Perce chief)

Henderson, Fletcher, 242, 246

Henry, Andrew, 106–109

Henry, Patrick, 49, 70, 71

Henry Street Settlement, 213, 232

Hickok, Lorena, 294

high schools, public, 300–301

Hill, A. P., 167

Hill, Daniel Harvey, 165

Hine, Lewis W., 207, 217

hippie culture, 402–417

Hirohito, 313, 314, 320, 326, 327, 328, 334

  biography, 330

Hiroshima, atomic bombing of, 309, 313, 321, 323, 333–334, 456

History of the Expedition of Captains Lewis and Clark (Biddle), 114

History of Woman Suffrage, 136

Hitchcock, Alfred, 361

Hitler, Adolf, 313, 320, 352

Ho Nee Yeath, 24

Hodson, William, 281

Holden v. Hardy (1898), 211, 213

Holiday, Billie, 254

Holiday, Jim, 119

Hollywood, *see* film industry

Hollywood Ten, 357

Home Owners Loan Corporation, 427

Homestead strike, 207

Hooker, Joseph, 165

Hoover, Herbert, 293, 310, 352

Hopkins, Harry, 278–295

  biography, 282

Horse Creek, 110

M

Photo Credits

We offer our thanks to those who shared their personal collections with us, as well as to all those archivists, too numerous to name, who generously responded to our sometimes multiple requests. In particular, we offer our compliments to Mary Carter of the Albertsons Library at Boise State University; Anthony Sullivan of Corbis; Amy Darlington of the Educational Testing Service; Chris Densmore of Friends Historical Library; Erin Hewitt of Genentech; Carolyn Bowler of the Idaho State Historical Society; Andrea Ashby of Independence Hall National Historical Park; Kelly Fearnow of Monticello; Charles Cummings of the Newark Public Library; Jamie Arbolino of the U.S. Senate Commission on Art; Trevor Bond of the Washington State University Libraries; and David Reel, Robert Fisch, and Michael McAfee of the West Point Museum.

All the images in *Days of Destiny* are from the collections of the Library of Congress, the National Archives, or Agincourt Press, with the exception of those reprinted with the permission of the following:

Gene Anthony: 402, 403, 406, 408, 410 (top), 411, 412–413, 416 (top), 416–417
Louis Armstrong Home and Archives at Queens College/CUNY: 234
Boise State University, Albertsons Library, Statesman Collection: 440, 447
Buffalo Bill Historical Center, Cody, Wyoming: 103, 108 (top)
Ananda Chakrabarty: 462
Chicago Historical Society: 41
Connecticut Historical Society, Hartford, Connecticut: 37
Corbis: 16, 18, 30, 32, 55 (top), 96 (right), 97 (top), 101, 121, 127, 162 (left), 182, 225, 242 (top), 246, 248, 251 (top), 255, 257 (bottom), 260 (top), 262, 263, 264, 267 (both), 269 (both), 271, 272, 273, 274, 277, 293, 299 (bottom), 305, 307, 322, 330, 339 (bottom), 340 (both), 341, 342, 343, 344 (both), 353, 365 (bottom), 371 (bottom), 375, 379 (both), 388 (bottom), 390 (top), 391, 393, 394 (top), 398, 420, 463
Denver Public Library: 102
Department of the Interior, National Park Service, Nez Perce National Historical Park: 185, 186 (bottom), 194 (top), 203
Department of the Interior, National Park Service, Yellowstone National Park: 196
Allen Derr: 441, 442 (both), 443, 445, 451
Donaldson, Lufkin & Jenrette Collection of Americana: 82
Educational Testing Service: 296, 298
Eli Lilly & Company: 452
Friends Historical Library, Swarthmore College: 125 (bottom), 131, 133, 137 (both), 140, 142
Fruitlands Museums: 23 (bottom)
Genentech, Inc.: 460, 461
Haffenreffer Museum of Anthropology: 14 (top)
Harvard University Archives: 302, 303
Historical Society of Frederick County: 159 (bottom)
Idaho State Historical Society, Boise: 189, 195, 202 (top)

Illinois State Historical Library, Springfield: 220

Independence Hall National Historical Park: 42, 48 (bottom), 56 (top), 68, 70 (top), 72, 74, 77, 94 (top), 100 (top)

Kenneth T. Jackson: 419, 422 (top), 437, 439

Lyndon Baines Johnson Library: 386, 388 (top), 396–397, 399, 401

Joslyn Art Museum, Omaha, Nebraska: 111

Kansas State Historical Society: 104

Daniel J. Kevles: 458

Jehane Kuhn: 377 (bottom), 378, 381, 382, 384, 385

Sarah Kuhn: 374, 377 (top)

Pamela Lappies: 221

Louisiana State Museum Collection: 238

Mashantucket Pequot Museum and Research Center: 17 (top)

Massachusetts Historical Society: 13, 22, 34, 130 (bottom)

Missouri Historical Society, St. Louis: 106 (bottom)

Montana Historical Society, Helena: 186 (top), 192 (top), 194 (bottom), 201

Monticello/Thomas Jefferson Memorial Foundation, Inc.: 79, 84, 92 (bottom), 95

Museum of American Political Life/University of Hartford: 91, 337

National Academy of Sciences: 455, 456 (both)

National Library of Medicine: 454

New Jersey Performing Arts Center: 438 (bottom)

Newark Public Library: 421, 422 (bottom), 426 (both), 427, 428, 431 (bottom), 432 (bottom left), 433 (bottom), 436

Newark *Star-Ledger*: 418, 429, 430, 431 (top), 433 (top), 434–435, 438 (top)

Pilgrim Society, Plymouth, Massachusetts: 15

Princeton University Libraries: 304, 444 (bottom)

Jack N. Rakove: 40

Donald Reilly © 2001 from cartoonbank.com (all rights reserved): 383

Tilman Reitzle: 297, 453

Franklin Delano Roosevelt Library: 279, 281, 291

Smithsonian Institution, National Museum of American History: 94 (bottom), 249

Smithsonian Institution, National Museum of the American Indian: 20

Smithsonian Institution, National Numismatics Collection, Douglas Mudd: 85

South Caroliniana Library, University of South Carolina, Columbia: 59

Stanford News Service: 459

Supreme Court of the United States Collection: 144, 146–147, 155, 215 (top), 444 (top), 446

Paul Szep: 457

Harry S. Truman Library: 310 (both), 315, 318, 319, 333

University of Chicago Press: 376

University of Massachusetts, Amherst, W. E. B. Du Bois Library: 222, 223, 224 (top), 233

U.S. Senate Commission on Art: 145, 146–147, 150 (bottom)

Walters Art Museum, Baltimore: 108 (bottom), 112–113

Washington State Historical Society, Tacoma: 184

Washington State University Libraries, Historical Photograph Collections: 188, 188–189, 190, 193 (bottom), 198–199

West Point Museum Collection, United States Military Academy: 55 (bottom), 56 (bottom), 58 (bottom), 62 (top), 63 (bottom), 64, 157, 160 (bottom), 166, 167, 187, 191 (both), 192 (bottom), 202 (bottom), 309, 326 (both), 332 (bottom), 387, 392, 394 (bottom)